POLITICAL PARTIES

A SOCIOLOGICAL STUDY OF THE OLIGARCHICAL TENDENCIES OF MODERN DEMOCRACY

By

ROBERT MICHELS

TRANSLATED BY
EDEN & CEDAR PAUL

DOVER PUBLICATIONS, INC.

NEW YORK

Published in Canada by General Publishing Company, Ltd., 30 Lesmill Road, Don Mills, Toronto, Ontario.
Published in the United Kingdom by Constable and Company, Ltd., 10 Orange Street, London WC 2.

This Dover edition, first published in 1959, is an unabridged and unaltered republication of the English translation first published in 1915 by Hearst's International Library.

Standard Book Number: 486-20569-X
Library of Congress Catalog Card Number: 59-65149

Manufactured in the United States of America
Dover Publications, Inc.
180 Varick Street
New York, N. Y. 10014

CONTENTS

CONTENTS

PREFACE

MANY of the most important problems of social life, though their causes have from the first been inherent in human psychology, have originated during the last hundred and fifty years; and even in so far as they have been handed down to us from an earlier epoch, they have of late come to press more urgently, have acquired a more precise formulation, and have gained fresh significance. Many of our leading minds have gladly devoted the best energies of their lives to attempts towards solving these problems. The so-called principle of nationality was discovered for the solution of the racial and linguistic problem which, unsolved, has continually threatened Europe with war and the majority of individual states with revolution. In the economic sphere, the social problem threatens the peace of the world even more seriously than do questions of nationality, and here "the labourer's right to the full produce of his labour" has become the rallying cry. Finally, the principle of self-government, the corner-stone of democracy, has come to be regarded as furnishing a solution of the problem of nationality, for the principle of nationality entails in practical working the acceptance of the idea of popular government. Now, experience has shown that not one of these solutions is as far-reaching in its effects as the respective discoverers imagined in the days of their first enthusiasm. The importance of the principle of nationality is undeniable, and most of the national questions of Western Europe can be and ought to be solved in accordance with this principle; but matters are complicated by geographical and strategical considerations, such as the difficulty of determining natural frontiers and the frequent need for the establishment of strategic frontiers; moreover, the principle of nationality cannot help us where nationalities can hardly be said to exist or where they are intertangled in inextricable confusion. As far as the economic problem is concerned, we have numerous solutions offered by the different schools of socialist thought, but the formula of the right to the whole produce of labour is one which can be comprehended more readily in the synthetic than in the analytic field; it is easy to formulate as a general principle and likely as such to command widespread sympathy, but it is exceedingly difficult to apply in actual practice. The present work aims at a critical discussion of the third question, the problem of democracy. It is the writer's opinion that democracy, at once as an intellectual theory and as a practical movement, has to-day entered upon a critical phase from which it will be extremely difficult to discover an exit. Democracy has encountered obstacles, not merely imposed from without, but spontaneously surgent from within. Only to a certain degree, perhaps, can these obstacles be surpassed or removed.

The present study makes no attempt to offer a "new system." It is not the principal aim of science to create systems, but rather to promote understanding. It is not the purpose of sociological science to discover, or rediscover, solutions, since numerous problems of the individual life and the life of social groups are not capable of "solution" at all, but must ever remain "open." The sociologist should aim rather at the dispassionate exposition of tendencies and counter-operating forces, of reasons and opposing reasons, at the display, in a word, of the warp and the woof of social life. Precise diagnosis is the logical and indispensable preliminary to any possible prognosis.

The unravelment and the detailed formulation of the complex of tendencies which oppose the realization of democracy are matters of exceeding difficulty. A preliminary analysis of these tendencies may, however, be attempted. They will be found to be classifiable as tendencies dependent (1) upon the nature of the human individual; (2) upon the nature of the political struggle; and (3) upon the nature of organization. Democracy leads to oligarchy, and necessarily contains an oligarchical nucleus. In making this assertion it is far from the author's intention to pass a moral judgment upon any political party or any system of government, to level an accusation of hypocrisy. The law that it is an essential characteristic of all human aggregates to constitute cliques and sub-classes is, like every other sociological law, beyond good and evil.

The study and analysis of political parties constitutes a new branch of science. It occupies an intermediate field between the social, the philosophico-psychological, and the historical disciplines, and may be termed a branch of applied sociology. In view of the present development of political parties, the *historical* aspect of this new branch of science has received considerable attention. Works have been written upon the history of almost every political party in the Western world. But when we come

to consider *the analysis of the nature of party,* we find that the
field has hardly been touched. To fill this gap in sociological
science is the aim of the present work.

The task has been by no means easy. So great was the extent
of the material which had to be discussed that the difficulties of
concise presentation might well seem almost insuperable. The
author has had to renounce the attempt to deal with the problem
in all its extension and all its complexity, and has confined
himself to the consideration of salient features. In the execution
of this design he has received the unwearied and invaluable help
of his wife, Gisela Michels.

This English translation is from the Italian edition, in the
preparation of which I had at my disposal the reviews of the
earlier German version. Opportunities for further emendation
of the present volume have also been afforded by the criticisms
of the recently published French and Japanese translations. But
the only event of outstanding importance in the political world
since my *Political Parties* was first drafted has been the outbreak of the war which still rages. The author's general conclusions as to the inevitability of oligarchy in party life, and
as to the difficulties which the growth of this oligarchy imposes
upon the realization of democracy, have been strikingly confirmed
in the political life of all the leading belligerent nations immediately before the outbreak of the war and during the progress
of the struggle. The penultimate chapter of the present volume,
specially written for the English edition, deals with *Party Life in
War-time.* It will be obvious that the writer has been compelled, in this new chapter, to confine himself to the discussion
of broad outlines, for we are still too near to the events under
consideration for accurate judgment to be possible. Moreover,
the flames of war, while throwing their sinister illumination upon
the military and economic organization of the states concerned,
leave political parties in the shadow. For the time being parties
are eclipsed by nations. It need hardly be said, however, that as
soon as the war is over party life will be resumed, and that the
war will be found to have effected a reinforcement of the tendencies characteristic of party.

ROBERT MICHELS.

Basle, 1915.

POLITICAL PARTIES

CHAPTER I

DEMOCRATIC ARISTOCRACY AND ARISTOCRATIC DEMOCRACY

THE most restricted form of oligarchy, absolute monarchy, is founded upon the will of a single individual. *Sic volo sic jubeo. Tel est mon bon plaisir.* One commands, all others obey. The will of one single person can countervail the will of the nation, and even to-day we have a relic of this in the constitutional monarch's right of veto. The legal justification of this regime derives its motives from transcendental metaphysics. The logical basis of every monarchy resides in an appeal to God. God is brought down from heaven to serve as a buttress to the monarchical stronghold, furnishing it with its foundation of constitutional law—the grace of God. Hence, inasmuch as it rests upon a supra-terrestrial element, the monarchical system, considered from the outlook of constitutional law, is eternal and immutable, and cannot be affected by human laws or by the human will. It follows that the legal, juridical, legitimate abolition of the monarchy is impossible, a fable of a foolish political dreamer. Lawfully, the monarchy can be abolished by God alone —and God's will is inscrutable.

At the antipodes of the monarchical principle, in theory, stands democracy, denying the right of one over others. *In abstracto,* it makes all citizens equal before the law. It gives to each one of them the possibility of ascending to the top of the social scale, and thus facilitates the way for the rights of the community, annulling before the law all privileges of birth, and desiring that in human society the struggle for preëminence should be decided solely in accordance with individual capacity. Whereas the principle of monarchy stakes everything upon the character of a single individual, whence it results that the best possible monarchical government offers to the people as a whole no guarantee for permanently benevolent and technically efficient rule,[1] democracy is, on principle, responsible to the community

---

[1] At the end of the eighteenth century this was far more clearly and

1

at large for the prevailing conditions of rule, of which it is the sole arbiter.

We know to-day that in the life of the nations the two theoretical principles of the ordering of the state are so elastic that they often come into reciprocal contact, "car la démocratie peut embrasser tout le peuple, ou se resserrer jusqu'à la moitié; l'aristocratie, à son tour, peut de la moitié du peuple se resserrer jusqu'au plus petit nombre indéterminément."[2] Thus the two forms of government do not exhibit an absolute antithesis, but meet at that point where the participants in power number fifty per cent.

Our age has destroyed once for all the ancient and rigid forms of aristocracy, has destroyed them, at least, in certain important regions of political constitutional life. Even conservatism assumes at times a democratic form. Before the assaults of the democratic masses it has long since abandoned its primitive aspect, and loves to change its disguise. To-day we find it absolutist, to-morrow constitutional, the next day parliamentary. Where its power is still comparatively unrestricted, as in Germany, it appeals exclusively to the grace of God. But when, as in Italy, it feels insecure, it adds to the appeal to the deity an appeal to the popular will. In its outward forms it is capable of the most extensive modifications. In monarchical France the *Franciae et Navarrae Rex* becomes the *Roy de France,* and the *Roy de France* becomes the *Roi des Français.*

The life of political parties, whether these are concerned chiefly with national or with local politics, must, in theory, necessarily

---

expressly recognized than it is to-day, when the *constitutional* monarchy has destroyed the essence of every political principle of government:—

"Servile dread, dependent upon the dazzling splendour of an inaccessible throne, upon myriads of satellites, upon innumerable armies, and upon the ever uplifted sword of vengeance, dependent in a word upon irresistible power, is the only thing that holds these monarchies together and secures the safety of the despots and their satraps. At times, indeed, fate sends a liberator to the unfortunate, a Cyrus who breaks the old fetters, and who rules a reconstituted kingdom with wisdom and a truly paternal spirit: but this rarely happens, and the good thus effected is for the most part personal and transient; for the prime source of the evil, the political structure, remains, and a succession of stupid or vicious monarchs will speedily destroy all that has been built up by the one benevolent sovereign" (C. M. Wieland, *Eine Lustreise ins Elysium,* Complete Works, Shrämbl, Vienna, 1803, vol. i, p. 209).

[2] J. J. Rousseau, *Le Contrat social,* Bibliothèque Nationale, 6th ed., Paris, 1871, p. 91.

exhibit an even stronger tendency towards democracy than that which is manifested by the state. The political party is founded in most cases on the principle of the majority, and is founded always on the principle of the mass. The result of this is that the parties of the aristocracy have irrevocably lost the aristocratic purity of their principles. While remaining essentially anti-democratic in nature, they find themselves compelled, at any rate in certain periods of political life, to make profession of the democratic faith, or at least to assume the democratic mask. Whereas the democratic principle, from its very nature, by reason of the mutability of the popular will and of the fluctuating character of the majority, tends in theory to transform the πάντα ρεῖ of Heraclitus into the reality of national and popular life, the conservative principle erects its edifice upon certain bases or norms which are immutable in their nature, determined by the test of experience to be the best or at any rate the least bad, and consequently claimed as valid *sub specie æternitatis*. Nevertheless, the conservative principle must not be understood in the sense of an unconditional maintenance of the *status quo*. If that principle consisted merely in the recognition of what already exists, above all in the matter of the legal forms prevailing in a given country or period, conservatism would lead to its own destruction.[3] In periods and among nations where the old conservative elements have been expelled from direct participation in power, and have been replaced by innovators fighting under the banner of democracy, the conservative party assumes an aspect hostile to the existing order of the state, and sometimes even a revolutionary character.[4] Thus, however, is

[3] Concerning the nature of conservatism, consult the interesting study of Oskar Stillich, *Die Politischen Parteien in Deutschland,*, vol. i, *Die Konservativen*, Klinkhardt, Leipzig, 1909, pp. 18 et seq.

[4] Or counter revolutionary? A definite historical signification is often associated with the word *revolution,* and the prototype of revolution in this sense is the great French Revolution. Thus the expression *revolutionary* is frequently applied simply to the struggle for liberty conducted by inferior classes of the population against superior, if this struggle assumes a violent form, whereas logically revolution implies nothing but a fundamental transformation, and the use of the term cannot be restricted to describe the acts of any particular class, nor should it be associated with any definite external form of violence. Consequently every class is revolutionary which, whether from above or from below, whether by force of arms, by legal means, or by economic methods, endeavours to bring about a radical change in the existing state of affairs. From this outlook, the concepts *revolutionary* and *reactionary* (*reactionary* as contrasted with

effected a metamorphosis of the conservative party, which, from
a clique cherishing an aristocratic exclusivism at once by instinct
and by conviction, now becomes a popular party. The recognition
that only the masses can help to reintroduce the ancient aristocracy in its pristine purity, and to make an end of the democratic
regime, transforms the very advocates of the conservative view
into democrats. They recognize unreservedly the sufferings of
the common people; they endeavour, as did very recently the
royalists in the French Republic, to ally themselves with the
revolutionary proletariat, promising to defend this against the
exploitation of democratic capitalism and to support and even to
extend labour organizations—all this in the hope of destroying
the Republic and restoring the Monarchy, the ultimate fruit of
the aristocratic principle.[5] *Le Roy et les camelots du Roy*—the
king and the king's poor—are to destroy the oligarchy of the
bloated plutocrats. Democracy must be eliminated by the democratic way of the popular will. The democratic method is the
sole one practicable by which an old aristocracy can attain to a
renewed dominion. Moreover, the conservatives do not usually
wait until they have been actually driven from power before

conservative), *revolution* and *counter-revolution,* fuse into a single whole.
It is moreover utterly unscientific to associate with these terms moral ideas
whose theoretical bearing is purely evolutionary. For example, Raumer,
writing from Paris in 1830, expressed the matter very well as follows:
"All these men [the liberals] regard as revolutionary the abolition of
anciently established institutions and evils, whereas by counter-revolution
they understand the restoration of these or of other abuses. Their adversaries, on the other hand, understand by revolution the aggregate of all
the follies and crimes that have ever been committed, whereas by counter-
revolution they mean the re-establishment of order, of authority, of religion, and so on" (Friedrich von Raumer, *Briefe aus Paris und Frankreich
im Jahre 1830,* F. A. Brockhaus, Leipzig, 1831, Part II, p. 26).—Cf. also
Wilhelm Roscher, *Politik, Geschichtliche Naturlehre der Monarchie, Aris-
tokratie und Demokratie,* Cotta, Stuttgart-Berlin, 1908, 3rd ed., p. 14.—Yet
we have to remember that in political matters such judgments of value may
be effective means of struggle towards political and sometimes also towards
moral ends; but they are apt to lead us astray if we use them to aid us in
defining historical tendencies or conceptions.
    [5] Cf. the royalist propagandist work by Georges Valois, a trade unionist,
La Monarchie et la Classe ouvrière, Nouvelle Librairie Nationale, Paris,
1909, pp. 45 et seq. Valois pays ardent court to French syndicalism as the
one great movement which now has the support of the masses. His conservatism is quite undisturbed by the contemplation of the idea that his king
can be established on the throne only by means of a revolution, becoming
king no longer by the grace of God, but by the grace of the revolutionary
socialists.

appealing to the masses. In countries where a democratic regime prevails, as in England, they spontaneously turn to the working class wherever this forms the most conspicuous constituent of the masses.[6] In other countries, also, where parliamentary government is unknown, but where there exists universal and equal suffrage, the parties of the aristocracy owe their political existence to the charity of the masses to whom in theory they deny political rights and political capacity.[7] The very instinct of self-preservation forces the old groups of rulers to descend, during the elections, from their lofty seats, and to avail themselves of the same democratic and demagogic methods as are employed by the youngest, the widest, and the most uncultured of our social classes, the proletariat.

The aristocracy to-day maintains itself in power by other means than parliamentary; at any rate in most of the monarchies

---

[6] In the violent electoral struggles in England in January 1910, it may be said that both parties, liberals and conservatives alike, in view of the manner in which they fought one another, were essentially working for socialist ideas and for the victory of the proletariat. The liberals did this by unfurling the flag of democracy, by working for the suppression of the House of Lords, and by advocating an extensive programme of far-reaching social reforms; while the conservatives displayed before the eyes of the workers all the misery of their existence in capitalist society; both parties did this by promising more than they could perform, and by recognizing in the whole conduct of their political agitation that the working class has become the decisive force in politics. The comments made at the time in the socialist papers of Germany were extremely apt: ''The English conservatives do not preach resignation to the workers, but discontent. Whereas the Prussian conservatives, for example, are in the habit of telling the working classes that nowhere in the world are they so well off as in Germany, the English conservatives assure their constituents that nowhere in the world are the workers worse off than in England.'' Naturally the aim of these assurances was to persuade the electorate to accept the abolition of the detested system of free trade, and to establish a protectionist system which would redound to their advantage. This idea has long been cherished by the English conservatives, but they cannot put it into practice except with the aid of the revolutionary labouring class.

[7] The merit of having recognized this truth with precision and of having applied it to the practice of the conservative party belongs especially to the great political leaders of ultra-conservative elements in Germany, Hammerstein and Stöcker. Hammerstein, from 1881 to 1895 editor of the ''Kreuzzeitung,'' was the first who clearly perceived the necessity, in order to save the life of his party, of acquiring the ''confidence of the masses'' (cf. Hans Leuss, *Wilhelm Freiherr von Hammerstein*, Walther, Berlin, 1905, p. 109). At the party congress held in Berlin in 1892, the proposal by a delegate from Chemnitz that the conservatives should become more ''demagogic'' received universal approval.

it does not need a parliamentary majority in order to be able to hold the reins by which is guided the political life of the state. But it does need, were it merely for decorative purposes and in order to influence public opinion in its favour, a respectable measure of parliamentary representation. It does not obtain this representation by divulging its true principles, or by making appeal to those who are truly of like mind with itself. A party of the landed gentry which should appeal only to the members of its own class and to those of identical economic interests, would not win a single seat, would not send a single representative to parliament. A conservative candidate who should present himself to his electors by declaring to them that he did not regard them as capable of playing an active part in influencing the destinies of the country, and should tell them that for this reason they ought to be deprived of the suffrage, would be a man of incomparable sincerity, but politically insane. If he is to find his way into parliament he can do so by one method only. With democratic mien he must descend into the electoral arena, must hail the farmers and agricultural labourers as professional colleagues, and must seek to convince them that their economic and social interests are identical with his own. Thus the aristocrat is constrained to secure his election in virtue of a principle which he does not himself accept, and which in his soul he abhors. His whole being demands authority, the maintenance of a restricted suffrage, the suppression of universal suffrage wherever it exists, since it touches his traditional privileges. Nevertheless, since he recognizes that in the democratic epoch by which he has been overwhelmed he stands alone with this political principle, and that by its open advocacy he could never hope to maintain a political party, he dissembles his true thoughts, and howls with the democratic wolves in order to secure the coveted majority.[8]

---

[8] Naumann writes very aptly: "We can readily understand that conservatives have no love for universal suffrage. It has an injurious influence upon their character, for no one can very well stand up before an electoral meeting and frankly enunciate the principle, *Authority, not Majority.* . . . It is only in certain privileged bodies, such as the Prussian Upper House, or the First Chamber of Saxony, that the conservative can show himself in his true colours. The modern conservative is a living compromise, an authoritarian in democratic gloves. . . . An aristocracy engaged in political agitation! If in this alone, we see the influence of the democratic tendency" (Friedrich Naumann, *Demokratie und Kaisertum, ein Handbuch für innere Politik,* Buchverlag der "Hilfe," Berlin-Schöne-

The influence of popular suffrage upon the outward behaviour of conservative candidates is so extensive that when two candidates of the same political views present themselves in a single constituency, each of them is forced to attempt to distinguish himself from his rival by a movement to the left, that is to say, by laying great stress upon his reputedly democratic principles.[9]

Such occurrences serve to confirm the experience that the conservatives also endeavour to regulate their actions in conformity with the fundamental principle of modern politics, a principle destined to replace the religious dictum that many are called but few are chosen, and to replace also the psychological theory that ideals are accessible solely to a minority of choice spirits: this principle may be summed up in the terms of Curtius, who said that the conservative cannot gain his ends with the aid of a small and select body of troops, but must control the masses and rule through the masses.[10] The conservative spirit of the old master-caste, however deeply rooted it may be, is forced to assume, at least during times of election, a specious democratic mask.

Nor does the theory of liberalism primarily base its aspirations upon the masses. It appeals for support to certain definite classes, which in other fields of activity have already ripened for mastery, but which do not yet possess political privileges—appeals, that is to say, to the cultured and possessing classes. For the liberals also, the masses pure and simple are no more than a necessary evil, whose only use is to help others to the attainment of ends to which they themselves are strangers. The first great liberal writer of Germany, Rotteck, reproaches the Queen of France for having, during the Revolution, forced the bourgeoisie to appeal to the common people for aid. He distinguishes be-

---

berg, 1904, p. 92). Cf. also Ludwig Gumplowicz (*Sozialphilosophie im Umriss,* Wagner, Innsbruck, 1910, p. 113), who regards the tendencies and the natural needs of landed property as one of the most essential props of conservatism.

[9] This applies equally to France. Cf. Aimé Berthod (Sous-chef de cabinet au Ministère des Affaires Etrangères), in a discussion upon Electoral Reform which took place at the society ''Union pour la vérité,'' and was published in the society's organ ''Libres Entretiens,'' 6th series, iv, *La Représentation proportionnelle et la Constitution des Partis politiques,* Paris, January 23, 1910, p. 212.

[10] Friedrich Curtius, *Ueber Gerechtigkeit und Politik,* ''Deutsche Rundschau,'' xxiii, 1897, fasc. 4, p. 46.

tween two kinds of democracy, the rule of representatives and the rule of the masses.[11]   During the revolution of June 1830, Raumer, who was in Paris, broke into vigorous lamentation because the masses possessed power, and said that it would be extremely difficult "to deprive them of this power without giving them offence and without provoking them to a fresh revolt against their new chiefs";[12] at the same time, in words expressing the dithyrambic spirit of romanticism, he refers to the conditions that obtain in his Prussian fatherland, where king and people "truly live in a higher and purer atmosphere," and where the contented bourgeoisie is not endeavouring to secure additional rights.   From the history of the origin of the North German Reichstag we learn that another eminent liberal leader and advocate of liberal views, the historian Heinrich von Sybel, declared himself opposed to universal, equal, and direct suffrage, on the ground (which can be understood solely with reference to the explanations given above regarding the peculiar conceptions the liberals have of the masses) that such a right must signify "the beginning of the end for every kind of parliamentarism"; such a right, he said, was eminently a right of dominion; and he was impelled to utter an urgent warning to the German monarchy not to introduce these dangerous elements of democratic dictatorship into the new federal state.[13]   The inward dislike of liberalism for the masses is also apparent in the attitude of the liberal leaders to the principles and institutions of aristocracy.   Since the inauguration of universal suffrage and the consequent prospect that there will in the near future be a majority of socialist tendencies among the electorate or in the Lower House, many liberals, so Roscher affirms, have

---

[11] "It was this opposition [of the ultra-monarchical friends of Louis XVI to the well-disposed liberals] which set itself against the idea of bourgeois and political freedom that was spreading, not in France alone, but in all the other civilized countries of Europe, that forced upon the Revolution (which otherwise might have been purely beneficial) its evil and destructive character. It was this which led the representatives of the people to endeavour to avoid the threatened ruin by calling the masses to their aid; it was this which led to the unchaining of the rough and lawless force of the mob, and thus threw open the box of Pandora" (Carl von Rotteck, *Allgemeine Geschichte vom Anfang der historischen Kenntniss bis auf unsere Zeiten*, Herdersche Buchhandlung, Freiburg, 1826, vol. ix, p. 83).

[12] Friedrich von Raumer, *Briefe aus Paris*, etc. Op. cit., vol. i, p. 176.

[13] Cf. Otto von Diest-Daber, *Geldmacht und Sozialismus*, Puttkammer u. Mühlbrecht, Berlin, 1875, p. 13.

come to take a different view of the powers of the Crown and of the Upper House,[14] as means by which it is possible to prevent decisions of the Lower House being immediately realized in legislative measures. The same author contends that an extension of the suffrage is undesirable "in the absence of a profound statistical inquiry," that is to say, in the absence of a laborious analysis of the numerical relationships that obtain among the various classes of the population. Recently, even in that liberal group which in Germany stands nearest to the socialists, the group of "national socialists," there has been evidence of a tendency to consider that it is by no means a bad thing "for obstacles to be imposed upon the influence in political affairs of the mutable and incalculable popular will which finds expression in the Reichstag, for the national socialists consider it desirable that there should exist also aristocratic elements, independent of the popular will, ever vigilant, armed with the right of veto, to constitute a permanent moderating element." [15]

For an entire century, from the days of Rotteck to those of Naumann, German writers have laboured in the sweat of their

---

[14] Roscher, op. cit., p. 321.

[15] Martin Rade, in a leading article (*Das Allgemeine Wahlrecht ein Königliches Recht*, "Hessische Landeszeitung," xxiii, No. 25, 1907) favouring the election of the national-socialist Helmuth von Gerlach at Marburg, wrote as follows in order to still the alarms of the adversaries of universal suffrage: "The case would be very different if our Reichstag were the actual director of the government, if it alone could decide the internal and external destinies of our people! But it is merely one among the elements of our constitution! Beside it, or rather above it, stands the Bundesrat (Federal Council), and not the most trifling proposition can become law unless with the assent of the Imperial Chancellor, the Emperor, and the Princes. Certainly the Federal Council will not permanently oppose a strong and reasonable expression of the popular will which is manifested in a constitutional manner in the Reichstag; but such resolutions of the Reichstag as it regards as injudicious it will reject, and often has rejected. By this means, precautions are taken to limit the power of universal suffrage, just as nature takes care that trees do not grow to touch the skies. It is well for our legislation that we have these two Chambers, and not the Reichstag alone." Such considerations run like a red thread through the entire history of bourgeois liberalism, of which they are, in fact, a congenital defect. Already in the work of Guizot, which in the literature of the young bourgeoisie occupies the place taken in socialist literature by the *Communist Manifesto* of Karl Marx, we read this praise of the French House of Peers, that its significance is to be "un privilège placé là où il peut servir" (F. Guizot, *Du Gouvernement de la France depuis la Restauration, et du Ministère actuel*, Librairie Française de Ladvocat, Paris, 1820, p. 14).

brow to effect a theoretical conciliation between democracy and
military monarchy, and to unite these natural opposites in a
higher unity. Hand in hand with their honourable endeavours
on behalf of this loftier aim have proceeded their attempts to
defeudalize the monarchy to the utmost, with the sole purpose
of substituting for the aristocratic guardians of the throne guardians speaking with professional authority. The task they set
themselves was to lay the theoretical foundations, if not of the
so-called social monarchy, at least of the popular monarchy. It
is evident that such an objective involves a political tendency
which has nothing in common with science, but which is not in
necessary opposition to or in contradiction with science (it is the
method which must decide this), being a political tendency which
is, quâ political, outside the domain of science. It cannot be
made a reason for blaming German men of science that there
exists in Germany a tendency towards the construction of something resembling the July Monarchy, for this tendency rests
within the orbit of politics. But it is plainly a matter for historical censure when we find an attempt to identify the monarchical principle which has for some decades been dominant in
Prussianized Germany with the cherished idea of the popular (or
social) monarchy. In committing such an error, the majority of
German liberal theorists and historians mistake dreams for reality. In this confusion rests the organic defect of all German
liberalism, which since 1866 has continually endeavoured to disguise its change of front (that is to say, its partisan struggle
against socialism and its simultaneous and voluntary renunciation of all attempts to complete the political emancipation of
the German bourgeoisie), by the fallacious assertion that with
the unification of Germany and the establishment of the empire
of the Hohenzollerns all or almost all the aspirations of its democratic youth have been realized. The fundamental principle of
modern monarchy (hereditary monarchy) is absolutely irreconcilable with the principles of democracy, even when these are
understood in the most elastic sense. Cæsarism is still democracy,
or may at least still claim the name, when it is based upon the
popular will; but automatic monarchy, never.

We may sum up the argument by saying that in modern party
life aristocracy gladly presents itself in democratic guise, whilst
the substance of democracy is permeated with aristocratic elements. On the one side we have aristocracy in a democratic
form, and on the other democracy with an aristocratic content.

The democratic external form which characterizes the life of political parties may readily veil from superficial observers the tendency towards aristocracy, or rather towards oligarchy, which is inherent in all party organization. If we wish to obtain light upon this tendency, the best field of observation is offered by the intimate structure of the democratic parties, and, among these, of the socialist and revolutionary labour party. In the conservative parties, except during elections, the tendency to oligarchy manifests itself with that spontaneous vigour and clearness which corresponds with the essentially oligarchical character of these parties. But the parties which are subversive in their aims exhibit the like phenomena no less markedly. The study of the oligarchical manifestations in party life is most valuable and most decisive in its results when undertaken in relation to the revolutionary parties, for the reason that these parties, in respect of origin and of programme, represent the negation of any such tendency, and have actually come into existence out of opposition thereto. Thus the appearance of oligarchical phenomena in the very bosom of the revolutionary parties is a conclusive proof of the existence of immanent oligarchical tendencies in every kind of human organization which strives for the attainment of definite ends.

In theory, the principle of social and democratic parties is the struggle against oligarchy in all its forms. The question therefore arises how we are to explain the development in such parties of the very tendencies against which they have declared war. To furnish an unprejudiced analytical answer to this question constitutes an important part of the task the author has undertaken.

In the society of to-day, the state of dependence that results from the existing economic and social conditions renders an ideal democracy impossible. This must be admitted without reserve. But the further question ensues, whether, and if so how far, within the contemporary social order, among the elements which are endeavouring to overthrow that order and to replace it by a new one, there may exist in the germ energies tending to approximate towards ideal democracy, to find outlet in that direction, or at least to work towards it as a necessary issue.

CHAPTER II

THE ETHICAL EMBELLISHMENT OF SOCIAL STRUGGLES

No one seriously engaged in historical studies can have failed to perceive that all classes which have ever attained to dominion have earnestly endeavoured to transmit to their descendants such political power as they have been able to acquire. The hereditary transmission of political power has always been the most efficacious means of maintaining class rule. Thus there is displayed in this field the same historical process which in the domain of the sexual life has given rise to the bourgeois family-order and its accessories, the indissolubility of marriage, the severe penalties inflicted upon the adulterous wife, and the right of primogeniture. In so far as we can draw sound conclusions from the scanty prehistoric data that are available, it seems that the bourgeois family owes its genesis to the innate tendency of man, as soon as he has attained a certain degree of economic well-being, to transmit his possessions by inheritance to the legitimate son whom he can with reasonable certainty regard as his own. The same tendency prevails in the field of politics, where it is kept active by all the peculiar and inherent instincts of mankind, and where it is vigorously nourished by an economic order based therefore, by a natural and psychological analogy, political power comes also to be considered as an object of private hereditary ownership. In the political field, as everywhere else, the paternal instinct to transmit this species of property to the son has been always strongly manifest throughout historic time. This has been one of the principal causes of the replacement of elective monarchy by hereditary monarchy. The desire to maintain a position acquired by the family in society has at all times been so intense that, as Gaetano Mosca has aptly noted, whenever certain members of the dominant class have not been able to have sons of their own (as, for example, was the case with the prelates of the Roman Church), there has arisen with spontaneous and dynamic force the institution of nepotism, as an extreme manifestation of the impulse to self-maintenance and to hereditary transmission.[1]

In a twofold manner aristocracy has introduced itself quite automatically in those states also from which it seemed to be excluded by constitutional principles, by historical considerations, or by reason of the peculiarities of national psychology— alike by way of a revived tradition and by way of the birth of new economic forces. The North Americans, democrats, living under a republican regime and knowing nothing of titles of nobility, by no means delivered themselves from aristocracy when they shook off the power of the English crown. This phenomenon is in part the simple effect of causes that have come into existence quite recently, such as capitalist concentration (with its associated heaping-up of the social power in the hands of the few and consequent formation of privileged minorities), and the progressive reconciliation of the old and rigid republican spirit with the ideas, the prejudices, and the ambitions of ancient Europe. The existence of an aristocracy of millionaires, railway kings, oil kings, cattle kings, etc., is now indisputable. But even at a time when the youthful democracy and the freedom of America had only just been sealed with the blood of its citizens, it was difficult (so we learn from Alexis de Tocqueville) to find a single American who did not plume himself with an idle vanity upon belonging to one of the first families which had colonized American soil.[2] So lively was "aristocratic prejudice" among these primitive republicans! Even at the present day the old families which are Dutch by name and origin constitute in the State of New York a stratum whose aristocratic preëminence is uncontested, a class of patricians lacking the outward attributes of nobility.

When, in the latter half of the seventeenth century, the French bourgeoisie was vigorously pressing upward, it knew no better how to adapt itself to its changed environment than by aping the usages, the mode of life, the tastes, and even the mentality of the feudal nobility. In 1670 Molière wrote his splendid comedy, *Le Bourgeois gentilhomme*. The Abbé de Choisy, who belonged to the *noblesse de robe*, and whose ancestors had filled the distinguished offices of *Maître des Requêtes* and *Conseiller*

---

[1] Gaetano Mosca, *Il Principio aristocratico e il democratico nel passato e nel' avvenire* (inaugural address), Stamperia Paravia, Turin, 1903, p. 22.
[2] Alexis de Tocqueville, *De la démocratie en Amérique*, Gosseliné, Paris, 1849, Part II, vol. ii, p. 19.

d'Etat, relates that his mother had given him as a maxim of conduct that he should be careful to frequent none but aristocratic salons.[3] With the fervour of the novice, the new arrivals assimilated the spirit and the principles of the class hitherto dominant, and the distinguished members of the bourgeoisie who had entered the service of the state, which was still predominantly feudal, hastened to take new names. The Fouquets, the Le Telliers, the Colberts, the Phélippeaux, and the Desmarets, became the Belle-Isles, the de Louvois, the de Seignelays, the de Maurepas, the de Maillebois, and the de Lavrillières.[4] In modern Germany, under our very eyes, there has for the last forty years been proceeding an absorption of the young industrial bourgeoisie into the old aristocracy of birth, and the process has of late been enormously accelerated.[5] The German bourgeoisie is becoming feudalized. Here the only result of the emancipation of the *roturier* has been to reinvigorate his old enemy the noble by the provision of new blood and new economic energy. The enriched bourgeois have no higher ambition than to fuse with the nobility, in order to derive from this fusion a kind of legitimate title for their connection with the dominant class, a title which can then be represented, not as acquired, but as existing by hereditary right. Thus we see that the hereditary principle (even when purely fictitious) greatly accelerates the process of social "training," accelerates, that is to say, the adaptation of the new social forces to the old aristocratic environment.

In the violent struggle between the new class of those who are rising and the old stratum of those who are undergoing a decadence partly apparent and partly real—a struggle at times waged with dramatic greatness, but often proceeding obscurely, so as hardly to attract attention—moral considerations are drawn into the dance, and pulled this way and that by the various contending parties, who use them in order to mask their true aims. In an era of democracy, ethics constitute a weapon which everyone can employ. In the old regime, the members of the ruling class and those who desired to become rulers continually spoke

---

[3] Abbé de Choisy, *Mémoires pour servir à l'Histoire de Louis XIV,* Van De Water, Utrecht, 1727, p. 23.

[4] Pierre Edouard Lémontey, *Essai sur l'établissement monarchique de Louis XIV,* Appendix to *Nouveaux mémoires de Dangeau,* republished by the author, Deterville, Paris, 1818, p. 392.

[5] Cf. the striking examples furnished by Werner Sombart, *Die deutsche Volkswirtschaft im XIX Jahrhundert,* Bondi, Berlin, 1903, pp. 545, et seq.

of their own personal rights. Democracy adopts a more diplomatic, a more prudent course. It has rejected such claims as unethical. To-day, all the factors of public life speak and struggle in the name of the people, of the community at large. The government and rebels against the government, kings and party-leaders, tyrants by the grace of God and usurpers, rabid idealists and calculating self-seekers, all are "the people," and all declare that in their actions they merely fulfil the will of the nation.

Thus, in the modern life of the classes and of the nations, moral considerations have become an accessory, a necessary fiction. Every government endeavours to support its power by a general ethical principle. The political forms in which the various social movements become crystallized also assume a philanthropic mask. There is not a single one among the young class-parties which fails, before starting on its march for the conquest of power, to declare solemnly to the world that its aim is to redeem, not so much itself as the whole of humanity, from the yoke of a tyrannical minority, and to substitute for the old and inequitable regime a new reign of justice. Democracies are always glib talkers. Their terminology is often comparable to a tissue of metaphors. The demagogue, that spontaneous fruit of democratic soil, overflows with sentimentality, and is profoundly moved by the sorrows of the people. "Les victimes soignent leurs mots, les bourreaux sont ivres de philosophie larmoyante," writes Alphonse Daudet in this connection.[6] Every new social class, when it gives the signal for an attack upon the privileges of a class already in possession of economic and political power, inscribes upon its banners the motto: "The Liberation of the entire Human Race!" When the young French bourgeoisie was girding its loins for the great struggle against the nobles and the clergy, it began with the solemn *Déclaration des Droits de l'Homme,* and hurled itself into the fray with the war-cry *Liberté, Egalité, Fraternité!* To-day we can ourselves hear the spokesmen of another great class-movement, that of the wage-earners, announce that they undertake the class-struggle from no egoistic motives, but on the contrary in order to exclude such motives for ever from the social process. For the refrain of its Hymn of Progress modern socialism ever reiterates the proud

---

[6] Léon A. Daudet, *Alphonse Daudet,* Bibliothèque Charpentier. E. Fasquelle, Paris, 1898, p. 142.

words: "Creation of a humane and fraternal society in which class will be unknown!"

The victorious bourgeoisie of the *Droits de l'Homme* did, indeed, realize the republic, but not democracy. The words *Liberté, Egalité, Fraternité* may be read to this day over the portals of all French prisons. The Commune was the first attempt, crowned by a transient success, at a proletarian-socialist government; and despite its communistic principles, and under the pressure of extreme financial stringency, the Commune respected the Bank of France as faithfully as could have done any syndicate of inexorable capitalists. There have been revolutions, but the world has never witnessed the establishment of logical democracy.

Political parties, however much they may be founded upon narrow class interests and however evidently they may work against the interests of the majority, love to identify themselves with the universe, or at least to present themselves as co-operating with all the citizens of the state, and to proclaim that they are fighting in the name of all and for the good of all.[7] It is only the socialist orators who are sometimes found to proclaim that their party is specifically a class party. But they tone down this assertion by adding that in ultimate analysis the interests of their party coincide with those of the entire people. It is, indeed, true that in protesting that it enters the lists in the interests of the whole of humanity the socialist party, representing the most numerous class of the population, is nearer to the truth than are the bourgeois parties when these make the same claim, for they by their very nature are parties of the minority.[8] But the

---

[7] The adherents of pessimism in sociology, writing for the most part independently of one another, have drawn express attention to the confusion, in part conscious and in part unconscious, characteristic of all revolutionary and reforming movements, between the interests or aims of class and of party and the interests or aims of the human race. Cf. more particularly Gaetano Mosca, *Elementi di Scienza politica*, Bocca, Turin, 1896, pp. 75 et seq.; Ludwig Gumplowicz, op. cit., pp. 23, 70, 71, 94, 123; Vilfredo Pareto, *Les Systèmes Socialistes*, Giard et Brière, Paris, 1892, vol. i, p. 59; Ludwig Woltmann, *Politische Anthropologie*, Thüringische Verlagsanstalt, Leipzig, 1903, pp. 299 et seq. Moreover, this confusion is not peculiar to democracy. Aristocracy also claims to represent on principle, not the interests of a small social group, but those of the entire people without distinction of class (as far as the German conservatives are concerned cf. Oskar Stillich, op. cit., p. 3). But it is here easier to recognize the true nature of the democratic mask.

[8] An extremely elaborate and able description of the intimate relation-

socialist claim is also far from the truth, seeing that the two terms *humanity* and *party* are far from being identical in extension, even if the party under consideration should embrace, or believe itself to embrace, the great majority of humanity. When for opportunist reasons the socialist party declares to the electors that socialism proposes to give to all, but to take nothing from any, it suffices to point out that the enormous differences of wealth which exist in society render it impossible to keep any such promise. The giving presupposes a taking away, and if the proletarians wish to bring about an equality of economic status between themselves on the one hand and the Rothschilds, Vanderbilts, and Rockefellers on the other, which could be done only by socializing the means of production and exchange to-day owned by these various millionaires, it is obvious that the wealth and power of these great bourgeois princes would be considerably diminished. To the same opportunist party tendency we must ascribe the formulation of the socialist theory which, in apparent accordance with the fundamental principle of the Marxist political economy, divides the population into owners of the means of production and non-owners dependent upon these, proceeding to the contention that all the owners must be capitalist in sentiment while all the dependents must be socialists, that is to say, must desire the triumph of socialism. This view is utterly fallacious, for it regards as the unique or most certain criterion for determining the class to which an individual belongs the amount of his income, which is a purely external characteristic, and then proceeds (in a manner which is perhaps effective in political life, but which is eminently contestable on theoretical grounds) to enlarge the concept of the proletariat so that all employees, governmental or private, may be claimed for the party of labour. According to this theory the directors of Krupp or the Minister-Presidents of Russia, since as such they are non-owners and employees, are dependents upon the means of production, ought to espouse with enthusiasm the cause of social-

---

ships between party and collectivity will be found in an essay by Karl Kautsky, *Klasseninteresse, Sonderinteresse, Parteiinteresse,* ''Neue Zeit'' xxi, vol. ii, Nos. 34 and 35. I may also refer those who care to study the relationship between the interests of humanity as a whole and the interests of the proletariat as a social class, to the consideration put forward in my own *Das Proletariat in der Wissenschaft und die Oekonomisch-Anthropologische Synthese,* published as preface to the German translation of Niceforo's work *Anthropologie der nichtbesitzenden Klassen, Studien und Untersuchungen,* Maas und van Suchtelen, Leipzig-Amsterdam, 1909.

ism—ought to do so, at least, in so far as they understand their true position in society, in so far as they have become what the socialists term "class-conscious."[9]

The ideal impetuosity of youthful movements aiming at emancipation is depicted by anti-democratic writers as a pious illusion, as the pursuit of a will-o'-the-wisp, arising from the need to make the particular good assume the aspect of the general good.[10] In the world of hard fact, every class-movement which professes to aim at the good of the entire community is stamped inevitably as self-contradictory. Humanity cannot dispense with "political classes," but from their very nature these classes are but fractions of society.

---

[9] The relationships between socialism and industrial bureaucracy were discussed by the present writer at considerable length in a paper read at the Italian Congress of the Sciences held at Florence in 1908, *Sulla decadenza della Classe media industriale antica e sul sorgere di una Classe media industriale moderna nei Paesi di economia spiccatamente capitalista*. This paper was published in the "Giornale degli Economisti," vol. xxxvii, Series 2, 1909.

[10] Cf. Gaetano Mosca, op. cit., p. 75.

PART ONE

LEADERSHIP IN DEMOCRATIC
ORGANIZATIONS

A. TECHNICAL AND ADMINISTRATIVE CAUSES OF LEADERSHIP

CHAPTER I

INTRODUCTORY—THE NEED FOR ORGANIZATION

DEMOCRACY is inconceivable without organization. A few words will suffice to demonstrate this proposition.[1]

A class which unfurls in face of society the banner of certain definite claims, and which aspires to be the realization of a complex of ideal aims deriving from the economic functions which that class fulfils, needs an organization. Be the claims economic or be they political, organization appears the only means for the creation of a collective will. Organization, based as it is upon the principle of least effort, that is to say, upon the greatest possible economy of energy, is the weapon of the weak in their struggle with the strong.[2]

The chances of success in any struggle will depend upon the degree to which this struggle is carried out upon a basis of solidarity between individuals whose interests are identical. In objecting, therefore, to the theories of the individualist anarchists that nothing could please the employers better than the dispersion and disaggregation of the forces of the workers, the socialists, the most fanatical of all the partisans of the idea of organization, enunciate an argument which harmonizes well with the results of scientific study of the nature of parties.

We live in a time in which the idea of coöperation has

---

[1] Moreover, the literature of this subject is exhaustive. Here we will refer merely to the following: Victor Griffuelhes, *L'Action syndicaliste*, Rivière, Paris, 1908, p. 8. Henriette Roland-Holst, *Generalstreik und Socialdemokratie*, Kaden u. Co., Dresden, 2nd ed., 1906, pp. 114 et seq. Attilio Cabiati, *Le Basi teoriche dell' organizzazione operaia*, Office of the "Critica Sociale," Milan, 1908, p. 19.

[2] A detailed study of the relations between the various aspects of coöperation and of the law of the minimal expenditure of effort will be found in an essay by the present writer, *L'Uomo economico e la Coöperazione*, Società Tip. Editr. Naz., Turin, 1909.

become so firmly established that even millionaires perceive the necessity of common action. It is easy to understand, then, that organization has become a vital principle in the working class, for in default of it their success is *a priori* impossible. The refusal of the worker to participate in the collective life of his class cannot fail to entail disastrous consequences. In respect of culture and of economic, physical, and physiological conditions, the proletarian is the weakest element of our society.[3] In fact, the isolated member of the working classes is defenceless in the hands of those who are economically stronger. It is only by combination to form a structural aggregate that the proletarians can acquire the faculty of political resistance and attain to a social dignity. The importance and the influence of the working class are directly proportional to its numerical strength. But for the representation of that numerical strength organization and coordination are indispensable. The principle of organization is an absolutely essential condition for the political struggle of the masses.

Yet this politically necessary principle of organization, while it overcomes that disorganization of forces which would be favourable to the adversary, brings other dangers in its train. We escape Scylla only to dash ourselves on Charybdis. Organization is, in fact, the source from which the conservative currents flow over the plain of democracy, occasioning there disastrous floods and rendering the plain unrecognizable.

---

[3] The inferiority of the proletarian alike in his anthropological and his cultural aspects is displayed by Niceforo in the work mentioned in a previous note.

CHAPTER II

MECHANICAL AND TECHNICAL IMPOSSIBILITY OF DIRECT GOVERNMENT BY THE MASSES

IT was a Rhenish Democrat, Moritz Rittinghausen, who first made a brilliant attempt to give a real basis for direct legislation by the people.[1]

According to this system the entire population was to be divided into sections, each containing a thousand inhabitants, as was done temporarily for some days in Prussia during the elections of the years 1848 and 1849. The members of each section were to assemble in some pre-arranged place—a school, a townhall, or other public building—and to elect a president. Every citizen was to have the right of speech. In this way the intelligence of every individual would be placed at the service of the fatherland. When the discussion was finished, each one would record his vote. The president would transmit the result to the burgomaster, who would notify the higher authorities. The will of the majority would be decisive.

No legislative proposal was to come from above. The government should have no further initiative than to determine that on a given day all the sections should discuss a given argument. Whenever a certain number of the citizens demanded a new law of any kind, or the reform of an existing law, the ministry concerned must invite the people to exercise its sovereignty within a stated time, and to pass for itself the law in question.[2] The law

---

[1] Moritz Rittinghausen, *Ueber die Organisation der direkten Gesetzgebung durch das Volk*, Social. Demokrat. Schriften, No. 4, Cöln, 1870, p. 10. The merit of having for the first time ventured to put forward practical proposals of this nature for the solution of the social problem unquestionably belongs to Rittinghausen. Victor Considérant, who subsequently resumed the attempt to establish direct popular government upon a wider basis and with a more far-reaching propagandist effect, expressly recognized Rittinghausen as his precursor (Victor Considérant, *La Solution ou Le Gouvernement Direct du Peuple*. Librairie Phalanstérienne, Paris, 1850, p. 61).

[2] In the American constitution those states only are termed *federalist* (the name being here used to imply a democratic character) in which the

takes organic form from the discussion itself. First of all, the president opens the debate upon the principal question. Subsequently subordinate points are discussed. Then comes the vote. That proposition which has received the majority of votes is adopted. As soon as all the returns of the voting have been sent to the ministry, a special commission must edit a clear and simple text of the law, formulating it in a manner which is not open to different interpretations, as is the case with most of the laws presented to modern parliaments, for these, as Rittinghausen sarcastically adds, would seem to incorporate a deliberate intention to favour the tendency of lawyers to ambiguity and hair-splitting.

The system here sketched is clear and concise, and it might seem at the first glance that its practical application would involve no serious difficulties. But if put to the test it would fail to fulfil the expectations of its creator.

The practical ideal of democracy consists in the self-government of the masses in conformity with the decisions of popular assemblies. But while this system limits the extension of the principle of delegation, it fails to provide any guarantee against the formation of an oligarchical camarilla. Undoubtedly it deprives the natural leaders of their quality as functionaries, for this quality is transferred to the people themselves. The crowd, however, is always subject to suggestion, being readily influenced by the eloquence of great popular orators; moreover, direct government by the people, admitting of no serious discussions or thoughtful deliberations, greatly facilitates *coups de main* of all kinds by men who are exceptionally bold, energetic, and adroit.[3]

It is easier to dominate a large crowd than a small audience. The adhesion of the crowd is tumultuous, summary, and unconditional. Once the suggestions have taken effect, the crowd does not readily tolerate contradiction from a small minority, and still less from isolated individuals. A great multitude assembled within a small area is unquestionably more accessible to panic

---

people assemble for such a legislative purpose, whilst the states with representative popular government are called *republics*.

[3] It often happens that by such a *coup de main* one leader will surprise and defeat the other. Thus Arturo Labriola, the well-known leader of the Italian syndicalists, during the general strike of 1904 at Milan induced the great meeting in the Arena to vote for the continuation of the strike, securing this by the sole power of his inflammatory eloquence, and in opposition to the desire of the representatives of the local labour organizations. (*I Gruppi Socialisti Milanesi al Congresso Socialista Nazionale di Roma, October 7-9, 1906.* Gruppi Socialisti, Milan, p. 11.)

alarms, to unreflective enthusiasm, and the like, than is a small meeting, whose members can quietly discuss matters among themselves (Roscher).[4]

It is a fact of everyday experience that enormous public meetings commonly carry resolutions by acclamation or by general assent, whilst these same assemblies, if divided into small sections, say of fifty persons each, would be much more guarded in their assent. Great party congresses, in which are present the *élite* of the membership, usually act in this way. Words and actions are far less deliberately weighed by the crowd than by the individuals or the little groups of which this crowd is composed. The fact is incontestable—a manifestation of the pathology of the crowd.[5] The individual disappears in the multitude, and therewith disappears also personality and sense of responsibility.[6]

The most formidable argument against the sovereignty of the masses is, however, derived from the mechanical and technical impossibility of its realization.

The sovereign masses are altogether incapable of undertaking the most necessary resolutions. The impotence of direct democracy, like the power of indirect democracy, is a direct outcome of the influence of number. In a polemic against Proudhon (1849), Louis Blanc asks whether it is possible for thirty-four millions of human beings (the population of France at that time) to carry on their affairs without accepting what the pettiest man of business finds necessary, the intermediation of representatives. He answers his own question by saying that one who declares direct action on this scale to be possible is a fool, and

---

[4] Roscher, op. cit., p. 358.

[5] This matter has been luminously discussed by French and Italian sociologists. Cf. Gabriel Tarde, *Les crimes des foules*, Storck, Lyons, 1892; Scipio Sighele, *I delitti della folla*, Fratelli Bocca, Turin, 1902. See also a discussion of the same question conducted with especial reference to the Chamber of Deputies, Scipio, Sighele, *Contro il parlamentarismo. Saggio di psicologia collettiva*, Treves, Milan, 1905.

[6] "It seems that the simple fact of aggregation brings out the sheeplike character of human beings, for wherever we observe great assemblies, whether in public meetings or in parliament, whether we have to do with shareholders' meetings, corporate meetings, or university convocations, we everywhere find that the majority is content to accept the leadership of single individuals, acting no longer in accordance with its own convictions, but enslaved by the phrases employed by the leaders" (Ludwig Gumplowicz, op. cit., p. 124).

that one who denies its possibility need not be an absolute opponent of the idea of the state.[7]   The same question and the same
answer could be repeated to-day in respect of party organization.
Above all in the great industrial centres, where the labour party
sometimes numbers its adherents by tens of thousands, it is impossible to carry on the affairs of this gigantic body without a
system of representation.   The great socialist organization of
Berlin, which embraces the six constituencies of the city, as well
as the two outlying areas of Niederbarnim and Teltow-Beeskow-
Charlottenburg, has a member-roll of more than ninety thousand.[8]

It is obvious that such a gigantic number of persons belonging
to a unitary organization cannot do any practical work upon a
system of direct discussion.[9]   The regular holding of deliberative
assemblies of a thousand members encounters the gravest difficulties in respect of room and distance; [10] while from the topographical point of view such an assembly would become altogether impossible if the members numbered ten thousand.   Even
if we imagined the means of communication to become much
better than those which now exist, how would it be possible to
assemble such a multitude in a given place, at a stated time,
and with the frequency demanded by the exigencies of party
life?   In addition must be considered the physiological impossibility even for the most powerful orator of making himself heard

---

[7] Louis Blanc, ''L'état dans une démocratie,'' *Questions d'aujourd'hui
et de demain*, Dentu, Paris, 1880, vol. iii, p. 150.

[8] Eduard Bernstein, *Die Demokratie in der Sozialdemokratie*, ''Sozialist.
Monatshefte,'' 1908, fasc. 18-19, p. 1109.

[9] ''Quiconque voudrait appliquer à une société nombreuse le premier principe (celui de faire concourir les individus à la formation des lois par eux-
mêmes), sans employer l'intermédiare, la bouleverserait infailliblement''
(Benjamin Constant, *Cours de politique constitutionnelle*, Société Typ.
Belge, Brussels, 1851, vol. iii, p. 246).

[10] Especially in northern climes, where the weather makes it impossible
to hold open-air meetings for the greater part of the year, and yet it is in
these very regions that political life attains its highest development.   In
some countries, again, as in Germany, the reactionary governments are most
unwilling to concede to the populace the right of public meeting in the
open air, and the use of the theatres for political purposes (as in Italy),
or of the town halls (as in England), is forbidden.   Bernstein is therefore
right when he says that in most towns it would be impossible, owing to the
absence of a sufficiently large hall, to unite in a general assembly even a
considerable proportion of the members of a party or society (Eduard
Bernstein, *Die Arbeiterbewegung*, Rütten u. Loening, Frankfort-on-the-
Main, 1910, p. 151).

by a crowd of ten thousand persons.[11] There are, however, other reasons of a technical and administrative character which render impossible the direct self-government of large groups. If Peter wrongs Paul, it is out of the question that all the other citizens should hasten to the spot to undertake a personal examination of the matter in dispute, and to take the part of Paul against Peter.[12] By parity of reasoning, in the modern democratic party, it is impossible for the collectivity to undertake the direct settlement of all the controversies that may arise.

Hence the need for delegation, for the system in which delegates represent the mass and carry out its will. Even in groups sincerely animated with the democratic spirit, current business, the preparation and the carrying out of the most important actions, is necessarily left in the hands of individuals. It is well known that the impossibility for the people to exercise a legislative power directly in popular assemblies led the democratic idealists of Spain to demand, as the least of evils, a system of popular representation and a parliamentary state.[13]

Originally the chief is merely the servant of the mass. The organization is based upon the absolute equality of all its members. Equality is here understood in its most general sense, as an equality of like men. In many countries, as in idealist Italy (and in certain regions in Germany where the socialist movement is still in its infancy), this equality is manifested, among other ways, by the mutual use of the familiar "thou," which is employed by the most poorly paid wage-labourer in addressing the most distinguished intellectual. This generic conception of equality is, however, gradually replaced by the idea of equality among comrades belonging to the same organization, all of whose members enjoy the same rights. The democratic principle aims at guaranteeing to all an equal influence and an equal participation in the regulation of the common interests. All are electors, and all are eligible for office. The fundamental postulate of the *Déclaration des Droits de l'Homme* finds here its theoretical application. All the offices are filled by election. The officials, executive organs of the general will, play a merely subordinate part, are always dependent upon the collectivity, and can be

---

[11] Roscher, op. cit., p. 351.

[12] Louis Blanc, op. cit., p. 144.

[13] Cf. the letter of Antonio Quiroga to King Ferdinand VII, dated January 7, 1820 (Don Juan van Halen, *Mémoires*, Renouard, Paris, 1827, Part II, p. 382).

deprived of their office at any moment. The mass of the party is omnipotent.

At the outset, the attempt is made to depart as little as possible from pure democracy by subordinating the delegates altogether to the will of the mass, by tying them hand and foot. In the early days of the movement of the Italian agricultural workers, the chief of the league required a majority of four-fifths of the votes to secure election. When disputes arose with the employers about wages, the representative of the organization, before undertaking any negotiations, had to be furnished with a written authority, authorized by the signature of every member of the corporation. All the accounts of the body were open to the examination of the members, at any time. There were two reasons for this. First of all, the desire was to avoid the spread of mistrust through the mass, "this poison which gradually destroys even the strongest organism." In the second place, this usage allowed each one of the members to learn bookkeeping, and to acquire such a general knowledge of the working of the corporation as to enable him at any time to take over its leadership.[14] It is obvious that democracy in this sense is applicable only on a very small scale. In the infancy of the English labour movement, in many of the trade-unions, the delegates were either appointed in rotation from among all the members, or were chosen by lot.[15] Gradually, however, the delegates' duties become more complicated; some individual ability becomes essential, a certain oratorical gift, and a considerable amount of objective knowledge. It thus becomes impossible to trust to blind chance, to the fortune of alphabetic succession, or to the order of priority, in the choice of a delegation whose members must possess certain peculiar personal aptitudes if they are to discharge their mission to the general advantage.

Such were the methods which prevailed in the early days of the labour movement to enable the masses to participate in party and trade-union administration. To-day they are falling into disuse, and in the development of the modern political aggregate there is a tendency to shorten and stereotype the process which transforms the led into a leader—a process which has hitherto developed by the natural course of events. Here

---

[14] Egidio Bernaroli, *Manuale per la costituzione e il funzionamento delle leghe dei contadini*, Libreria Soc. Ital., Rome, 1902, pp. 20, 26, 27, 52.

[15] Sidney and Beatrice Webb, *Industrial Democracy* (German edition), Stuttgart, 1898, vol. i, p. 6.

and there voices make themselves heard demanding a sort of official consecration for the leaders, insisting that it is necessary to constitute a class of professional politicians, of approved and registered experts in political life. Ferdinand Tönnies advocates that the party should institute regular examinations for the nomination of socialist parliamentary candidates, and for the appointment of party secretaries.[16] Heinrich Herkner goes even farther. He contends that the great trade-unions cannot long maintain their existence if they persist in entrusting the management of their affairs to persons drawn from the rank and file, who have risen to command stage by stage solely in consequence of practical aptitudes acquired in the service of the organization. He refers, in this connection, to the unions that are controlled by the employers, whose officials are for the most part university men. He foresees that in the near future all the labour organizations will be forced to abandon proletarian exclusiveness, and in the choice of their officials to give the preference to persons of an education that is superior alike in economic, legal, technical, and commercial respects.[17]

Even to-day, the candidates for the secretaryship of a trade-union are subject to examination as to their knowledge of legal matters and their capacity as letter-writers. The socialist organizations engaged in political action also directly undertake the training of their own officials. Everywhere there are coming into existence "nurseries" for the rapid supply of officials possessing a certain amount of "scientific culture." Since 1906 there has existed in Berlin a Party-School in which courses of instruction are given for the training of those who wish to take office in the socialist party or in the trade-unions. The instructors are paid out of the funds of the socialist party, which was directly responsible for the foundation of the school. The other expenses of the undertaking, including the maintenance of the pupils, are furnished from a common fund supplied by the party and the various trade-unions interested. In addition, the families of the pupils, in so far as the attendance of these at the school deprives the families of their bread-winners, receive an allowance from the provincial branch of the party or from the local branch of the union to which each pupil belongs. The

---

[16] Ferdinand Tönnies, *Politik und Moral*, Neuer Frankf. Verl., Frankfort, 1901, p. 46.

[17] Heinrich Herkner, *Die Arbeiterfrage*, Guttentag, Berlin, 1908, 5th ed., pp. 116, 117.

third course of this school, from October 1, 1908, to April 3, 1909, was attended by twenty-six pupils, while the first year there had been thirty-one and the second year thirty-three. As pupils, preference is given to comrades who already hold office in the party or in one of the labour unions.[18] Those who do not already belong to the labour bureaucracy make it their aim to enter that body, and cherish the secret hope that attendance at the school will smooth their path. Those who fail to attain this end are apt to exhibit a certain discontent with the party which, after having encouraged their studies, has sent them back to manual labour. Among the 141 students of the year 1910-11, three classes were to be distinguished: one of these consisted of old and tried employees in the different branches of the labour movement (fifty-two persons); a second consisted of those who obtained employment in the party or the trade-unions directly the course was finished (forty-nine persons); the third consisted of those who had to return to manual labour (forty persons).[19]

In Italy, *L'Umanitaria*, a philanthropic organization run by the socialists, founded at Milan in 1905 a "Practical School of Social Legislation," whose aim it is to give to a certain number of workers an education which will fit them for becoming factory inspectors, or for taking official positions in the various labour organizations, in the friendly societies, or in the labour exchanges.[20] The course of instruction lasts for two years, and at its close the pupils receive, after examination, a diploma which entitles them to the title of "Labour Expert." In 1908 there were two hundred and two pupils, thirty-seven of whom were employees of trade unions or of co-operative societies, four were secretaries of labour exchanges, forty-five employees in or members of the liberal professions, and a hundred and twelve working men.[21] At the outset most of the pupils came to the school as a matter of personal taste, or with the aim of obtaining the diploma in order to secure some comparatively lucrative private employment. But quite recently the governing body has determined to suppress the diploma, and to institute a supplementary

---

[18] *Protokoll des Parteitags zu Leipzig*, 1909, "Vorwärts," Berlin, 1909, p. 48.

[19] Heinrich Schulz, *Fünf Jahre Parteischule*, "Neue Zeit," Anno xxix, vol. ii, fasc. 49, p. 807.

[20] *Scuola Prat. di Legislaz. Sociale* (Programma e Norme), anno iii, Soc. Umanitaria, Milan, 1908.

[21] Ibid., anno iv, Milan, 1909, p. 5.

course open to those only who are already employed by some labour organization or who definitely intend to enter such employment. For those engaged upon this special course of study there will be provided scholarships of £2 a week, the funds for this purpose being supplied in part by *L'Umanitaria* and in part by the labour organizations which wish to send their employees to the school.[22] In the year 1909, under the auspices of the *Bourse du Travail*, there was founded at Turin a similar school (*Scuola Pratica di Cultura e Legislazione Sociale*), which, however, soon succumbed.

In England the trade-unions and co-operative societies make use of Ruskin College, Oxford, sending thither those of their members who aspire to office in the labour organizations, and who have displayed special aptitudes for this career.[23] In Austria it is proposed to found a party school upon the German model.[24]

It is undeniable that all these educational institutions for the officials of the party and of the labour organizations tend, above all, towards the artificial creation of an *élite* of the working-class, of a caste of cadets composed of persons who aspire to the command of the proletarian rank and file. Without wishing it, there is thus effected a continuous enlargement of the gulf which divides the leaders from the masses.

The technical specialization that inevitably results from all extensive organization renders necessary what is called expert leadership. Consequently the power of determination comes to be considered one of the specific attributes of leadership, and is gradually withdrawn from the masses to be concentrated in the hands of the leaders alone.[25] Thus the leaders, who were at first

---

[22] Rinaldo Rigola, *I funzionari delle organizzazioni,* "Avanti," anno xiv, No. 341.

[23] See the admirable description given by Lily Braun in her *Londoner Tagebuch,* "Neue Gesellschaft," anno ii, fasc. xxix, 1906.—More recently, in England, another body with similar objects to Ruskin College, but more definitely socialist in tendency, has come into existence, and is known as the Central Labour College. It was founded in Oxford in 1909, to some extent in opposition to Ruskin College, since the education given at this latter was regarded as being unduly influenced by the Oxford outlook, by the views of the dominant class. The Central Labour College insists on the labour point of view in all its educational work. Owing to the opposition of the University landowners it was removed to London in 1911.

[24] Otto Bauer, *Eine Parteischule für Oesterreich,* "Der Kampf," Vienna, anno iii, fasc. 4.

[25] "In intimate connection with these theoretical tendencies, there results

no more than the executive organs of the collective will, soon emancipate themselves from the mass and become independent of its control.

Organization implies the tendency to oligarchy. In every organization, whether it be a political party, a professional union, or any other association of the kind, the aristocratic tendency manifests itself very clearly. The mechanism of the organization, while conferring a solidity of structure, induces serious changes in the organized mass, completely inverting the respective position of the leaders and the led. As a result of organization, every party or professional union becomes divided into a minority of directors and a majority of directed.

It has been remarked that in the lower stages of civilization tyranny is dominant. Democracy cannot come into existence until there is attained a subsequent and more highly developed stage of social life. Freedoms and privileges, and among these latter the privilege of taking part in the direction of public

---

a change in the relationship between the leaders and the mass. For the comradely leadership of local committees with all its undeniable defects there is substituted the professional leadership of the trade-union officials. Initiative and capacity for decision thus become what may be called a professional speciality, whilst for the rank and file is left the passive virtue of discipline. There can be no doubt that this seamy side of officialism involves serious dangers for the party. The latest innovation in this direction, in the German social democratic party, is the appointment of salaried secretaries to the local branches. Unless the rank and file of the party keep very much on the alert, unless they are careful that these secretaries shall be restricted to purely executive functions, the secretaries will come to be regarded as the natural and sole depositaries of all power of initiative, and as the exclusive leaders of local party life. In the socialist party, however, by the nature of things, by the very character of the political struggle, narrower limits are imposed upon bureaucracy than in the case of the trade-unions. In these latter, the technical specialization of the wage-struggle (the need, for example, for the drafting of complicated sliding scales and the like) often leads the chiefs to deny that the mass of organized workers can possess ''a general view of the economic life of the country as a whole,'' and to deny, therefore, their capacity of judgment in such matters. The most typical outcome of this conception is afforded by the argument with which the leaders are accustomed to forbid all theoretical criticism of the prospects and possibilities of practical trade-unionism, asserting that such criticism involves a danger for the spirit of organization. This reasoning starts from the assumption that the workers can be won for organization and can be induced to remain faithful to their trade-unions only by a blind and artless belief in the saving efficacy of the trade-union struggle'' (Rosa Luxemburg, *Massenstreik, Partei u. Gewerkschaften*, Erdmann Dubber, Hamburg, 1906, p. 61).

affairs, are at first restricted to the few. Recent times have
been characterized by the gradual extension of these privileges
to a widening circle. This is what we know as the era of
democracy. But if we pass from the sphere of the state to the
sphere of party, we may observe that as democracy continues to
develop, a backwash sets in. With the advance of organization,
democracy tends to decline. Democratic evolution has a para-
bolic course. At the present time, at any rate as far as party
life is concerned, democracy is in the descending phase. It may
be enunciated as a general rule that the increase in the power
of the leaders is directly proportional with the extension of the
organization. In the various parties and labour organizations
of different countries the influence of the leaders is mainly determined (apart from racial and individual grounds) by the varying development of organization. Where organization is stronger,
we find that there is a lesser degree of applied democracy.

Every solidly constructed organization, whether it be a democratic state, a political party, or a league of proletarians for the
resistance of economic oppression, presents a soil eminently
favourable for the differentiation of organs and of functions.
The more extended and the more ramified the official apparatus
of the organization, the greater the number of its members, the
fuller its treasury, and the more widely circulated its press, the
less efficient becomes the direct control exercised by the rank and
file, and the more is this control replaced by the increasing
power of committees.[26] Into all parties there insinuates itself
that indirect electoral system which in public life the democratic
parties fight against with all possible vigour. Yet in party life
the influence of this system must be more disastrous than in the
far more extensive life of the state. Even in the party congresses, which represent the party-life seven times sifted, we
find that it becomes more and more general to refer all important
questions to committees which debate in camera.

As organization develops, not only do the tasks of the administration become more difficult and more complicated, but, further, its duties become enlarged and specialized to such a degree
that it is no longer possible to take them all in at a single glance.

---

[26] ''Here we see the beginning of a danger which is imminent in all popular administration, namely, that in place of true democracy there should
develop an omnipotent influence of committees'' (Wolfgang Heine, *Demokratische Randbemerkungen zum Fall Göhre*, ''Sozialistische Monatshefte,''
viii (x), fasc. 4, p. 254).

In a rapidly progressive movement, it is not only the growth in the number of duties, but also the higher quality of these, which imposes a more extensive differentiation of function. Nominally, and according to the letter of the rules, all the acts of the leaders are subject to the ever vigilant criticism of the rank and file. In theory the leader is merely an employee bound by the instructions he receives. He has to carry out the orders of the mass, of which he is no more than the executive organ. But in actual fact, as the organization increases in size, this control becomes purely fictitious. The members have to give up the idea of themselves conducting or even supervising the whole administration, and are compelled to hand these tasks over to trustworthy persons specially nominated for the purpose, to salaried officials. The rank and file must content themselves with summary reports, and with the appointment of occasional special committees of inquiry. Yet this does not derive from any special change in the rules of the organization. It is by very necessity that a simple employee gradually becomes a "leader," acquiring a freedom of action which he ought not to possess. The chief then becomes accustomed to despatch important business on his own responsibility, and to decide various questions relating to the life of the party without any attempt to consult the rank and file. It is obvious that democratic control thus undergoes a progressive diminution, and is ultimately reduced to an infinitesimal minimum. In all the socialist parties there is a continual increase in the number of functions withdrawn from the electoral assemblies and transferred to the executive committees. In this way there is constructed a powerful and complicated edifice. The principle of division of labour coming more and more into operation, executive authority undergoes division and subdivision. There is thus constituted a rigorously defined and hierarchical bureaucracy.[27] In the catechism of party duties, the strict observance of hierar-

---

[27] Achille Loria has drawn attention to the numerous resemblances between *administrative* hierarchy and *economic*. The chief point of resemblance is found, according to him, in the echeloned pyramidal structure of both. He writes: "Just as in the executive we have a limited number of chiefs commanding a larger number of sub-chiefs, and these a still larger number of subordinates, down to the lowest employees who exhibit the maximum numerical density, in the same way a small handful of the greatest recipients of income rules a larger number of less wealthy recipients of income, these rule a still greater number of recipients of more modest incomes, and so on down to the incomes of the lowest degree, which are the most numerous" (Achille Loria, *La Sintesi economica*, Bocca, Turin, 1909,

chical rules becomes the first article. This hierarchy comes into existence as the outcome of technical conditions, and its constitution is an essential postulate of the regular functioning of the party machine.

It is indisputable that the oligarchical and bureaucratic tendency of party organization is a matter of technical and practical necessity. It is the inevitable product of the very principle of organization. Not even the most radical wing of the various socialist parties raises any objection to this retrogressive evolution, the contention being that democracy is only a form of organization and that where it ceases to be possible to harmonize democracy with organization, it is better to abandon the former than the latter. Organization, since it is the only means of attaining the ends of socialism, is considered to comprise within itself the revolutionary content of the party, and this essential content must never be sacrificed for the sake of form.[28]

In all times, in all phases of development, in all branches of human activity, there have been leaders.[29] It is true that certain socialists, above all the orthodox Marxists of Germany, seek to convince us that socialism knows nothing of "leaders," that the party has "employees" merely, being a democratic party, and the existence of leaders being incompatible with democracy. But a false assertion such as this cannot override a sociological law. Its only result is, in fact, to strengthen the rule of the leaders, for it serves to conceal from the mass a danger which really threatens democracy.

For technical and administrative reasons, no less than for

---

p. 348.—Eng. trans., *The Economic Synthesis*, Allen, London, 1914, p. 317). Loria might have added that the two species of hierarchy differ in respect of their apices, for one terminates in a point, being dynastic, while in the other the apex is truncated, the hierarchy being plutocratic. The administration of political parties does not come into the scope of Loria's considerations. As far as the pyramid of the party hierarchy is concerned, its apex is certainly less conspicuously pointed than that of a monarchical regime, but none the less in the political party the administration is in the hands of chiefs whose number is comparatively restricted, so that the apex of this pyramid is more acute than that of the pyramid which represents the hierarchy of economic powers in a country far advanced in capitalist development.

[28] Cf. Hans Block, *Ueberspannung der Demokratie,* "Neue Zeit," xxvi, No. 8, pp. 264 et seq.

[29] Eben Mumford (*The Origins of Leadership*, University Press, Chicago, 1909, pp. 1-12) has developed this thesis especially in relation to primitive times.

tactical reasons, a strong organization needs an equally strong leadership. As long as an organization is loosely constructed and vague in its outlines, no professional leadership can arise. The anarchists, who have a horror of all fixed organization, have no regular leaders. In the early days of German socialism, the *Vertrauensmann* (homme de confiance) continued to exercise his ordinary occupation. If he received any pay for his work for the party, the remuneration was on an extremely modest scale, and was no more than a temporary grant. His function could never be regarded by him as a regular source of income. The employee of the organization was still a simple workmate, sharing the mode of life and the social condition of his fellows.[30] To-day he has been replaced for the most part by the professional politician, *Berzirksleiter* (U.S. ward-boss), etc. The more solid the structure of an organization becomes in the course of the evolution of the modern political party, the more marked becomes the tendency to replace the emergency leader by the professional leader. Every party organization which has attained to a considerable degree of complication demands that there should be a certain number of persons who devote all their activities to the work of the party. The mass provides these by delegation, and the delegates, regularly appointed, become permanent representatives of the mass for the direction of its affairs.

For democracy, however, the first appearance of professional leadership marks the beginning of the end, and this, above all, on account of the logical impossibility of the ''representative'' system, whether in parliamentary life or in party delegation. Jean Jacques Rousseau may be considered as the founder of this aspect of the criticism of democracy. He defines popular government as ''l'exercice de la volonté générale,'' and draws from this the logical inference, ''elle ne peut jamais s'aliéner, et le souverain, qui n'est qu'un être collectif, ne peut être représenté que par lui-même.'' Consequently, ''à l'instant qu'un peuple se donne des représentants, il n'est plus libre, il n'est plus.''[31] A mass which delegates its sovereignty, that is to say transfers its sovereignty to the hands of a few individuals, abdicates its sov-

---

[30] Cf. Eduard Bernstein, *Die Arbeiterbewegung*, Rütten u. Loening, Frankfort-on-the-Main, 1910, p. 141. For the historical counterpart that is offered by the evolution of officialdom within the state, cf. Gustav Schmoller, *Umrisse u. Untersuchungen zur Verfassungs- Verwaltungs- u. Wirtschaftsgeschichte*, Dunker u. Humblot, Leipzig, 1898, p. 291.
[31] Jean Jacques Rousseau, *Le Contrat social* (lib. cit., pp. 40 et seq.).

ereign functions.[32] For the will of the people is not transferable, nor even the will of the single individual. However much in practice, during the confused years of the Terror, the doctrine was abandoned by the disciples of the philosopher of Geneva, it was at this time in theory universally admitted as incontrovertible. Robespierre himself accepted it, making a subtle distinction between the "représentant du peuple," who has no right to exist, "parce que la volonté ne peut se représenter," and "le mandataire du peuple, à qui le peuple a donné la première puissance."

The experience of attentive observers of the working of the first attempts at a representative system, contributed to establish more firmly the theory of the limits of democracy. Towards the middle of the nineteenth century this theory, the outcome of an empirical psychology, was notably enlarged, its claim to general validity was sustained, and it was formulated as the basis of definite rules and precepts. Carlo Pisacane, the theorist, too soon forgotten, of the national and social revolution in Italy, expounds in his *Saggio sulla Rivoluzione* how the men in whose hands supreme political power is placed must, from their very nature as human beings, be subject to passions and to the physical and mental imperfections therefrom resulting. For this reason the tendency and the acts of their rule are in direct contrast with the tendency and the acts of the mass, "for the latter represent the mean of all individual judgments and determinations, and are therefore free from the operation of such influences." To maintain of a government that it represents public opinion and the will of the nation is simply to mistake a part for the whole.[33] He thus considers delegation to be an absurdity. Victor Considérant, a contemporary of Pisacane and the representative of a similar tendency, also followed in the tracks of Rousseau: "Si le peuple délègue sa souveraineté, il l'abdique. Le peuple ne se gouverne plus lui-même, on le gouverne. . . . Peuple, délègue donc ta souveraineté! Cela fait, je te garantis, à ta souveraineté le sort inverse de celui de Saturne: ta souveraineté sera devorée par la Délégation, ta fille."[34] The theorists

---

[32] Quite recently some of the most notable of the revisionists have come to hold this opinion. Cf., for example, Eugène Fournière, *La Sociocratie. Essai de Politique positive,* Giard et Brière, Paris, 1910, pp. 98 et seq.

[33] Carlo Pisacane, *Saggio sulla Rivoluzione,* with a preface by Napoleone Colajanni, Lib. Treves di Pietro Virano, Bologna, 1894, pp. 121-5.

[34] Victor Considérant, op. cit., pp. 13-15.

of democracy are never tired of asserting that, when voting, the people is at one and the same time exercising its sovereignty and renouncing it. The great democrat Ledru-Rollin, the father of universal and equal suffrage in France, goes so far as to demand the suppression of president and parliament, and the recognition of the general assembly of the people as the sole legislative organ. If people, he continues, find it possible in the course of the year to waste so much time upon public entertainments, holidays, and loafing, they could surely make a better use of their time by devoting it ''à cimenter son indépendance, sa grandeur et sa prospérité.'' [35]

Victor Considérant fiercely opposed the theory that popular sovereignty is guaranteed by the representative system. Even if we make the theoretical admission that *in abstracto* parliamentary government does indeed embody government by the masses, in practical life it is nothing but a continuous fraud on the part of the dominant class. Under representative government the difference between democracy and monarchy, which are both rooted in the representative system, is altogether insignificant—a difference not in substance but in form. The sovereign people elects, in place of a king, a number of kinglets. Not possessing sufficient freedom and independence to direct the life of the state, it tamely allows itself to be despoiled of its fundamental right. The one right which the people reserves is the ''climatérique et dérisoire'' privilege of choosing from time to time a new set of masters.[36] To this criticism of the representative system may be appended the remark of Proudhon, to the effect that the representatives of the people have no sooner been raised to power than they set to work to consolidate and reinforce their influence. They continue unceasingly to surround their positions by new lines of defence, until they have succeeded in emancipating themselves completely from popular control. All power thus proceeds in a natural cycle: issuing from the people, it ends by raising itself above the people.[37] In the forties of the last century these ideas were widely diffused and their truth was almost universally admitted, and in France more particularly by students of social science and by democratic states-

---

[35] A. A. Ledru-Rollin, *Plus de Président, plus de Représentants,* ed. de ''La Voix du Proscrit,'' Paris, 1851, 2nd ed., p. 7.

[36] Victor Considérant, op. cit., pp. 11-12.

[37] Cf. P. J. Proudhon, *Les Confessions d'un Révolutionnaire. Pour servir à la Révolution de Février,* Verboeckhoven, Paris, 1868, new ed., p. 286.

men. Even the clericals mingled their voices with those which condemned the representative system. Louis Veuillot, the Catholic, said: "Quand j'ai voté, mon égalité tombe dans la boîte avec mon bulletin; ils disparaissent ensemble." [38] To-day this theory is the central feature of the political criticism of the various schools of anarchists, who often expound it eloquently and acutely.[39] Finally Marx and his followers, who in theory regard parliamentary action as but one weapon among many, but who in practice employ this weapon alone, do not fail to recognize incidentally the perils of the representative system, even when based upon universal suffrage. But the Marxists hasten to add that the socialist party is quite free from these dangers.[40]

Popular sovereignty has recently been subjected to a profound criticism by a group of Italian writers conservative in their tendency. Gaetano Mosca speaks of "the falsity of the parliamentary legend." He says that the idea of popular representation as a free and spontaneous transference of the sovereignty of the electors (collectivity) to a certain number of elected persons (minority) is based upon the absurd premise that the minority can be bound to the collective will by unbreakable bonds.[41] In actual fact, directly the election is finished, the power of the mass of electors over the delegate comes to an end. The deputy regards himself as authorized arbiter of the situation, and really is such. If among the electors any are to be found who possess some influence over the representative of the people, their number is very small; they are the big guns of the constituency or of the local branch of the party. In other words, they are persons who, whilst belonging by social position to the class of the ruled, have in fact come to form part of the ruling oligarchy.[42]

[38] Louis Veuillot, *Ça et là*, Caume Frères et Duprey, Paris, 1860, 2nd ed., vol. i, p. 368.

[39] Cf., for example, Enrico Malatesta in two pamphlets: *L'anarchia* (Casa ed. Pensiero, Rome, 6th ed., 1907), and *La Politica parlamentare del Partito socialista* (ediz. dell' "Allarme," Turin, 1903). Cf. also Ferdinand Domela Nieuwenhuis, *Het Parlamentarisme in zijn Wezen en Toepassing*, W. Sligting, Amsterdam, 1906, pp. 149 et seq.

[40] Cf. Karl Kautsky, Rosa Luxemburg, and others. In the works of Karl Marx we find traces here and there of a theoretical mistrust of the representative system; see especially this writer's *Revolution u. Kontre-Revolution in Deutschland*, Dietz, Stuttgart, 1896, p. 107.

[41] Cf. Gaetano Mosca, *Questioni pratiche di Diritto costituzionale*, Fratelli Bocca, Turin, 1898, pp. 81 et seq. Also *Sulla Teorica dei Governi e sul Governo parlamentare*, Loescher, Rome, 1884, pp. 120 et seq.

[42] "An electional system simply places power in the hands of the most

This criticism of the representative system is applicable above all in our own days, in which political life continually assumes more complex forms. As this complexity increases, it becomes more and more absurd to attempt to "represent" a heterogeneous mass in all the innumerable problems which arise out of the increasing differentiation of our political and economic life. To represent, in this sense, comes to mean that the purely individual desire masquerades and is accepted as the will of the mass.[43] In certain isolated cases, where the questions involved are extremely simple, and where the delegated authority is of brief duration, representation is possible. But permanent representation will always be tantamount to the exercise of dominion by the representatives over the represented.

---

skilful electioneers'' (H. G. Wells, *Anticipations of the Reaction of Mechanical and Scientific Progress upon Human Life and Thought,* Chapman and Hall, London, 1904, p. 58). Of course, this applies only to countries with a republican-democratic constitution.

[43] Fouillée writes aptly in this connection: ''Si j'use personnellement de mon droit civil d'aller et de venir pour me rendre de Marseille à Paris, je ne vous empêche pas, vous, d'aller de Paris à Marseille; l'exercice de ma liberté civile ne vous enlève rien de la vôtre. Mais, quand j'envoie à la Chambre un député qui appliquera à vos dépens des mesures contre lesquelles vous avez toujours protesté, cette façon de me gouverner implique une façon de vous gouverner qui vous est pénible et qui peut être injuste. Le droit civil est une liberté pour soi et sur soi; le droit politique est un droit sur autrui et sur le tout en même temps que sur moi-même'' (Alfred Fouillée, *Erreurs sociologiques et morales de la Sociologie,* ''Revue des deux Mondes,'' liv, p. 330).

CHAPTER III

THE MODERN DEMOCRATIC PARTY AS A FIGHTING PARTY, DOMINATED BY MILITARIST IDEAS AND METHODS

Louis XIV understood the art of government as have few princes either before or since, and this was the case above all in the first half of his reign, when his spirit was still young and fresh. In his memoirs of the year 1666, he lays down for every branch of the administration, and more especially for the conduct of military affairs, the following essential rules: "que les résolutions doivent être promptes, la discipline exact, les commandements absolus, l'obéissance ponctuelle."[1] The essentials thus enumerated by the *Roi Soleil* (promptness of decision, unity of command, and strictness of discipline) are equally applicable, *mutatis mutandis*, to the various aggregates of modern political life, for these are in a perpetual condition of latent warfare.

The modern party is a fighting organization in the political sense of the term, and must as such conform to the laws of tactics. Now the first article of these laws is facility of mobilization. Ferdinand Lassalle, the founder of a revolutionary labour party, recognized this long ago, contending that the dictatorship which existed in fact in the society over which he presided was as thoroughly justified in theory as it was indispensable in practice. The rank and file, he said, must follow their chief blindly, and the whole organization must be like a hammer in the hands of its president.

This view of the matter was in correspondence with political necessity, especially in Lassalle's day, when the labour movement was in its infancy, and when it was only by a rigorous discipline that this movement could hope to obtain respect and consideration from the bourgeois parties. Centralization guaranteed, and always guarantees, the rapid formation of resolutions. An extensive organization is *per se* a heavy piece of

---

[1] *Mémoires de Louis XIV pour l'instruction du Dauphin,* annotées par Charles Deyss, Paris, 1860, vol. ii, p. 123.

mechanism, and one difficult to put in operation. When we have to do with a mass distributed over a considerable area, to consult the rank and file upon every question would involve an enormous loss of time, and the opinion thus obtained would moreover be summary and vague. But the problems of the hour need a speedy decision, and this is why democracy can no longer function in its primitive and genuine form, unless the policy pursued is to be temporizing, involving the loss of the most favourable opportunities for action. Under such guidance, the party becomes incapable of acting in alliance with others, and loses its political elasticity. A fighting party needs a hierarchical structure. In the absence of such a structure, the party will be comparable to a savage and shapeless negro army, which is unable to withstand a single well-disciplined and well-drilled battalion of European soldiers.

In the daily struggle, nothing but a certain degree of cæsarism will ensure the rapid transmission and the precise execution of orders. The Dutch socialist, Van Kol, frankly declares that true democracy cannot be installed until the fight is over. Meanwhile, even a socialist leadership must possess authority, and sufficient force to maintain itself in power. A provisional despotism is, he contends, essential, and liberty itself must yield to the need for prompt action. Thus the submission of the masses to the will of a few individuals comes to be considered one of the highest of democratic virtues. "A ceux que sont appelés à nous conduire, nous promettons fidélité et soumission et nous leur disons: Hommes ennoblis par le choix du peuple, montrez nous le chemin, nous vous suivrons."[2] It is such utterances as this which reveal to us the true nature of the modern party. In a party, and above all in a fighting political party, democracy is not for home consumption, but is rather an article made for export. Every political organization has need of "a light equipment which will not hamper its movements." Democracy is utterly incompatible with strategic promptness, and the forces of democracy do not lend themselves to the rapid opening of a campaign. This is why political parties, even when democratic, exhibit so much hostility to the referendum and to all other measures for the safeguard of real democracy; and this is why in their constitution these parties exhibit, if not uncondi-

---

[2] Rienzi [van Kol], *Socialisme et Liberté,* Giard et Brière, Paris, 1898, pp. 243-53.

tional cæsarism, at least extremely strong centralizing and oligarchical tendencies. Lagardelle puts the finishing touches to the picture in the following words: "Et ils ont reproduit à l'usage des prolétaires les moyens de domination des capitalistes; ils ont constitué un gouvernement ouvrier aussi dur que le gouvernement bourgeois, une bureaucratie ouvrière aussi lourde que la bureaucratie bourgeoise, un pouvoir central qui dit aux ouvriers ce qu'ils peuvent et ce qu'ils ne peuvent pas faire, qui brisent dans les syndicats et chez les syndiqués toute indépendance et toute initiative et qui doit parfois inspirer à ses victimes le regret des modes capitalistes de l'autorité." [3]

The close resemblance between a fighting democratic party and a military organization is reflected in socialist terminology, which is largely borrowed, and especially in Germany, from military science. There is hardly one expression of military tactics and strategy, hardly even a phrase of barrack slang, which does not recur again and again in the leading articles of the socialist press.[4] In the daily practice of the socialist struggle it is true that preference is almost invariably given to the temporizing tactics of Fabius Cunctator, but this depends upon special circumstances, which will be subsequently discussed (Part VI, chap.

---

[3] Hubert Lagardelle, *Le Parti Socialiste et la Confédération du Travail*, Discussion avec J. Guesde, Rivière, Paris, 1907, p. 24.

[4] As typical may be instanced the expressions used by Kautsky in his article *Was nun?*, "Neue Zeit," xxviii, No. 29, p. 68. "Like all other strategy, the Fabian strategy is dependent upon certain conditions which alone make it possible and appropriate. It would be foolish to wish to apply it in all circumstances, and the fact that we have for many years used it with brilliant success is no reason why we should continue to use it for all time. When circumstances change, a new strategical method may be necessary. In war, the Fabian strategy becomes impossible or undesirable when the enemy is threatening to cut us off from our base or even to occupy that base. Direct attack then becomes a matter of self-preservation. Similarly the Fabian strategy must be abandoned when it demoralizes and discourages our own troops, when it threatens to induce cowardice and desertion, and when only a policy of vigorous attack can hold the army together. It also becomes impossible to avoid assuming the offensive when we are caught in a blind alley, where our only choice is between giving battle and a shameful capitulation. Finally, the change to an offensive strategy is indicated when the enemy himself is in a tight corner, so that the situation is favourable to our side, and by a rapid and energetic use of our opportunity we can deliver a vigorous and perhaps fatal blow. The transference of these considerations from the military to the political field does not require lengthy explanations." It is perhaps worthy of note that the French socialists of anti-militarist tendency are in the habit of referring to their leader Gustave Hervé as "notre Général."

i). The intimate association between party life and military life is manifested also by the passionate interest which some of the most distinguished leaders of German socialism take in military affairs. During his residence in England, the German merchant Frederick Engels, who had once served in the Guards as a volunteer, devoted his leisure to the simultaneous exposition of socialist and of militarist theory.[5] To Bebel, the son of a Prussian non-commissioned officer, the world is indebted for a number of ideas of reform in matters of military technique which have nothing in common with the theoretical socialist anti-militarism.[6] Bebel and Engels, and especially the latter, may even be considered as essentially military writers. This tendency on the part of socialist leaders is not the outcome of mere chance, but depends upon an instinct of elective affinity.

[5] See in particular Engels' works: *Po und Rhein* (1859); *Savoyen, Nizza und der Rhein* (1860); *Die preussische Militärfrage und die deutsche Arbeiterpartei* (1865); *Der deutsche Bauernkrieg* (1875, Vorwärts-Verlag, Berlin, 1909, 3rd ed. edited by Mehring); *Kann Europa abrüsten?* (Nuremberg, 1893).

[6] Cf., for example, the pamphlet *Nicht stehendes Heer, sondern Volkswehr*, Dietz, Stuttgart, 1908, p. 80; also a large number of speeches in the Reichstag on the military estimates, in which he is never tired of discussing the minutiæ of army reform, and in which in especial he advocates changes in military equipment to render the army more efficient.

CHAPTER IV

THE ESTABLISHMENT OF A CUSTOMARY RIGHT TO THE OFFICE OF DELEGATE

ONE who holds the office of delegate acquires a moral right to that office, and delegates remain in office unless removed by extraordinary circumstances or in obedience to rules observed with exceptional strictness. An election made for a definite purpose becomes a life incumbency. Custom becomes a right. One who has for a certain time held the office of delegate ends by regarding that office as his own property. If refused reinstatement, he threatens reprisals (the threat of resignation being the least serious among these) which will tend to sow confusion among his comrades, and this confusion will continue until he is victorious.

Resignation of office, in so far as it is not a mere expression of discouragement or protest (such as disinclination to accept a candidature in an unpromising constituency), is in most cases a means for the retention and fortification of leadership. Even in political organizations greater than party, the leaders often employ this stratagem, thus disarming their adversaries by a deference which does not lack a specious democratic colour. The opponent is forced to exhibit in return an even greater deference, and this above all when the leader who makes use of the method is really indispensable or is considered indispensable by the mass. The recent history of Germany affords numerous examples showing the infallibility of this machiavellian device for the maintenance of leadership. During the troubled period of transition from absolute to constitutional monarchy, during the ministry of Ludolf Camphausen, King Frederick William IV of Prussia threatened to abdicate whenever liberal ideas were tending in Prussian politics to gain the upper hand over the romanticist conservatism which was dear to his heart. By this threat the liberals were placed in a dilemma. Either they must accept the king's abdication, which would involve the accession to the throne of Prince William of Prussia, a man of ultra-reactionary tendencies, whose reign was likely to be initiated by an uprising among the lower classes; or else they must abandon their liberal schemes, and maintain in power the king now become indispensable. Thus Frederick William always succeeded in getting his own way and in defeating the schemes of his political opponents.[1] Thirty-five years later Prince Bismarck, establishing his strength with the weapon of his indispensability, consolidated his omnipotence over the German empire which he had recently created, by again and again handing in his resignation to the Emperor William I. His aim was to reduce the old monarch to obedience, whenever the latter showed any signs of exercising an independent will, by suggesting the chaos in internal and external policy which would necessarily result from the retirement of the "founder of the empire," since the aged emperor was not competent to undertake the personal direction of affairs.[2] The present president of the Brazilian republic, Hermes da Fonseca, owes his position chiefly to a timely threat of resignation. Having been appointed Minister of War in 1907, Fonseca undertook the reorganization of the Brazilian army. He brought forward a bill for the introduction of universal compulsory military service, which was fiercely resisted in both houses of parliament. Through his energetic personal advocacy, sustained by a threat of resignation, the measure was ultimately carried, and secured for its promoter such renown, that not only did he remain in office, but in the year 1910 was elected President of the Republic by 102,000 votes against 52,000.

It is the same in all political parties. Whenever an obstacle is encountered, the leaders are apt to offer to resign, professing that they are weary of office, but really aiming to show to the dissentients the indispensability of their own leadership. In 1864, when Vahlteich proposed a change in the rules of the General Association of German Workers, Lassalle, the president, was very angry, and, conscious of his own value to the movement, propounded the following alternative: Either you protect me

---

[1] *König Friedrich Wilhelm IV. Briefwechsel mit Ludolf Camphausen*, edited and annotated by Erich Brandenburg, Gebr. Paetel, Berlin, 1906, pp. 112 et seq.

[2] *Denkwürdigkeiten des Fürsten Chlodwig zu Hohenlohe-Schillingsfürst*, ed. by Friedrich Curtius, Deutsche Verlagsanstalt, Stuttgart and Leipzig, 1907, vol. ii.

from the recurrence of such friction as this, or I throw up my office. The immediate result was the expulsion of the importunate critic.[3] In Holland to-day, Troelstra, the Dutch Lassalle, likewise succeeds in disarming his opponents within the party by pathetically threatening to retire into private life, saying that if they go on subjecting his actions to an inopportune criticism, his injured idealism will force him to withdraw from the daily struggles of party life.[4] The same thing has occurred more than once in the history of the Italian socialist party. It often happens that the socialist members of parliament find themselves in disagreement with the majority of the party upon some question of importance, such as that of the opportuneness of a general strike; or in the party congresses they may wish to record their votes in opposition to the views of their respective branches. It is easy for them to get their own way and to silence their opponents by threatening to resign. If necessary, they go still further, and actually resign their seats, appealing to the electors as the only authority competent to decide the question in dispute. In such cases they are nearly always re-elected, and thus attain to an incontestable position of power. At the socialist congress held at Bologna in 1904, some of the deputies voted in favour of the reformist resolution, in opposition to the wishes of the majority of the comrades whose views they were supposed to represent. When called to account, they offered to resign their seats, and the party electors, wishing to avoid the expense and trouble of a new election, and afraid of the loss of party seats, hastened to condone the deputies' action. In May, 1906, twenty-four out of the twenty-seven members of the socialist group in the Chamber resigned their seats, in consequence of the difference of views between themselves and the rank and file on the subject of the general strike, which the deputies had repudiated. All but three were re-elected.

Such actions have a fine democratic air, and yet hardly serve to conceal the dictatorial spirit of those who perform them. The leader who asks for a vote of confidence is in appearance submitting to the judgment of his followers, but in reality he throws into the scale the entire weight of his own indispensability, real

---

[3] Julius Vahlteich, *Ferdinand Lassalle und die Anfänge der deutschen Arbeiterbewegung*. Birk, Munich, 1904, p. 74.
[4] This occurred at the party congress at Utrecht in 1906. Cf. the account given in the "Nieuwe Arnhemsche Courant," vol. vii, No. 4639, and P. J. Troelstra, *Inzaken Partijleiding*, Wakker, Rotterdam, 1906, pp. 103-4.

or supposed, and thus commonly forces submission to his will.[5] The leaders are extremely careful never to admit that the true aim of their threat to resign is the reinforcement of their power over the rank and file.[6] They declare, on the contrary, that their conduct is determined by the purest democratic spirit, that it is a striking proof of their fineness of feeling, of their sense of personal dignity, and of their deference for the mass. Yet if we really look into the matter we cannot fail to see that, whether they desire it or not, their action is an oligarchical demonstration, the manifestation of a tendency to enfranchise themselves from the control of the rank and file. Such resignations, even if not dictated by a self-seeking policy, but offered solely in order to prevent differences of opinion between the leaders and the mass, and in order to maintain the necessary harmony of views, always have as their practical outcome the subjection of the mass to the authority of the leader.

---

[5] Schweitzer knew this very well when he declared to the general assembly of the Allgemeiner Deutscher Arbeiterverein that he would resign his position if he were not allowed to call a congress of the association in order to discuss the foundation of trade-unions. His biographer writes very justly: "Schweitzer must have felt his position to be extremely strong. Otherwise he would never have ventured to deliver such an ultimatum, for his defeat on a vote would have made it almost impossible for him to retain his office, to which he was greatly attached. He had not, however, overestimated his influence, and when he was reproached with exercising an improper pressure on the delegates, this was in itself an indirect recognition of his indispensability. This time, in fact, he got his own way'' (Gustav Mayer, *J. B. von Schweitzer und die Sozialdemocratie*, Fischer, Jena, 1909, p. 223).

[6] In the tactical struggles in the Italian party during the year 1904, the Florentine reformist socialist, Professor Gaetano Pieraccini, declared that he would not withdraw the resignation of his position as a party-leader unless the adherents of the revolutionary tendency were expelled from the party (''Avanguardia Socialista,'' anno ii, No. 76).

CHAPTER V

THE NEED FOR LEADERSHIP FELT BY THE MASS

A DISTINGUISHED French dramatist who devoted his leisure to writing prose studies of serious social questions, Alexandre Dumas fils, once observed that every human advance was, at its outset, opposed by ninety-nine per cent of humanity. "Mais c'est sans aucune importance puisque ce centième auquel nous appartenons, depuis le commencement du monde a fait faire aux quatre-vingt-dix-neuf autres toutes les réformes dont ils se trouvent très bien aujourd'hui tout en protestant contre celles qui restent à faire." In another passage he adds: "Les majorités ne sont que la preuve de ce qui est," whereas "les minorités sont souvent le germe de ce qui sera." [1]

There is no exaggeration in the assertion that among the citizens who enjoy political rights the number of those who have a lively interest in public affairs is insignificant. In the majority of human beings the sense of an intimate relationship between the good of the individual and the good of the collectivity is but little developed. Most people are altogether devoid of understanding of the actions and reactions between that organism we call the state and their private interests, their prosperity, and their life. As de Tocqueville expresses it, they regard it as far more important to consider "s'il faut faire passer un chemin au bout de leur domaine" [2] than to interest themselves in the general work of public administration. The majority is content, with Stirner, to call out to the state, "Get away from between me and the sun!" Stirner makes fun of all those who, in accordance with the views of Kant, preach it to humanity as a "sacred duty" to take an interest in public affairs. "Let those persons who have a personal interest in political changes concern themselves with these. Neither now nor at any future time will 'sacred duty' lead people to trouble themselves about the

---

[1] Alexandre Dumas fils, *Les Femmes qui tuent et les Femmes qui votent,* Calman Lévy, Paris, 1880, pp. 54 and 214.
[2] Alexis de Tocqueville, op. cit., vol. i, p. 167.

state, just as little as it is by 'sacred duty' that they become men
of science, artists, etc. Egoism alone can spur people to an interest in public affairs, and will spur them—when matters grow
a good deal worse.''[3]

In the life of modern democratic parties we may observe signs
of similar indifference. It is only a minority which participates
in party decisions, and sometimes that minority is ludicrously
small. The most important resolutions taken by the most democratic of all parties, the socialist party, always emanate from a
handful of the members. It is true that the renouncement of
the exercise of democratic rights is voluntary; except in those
cases, which are common enough, where the active participation of the organized mass in party life is prevented by geographical or topographical conditions. Speaking generally, it is
the urban part of the organization which decides everything;
the duties of the members living in country districts and in remote provincial towns are greatly restricted; they are expected
to pay their subscriptions and to vote during elections in favour
of the candidates selected by the organization of the great town.
There is here at work the influence of tactical considerations as
well as that of local conditions. The preponderance of the towns-
men over the scattered country members corresponds to the necessity of promptness in decision and speed in action to which allusion was made in an earlier chapter.

Within the large towns there goes on a process of spontaneous
selection, in virtue of which there is separated from the organized mass a certain number of members who participate more
diligently than the others in the work of the organization. This
inner group is composed, like that of the pious frequenters of
the churches, of two very distinct categories: the category of
those who are animated by a fine sense of duty, and the category of those whose attendance is merely a matter of habit.
In all countries the number of this inner circle is comparatively
small.[4] The majority of the members are as indifferent to the

---

[3] Max Stirner (Kaspar Schmidt), *Der Einzige und sein Eigentum*, Reclam,
Leipzig, 1892, p. 272.

[4] Here is a typical example. The deputy Leonida Bissolati, a leading
Italian socialist and one of the founders of the party, was on November 5,
1905 (with other distinguished members), expelled from the party. The
expulsion was effected at a meeting of the Roman branch. The full membership of this branch was seven hundred, but only one hundred were present at the meeting; of these fifty-five voted for the exclusion and forty-five
against (''Azione Socialista,'' i, No. 28). In May 1910, the same branch,

organization as the majority of the electors are to parliament.[5]
Even in countries like France, where collective political education is of older date, the majority renounces all active participation in tactical and administrative questions, leaving these to
the little group which makes a practice of attending meetings.
The great struggles which go on among the leaders on behalf
of one tactical method or another, struggles in fact for supremacy in the party, but carried out in the name of Marxism,
reformism, or syndicalism, are not merely beyond the understanding of the rank and file, but leave them altogether cold.
In almost all countries it is easy to observe that meetings held
to discuss questions of the hour, whether political, sensational,
or sentimental (such as protection, an attack upon the Government, the Russian revolution, and the like), or those for the
discussion of matters of general interest (the discovery of the
North Pole, personal hygiene, spiritualism), attract a far larger
audience, even when reserved to members of the party, than do
meetings for the discussion of tactical or theoretical questions,
although these are of vital importance to the doctrine or to the
organization. The present writer knows this from personal experience in three typical great cities, Paris, Frankfort-on-the-
Main, and Turin. Notwithstanding differences of atmosphere,
there was observable in each of these three centres the same indifference to party affairs and the same slackness of attendance
at ordinary meetings.[6] The great majority of the members will
not attend meetings unless some noted orator is to speak, or un-

---

then containing about six hundred members, passed a resolution fiercely
condemning the socialist deputies on account of their being too friendly
with the ministry. The resolution was carried by forty-one votes against
twenty-four ("Stampa," liv, No. 134).

[5] In trade-union circles loud complaints are also heard regarding this human, all-too-human, tendency. Thus, of the bakers' union we read: "In
every strike we have the same experience, that in the distribution of leaflets,
in picketing, in the whole work of agitation which a strike necessitates, it is
only a few of the members who do their share, while the great mass of the
strikers, and especially the younger ones, shirk all these duties" (O. Allmann, *Die Entwicklung des Verbandes der Bäcker und Berufsgenossen
Deutschlands und die Lohnbewegungen und Streiks im Bäckergewerbe*, Verlag von O. Allmann, 1900, p. 68).

[6] The same phenomenon is seen in the trade-union movement. "In Germany the Bourses du Travail numbering 5,000 members think themselves
happy if they can get together 500 of these at a meeting. The other nine-
tenths of the organized workers habitually lack all interest in the intimate
life of *their* corporation" (Bernhard Schildbach, *Verfassungsfragen in den
Gewerkschaften*, "Neue Zeit," xxix, fasc. 10).

less some extremely striking war-cry is sounded for their attraction, such as, in France, "A bas la vie chère!", or, in Germany, "Down with personal government!" A good meeting can also be held when there is a cinema-show, or a popular scientific lecture illustrated by lantern-slides. In a word, the ordinary members have a weakness for everything which appeals to their eyes and for such spectacles as will always attract a gaping crowd.[7]

It may be added that the regular attendants at public meetings and committees are by no means always proletarians—especially where the smaller centres are concerned. When his work is finished, the proletarian can think only of rest, and of getting to bed in good time. His place at meetings is taken by petty bourgeois, by those who come to sell newspapers and picture-postcards, by clerks, by young intellectuals who have not yet got a position in their own circle, people who are all glad to hear themselves spoken of as authentic proletarians and to be glorified as the class of the future.[8]

The same thing happens in party life as happens in the state. In both, the demand for monetary supplies is upon a coercive foundation, but the electoral system has no established sanction. An electoral right exists, but no electoral duty. Until this duty is superimposed upon the right, it appears probable that a small minority only will continue to avail itself of the right which the majority voluntarily renounces, and that the minority will always dictate laws for the indifferent and apathetic mass. The consequence is that, in the political groupings of democracy, the participation in party life has an echeloned aspect. The extensive base consists of the great mass of electors; upon this is superimposed the enormously smaller mass of enrolled members of the local branch of the party, numbering perhaps one-tenth or even as few as one-thirtieth of the electors; above this, again, comes the much smaller number of the members who regularly attend meetings; next comes the group of officials of the party; and highest of all, consisting in part of the same individuals as the last group, come the half-dozen or so members of the executive committee. Effective power is here in inverse ratio to the number of those who exercise it. Thus practical democracy is represented by the following diagram:—

---

[7] Cf., as far as Italian conditions are concerned, Giulio Casalini, *Crisi di Impreparazione*, "Critica Sociale," 1904, xiv, No. 1.

[8] Cf. the vigorous criticism of Filippo Turati, *Ancora la Propaganda improduttiva*, "Critica Sociale," 1903, xiii, No. 14.

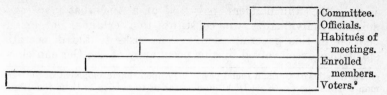

Committee.
Officials.
Habitués of
meetings.
Enrolled
members.
Voters.[9]

Though it grumbles occasionally, the majority is really delighted to find persons who will take the trouble to look after its affairs. In the mass, and even in the organized mass of the labour parties, there is an immense need for direction and guidance. This need is accompanied by a genuine cult for the leaders, who are regarded as heroes. Misoneism, the rock upon which so many serious reforms have at all times been wrecked, is at present rather increasing than diminishing. This increase is explicable owing to the more extensive division of labour in modern civilized society, which renders it more and more impossible to embrace in a single glance the totality of the political organization of the state and its ever more complicated mechanism. To this misoneism are superadded, and more particularly in the popular parties, profound differences of culture and education among the members. These differences give to the need for leadership felt by the masses a continually increasing dynamic tendency.

This tendency is manifest in the political parties of all countries. It is true that its intensity varies as between one nation and another, in accordance with contingencies of a historical character or with the influences of racial psychology. The German people in especial exhibits to an extreme degree the need for some one to point out the way and to issue orders. This peculiarity, common to all classes not excepting the proletariat, furnishes a psychological soil upon which a powerful directive hegemony can flourish luxuriantly. There exist among the Germans all the preconditions necessary for such a development: a psychical predisposition to subordination, a profound instinct for discipline, in a word, the whole still-persistent inheritance of the influence of the Prussian drill-sergeant, with all its advantages and all its disadvantages; in addition, a trust in authority which verges on the complete absence of a critical faculty.[10] It

[9] This figure must not be regarded as intended to represent such relationships according to scale, for this would require an entire page. It is purely diagrammatic.

[10] Native and foreign writers alike have referred to the influence of these

is only the Rhinelanders, possessed of a somewhat more conspicuous individuality, who constitute, to a certain extent, an exception to this generalization.[11] The risks to the democratic spirit that are involved by this peculiarity of the German char-

characteristics of German racial psychology upon the development of the German socialist party. Karl Diehl goes so far as to ascribe to them the origin and importance of the German labour party. He writes: "If we find that in Germany a socialist party has come into existence greater than that found anywhere else in the world, this is dependent upon the whole historical evolution of the labour movement. . . . A certain political immaturity, and the ease with which the Germans are disciplined and subordinated, were the factors which enabled socialism to gain in this country so extraordinary a number of adherents" (Karl Diehl, *Ueber Sozialismus, Kommunismus und Anarchismus*, Fischer, Jena, 1906, p. 226). Another writer well acquainted with the German labour movement, rightly points out the contradiction between the official doctrine of historic materialism and the actual overvaluation of great men in the movement: "However earnestly German socialism has desired, however fundamentally its philosophy of history has laboured, to undermine the influence of great personalities, the members of the socialist party have in practice paid little attention to such theories. From 1860 down to our own day, the masses have always sworn by their masters. If it has been made a just reproach to the German people that there exists among us an excessive belief in authority, to the labour movement, even in its international dress, there must attach considerable responsibility for this error" (Gustav Mayer, *Die Lösung der deutschen Frage im Jahre 1866 und die Arbeiterbewegung*, "Festgaben für Wilhelm Lexis," Fischer, Jena, 1906, p. 227). A Portuguese socialist describes with great acuteness the authoritarian leanings of the German party: "In Germany, the militarist tendencies which may be observed in the other camps are, with greater or less intensity, reflected in the socialist party. This is especially noticeable in the congresses, where, at a simple sign given by the deputy Singer, all the delegates approve or disapprove in accordance with the instructions they have received. The same military discipline extends to the parties and to the political groupings. And woe to him who transgresses these rules: he runs the risk of being expelled without chance of appeal" (Magalhaes Lima, *O primeiro de Maio*, Typ. de la Companhia Nacional Editora, Lisbon, 1894, p. 40).

[11] In the Rhenish districts, the active and vivacious character of the population is, according to many trade-union leaders, a matter of considerable significance: "More inclined to form societies for recreation than for serious undertakings, the Rhenish workers are difficult to organize. Those who have been induced to join a union can be retained in that body only when led by some one whose personality is sympathetic to them, and who understands on suitable occasions to flavour seriousness with humour. If the central organization of the trade-union brings about a change in the local leadership without paying due attention to this consideration, the anti-authoritarian tendency of the Rhinelanders comes into play, and the membership falls off greatly" (Walter Troeltsch and P. Hirschfeld, *Die deutschen Sozialdemokratischen Gewerkschaften. Untersuchungen u. Materialen über ihre geographische Verbreitung*, Carl Heymanns Verlag, Berlin, 1905, p. 71).

acter were well known to Karl Marx. Although himself a party leader in the fullest sense of the term, and although endowed to the highest degree with the qualities necessary for leadership, he thought it necessary to warn the German workers against entertaining too rigid a conception of organization. In a letter from Marx to Schweitzer we are told that in Germany, where the workers are bureaucratically controlled from birth upwards, and for this reason have a blind faith in constituted authority, it is above all necessary to teach them to walk by themselves.[12]

The indifference which in normal times the mass is accustomed to display in ordinary political life becomes, in certain cases of particular importance, an obstacle to the extension of the party influence. The crowd may abandon the leaders at the very moment when these are preparing for energetic action. This happens even in connection with the organization of demonstrations of protest. At the Austrian socialist congress held at Salzburg in 1904, Dr. Ellenbogen complained: "I am always anxious when the party leaders undertake any kind of action. It seems simply impossible to arouse the interest of the workers even in matters which one would have expected them to understand. In the agitation against the new military schemes, we found it impossible to organize meetings of a respectable size."[13] In Saxony, in 1895, when it was proposed to restrict the suffrage, the socialist leaders vainly endeavoured to arouse a general agitation, their attempts being rendered nugatory by the general apathy of the masses. The language of the press was inflammatory. Millions of leaflets were distributed. Within the space of a few days a hundred and fifty meetings of protest were held. All was without effect. There was no genuine agitation. The meetings, especially in the outlying districts, were very scantily attended.[14] The leaders, alike the Central Committee and the district organizers, were overwhelmed with disgust at the calm indifference of the mass, which rendered serious agitation altogether impossible.[15] The failure of the movement was

---

[12] Letter from Karl Marx to J. B. von Schweitzer, dated London, October 13, 1868, published, with comments, by Ed. Bernstein of "Neue Zeit," xv, 1897, p. 9. Bernstein himself appears to share the views of Marx. (Cf. Ed. Bernstein, *Gewerkschaftsdemokratie*, "Sozial. Monatshefte," 1909, p. 83.)

[13] *Protokoll der Verhandlungen*, etc., J. Brand, Vienna, 1904, p. 90.

[14] Edmund Fischer, *Der Widerstand des deutschen Volkes gegen Wahlentrechtungen*, "Sozial. Monatshefte," viii (x), fasc. 10.

[15] Edmund Fischer, *Die Sächsische Probe*, "Sozial. Monatshefte," viii (x), fasc. 12.

due to an error of omission on the part of the leaders. The
rank and file did not recognize the importance of the loss they
were to suffer because the leaders had neglected to point out
all its consequences. Accustomed to being ruled, the rank and
file need a considerable work of preparation before they can be
set in motion. In default of this, and when signals which the
rank and file do not understand are unexpectedly made by the
leaders, they pay no attention.

The most striking proof of the organic weakness of the mass
is furnished by the way in which, when deprived of their leaders
in time of action, they abandon the field of battle in disordered
flight; they seem to have no power of instinctive reorganization,
and are useless until new captains arise capable of replacing
those that have been lost. The failure of innumerable strikes
and political agitations is explained very simply by the opportune action of the authorities, who have placed the leaders under
lock and key.[16] It is this experience which has given rise to the
view that popular movements are, generally speaking, artificial
products, the work of isolated individuals termed agitators
(Aufwiegler, Hetzer, Meneurs, Sobillatori), and that it suffices
to suppress the agitators to get the upper hand of the agitation.
This opinion is especially favoured by certain narrow-minded
conservatives. But such an idea shows only the incapacity of
those who profess to understand the intimate nature of the mass.

---

[16] The most conspicuous example of this is furnished by an episode in the
history of the Danish labour movement. The condemnation and subsequent
exile in America of the socialist leader, Louis Pio, in the seventies, sufficed
to check for years the growth of the labour movement, then in its infancy
(Rud. Meyer, *Der Sozialismus in Dänemark,* Aug. Schindler, Berlin, 1875,
pp. 13 et seq.). Gustav Bang describes the collapse of the movement in the
following terms: ''He [Pio] had become fatigued, and was too weak to
continue the struggle. In the spring of 1877 he allowed himself to be bribed
by the police, who induced him to leave the country for ever; with him went
Geleff, who had also been bribed. Pio died in America in 1894. This was
disastrous for the party. It had trusted Pio too blindly, believed in him
too earnestly, to be able to stand on its own feet. . . . There were no
new men to fill the empty place, and the party was too loosely constructed,
too weakly combined, to be able to hold together. The unions dissolved
or faded out of existence'' (G. Bang, *Ein Blick auf die Geschichte der
dänischen Sozialdemocratie,* ''Neue Zeit,'' December 25, 1897, xvi, vol. i,
No. 13, pp. 404-5). Another notable example, and a more recent one, belongs to the history of the labour movement in France, where in 1909 the
attempt at a general strike of railway men failed because Briand, the
Prime Minister, had suddenly imprisoned some of the most influential leaders of the railway workers.

In collective movements, with rare exceptions, the process is natural and not "artificial." Natural above all is the movement itself, at whose head the leader takes his place, not as a rule of his own initiative, but by force of circumstances. No less natural is the sudden collapse of the agitation as soon as the army is deprived of its chiefs.

The need which the mass feels for guidance, and its incapacity for acting in default of an initiative from without and from above, impose, however, heavy burdens upon the chiefs. The leaders of modern democratic parties do not lead an idle life. Their positions are anything but sinecures, and they have acquired their supremacy at the cost of extremely hard work. Their life is one of incessant effort. The tenacious, persistent, and indefatigable agitation characteristic of the socialist party, particularly in Germany, never relaxed in consequence of casual failures, nor ever abandoned because of casual successes, and which no other party has yet succeeded in imitating, has justly aroused the admiration even of critics and of bourgeois opponents.[17] In democratic organizations the activity of the professional leader is extremely fatiguing, often destructive to health, and in general (despite the division of labour) highly complex.[18]

---

[17] In a controversial article directed against a Catholic periodical of conservative tendencies, the "Germania" of Berlin, another Catholic paper, the "Westdeutsche Arbeiterzeitung," the organ of the Catholic workers of the Rhineland, publishes the following appreciation of its socialist opponents: "We could wish that our own party would take example by the sentiment of sacrifice for the party welfare with which the socialist workers are animated. We cannot venture to assert, as does the 'Germania,' that in the socialist party there is a larger number of arrivists than in any other, for we must confess that we lack materials to prove such a proposition. It is indeed our own impression, based upon considerable experience, that the socialist workers demand from their paid employees a notable amount of intellectual labour and of propagandist activity. In fact, the leaders commonly fulfil the desires of the mass" (quoted from the "Frankfurter Volksstimme," 1910, No. 248, 5th supplement). In the same vein writes the Catholic priest Engelbert Kaeser, *Der Sozialdemokrat hat's Wort!*, Herder, Freiburg i. B., 1905, 3rd ed., p. 201.

[18] The capitalist press is in the habit of describing socialist leaders as debauchees and parasites who batten upon the funds extracted from the toilers. The first part of the accusation is absurd. The second is, of course, substantially true, but does not, to the sociologist, involve condemnation on that account. Certainly the leaders live at the cost of the workers, but with the full knowledge of these, and, in so far as the workers are organized, by their deliberate will. The leaders are selected and paid to render in return inestimable service. Another reflection may be made in passing. The fact that the workers are able permanently to maintain out of their savings so

He has continually to sacrifice his own vitality in the struggle, and when for reasons of health he ought to slacken his activities, he is not free to do so. The claims made upon him never wane. The crowd has an incurable passion for distinguished orators, for men of a great name, and if these are not obtainable, they insist at least upon an M.P. At anniversaries and other celebrations of which the democratic masses are so fond, and always during electoral meetings, demands pour in to the central organization, and close always on the same note, "we must have an M.P.!"[19] In addition, the leaders have to undertake all kinds of literary work, and should they happen to be barristers, they must give their time to the numerous legal proceedings which are of importance to the party. As for the leaders of the highest grade, they are simply stifled under the honorary positions which are showered upon them. Accumulation of functions is, in fact, one of the characteristics of modern democratic parties. In the German socialist party we not infrequently find that the same individual is a town-councillor, a member of the diet, and a member of the Reichstag, or that, in addition to two of these functions, he is editor of a newspaper, secretary of a trade union, or secretary of a co-operative society;[20] the same thing is true of Belgium, of Holland,[21] and of Italy. All this brings

---

enormous a party-apparatus as that of the German social democracy, contradicts the Theory of Increasing Misery, and contradicts even more plainly Lassalle's theory (now, indeed, almost universally abandoned) of the Iron Law of Wages. (Cf. the present writer's address to the third Italian Congress of the Sciences held at Padua in 1909, *Dilucidazioni sulla teoria dell' immiserimento*, "Giornale degli Economisti," xxxix, series 2, 1909.)

[19] In Italy, requests for an M.P. are often sent to the head office when the matter in question is no more than the proclamation of a strike. One of the country branches once asked for the exclusive services of a socialist deputy for an entire fortnight. He was to study the local working conditions of the agricultural labourers, to discover possibilities of improvement, to draft a memorial to the local landowners, and so on (Varazzani and Costa, *Relazione della Direzione del Partito al Congresso d'Imola*, September 1902, Co-operativa Tip.-editrice, Imola, 1902, p. 7).

[20] Oehme, referring to the labour movement in Bremen, writes: "My position was certainly not one to be envied, for I was publisher, editor, distributor, advertising agent, and cashier, not to mention maid-of-all-work. Throughout the year I had not a single Sunday free, for I spent all my Sundays running up and down stairs in order to collect the monthly subscriptions to the paper, a task not accomplished without difficulty." This refers to an earlier date when the anti-socialist laws were still in force, and when the division of labour in the movement had not attained its present degree ("Bremer Burger-Zeitung," September 23, 1904, xv, No. 225).

[21] In Holland, Willem Hubertus Vliegen was at one and the same time

honour to the leader, gives him power over the mass, makes him more and more indispensable; but it also involves continuous overwork; for those who are not of exceptionally strong constitution it is apt to involve a premature death.[22]

---

socialist deputy, editor in chief of the central organ of the party (''Het Volk''), county councillor of N. Holland, municipal councillor of Amsterdam, president of the party executive, and chairman in ordinary in all the congresses—six functions in all (Leeuwenburg, ''Nieuwe Arnhemsche Courant,'' No. 4659).

[22] It is remarkable how large a percentage of socialist agitators and organizers have succumbed to mental disorder. Carlo Cafiero, Jean Volders, Bruno Schönlank, Georg Jaeckh, died in asylums. Lassalle was on the verge of physical and mental collapse when he determined to devote his life to Helene von Dönniges. This predisposition to insanity is a result of the overwork which the party life imposes upon its leaders.

CHAPTER VI

THE POLITICAL GRATITUDE OF THE MASSES

IN addition to the political indifference of the masses and to their need for guidance, there is another factor, and one of a loftier moral quality, which contributes to the supremacy of the leaders, and this is the gratitude felt by the crowd for those who speak and write on their behalf. The leaders acquire fame as defenders and advisers of the people; and while the mass, economically indispensable, goes quietly about its daily work, the leaders, for love of the cause, must often suffer persecution, imprisonment, and exile.[1]

These men, who have often acquired, as it were, an aureole of sanctity and martyrdom, ask one reward only for their services, gratitude.[2] Sometimes this demand for gratitude finds written

---

[1] "It is the privilege of the leaders to march in the van, and to be the first to receive the blows directed against the party by our adversaries" (Auguste Bebel, *Ein Nachwort zur Vizepräsidentenfrage und Verwandtem,* reprint from "Neue Zeit," 1903, p. 21). Naturally this applies chiefly to times of comparative political calm.

[2] The appeal to gratitude is an effective means of domination, an admirable platform upon which to base further claims. The poet aptly puts in the mouth of a spokesman of the masses the following words, directed against a victorious leader who is vaunting his own merits: "Neither the money in our money-boxes, nor the words in our mouths, nor the wine in our cellars, nor the wives in our beds, will be safe from him. He will always be telling us, 'I delivered you from the Genoese, I am the victor of Aliscampo'" (Rudolph Lothar, *König Harlekin,* G. H. Meyer, Leipzig-Berlin, 1900, p. 39).—The part which gratitude has played in the political life of great national organizations still lacks adequate recognition. The omnipotence of Bismarck, the founder of the modern German Empire, an omnipotence which endured for nearly thirty years, was largely based upon this sentiment. Max Nordau writes with perfect justice: "Unprincipled advantage is taken of the most touching and amiable characteristic of our nation, its gratitude" (Max Nordau, *Die Krankheit des Jahrhunderts,* B. Elischer, Leipzig, 1888, p. 247).—In Italy, many patriots who had rendered great services in the struggles on behalf of United Italy were, after the constitution of the kingdom, elected deputies, and were subsequently re-elected again and again, simply out of gratitude for their ancient services. (Cf. Pasquale Turiello, *Governo e Governati in Italia, Fatti,* N. Zanichelli, Bologna, 1889, 2nd revised edition, p. 325.)

expression.[3]   Among the masses themselves this sentiment of
gratitude is extremely strong.[4]   If from time to time we encounter exceptions to this rule, if the masses display the blackest
ingratitude towards their chosen leaders, we may be certain
that there is on such occasions a drama of jealousy being played
beneath the surface.   There is a demagogic struggle, fierce,
masked, and obstinate, between one leader and another, and the
mass has to intervene in this struggle, and to decide between the
adversaries.   But in favouring one competitor, it necessarily displays "ingratitude" towards the other.   Putting aside these exceptional cases, the mass is sincerely grateful to its leaders, regarding gratitude as a sacred duty.[5]   As a rule, this sentiment
of gratitude is displayed in the continual re-election of the

---

[3] Cf. a catechism for the use of the Belgian workers (Alphonse Octors,
De Catechismus van den Werkman, Volksdrukkerij, Ghent, 1905, p. 6), in
which we read, in reply to the question, ''Has there not been considerable
change for the better of late?'' the answer, ''Yes, thanks to the unwearying
propaganda of De Paepe, Jean Volders, G. Defnet, Leon and Alfred De
Fuisseaux, Vandervelde, Anseele, and many others, the workers have secured
the legal recognition of their civil equality.''

[4] The leaders often maintain that the democratic masses are ungrateful,
but this is far from being true.   Roscher writes of democracy in the life
of the state, that whereas the ingratitude of the monarchy and of the aristocracy is conscious and deliberate, when the democracy is ungrateful, this
usually arises from an involuntary forgetfulness, dependent upon the frequent party changes characteristic of democratic government, and is altogether uncalculating and devoid of personal intention (Roscher, op. cit., p.
396).   In the internal life of the democratic party, since here ''party
changes'' are much rarer than in the national life of democracy, there
is far less likelihood of the display of ingratitude.

[5] The German socialist party showed a fine spirit of gratitude towards the
elder Liebknecht, appointing him, when his intellectual powers were already
beginning to fail, to the editorship of ''Vorwärts,'' and voting him, though
not without opposition, a salary of £360 (*Protokoll des sozialdemokratischen
Parteitags zu Frankfurt,* 1894, p. 33).   When Liebknecht died and his
family was left badly off, the party provided funds for the continuance of
his sons' education.

Eduard Bernstein considers that it was simply on account of a sense of
gratitude that Max Schippel, the deputy, was not expelled from the party
at the Bremen Congress of 1904.   ''A fine human sentiment, whose working has been seen in earlier congresses, was here once more manifest.   I
refer to the obvious disinclination to pass a political death-sentence upon
one who has done important services for the party. . . . These are certainly among the choicest feelings of which the human heart is capable:
respect for merit, and antipathy to the idea of brutal expulsion'' (Eduard
Bernstein, *Was Bremen gebracht hat,* ''Neue Montagsblatt,'' i, No. 22,
September 26, 1904.

leaders who have deserved well of the party, so that leadership commonly becomes perpetual. It is the general feeling of the mass that it would be "ungrateful" if they failed to confirm in his functions every leader of long service.[6]

---

[6] It is to this sentiment that Bernstein refers the indignation which was displayed at the Dresden Congress (1903) by the majority of the delegates, when it was reported that a number of the more revolutionary elements had decided to vote against the re-election of the reformist Ignatz Auer as a member of the Executive Committee. The general feeling in the party was that of eternal gratitude towards Auer because he had been one of the founders of the party, and because to the rank and file he seemed the personification of a most interesting period in the history of the social democracy (Eduard Bernstein, *Die Demokratie in der Sozialdemokratie,* "Sozial. Monatsh.," September 3, 1908, p. 1109). In the opinion of the present writer, the case of Auer manifests also, gratitude apart, the general disinclination of the masses to change their leaders. (Cf. Part II, Chap. I.)

CHAPTER VII

THE CULT OF VENERATION AMONG THE MASSES

THE socialist parties often identify themselves with their leaders to the extent of adopting the leaders' names. Thus, in Germany from 1863 to 1875 there were Lassallists and Marxists; whilst in France until quite recently there were Broussists, Allemanists, Guesdists, and Jaurèsists.[1] The fact that these personal descriptive terms tend to pass out of use in such countries as Germany may be attributed to two distinct causes: in the first place, there has been an enormous increase in the membership and especially in the voting strength of the party; and secondly, within the party, dictatorship has given place to oligarchy, and the leaders of this oligarchy are inspired by sentiments of mutual jealousy. As a supplementary cause may be mentioned the general lack of leaders of conspicuous ability, capable of securing and maintaining an absolute and indisputable authority.[2]

The English anthropo-sociologist Frazer contends that the maintenance of the order and authority of the state is to a large extent dependent upon the superstitious ideas of the masses, this being, in his view, a bad means used to a good end. Among such superstitious notions, Frazer draws attention to the belief so frequent among the people that their leaders belong to a

---

[1] In this we see the analogy of party with religious sects and monastic orders. Yves Guyot rightly points out that the members of the modern party imitate the practice of the medieval monks, who, while faithfully following the teachings of their respective masters, called themselves after St. Dominic, St. Benedict, St. Augustine, and St. Francis (Yves Guyot, *La Comédie socialiste*, Bibl. Charpentier, Paris, 1897, p. 111).

[2] According to Sombart, there has occurred in the German socialist party, concurrently with its numerical increase, a decline in quality. He writes: "The socialist democracy found it necessary to reduce to impotence the men of real talent, and to replace them by vigorous routinists. What could Marx do to-day as editor of the 'Neue Zeit' or even of the 'Sozialistische Monatshefte'; what could Lassalle do in the Reichstag?" (Werner Sombart, *Die Deutsche Volkswirtschaft im 19 Jahrhundert*, Bondi, Berlin, 1903, p. 528.)

higher order of humanity than themselves.[3] The phenomenon
is, in fact, conspicuous in the history of the socialist parties
during the last fifty years. The supremacy of the leaders over
the mass depends, not solely upon the factors already discussed,
but also upon the widespread superstitious reverence paid to the
leaders on account of their superiority in formal culture—for
which a much greater respect is commonly felt than for true
intellectual worth.

The adoration of the led for the leaders is commonly latent.
It reveals itself by signs that are barely perceptible, such as
the tone of veneration in which the idol's name is pronounced,
the perfect docility with which the least of his signs is obeyed,
and the indignation which is aroused by any critical attack upon
his personality. But where the individuality of the leader is
truly exceptional, and also in periods of lively excitement, the
latent fervour is conspicuously manifested with the violence of
an acute paroxysm. In June 1864, the hot-blooded Rhinelanders
received Lassalle like a god. Garlands were hung across the
streets. Maids of honour showered flowers over him. Interminable lines of carriages followed the chariot of the "president."
With overflowing and irresistible enthusiasm and with frenzied
applause were received the words of the hero of the triumph,
often extravagant and in the vein of the charlatan, for he spoke
rather as if he wished to defy criticism than to provoke applause.
It was in truth a triumphal march. Nothing was lacking—triumphal arches, hymns of welcome, solemn receptions of foreign
deputations.[4] Lassalle was ambitious in the grand style, and,
as Bismarck said of him at a later date, his thoughts did not
go far short of asking whether the future German Empire, in
which he was greatly interested, ought to be ruled by a dynasty
of Hohenzollerns or of Lassalles.[5] We need feel no surprise that
all this adulation excited Lassalle's imagination to such a degree
that he soon afterwards felt able to promise his affianced that
he would one day enter the capital as president of the German
republic, seated in a chariot drawn by six white horses.[6]

---

[3] J. G. Frazer, *Psyche's Task*, Macmillan, London, 1909, p. 56.

[4] See the accounts in the contemporary papers, which appear as preface
to the speech delivered by Lassalle at Ronsdorf, May 22, 1864, in *Ferdinand
Lassalles Gesamtwerken*, edited by Erich Blum, Pfau, Leipzig, vol. ii, p. 301.

[5] Bismarck, in the Reichstag, September 17, 1878 (*Fürst Bismarck's Reden*, edited by Philippe Stein, Reclam, Leipzig, vol. vii, p. 85).

[6] J. Vahlteich, op. cit., p. 58.

In Sicily, in 1892, when the first agricultural labourers' unions, known as *fasci,* were constituted, the members had an almost supernatural faith in their leaders. In an ingenuous confusion of the social question with their religious practices, they often in their processions carried the crucifix side by side with the red flag and with placards inscribed with sentences from the works of Marx. The leaders were escorted on their way to the meetings with music, torches, and Japanese lanterns. Many, drunk with the sentiment of adoration, prostrated themselves before their leaders, as in former days they had prostrated themselves before their bishops.[7] A bourgeois journalist once asked an old peasant, member of a socialist *fascio,* if the proletarians did not think that Giuseppe De Felice Giuffrida, Garibaldi Bosco, and the other young students or lawyers who, though of bourgeois origin, were working on behalf of the *fasci,* were not really doing this with the sole aim of securing their own election as county councillors and deputies. "De Felice and Bosco are angels come down from heaven!" was the peasant's brief and eloquent reply.[8]

It may be admitted that not all the workers would have replied to such a question in this way, for the Sicilian populace has always had a peculiar tendency to hero-worship. But throughout southern Italy, and to some extent in central Italy, the leaders are even to-day revered by the masses with rites of a semi-religious character. In Calabria, Enrico Ferri was for some time adored as a tutelary saint against governmental corruption. In Rome also, where the tradition of the classic forms of paganism still survives, Ferri was hailed in a public hall, in the name of all the "proletarian quirites," as "the greatest among the great." The occasion for this demonstration was that Ferri had broken a window as a sign of protest against a censure uttered by the President of the Chamber (1901).[9] In Holland, in the year 1886, when Domela Nieuwenhuis was liberated from prison, he received from the people, as he himself records,

---

[7] Adolfo Rossi, *Die Bewegung in Sicilien,* Dietz, Stuttgart, 1894, pp. 8 and 35.

[8] Rossi, op. cit., p. 34. Even to-day, De Felice is venerated as a demigod, especially in Catagna, where, as Syndic, he has carried on an extensive and many-sided activity in the field of municipal socialism. (Cf. Gisella Michels-Lindner, *Geschichte der modernen Gemeindebetriebe in Italien,* Dunke u. Humblot, Leipzig, 1909, pp. 77 et seq.)

[9] Enrico Ferri, *La Questione meridionale,* "Asino," Rome, 1902, p. 4.

greater honours than had ever been paid to any sovereign, and the halls in which he addressed meetings were profusely adorned with flowers.[10] Such an attitude on the part of the mass is not peculiar to backward countries or remote periods; it is an atavistic survival of primitive psychology. A proof of this is afforded by the idolatrous worship paid to-day in the department of the Nord (the most advanced industrial region in France) to the Marxist prophet, Jules Guesde. Moreover, in certain parts of England, we find that the working classes give their leaders a reception which recalls the days of Lassalle.[11]

The adoration of the chiefs survives their death. The greatest among them are canonized. After the death of Lassalle, the Allgemeiner Deutscher Arbeiterverein, of which he had been absolute monarch, broke up into two sections, the "fraction of the Countess Hatzfeld" or "female line," as the Marxist adversaries sarcastically styled it, and the "male line" led by J. B. von Schweitzer. While quarrelling fiercely with one another, these two groups were at one, not only in respect of the honour they paid to Lassalle's memory, but also in their faithful observance of every letter of his programme. Nor has Karl Marx escaped this sort of socialist canonization, and the fanatical zeal with which some of his followers defend him to this day strongly recalls the hero-worship paid to Lassalle.[12] Just as Christians used to give and still give to their infants the names of the founders of their religion, St. Peter and St. Paul, so socialist parents in certain parts of central Italy call their boys Lassallo and their girls Marxina, as an emblem of the new faith. Moreover, the zealots often have to pay heavily for their devotion, in quarrels with angry relatives and with recalcitrant registration-officials, and sometimes even in the form of serious material injury, such as loss of employment. Whilst this practice is at times no more than a manifestation of that intellectual snobbery from which even the working-class environment is not wholly free, it is often the outward sign of a profound and sincere ideal-

---

[10] Ferdinand Domela Nieuwenhuis, *Van Christen tot Anarchist, Gedenkschriften,* Van Holkema en Warandorp, Amsterdam, 1911, p. 198. Cf. also P. J. Troelstra, "De Wording der S.D.A.P.," *Na tien jaar (1894-1904) Gedenkschriften,* Soep, Amsterdam, 1904, p. 97.

[11] Cf. a report by H. M. Hyndman of his visit to Burnley, "Justice," 1910, xxviii, No. 1355.

[12] An analogous spirit is manifested by the phrase long current among the militant Italian democracy, "He spoke evil of Garibaldi," signifying "He committed the most horrible of crimes."

ism.[13] Whatever its cause, it proves the adoration felt by the masses for the leaders, an adoration transcending the limits of a simple sense of obligation for services rendered. Sometimes this sentiment of hero-worship is turned to practical account by speculative tradesmen, so that we see in the newspapers (especially in America, Italy, and the southern Slav lands) advertisements of "Karl Marx liqueurs" and "Karl Marx buttons"; and such articles are offered for sale at public meetings.[14] A clear light is thrown upon the childish character of proletarian psychology by the fact that these speculative activities often prove extremely lucrative.

The masses experience a profound need to prostrate themselves, not simply before great ideals, but also before the individuals who in their eyes incorporate such ideals. Their adoration for these temporal divinities is the more blind in proportion as their lives are rude. There is considerable truth in the paradoxical phrase of Bernard Shaw, who defines democracy as a collection of idolators, in contradistinction to aristocracy, which is a collection of idols.[15] This need to pay adoring worship is often the sole permanent element which survives all the changes in the ideas of the masses. The industrial workers of Saxony have during recent years passed from fervent Protestantism to socialism. It is possible that in the case of some of them this evolution has been accompanied by a complete reversal of all their former intellectual and moral valuations; but it is certain that if from their domestic shrines they have expelled the traditional image of Luther, it has only been in order to replace it by one of Bebel. In Emilia, where the peasantry has undergone a similar evolution, the oleograph of the Blessed Virgin has simply given place to one of Prampolini; and in southern Italy, faith in the annual miracle of the liquefaction of the blood of St. Januarius has yielded before a faith in the miracle of the superhuman power of Enrico Ferri, "the Scourge of the Camorra." Amid the ruins of the old moral world of the masses, there remains intact the triumphal column of religious need. They often behave towards their leaders after the manner of the sculptor of ancient Greece who, having modelled a Jupiter To-

---

[13] Cf. the articles by Savino Varazzani, *Una famiglia socialista,* and *Reo di leso-Socialismo,* "Avanti della Domenica," ii, Nos. 67 and 68.

[14] Robert Michels, *Storia del Marxismo in Italia,* Mongini, Rome, 1910, pp. 148 et seq.

[15] Bernard Shaw, *The Revolutionist's Handbook.*

nans, prostrated himself in adoration before the work of his own hands.

In the object of such adoration, megalomania is apt to ensue.[16] The immeasurable presumption, which is not without its comic side, sometimes found in modern popular leaders, is not dependent solely on their being self-made men, but also upon the atmosphere of adulation in which they live and breathe. This overweening self-esteem on the part of the leaders diffuses a powerful suggestive influence, whereby the masses are confirmed in their admiration for their leaders, and it thus proves a source of enhanced power.

---

[16] George Sand writes: ''J'ai travaillé toute ma vie à être modeste. Je déclare que je ne voudrais pas vivre quinze jours entourée de quinze personnes persuadées que je ne peux pas me tromper. J'arriverais peut-être à me le persuader à moi-même'' (George Sand, *Journal d'un voyageur pendant la guerre*, M. Lévy Frères, Paris, 1871, pp. 216-17).

CHAPTER VIII

ACCESSORY QUALITIES REQUISITE TO LEADERSHIP

IN the opening days of the labour movement, the foundation of leadership consisted mainly, if not exclusively, in oratorical skill. It is impossible for the crowd to escape the æsthetic and emotional influence of words. The fineness of the oratory exercises a suggestive influence whereby the crowd is completely subordinated to the will of the orator.[1] Now the essential characteristic of democracy is found in the readiness with which it succumbs to the magic of words, written as well as spoken. In a democratic regime, the born leaders are orators and journalists. It suffices to mention Gambetta and Clemenceau in France; Gladstone and Lloyd George in England; Crispi and Luzzatti in Italy. In states under democratic rule it is a general belief that oratorical power is the only thing which renders a man competent for the direction of public affairs. The same maxim applies even more definitely to the control of the great democratic parties. The influence of the spoken word has been obvious above all in the country in which a democratic regime first came into existence. This was pointed out in 1826 by an acute Italian observer: "The English people, so prudent in the use of its time, experiences, in listening to a public speaker,

---

[1] The suggestive force of the oratory of the cultured leader is described in the following terms by one who was himself a master in its exercise: "In a political orator the principal matter is neither his command of the subject nor the mode in which he presents it; his power is established from the moment when he begins, no longer to speak, but rather to be carried forward upon a thousand glances, friendly it may be or hostile, but always vibrant with a metallic sheen, and launched by a thousand palpitating hearts. There is always in the orator's mind, even in that of the greatest, a sense of extreme tension . . . until at last the moment comes when one's blood suddenly warms up, and one sails on a cloud, or soars like a lark, higher, always higher. . . . The orator on the platform reacts to the gaze of the audience. He sees the red hearts of the crowd palpitating towards him, their thoughts concentrating towards him like a thousand threads uniting in one" (Adolf Köster, *Die zehn Schornsteine,* Langen, Munich, 1909, p. 113).

the same pleasure which it enjoys at the theatre when the works of the most celebrated dramatists are being played."[2] A quarter of a century later, Carlyle wrote: "No British man can attain to be a statesman or chief of workers till he has first proved himself a chief of talkers."[3] In France, Ernest-Charles, making a statistical study of the professions of the deputies, showed that, as far as the young, impetuous, lively, and progressive parties are concerned, almost all the parliamentary representatives are journalists and able speakers.[4] This applies not only to the socialists, but also to the nationalists and to the antisemites. The whole modern history of the political labour movement confirms the observation. Jaurès,[5] Guesde, Lagardelle, Hervé, Bebel, Ferri, Turati, Labriola, Ramsay Macdonald, Troelstra, Henriette Roland-Holst, Adler, Daszynski[6]—all, each in his own fashion, are powerful orators.

On the other hand, it is the lack of oratorical talent which largely explains why, in Germany, such a personality as that of Eduard Bernstein has remained in comparative obscurity, notwithstanding the vigour of his doctrinal views and his great intellectual influence; why, in Holland, Domela Nieuwenhuis has in the end lost his leading position; why, in France, a man possessed of so much talent and cultivation as Paul Lafargue,

---

[2] Giuseppe Pecchio, *Un' Elezione di Membri del Parlamento in Inghilterra*, Lugano, 1826, p. 109.

[3] Thomas Carlyle, *Latter Day Pamphlets*, No. V, "Stump-Orator," Thomas Carlyle's Works, "The Standard Edition," Chapman and Hall, London, 1906, vol. iii, p. 167.

[4] J. Ernest-Charles, *Les Lettrés du Parlement*, "La Revue," 1901, vol. xxxix, p. 361.

[5] A critic says of Jaurès that he "governs by eloquence." "Jaurès est orateur; c'est un vaste orateur, et son éloquence est lyrique, s'étale en larges périodes, pour l'essort desquelles il faut de larges amphithéâtres. La société, l'universe, toute la société, si possible, dans sa majestueuse unité, et l'universe dans sa prodigieuse immensité, ce serait mieux encore, sont les amphithéâtres naturels, les auditoires nécessaires, devant qui Jaurès se sent de taille à discourir" (Edouard Berth, *Les discours de Jaurès*, "Mouvement Socialiste," series 2, iv, No. 144, December 1, 1904, pp. 215 and 218). Another biographer believes that in Jaurès' skull he can recognize the anthropological type of the "born orator": "il a la tête faite pour parler au loin et regarder en l'air" (Gustave Téry, *Jean Jaurès, le poète lyrique*, "L'Œuvre," Paris, 1904, viii, p. 11). Cf. also the view expressed by Urbain Gohier, *Histoire d'une trahison, 1899-1903*, Société Parisienne d'édition, Paris, 1903, pp. 28-9.

[6] Richard Chamarz, *Charakterskizzen Oesterreichischer Politiker*, "Die Zeit," Naumann, 1902, p. 493.

closely connected by family ties with Karl Marx, failed to attain such a position in the councils of the party as Guesde, who is far from being a man of science, or even a man of very powerful intelligence, but who is a notable orator. Those who aspire to leadership in the labour organizations fully recognize the importance of the oratorical art. In March, 1909, the socialist students of Ruskin College, Oxford, expressed discontent with their professors because these gave to sociology and to pure logic a more important place in the curriculum than to oratorical exercises. Embryo politicians, the students fully recognized the profit they would derive from oratory in their chosen career. Resolving to back up their complaint by energetic action, they went on strike until they had got their own way.[7]

The prestige acquired by the orator in the minds of the crowd is almost unlimited. What the masses appreciate above all are oratorical gifts as such, beauty and strength of voice, suppleness of mind, badinage; whilst the content of the speech is of quite secondary importance. A spouter who, as if bitten by a tarantula, rushes hither and thither to speak to the people, is apt to be regarded as a zealous and active comrade, whereas one who, speaking little but working much, does valuable service for the party, is regarded with disdain, and considered but an incomplete socialist.[8]

Unquestionably, the fascination exercised by the beauty of a sonorous eloquence is often, for the masses, no more than the prelude to a long series of disillusionments, either because the speaker's practical activities bear no proportion to his oratorical abilities, or simply because he is a person of altogether common character. In most cases, however, the masses, intoxicated by the speaker's powers, are hypnotized to such a degree that for long periods to come they see in him a magnified image of their own ego.[9] Their admiration and enthusiasm for the orator are, in ultimate analysis, no more than admiration and enthusiasm for their own personalities, and these sentiments are fostered by

---

[7] Cf. a notice in "The Westminster Gazette," March 30, 1909.

[8] Adolfo Zerboglio, *Ancora la Propaganda improduttiva,* "Critica Sociale," xiii, No. 14.

[9] Cf. regarding the emotional relationships between leaders and the masses a sketch by J. K. Kochanowski, *Urzeitklänge und Wetterleuchten Geschichtlicher Gesetze in den Ereignissen der Gegenwart,* Wagner, Innsbruck, 1910, p. 19.

the orator in that he undertakes to speak and to act in the name of the mass, in the name, that is, of every individual. In responding to the appeal of the great orator, the mass is unconsciously influenced by its own egoism.

Numerous and varied are the personal qualities thanks to which certain individuals succeed in ruling the masses. These qualities, which may be considered as specific qualities of leadership, are not necessarily all assembled in every leader. Among them, the chief is the force of will which reduces to obedience less powerful wills. Next in importance come the following: a wider extent of knowledge which impresses the members of the leaders' environment; a catonian strength of conviction, a force of ideas often verging on fanaticism, and which arouses the respect of the masses by its very intensity; self-sufficiency, even if accompanied by arrogant pride, so long as the leader knows how to make the crowd share his own pride in himself;[10] in exceptional cases, finally, goodness of heart and disinterestedness, qualities which recall in the minds of the crowd the figure of Christ, and reawaken religious sentiments which are decayed but not extinct.

The quality, however, which most of all impresses the crowd is the prestige of celebrity. As we learn from modern psychology, a notable factor in the suggestive influence exercised by a man is found in the elevation to which he has climbed on the path leading to the Parnassus of celebrity. Tarde writes: "En réalité, quand un esprit agit sur notre pensée, c'est avec la collaboration de beaucoup d'autres esprits à travers lesquels nous le voyons et dont l'opinion se réflète dans la nôtre, à notre insu. Nous songeons vaguement à la considération qu'on a pour lui . . . à l'admiration qu'il inspire. . . . S'il s'agit d'un homme célèbre, c'est en masse et confusément que le nombre considérable de ses appréciateurs nous impressionne, et cet influence revêt un air de solidarité objective, de réalité impersonnelle, qui fait le prestige propre aux personnes glorieuses."[11] It suffices for the celebrated man to raise a finger to make for himself a political position. It is a point of honour with the masses to put the conduct of their affairs in the hands of a ce-

---

[10] Cf. Rienzi (H. van Kol), op. cit., p. 250; Gabriel Tarde, *L'Action intermentale,* "Grande Revue," Paris, 1900, iv, No. 11, p. 331; Ettore Ciccotti, *Psicologia del Movimento socialista,* Laterza, Bari, 1903, p. 128; E. Fournière, op. cit., p. 128.

[11] G. Tarde, *L'Action intermentale,* p. 334.

lebrity. The crowd always submits willingly to the control of distinguished individuals. The man who appears before them crowned with laurels is considered a priori to be a demi-god. If he consents to place himself at their head it matters little where he has gained his laurels, for he can count upon their applause and enthusiasm. It was because Lassalle was celebrated at once as poet, philosopher, and barrister that he was able to awaken the toiling masses, ordinarily slumbering or drawn in the wake of the bourgeois democracy, to group them round his own person. Lassalle was himself well aware of the effect which great names produce upon the crowd, and for this reason he always endeavoured to secure for his party the adhesion of men of note.[12] In Italy, Enrico Ferri, who while still a young man was already a university professor, and had at the same time acquired wide distinction as the founder of the new Italian school of criminology, had merely to present himself at the Socialist Congress of Reggio Emilia in the year 1893 to secure the leadership of the Italian socialist party, a leadership which he retained for fifteen years. In like manner, Cesare Lombroso, the anthropologist, and Edmondo De Amicis, the author, had no sooner given in their adhesion to the socialist party than they were immediately raised to positions of honour, one becoming the confidential adviser and the other the official Homer of the militant Italian proletariat. Yet not one of these distinguished men had become a regular subscribing member; they had merely sent certain congratulatory telegrams and letters.[13]

---

[12] Lassalle, who had a keen sense of theatrical pomp, and wished to display the results obtained by his energies, endeavoured to introduce as many bourgeois as he could into the Allgemeiner Deutscher Arbeiterverein. In his famous last speech he plumed himself upon having in the union a considerable number of men "who belong to the bourgeois class . . . a whole series of authors and thinkers" (Ferdinand Lassalle, *Die Agitation des Allgemeinen Deutschen Arbeitervereins und das Versprechen des Königs von Preussen*, a speech at Ronsdorf, 1864. Edition "Vorwärts," Berlin, 1892, p. 40). Even Bernstein, whose judgment of Lassalle is otherwise so extremely favourable, admits the president's excessive inclination for the attraction of brilliant names into the Verein (Eduard Bernstein, *Ferdinand Lassalle und seine Bedeutung für die Arbeiterklasse*. Edition "Vorwärts," Berlin, 1909, p. 55).

[13] Regarding the relationships of these two distinguished men with Italian socialism, consult Robert Michels, *Edmondo De Amicis*, "Sozialistische Monatshefte," 1909, fasc. 6, p. 361; and *Cesare Lombroso, Note sull' Uomo politico e sull' Uomo privato*, Archiv. di Anthrop. Criminale, xxxii, fasc. iv-v.

In France, Jean Jaurès, already distinguished as an academic philosopher and as a radical politician, and Anatole France, the celebrated novelist, attained to leading positions in the labour movement as soon as they decided to join it, without having to undergo any period of probation. In England, when the poet William Morris, at the age of forty-eight, became a socialist, he immediately acquired great popularity in the socialist movement. Similar was the case in Holland of Herman Gorter, author of the fine lyric poem *Mei*, and of the poetess Henriette Roland-Holst. In contemporary Germany there are certain great men, at the zenith of their fame, who are intimate sympathizers with the party, but have not decided to join it. It may, however, be regarded as certain that if Gerhard Hauptmann, after the success of his *Weavers*, and Werner Sombart, when his first published writings had attracted such wide attention, had given in their official adhesion to the German socialist party, they would now be amongst the most honoured leaders of the famous three million socialists of Germany. In the popular view, to bear a name which is already familiar in certain respects constitutes the best title to leadership. Among the party leaders will be found men who have acquired fame solely within the ranks of the party, at the price of long and arduous struggles, but the masses have always instinctively preferred to these those leaders who have joined them when already full of honour and glory and possessing independent claims to immortality. Such fame won in other fields seems to them of greater value than that which is won under their own eyes and solely in the field of socialism.

Certain accessory facts are worth mentioning in this connection. History teaches that between the chiefs who have acquired high rank solely in consequence of work for the party and those who have entered the party with a prestige acquired in other fields, a conflict speedily arises, and there often ensues a prolonged struggle for dominion between two factions. As motives for this struggle, we have, on the one side, envy and jealousy, and, on the other, presumption and ambition. In addition to these subjective factors, objective and tactical factors are also in operation. The great man who has attained distinction solely within the party commonly possesses, when compared with the "outsider," the advantage of a keener sense for the immediately practical, a better understanding of mass-psychology, a fuller knowledge of the history of the labour movement, and in many cases clearer ideas concerning the doctrinal content of the party programme.

In this struggle between the two groups of leaders, two phases may almost always be distinguished. The new arrivals begin by detaching the masses from the power of the old leaders, and by preaching a new evangel which the crowd accepts with delirious enthusiasm. This evangel, however, is no longer illuminated by the treasury of ideas which as a whole constitute socialism properly so-called, but by ideas drawn from the science or from the art in which these great men have previously acquired fame, and it is given a suggestive weight owing to the admiration of the great amorphous public. Meanwhile, the old leaders, filled with rancour, having first organized for defence, end by openly assuming the offensive. They have the natural advantage of numbers. It often happens that the new leaders lose their heads because, as great men, they have cherished the illusion that they are quite safe from such surprises. Are not the old leaders persons of mediocre ability, who have acquired their present position only at the price of a long and arduous apprenticeship? In the view of the new-comers, this apprenticeship does not demand any distinguished intellectual qualities, and from their superior platform they look down with mingled disdain and compassion. There are, however, additional reasons why the men of independent distinction almost invariably succumb in such a struggle. Poets, æsthetes, or men of science, they refuse to submit to the general discipline of the party, and attack the external forms of democracy. But this weakens their position, for the mass cherishes such forms, even when it is ruled by an oligarchy. Consequently their adversaries, though no more truly democratic, since they are much cleverer in preserving the appearance of democracy, gain credit with the crowd. It may be added that the great men are not accustomed to confront systematic opposition. They become enervated when prolonged resistance is forced upon them. It is thus easy to understand why, in disgust and disillusion, they so often abandon the struggle, or create a little private clique for separate political action. The few among them who remain in the party are inevitably overthrown and thrust into the background by the old leaders. The great Lassalle had already found a dangerous competitor in the person of the simple ex-workman, Julius Vahlteich. It is true that Lassalle succeeded in disembarrassing himself of this opponent, but had he lived longer, he would have had to sustain a merciless struggle against Liebknecht and Bebel. William Morris, after he had broken with the old professional leaders of the English labour movement, was reduced to the leadership of his little guard of intellectuals at Hammersmith. Enrico Ferri, who at his first entrance into the party had to encounter the tenacious mistrust of the old leaders, subsequently committed theoretical and practical errors which ended by depriving him once for all of his position as official chief of the Italian socialists. Gorter and Henriette Roland-Holst, after having for some years aroused intense enthusiasm, were finally overthrown and reduced to complete impotence by the old notables of the party.

Thus the dominion dependent upon distinction acquired outside the party is comparatively ephemeral. But age in itself is no barrier whatever to the power of the leaders. The ancient Greeks said that white hairs were the first crown which must decorate the leaders' foreheads. To-day, however, we live in an epoch in which there is less need for accumulated personal experience of life, for science puts at every one's disposal efficient means of instruction that even the youngest may speedily become thoroughly well instructed. To-day everything is quickly acquired, even that experience in which formerly consisted the sole and genuine superiority of the old over the young. Thus, not in consequence of democracy, but simply owing to the technical type of modern civilization, age has lost much of its value, and therefore has lost, in addition, the respect which it inspired and the influence which it exercised. It might rather be said that age is a hindrance to progress within the party, just as in any other career which it is better to enter in youth because there are so many steps to mount. This is true at least in the case of well organized parties, and where there is a great influx of new members. It is certainly different as far as concerns leaders who have grown old in the service of the party. Age here constitutes an element of superiority. Apart from the gratitude which the masses feel towards the old fighter on account of the services he has rendered to the cause, he also possesses this great advantage over the novice, that he has a better knowledge of his trade. David Hume tells us that in practical agriculture the superiority of the old farmer over the young arises in consequence of a certain uniformity in the effects of the sun, the rain, and the soil upon the growth of plants, and because practical experience teaches the rules that determine and guide these influences.[14] In party life, the old hand has a similar advantage. He possesses a profounder understanding of the relationships between cause and effect which form the framework of popular political life and the substance of popular psychology. The result is that his conduct is guided by a fineness of perception to which the young have not yet attained.

---

[14] "Why is the aged husbandman more skilful in his calling than the young beginner but because there is a certain uniformity in the operation of the sun, rain, and earth towards the production of vegetables; and experience teaches the old practitioner the rules by which this operation is governed and directed" (David Hume, *Enquiries Concerning the Human Understanding*, viii, i, 65, Ed. Clar. Press, Oxford, 1902, p. 85).

CHAPTER IX

ACCESSORY PECULIARITIES OF THE MASSES

To enable us to understand and properly to appreciate the superiority of the leaders over the mass it is necessary to turn our attention to the characteristics of the rank and file. The question arises, what are these masses?

It has already been shown that a general sentiment of indifference towards the management of its own affairs is natural to the crowd, even when organized to form political parties.

The very composition of the mass is such as to render it unable to resist the power of an order of leaders aware of its own strength. An analysis of the German trade unions in respect of the age of their members gives a sufficiently faithful picture of the composition also of the various socialist parties. The great majority of the membership ranges in age from 25 to 39 years.[1] Quite young men find other ways of employing their leisure; they are heedless, their thoughts run in erotic channels, they are always hoping that some miracle will deliver them from the need of passing their whole lives as simple wage-earners, and for these reasons they are slow to join a trade union. The men over forty, weary and disillusioned, commonly resign their membership (unless retained in the union by purely personal interest, to secure out-of-work pay, insurance against illness, and the like). Consequently there is lacking in the organization the force of control of ardent and irreverent youth and also that of experienced maturity. In other words, the leaders have to do with a mass of members to whom they are superior in respect of age and experience of life, whilst they have nothing to fear from the relentless criticism which is so peculiarly characteristic of men who have just attained to virility.

Another important consideration as to the composition of the rank and file who have to be led is its fluctuating character. It seems, at any rate, that this may be deduced from a report

---

[1] Adolf Braun, *Organisierbarkeit der Arbeiter,* "Annalen für soziale Politik und Gesetzebung," i, No. 1, p. 47.

of the socialist section of Munich for the year 1906. It contains statistics, showing analytically the individual duration of membership. The figures in parenthesis indicate the total number of members, including those members who had previously belonged to other sections.

MEMBERSHIP CLASSIFIED ACCORDING TO DURATION.

		%	
Less than 6 months	1,502	about 23	(1,582)
From 6 months to 2 years	1,620	" 24	(1,816)
" 2 to 3 years	684	" 10	(995)
" 3 to 4 "	1,020	" 15	(1,965)
" 4 to 5 "	507	" 7½	(891)
" 5 to 6 "	270	" 4	(844)
" 6 to 7 "	127	" 2	(604)
" 7 to 8 "	131	" 2	(1,289)
More than 8 "	833	" 12½	(1,666)[2]

The fluctuating character of the membership is manifest in even greater degree in the German trade unions. This has given rise to the saying that a trade union is like a pigeon-house where the pigeons enter and leave at their caprice. The German Metalworkers' Federation (Deutscher Metallarbeiterverband) had, during the years 1906 to 1908, 210,561 new members. But the percentage of withdrawals increased in 1906 to 60, in 1907 to 83, and in 1908 to 100.[3] This shows us that the bonds connecting the bulk of the masses to their organization are extremely slender, and that it is only a small proportion of the organized workers who feel themselves really at one with their unions. Hence the leaders, when compared with the masses, whose composition varies from moment to moment, constitute a more stable and more constant element of the organized membership.

---

[2] Robert Michels, *Die deutsche Sozialdemocratie, I, Soziale Zusammensetzung,* "Arch. für Sozialwissenschaft," xxiii, fasc. 2.

[3] A. von Elm, *Führer und Massen,* "Korrespondenzblatt der Generalkommission," xxi, No. 9.

C. INTELLECTUAL FACTORS

CHAPTER X

SUPERIORITY OF THE PROFESSIONAL LEADERS IN RESPECT OF CULTURE, AND THEIR INDISPEN-SABILITY; THE FORMAL AND REAL INCOMPE-TENCE OF THE MASS

IN the infancy of the socialist party, when the organization is still weak, when its membership is scanty, and when its principal aim is to diffuse a knowledge of the elementary principles of socialism, professional leaders are less numerous than are leaders whose work in this department is no more than an accessory occupation. But with the further progress of the organization, new needs continually arise, at once within the party and in respect of its relationships with the outer world. Thus the moment inevitably comes when neither the idealism and enthusiasm of the intellectuals, nor yet the goodwill with which the proletarians devote their free time on Sundays to the work of the party, suffice any longer to meet the requirements of the case. The provisional must then give place to the permanent, and dilettantism must yield to professionalism.

With the appearance of professional leadership, there ensues a great accentuation of the cultural differences between the leaders and the led. Long experience has shown that among the factors which secure the dominion of minorities over majorities—money and its equivalents (economic superiority), tradition and hereditary transmission (historical superiority)—the first place must be given to the formal instruction of the leaders (so-called intellectual superiority). Now the most superficial observation shows that in the parties of the proletariat the leaders are, in matters of education, greatly superior to the led.

Essentially, this superiority is purely formal. Its existence is plainly manifest in those countries in which, as in Italy, the course of political evolution and a wide-spread psychological predisposition have caused an afflux into the labour party of a great number of barristers, doctors, and university professors. The deserters from the bourgeoisie become leaders of the proletariat, not in spite of, but because of, that superiority of formal instruction which they have acquired in the camp of the enemy and have brought with them thence.

It is obvious that the dynamic influence of these newcomers over the mass of workers will diminish in proportion as their own number increases, that a small nucleus of doctors and barristers in a great popular party will be more influential than a considerable quantity of intellectuals who are fiercely contending for supremacy.[1] In other countries, however, such as Germany, whilst we find a few intellectuals among the leaders, by far the greater number of these are ex-manual workers. In these lands the bourgeois classes present so firm a front against the revolutionary workers that the deserters from the bourgeoisie who pass over to the socialist camp are exposed to a thoroughgoing social and political boycott, and, on the other hand, the proletarians, thanks to the wonderful organization of the state, and because highly developed capitalist manufacturing industry demands from its servitors high intelligence, have attained to the possession of a considerable, if elementary, degree of scholastic instruction, which they earnestly endeavour to amplify by private study. But the level of instruction among the leaders of working-class origin is no longer the same as that of their former workmates. The party mechanism, which, through the abundance of paid and honorary posts at its disposal, offers a career to the workers, and which consequently exercises a powerful attractive force, determines the transformation of a number of proletarians with considerable intellectual gifts into employees whose mode of life becomes that of the petty bourgeois. This change of condition at once creates the need and provides the opportunity for the acquisition, at the expense of the mass, of more elaborate instruction and a clearer view of existing social relationships.[2] Whilst their occupation and the needs of daily life render it impossible for the masses to attain to a profound knowledge of the social machinery, and above all of the working

---

[1] In the earliest days of the Dutch socialist movement, the leaders, all of bourgeois origin, were extremely restricted in number. For this very reason, it seems, they resisted in every possible way the adhesion to the party of new intellectuals whose competition they might have reason to fear. (Cf. Frank van der Goes, *Van de Oude Partij*, "Na Tien Jaar," pp. 52 et seq.)

[2] Cf. Part IV, Chap. V.

of the political machine, the leader of working-class origin is enabled, thanks to his new situation, to make himself intimately familiar with all the technical details of public life, and thus to increase his superiority over the rank and file. In proportion as the profession of politician becomes a more complicated one, and in proportion as the rules of social legislation become more numerous, it is necessary for one who would understand politics to possess wider experience and more extensive knowledge. Thus the gulf between the leaders and the rest of the party becomes ever wider, until the moment arrives in which the leaders lose all true sense of solidarity with the class from which they have sprung, and there ensues a new class-division between ex-proletarian captains and proletarian common soldiers.[3] When the workers choose leaders for themselves, they are with their own hands creating new masters whose principal means of dominion is found in their better instructed minds.

It is not only in the trade-union organization, in the party administration, and in the party press, that these new masters make their influence felt. Whether of working-class or of bourgeois origin, they also monopolize the party representation in parliament.

All parties to-day have a parliamentary aim. (There is only one exception, that of the anarchists, who are almost without political influence, and who, moreover, since they are the declared enemies of all organization, and who, when they form organizations, do so in defiance of their own principles, cannot be considered to constitute a political party in the proper sense of the term.) They pursue legal methods, appealing to the electors, making it their first aim to acquire parliamentary influence, and having for their ultimate goal "the conquest of political power." It is for this reason that even the representatives of the revolutionary parties enter the legislature. Their parliamentary labours, undertaken at first with reluctance,[4] but sub-

---

[3] Cf. Part VI, Chap. I.

[4] It is well known that in all countries the socialists at first took part in elections almost in spite of themselves, and full of scruples and theoretical reserves which have nothing in common with the conception of parliamentarism held by socialist deputies to-day. Thus in Germany, in 1869, some years after the first participation of the socialists in the elections to the Reichstag of the North German Federation, Wilhelm Liebknecht thought it necessary to justify this action in special writings, in which express reference was made to the fact that, notwithstanding this participation in the elections, parliament was for the socialists an institution of

sequently with increasing satisfaction and increasing professional zeal, remove them further and further from their electors. The questions which they have to decide, and whose effective decision demand on their part a serious work of preparation, involve an increase in their own technical competence, and a consequent increase in the distance between themselves and their comrades of the rank and file. Thus the leaders, if they were not "cultured" already, soon become so. But culture exercises a suggestive influence over the masses.

In proportion as they become initiated into the details of political life, as they become familiarized with the different aspects of the fiscal problem and with questions of foreign policy, the leaders gain an importance which renders them indispensable so long as their party continues to practise a parliamentary tactic, and which will perhaps render them important even should this tactic be abandoned. This is perfectly natural, for the leaders cannot be replaced at a moment's notice, since all the other members of the party are absorbed in their every-day occupations and are strangers to the bureaucratic mechanism.[5] This

quite subordinate importance. In Italy, in 1882, when the extension of the suffrage induced the Italian workers to abandon the policy of abstention from voting which they had hitherto practised, Enrico Bignami published a similar apologia. Liebknecht wrote: "By our speeches in the Reichstag we cannot diffuse among the masses any truths that could not be much better diffused in some other way. Then what 'practical' purpose have we in speaking in the Reichstag? None whatever! And to speak without purpose is folly. We gain no advantage, whilst we incur the obvious disadvantage of sacrificing our principles, of debasing our serious political struggle to the level of the parliamentary game, and of encouraging the people to cherish the illusion that the Bismarckian Reichstag is destined to solve the social problem" (Wilhelm Liebknecht, *Ueber die politische Stellung der Sozialdemokratie insbesondere mit Bezug auf den Reichstag*, Vorwärts-Verlag, Berlin, 1893, p. 15). Bignami's view was a very similar one. In recommending electoral activity, he contended that the socialist deputy should always refrain from active participation in legislation, and that the only purpose of his presence in parliament should be to proclaim from this lofty tribune the annihilation of the very privilege in virtue of which he had himself mounted that tribune (Enrico Bignami, *Il Candidato socialista*, Plebe, Milan, 1882, p. 3). It will readily be understood that so long as the socialist deputies continued to hold such views of their parliamentary position they could take no part in "practical politics."

[5]It must not be supposed that the technical competence of the leaders is necessarily profound, and it may be quite superficial. It has been justly observed that the deputies (especially in countries in which the government is responsible to parliament) have to spend a great deal of

special competence, this expert knowledge, which the leader acquires in matters inaccessible, or almost inaccessible, to the mass, gives him a security of tenure which conflicts with the essential principles of democracy.

The technical competence which definitely elevates the leaders above the mass and subjects the mass to the leaders, has its influence reinforced by certain other factors, such as routine, the social education which the deputies gain in the chamber, and their special training in the work of parliamentary committees.[6] The leaders naturally endeavour to apply in the normal life of the parties the manœuvres they have learned in the parliamentary environment, and in this way they often succeed in diverting currents of opposition to their own dominance.[7] The parliamentarians are past masters in the art of controlling meetings, of applying and interpreting rules, of proposing mo-

---

their valuable time in intrigues, and that just as journalists must often write, so deputies must often speak, impromptu, discussing subjects with which they are very little acquainted. "Pour qui examine, sait écouter et observe, ce n'est pas uniquement le cabinet actuel qui chancelle; la désaffection, une certaine désaffection, il ne faut rien exagérer, s'adresse à l'outil parlementaire lui-même. Les républicains devraient renoncer, de leur propre initiative, à ce régime, usé de palabres, où un député passe tout son temps à harceler un Ministre lequel emploie tout le sien, même ses veilles, à ne pas se laisser désarçonner. Toute minute se dépense en réceptions, en paroles, et en préparation de discours. Nul n'a le loisir de contrôler, de réfléchir, de diriger. La qualité première d'un député et d'un Ministre est de posséder l'organe et le talent d'un avocat capable de causer de tout, à toute heure, en tous lieux. De ce régime qui a succédé au noble règne de l'épée et qui précède celui du travail, de ce règne de la parlotte, l'opinion a déjà donné une forte preuve de dégoût" (Paul Brousse, "Petit Meridional," April 12, 1909).

[6] Cf. Ettore Ciccotti, *Montecitorio. Noterelle di uno che c'è stato*, Mongini, Rome, 1908, pp. 44, 45, and 74. Ciccotti regards the committees as the seat or as the point of origin of an oligarchy within parliament, that is to say, of an oligarchy within an oligarchy.

[7] Bearing upon this point, a striking passage may be quoted from the London correspondence of the socialist "Volksstimme," of Frankfort-on-the-Main, of February 2, 1909, concerning the Ninth Congress of the English Labour Party. "All expectations to the contrary notwithstanding, the two closing days of the Congress were peaceful, and were marked by no great discussions. This shows above all how united are the principal party leaders upon matters of tactics; but it shows also the extraordinary adroitness of the party executive, which had arranged the Agenda in such a way that it was possible for the chairman to steer the Congress past all the danger points almost without attracting attention. . . . The first preventive measure adopted by the standing orders committee was to rule out of the Agenda certain resolutions whose discussion was regarded as

tions at opportune moments; in a word, they are skilled in the
use of artifices of all kinds in order to avoid the discussion of
controversial points, in order to extract from a hostile majority
a vote favourable to themselves, or at least, if the worst comes
to the worst, to reduce the hostile majority to silence. There
is no lack of means, varying from an ingenious and often ambiguous manner of putting the question when the vote is to be
taken, to the exercise on the crowd of a suggestive influence by
insinuations which, while they have no real bearing on the question at issue, none the less produce a strong impression. As
referendaries (*rapporteurs*) and experts, intimately acquainted
with all the hidden aspects of the subject under discussion, many
of the deputies are adepts in the art of employing digressions,
periphrases, and terminological subtleties, by means of which
they surround the simplest matter with a maze of obscurity
to which they alone have the clue. In this way, whether acting
in good faith or in bad, they render it impossible for the masses,
whose "theoretical interpreters" they should be, to follow them,
and to understand them, and they thus elude all possibility of
technical control. They are masters of the situation.[8]

The intangibility of the deputies is increased and their privileged position is further consolidated by the renown which they
acquire, at once among their political adversaries and among
their own partisans, by their oratorical talent, by their specialized aptitudes, or by the charm of their intellectual or even of
their physical personalities. The dismissal by the organized
masses of a universally esteemed leader would discredit the party
throughout the country. Not only would the party suffer from
being deprived of its leaders, if matters were thus pushed to an
extreme, but the political reaction upon the status of the party
would be immeasurably disastrous. Not only would it be necessary to find substitutes without delay for the dismissed leaders,

---

needless or undesirable." Neither the correspondent nor the editor of the
"Volksstimme" thought it necessary to make any comment on this procedure.

[8] It is interesting to note that the developing bourgeoisie of the seventeenth century found itself in relation to the monarchy in the same state
of intellectual inferiority as that in which to-day are the democratic
masses in relation to their leaders, and for very similar reasons. The ingenious Louis XIV expressed the point in the following words: "Toute
l'autorité se trouvait alors [en Franche Comté] entre les mains du Parlement qui, comme une assemblée de simple bourgeois, serait facile et à
tromper et à intimider" (Dreyss, op. cit., vol. ii, p. 328).

who have only become familiar with political affairs after many years of arduous and unremitting toil (and where is the party which between one day and the next would be able to provide efficient substitutes?) ; but also it has to be remembered that it is largely to the personal influence of their old parliamentary chiefs that the masses owe their success in social legislation and in the struggle for the conquest of general political freedom.

The democratic masses are thus compelled to submit to a restriction of their own wills when they are forced to give to their leaders an authority which is in the long run destructive to the very principle of democracy. The leader's principal source of power is found in his indispensability. One who is indispensable has in his power all the lords and masters of the earth.[9] The history of the working-class parties continually furnishes instances in which the leader has been in flagrant contradiction with the fundamental principles of the movement, but in which the rank and file have not been able to make up their minds to draw the logical consequences of this conflict, because they feel that they cannot get along without the leader, and cannot dispense with the qualities he has acquired in virtue of the very position to which they have themselves elevated him, and because they do not see their way to find an adequate substitute. Numerous are the parliamentary orators and the trade-union leaders who are in opposition to the rank and file at once theoretically and practically, and who, none the less, continue to think and to act tranquilly on behalf of the rank and file. These latter, disconcerted and uneasy, look on at the behaviour of the "great men," but seldom dare to throw off their authority and to give them their dismissal.

The incompetence of the masses is almost universal throughout the domains of political life, and this constitutes the most solid foundation of the power of the leaders. The incompetence furnishes the leaders with a practical and to some extent with a moral justification. Since the rank and file are incapable of looking after their own interests, it is necessary that they should

---

[9] One who is indispensable can submit even the hereditary leader to his will. Roscher relates that a despotic prince in North Germany, when one of his best officials was offered a position in a neighbouring state, asked the minister who advised the prince to retain the official in his own service, "Is he indispensable?" When the minister replied in the affirmative, the prince said, "Let him go then, for I have no use for an indispensable servant" (Roscher, op. cit., p. 359).

have experts to attend to their affairs. From this point of view it cannot be always considered a bad thing that the leaders should really lead. The free election of leaders by the rank and file presupposes that the latter possess the competence requisite for the recognition and appreciation of the competence of the leaders. To express it in French, la désignation des capacités suppose elle-même la capacité de la désignation.

The recognition of the political immaturity of the mass and of the impossibility of a complete practical application of the principle of mass-sovereignty, has led certain distinguished thinkers to propose that democracy should be limited by democracy itself.[10] Condorcet wished that the mass should itself decide in what matters it was to renounce its right of direct control.[11] This would be the voluntary renunciation of sovereignty on the part of the sovereign mass. The French Revolution, which claimed to translate into practice the principle of free popular government and of human equality, and according to which the mutable will of the masses was in the abstract the supreme law, established through its National Assembly that the mere proposal to restore a monarchical form of government should be punishable by death.[12] In a point of such essential importance the deliberative power of the masses must yield to the threat of martial law. Even so fanatical an advocate of popular sovereignty as Victor Considérant was forced to acknowledge that at the first glance the machinery of government seemed too ponderous for it to appear possible for the people as such to make the machine work, and he therefore proposed the election of a group of specialists whose duty it should be to elaborate the text of the laws which the sovereign people had voted in principle.[13] Bernstein also denies that the average man has sufficient political competence to render unrestricted popular sovereignty legitimate. He considers that a great part of the questions that have to be decided consist of peculiar problems concerning which, until all men become living encyclopædias, a

---

[10] Cf. Part III, Chap. IV.

[11] Condorcet, *Progrès de l'Esprit humain*, ed. de la Bib. Nat., p. 186.

[12] Adolphe Thiers, *Histoire de la Révolution Française*, Brockhaus, Leipzig, 1846, vol. ii, p. 141. The same spirit of illogical amalgamation of unlimited popular sovereignty with the most rigid and despotic tutelage exercised over this alleged sovereign by its leaders, dominates most of the speeches of the Jacobins. (Cf., for example, *Œuvres de Danton*, recueillies et annotées par A. Vermorel, Cournol, Paris, pp. 119 et seq.)

[13] Victor Considérant, op. cit., p. 41.

few only will have interest and knowledge. To attain to an adequate degree of information regarding such questions, so that a carefully considered judgment can be given, requires a rare sense of responsibility such as cannot at present be attributed to the majority of the citizens.[14] Even Kautsky could not but recognize the difficulty of the problem thus presented to the labour movement; he has pointed out that it is not every province of social life which is suitable for democratic administration, and that democracy must be introduced gradually, and will not be completely realized until those interested shall have become capable of forming an independent judgment upon all decisive questions; and he shows that the possibility of realizing democratic administration will be greater in proportion as the co-operation of all the persons concerned in the decision of the issues becomes possible.[15]

The incompetence of the masses, which is in last analysis always recognized by the leaders, serves to provide a theoretical justification for the dominion of these. In England, which owes to Thomas Carlyle the theory of the supreme importance of great men, or "heroes," and where that theory has not, as in Germany, been utterly expelled from the official doctrine of socialism by the theory of historical materialism, even socialist thought has been profoundly influenced by the great-men theory. The English socialists, in fact, including those of the most various tendencies, have openly declared that if democracy is to be effective it must assume the aspect of a benevolent despotism. "He [the leader] has a scheme to which he works, and he has the power to make his will effective."[16] In all the affairs of management for whose decision there is requisite specialized knowledge, and for whose performance a certain degree of authority is essential, a measure of despotism must be allowed, and thereby a deviation from the principles of pure democracy. From the democratic point of view this is perhaps an evil, but it is a necessary evil. Socialism does not signify everything *by* the people, but everything *for* the people.[17] Consequently the

[14] Eduard Bernstein, *Zur Geschichte und Theorie des Sozialismus*, Edelheim, Berlin, 1910, p. 204.

[15] Karl Kautsky, *Consumvereine und Arbeiterbewegung*, Ignaz Brand, Erste Wiener Volksbuchhandlung, Vienna, 1897, p. 16.

[16] James Ramsay Macdonald, *Socialism and Society*, Independent Labour Party, London, 1905, pp. xvi, xvii.

[17] Ernest Belfort Bax, *Essays in Socialism New and Old*, Grant Richards, London, 1906, pp. 174, 182.

English socialists entrust the salvation of democracy solely to the good will and to the insight of the leaders. The majority determined by the counting of heads can do no more than lay down the general lines; all the rest, which is tactically of greater importance, devolves upon the leaders. The result is that quite a small number of individuals—three, suggests Bax—effectively controls the policy of the whole party. Social democracy is not democracy, but a party fighting to attain to democracy. In other words, democracy is the end, but not the means.[18] The impossibility of the means' being really democratic is conspicuously shown by the character of the socialist party as an undertaking endowed with certain financial characteristics, and one which, though created for ideological aims, depends for its success, not only upon the play of economic forces, but also upon the quality of the persons who have assumed leadership and responsibility.

Here, as elsewhere, the saying is true that no undertaking can succeed without leaders, without managers. In parallelism with the corresponding phenomena in industrial and commercial life, it is evident that with the growth of working-class organization there must be an accompanying growth in the value, the importance, and the authority of the leaders.[19] The principle of the division of labour creates specialism, and it is with good reason that the necessity for expert leadership has been compared with that which gives rise to specialism in the medical profession and in technical chemistry.[20]

Specialism, however, implies authority. Just as the patient obeys the doctor, because the doctor knows better than the patient, having made a special study of the human body in health and disease, so must the political patient submit to the guidance of his party leaders, who possess a political competence impossible of attainment by the rank and file.

Thus democracy ends by undergoing transformation into a form of government by the best, into an aristocracy. At once materially and morally, the leaders are those who must be regarded as the most capable and the most mature.

Is it not, therefore, their duty as well as their right to put

---

[18] Bax, ibid.
[19] Fausto Pagliari, *Le organizzazione e i loro Impiegati,* relazione al VII Congresso Nazionale delle società di resistenza, Tip. Coop., Turin, 1908, pp. 3, 5, 8.
[20] Rienzi (H. van Kol), op. cit., p. 250.

themselves at the head, and to lead not merely as representatives of the party, but as individuals proudly conscious of their own personal value? [21]

---

[21] Such was in actual fact the thesis of a Milanese politician, Guglielmo Gambarotta. Cf. his article *La Funzione dell' Uomo politico*, "Rivista critica del Socialismo," Rome, 1899, anno I, fasc. 9, p. 888. Gambarotta, not having succeeded in becoming a socialist deputy, abandoned the socialists to join the bourgeois radicals.

PART TWO

AUTOCRATIC TENDENCIES OF LEADERS

CHAPTER I

THE STABILITY OF LEADERSHIP

No one who studies the history of the socialist movement in Germany can fail to be greatly struck by the stability of the group of persons leading the party.

In 1870–71, in the year of the foundation of the German Empire, we see two great personalities, those of Wilhelm Liebknecht and August Bebel, emerge from the little group of the faithful to the new socialist religion to acquire leadership of the infant movement by their energy and their intelligence. Thirty years later, at the dawn of the new century, we find them still occupying the position of the most prominent leaders of the German workers.[1] This stability in the party leadership in Germany is very striking to the historian when he compares it with what has happened in the working-class parties elsewhere in Europe. The Italian socialist party, indeed, for the same reasons as in Germany, has exhibited a similar stability. Elsewhere, however, among the members of the Old International, a few individualities only of minor importance have retained their faith in socialism intact into the new century. In Germany, it may be said that the socialist leaders live in the party, grow old and die in its service.

We shall subsequently have occasion to refer to the smallness, in Germany, of the number of deserters from the socialist camp to join the other parties.[2] In addition to these few who have

---

[1] In the minutes of the Congress of Unification held at Gotha in 1875, at which the existing German socialist party was born, we find among the seventy-three delegates the following names of persons, who all remained faithful to the party, and of whom those yet alive are still prominent and active workers on its behalf: Auer, Bock, Blos, Geib, Grillenberger, Liebknecht, Loewenstein, Dreesbach, A. Kapell, Molkenbuhr, Hoffmann, Bebel, Motteler and Stolle. (Cf. Protokoll reissued by the Frankfort "Volksstimme," *Waffenkammer des Sozialismus,* eine Sammlung alter und neuer Propagandaschriften. Sixth half-yearly issue, January to June, 1906, p. 122.)—The facts recorded on p. 85 show that the stability in the rank and file of the party is far less marked than the stability of the leadership.

[2] Vide infra, pp. 107 et seq.

completely abandoned socialism, there are some, who, after working on behalf of the party for a time, have left politics to devote their energies to other fields. There are certain men of letters, who rose in the party like rockets, to disappear with corresponding rapidity. After a brief and sometimes stormy activity, they have quitted the rude political stage to return to the peaceful atmosphere of the study; and often their retirement from active political life has been accomplished by a mental estrangement from the world of socialist thought, whose scientific content they had perhaps never assimilated. Among such may be mentioned: Dr. Paul Ernst, at one time editor of the "Volkstribüne"; Dr. Bruno Wille, who led the section of *Die Jungen* (the Young Men) to the assault upon the veterans of the party who were captained by Bebel and Liebknecht (1890) ; Dr. Otto Erich Hartleben, once dramatic critic of "Vorwärts," but never a conspicuous member of the party; Dr. Ludwig Woltmann, delegate of the Rhenish manufacturing town of Barmen to the Congress of Hanover in 1899, where he was engaged in the defence of Bernstein, and who, after writing some socialist books which constitute notable contributions to sociology, subsequently devoted himself entirely to "political anthropology" with a strong nationalist flavour;[3] Ernst Gystrow (Dr. Willy Hellpach) ; and several others, for the most part talented and highly cultured men who have made names for themselves in German belletristic literature or in German science, but who were not suited for enduring political activities. It has also happened more than once in the history of the social democracy that men dominated by a fixed idea, and inspired by the hope of concentrating upon the realization of this idea the whole activity of socialist propaganda, or of simply annexing socialism to the service of this obsession,

---

[3] We owe to Paul Ernst a little work on social science, *Die Gesellschaftlicher Produktion des Kapitals bei gesteigerter Produktivität der Arbeit* (1894), and also two literary studies, *Lumpenbagasch* and *Im Chambre séparée*, which belong to socialist imaginative literature.—To the socialist phase of Otto Erich Hartleben belong the interesting description of social life *Um den Glauben, ein Tagebuch* (known also under the title *Die Serényi*), published in "Zwei Novellen," Wilhelm Friedrich, Leipzig, 1887. —Ludwig Woltmann wrote *Die Darwinsche Theorie und der Sozialismus, Beitrag zur Naturgeschichte der menschlichen Gesellschaft* (Düsseldorf, 1889), and *Der historische Materialismus, Darstellung und Kritik der Marxistischen Weltanschauung* (Düsseldorf, 1900). His brief but able and bold defence of Bernstein will be found in the *Protokoll* of the Congress of Hanover (Buchhandlung "Vorwärts," Berlin, 1899, pp. 147 et seq.).

have rushed into the party, only to leave it as suddenly with a chilled enthusiasm as soon as they perceived that they were attempting the impossible. At the Munich Congress of 1902, the pastor Georg Welker of Wiesbaden, a member of the sect of *Freireligiosen* (Broad Church), inspired by all the ardour of a neophyte, wished to substitute for the accepted socialist principle that religion is to be considered as a private matter the tactically dangerous device *Ecrasez l'infâme*. Again, at the first Congress of Socialist Women, which was held contemporaneously with the Munich Socialist Congress, Dr. Karl von Oppel, who had recently returned from Cape Colony and was a new member of the socialist party, emphasized the need for the study by socialists of foreign languages, and even foreign dialects, to enable them to come into more intimate contact with their brethren in other lands, and in his peroration insisted that the use of the familiar "thou" should be made universal and compulsory in the intercourse of socialist comrades. Such phenomena are characteristic of the life of all parties, but are especially common among socialists, since socialism exercises a natural force of attraction for cranks of all kinds. Every vigorous political party which is subversive in its aims is predestined to become for a time an exercise ground for all sorts of innovators and quacksalvers, for persons who wish to cure the ills of travailing humanity by the use of their chosen specifics, employed exclusively in smaller or larger doses—the substitution of friction with oil for washing with soap and water, the wearing of all-wool underclothing, vegetarianism, Christian science, neo-Malthusianism, and other fantasies.

More serious than the loss of such casual socialists were the losses which the party sustained during the period of the early and fierce application of the anti-socialist laws. At this time, in the period of reaction from 1840 to 1850, a large proportion of the leaders were forced to emigrate to America.[4] Still more serious were the losses sustained by the party during the Bismarckian regime. Bebel declares that at this time the number of those

---

[4] Among these refugees, in the early fifties, was F. A. Sorge, one of the founders of the "Neue Zeit." When by the influence of Marx the General Council of the International had in 1872 been transferred from London to New York, Sorge assumed the largely imaginary function of secretary of the Council, and subsequently, after the extinction of the Old International, devoted himself entirely to music. Another refugee was the poet Robert Schweichel, who returned to Germany after fifty years in America.

who were deprived of their means of livelihood and were forced to seek work and asylum on foreign soil ran into several hundreds. Of the nucleus of those who before the passing of the anti-socialist laws which unchained the tempest against the socialists, had worked actively in the party as propagandists, editors, and deputies, more than eighty left Germany, which most of them never revisited. "This involved a great draining of our energies."[5] In the worst years the exodus was particularly strong. Thus in the year 1881, just before the elections had demonstrated the indomitable vitality of the German socialist party, Friedrich Wilhelm Fritzsche (ob. 1905) and Julius Vahlteich, the critic of Lassalle, both of them at one time leaders in the party of Lassalle and socialist deputies to the Reichstag, crossed the Atlantic never to return.[6] Notwithstanding the storm which raged for more than ten years against the socialist party, the number of those whose socialist activity survived this period of terror was very large. Obviously, then, in times of comparative calm the stability of the leaders must be considerably greater. The author has examined the lists of those present at the congresses held in 1893 by three of the international socialist parties, namely, the German social democrats, the Parti Ouvrier (Guesdistes) in France, and the Italian socialist party, in order to ascertain the names of those who in the year 1910 were still in the first rank of the fighters on behalf of socialism in their respective countries. The results of this enquiry, which cannot claim absolute scientific precision, but which have none the less considerable practical value, are as follows. Of the 200 delegates to the Congress of Cologne, 60 were still fighting in the breach in 1910; of the 93 delegates of the Congress of Paris, 12; and of the 311 delegates to the Congress of Reggio Emilia, 102.[7] This shows a very high percentage of survivals, above all for the proletarian parties of Italy and Germany, but to a less extent for the Parti

---

[5] *Protokoll der Verhandlungen des Parteitags zu Halle a/S.*, 1890, p. 29.

[6] Vahlteich, however, though lost to the German labour movement, was not lost to socialism, for as editor of the German socialist daily published in New York he continued to play an active part in the life of the party until his death in 1915.

[7] Cf. the lists of delegates published in the *Protokoll über die Verhandlungen des Parteitages zu Cöln* (Verlag Vorwärts, Berlin, 1893, pp. 280 et seq.); *Onzième Congrès National du Parti Ouvrier tenu à Paris du 7 au 9 octobre, 1893* (Imp. Ouvrière S. Delory, Lille, 1893, p. 9); *Il Congresso di Reggio Emilia, Verbale stenografico* (Tip. degli Operai [Società Cooperativa], Milan, 1893, p. 57).

Ouvrier.[8] The bourgeois parties of the left on the Continent will hardly find it possible to boast of a similar continuity in the personnel of their leaders great and small. In the working-class parties we find that the personnel of the officials is even more stable than that of the leaders in general. The causes of this stability, as will be shown in the sequel, depend upon a complex of numerous phenomena.

Long tenure of office involves dangers for democracy. For this reason those organizations which are anxious to retain their democratic essence make it a rule that all the offices at their disposal shall be conferred for brief periods only.[9] If we take into account the number of offices to be filled by universal suffrage and the frequency of elections, the American citizen is the one who enjoys the largest measure of democracy. In the United States, not only the legislative bodies, but all the higher administrative and judicial officials are elected by popular vote. It has been calculated that every American citizen must on an average exercise his function as a voter twenty-two times a year.[10] The members of the socialist parties in the various countries must to-day exercise similarly extensive electoral activities: nomination of candidates for parliament, county councils, and munici-

[8] It would obviously be altogether erroneous to deduce from this the existence in the French national character of any particular fickleness or instability. The reasons for the comparative instability of the French leadership are connected with various tendencies of historical tradition and political democracy in France, the discussion of which would lead us too far from our subject.

[9] The third French Republic, wishing to guard against the danger of a military dictatorship and a new Cæsarism, has decreed that no general shall remain in command of an army corps for more than three years in succession.—In periods especially inspired with democratic ideas the very chambers of commerce have been moved to similar preventive measures. In the time of Napoleon, the Cologne chamber of commerce made a rule that all the officers must be re-elected annually, except the president, who must be changed every three months. It soon appeared, however, that the strict application of such a system was impossible. The frequent changes in the presidency were extremely injurious to the conduct of business, and deprived the chamber of commerce of the services of its best elements, thus reducing all reformatory energy to impotence (Mathieu Schwann, *Geschichte der Kölner Handelskammer*, Neubner, Cologne, 1906, p. 444). Schmoller considers that this election to offices in rotation is a peculiar blessing of urban civilization, municipal in its origin. (Cf. Schmoller, *Umrisse und Untersuchungen zur Verfassungs-, Verwaltungs- und Wirtschaftsgeschichte*, 1898, p. 291.)

[10] Werner Sombart, *Warum giebt es in der Vereinigten Staaten keinen Sozialismus?*, J. C. B. Mohr (Siebeck), Tübingen, 1906, p. 43.

palities; nomination of delegates to local and national party congresses; election of committees; re-election of the same; and so on, *da capo*. In almost all the socialist parties and trade unions the officers are elected for a brief term, and must be re-elected at least every two years. The longer the tenure of office, the greater becomes the influence of the leader over the masses and the greater therefore his independence. Consequently a frequent repetition of election is an elementary precaution on the part of democracy against the virus of oligarchy.

Since in the democratic parties the leaders owe their position to election by the mass, and are exposed to the chance of being dispossessed at no distant date, when forced to seek re-election, it would seem at first sight as if the democratic working of these parties were indeed secured. A persevering and logical application of democratic principles should in fact get rid of all personal considerations and of all attachment to tradition. Just as in the political life of constitutional states the ministry must consist of members of that party which possesses a parliamentary majority, so also in the socialist party the principal offices ought always to be filled by the partisans of those tendencies which have prevailed at the congresses.[11] Thus the old party dignitaries ought always to yield before youthful forces, before those who have acquired that numerical preponderance which is represented by at least half the membership plus one. It must, moreover, be a natural endeavour not to leave the same comrades too long in occupation of important offices, lest the holders of these should stick in their grooves, and should come to regard themselves as God-given leaders. But in those parties which are solidly organized, the actual state of affairs is far from corresponding to this theory. The sentiment of tradition, in co-operation with an instinctive need for stability, has as its result that the leadership represents always the past rather than the present. Leadership is indefinitely retained, not because it is the tangible expression of the relationships between the forces existing in the party at any given moment, but simply because it is already constituted. It is through gregarious idleness, or, if we may employ the euphuism, it is in virtue of the law of inertia, that the leaders are so often confirmed in their office as long as they like. These tendencies are particularly evident in the German social democracy, where the leaders are practically irremovable. The

---

[11] This has recently been laid down as a rule by the Dutch socialist party.

practice of choosing an entirely new set of leaders every two years ought long ago to have become general in the socialist party, as prototype of all democratic parties. Yet, as far as the German socialists are concerned, not merely does no such practice exist, but any attempt to introduce it provokes great discontent among the rank and file. It is true that one of the fundamental rules of the party, voted at the Mainz congress in 1900, lays down that at every annual congress the party must "renew," by ballot and by absolute majority, the whole of the executive committee, consisting of seven persons (two presidents, two vice-presidents, two secretaries, and a treasurer). This would be the true application of the democratic principle, but so little is it commonly observed in practice, that at every congress there are distributed to the delegates who are about to elect their new leaders printed ballot papers bearing the names of all the members of the retiring committee. This proves, not merely that the re-election of these leaders is taken as a matter of course, but even that a certain pressure is exercised in order to secure their re-election. It is true that in theory every elector is free to erase the printed names and to write in others, and that this is all the easier since the vote is secret. None the less, the printed ballot paper remains an effective expedient. There is a French phrase, *corriger la fortune;* this method enables the leaders to *corriger la democratie.*[12] A change in the list of names, although this is simply the exercise of an electoral right established by the rules, is even regarded as a nuisance by most of the delegates, and is censured by them should it occur. This was characteristically shown at the Dresden congress in 1903.[13] When the report spread through the congress that the revolutionary socialists of Berlin intended to remove from among the names on the ballot paper the name of Ignaz Auer, of whom they disapproved on account of his revisionist tendencies (an accusation which they subsequently repelled with indignation), the widespread anger aroused by the proposed sacrilege sufficed to overthrow the scheme.[14]

It is in this manner that the leaders of an eminently democratic party, nominated by indirect suffrage, prolong throughout

---

[12] Regarding identical practices employed by the "party machine" in America, cf. Ostrogorsky, *La Democratie et l'Organisation des Partis politiques,* Calman Lévy, Paris, 1903, vol. ii, p. 200.

[13] See p. 62, note 6.

[14] Cf. *Protokoll des Parteitages zu Dresden,* pp. 361, 373 et seq., 403.

their lives the powers with which they have once been invested. The re-election demanded by the rules becomes a pure formality. The temporary commission becomes a permanent one, and the tenure of office an established right. The democratic leaders are more firmly established in their seats than were ever the leaders of an aristocratic body. Their term of office comes greatly to exceed the mean duration of ministerial life in monarchical states. It has been calculated that in the German Empire the average official life of a minister of state is four years and three months. In the leadership, that is to say in the ministry, of the socialist party we see the same persons occupying the same posts for forty years in succession.[15] Naumann writes of the democratic parties: "Here changes in the leading offices occur less rapidly than in those of the secretaries of state and of the ministers. The democratic method of election has its own peculiar loyalty. As far as individual details are concerned it is incalculable, and yet on general lines we can count upon its activity with more certainty than upon the policy of princes. Through all democracy there runs a current of slow-moving tradition, for the ideas of the masses change only step by step and by gentle gradations. While in the monarchical organism there is an abundance of ancient forms, we find no less in the democratic organism that the longer it exists the more does it become dominated by tenaciously established phrases, programmes, and customs. It is not until new ideas have been in progress up and down the country for a considerable time that these ideas can penetrate the constituted parties through the activity of particular groups that have adopted them, or as an outcome of a spontaneous change of opinion among the rank and file. This natural tenacity of parliaments which are the outcome of popular election is indisputable, be it advantageous or disadvantageous to the community."[16] In democratically constituted bodies elsewhere than in Germany a similar phenomenon is manifest. In proof of this, reference may be made to a paragraph in the rules drawn up on February 3, 1910, by the Italian General Confederation of Labour as to the proclamation of the general strike.

---

[15] "We hear a great deal of the capriciousness and fickleness of popular favour. But it is certain that a leader who does his duty conscientiously is more secure in his position in the labour movement than is a minister in the Prussian monarchy founded upon the grace of God" (Eduard Bernstein, *Die Arbeiterbewegung*, ed. cit., p. 149).

[16] Friedrich Naumann, *Demokratie und Kaisertum*, ed. cit., p. 53.

The rule begins by declaring, in perfect conformity with democratic principles, that the declaration of a general strike must always be preceded by a referendum to the branches. To the terms of this referendum were to be appended the minutes of the session at which the Confederation of Labour had decided to submit the question. But the rule adds that if there should be disagreement between the executive council of the Federation and the results of the reference to the branches, if, for instance, the council had rejected the general strike while the referendum showed that the rank and file favoured it, this difference must not be taken to imply a vote of censure on the leaders.[17] This shows that in the working-class organizations of Italy ministerial responsibility is not so strongly established as in the Italian state, where the ministry feels that it must resign if, when it has brought forward a bill, this bill is rejected by the majority of the Chamber. As far as concerns England, we learn from the Webbs that the stability of the officials in the labour organizations is superior to that of the employees in the civil service. In the Amalgamated Association of Operative Cotton-Spinners we actually find that there is a rule to the effect that the officials shall remain in office indefinitely, as long as the members are satisfied with them.[18]

An explanation of this phenomenon is doubtless to be found in the force of tradition, whose influence assimilates, in this respect, the revolutionary masses to the conservatives. A contributory cause is one to which we have already referred, the noble human sentiment of gratitude.[19] The failure to re-elect a comrade who has assisted in the birth of the party, who has suffered with it many adversities, and has rendered it a thousand services, would be regarded as a cruelty and as an action to be condemned. Yet it is not so much the deserving comrade as one who is tried and expert whom the collectivity approves above all others, and whose collaboration must on no account be renounced. Certain individuals, simply for the reason that they have been invested with determinate functions, become irremovable, or at least difficult to replace. Every democratic organization rests, by its very nature, upon a division of labour. But wherever division of labour prevails, there is necessarily specialization, and the specialists become indispensable. This is especially true of such states as

---

[17] "Stampa," February 3, 1910.
[18] Sidney and Beatrice Webb, op. cit., vol. i, p. 16.
[19] Cf. supra, pp. 60 et seq.

Germany, where the Prussian spirit rules, where, in order that the party may be safely steered through all the shoals and breakers that result from police and other official interference and from the threats of the penal laws, the party can be assured of a certain continuity only when a high degree of stability characterizes the leadership.

There is an additional motive in operation. In the working-class organization, whether founded for political or for economic ends, just as much as in the life of the state, it is indispensable that the official should remain in office for a considerable time, so that he may familiarize himself with the work he has to do, may gain practical experience, for he cannot become a useful official until he has been given time to work himself into his new office. Moreover, he will not devote himself zealously to his task, he will not feel himself thoroughly at one with the aim he is intended to pursue, if he is likely to be dismissed at any moment; he needs the sense of security provided by the thought that nothing but circumstances of an unforeseen and altogether extraordinary character will deprive him of his position. Appointment to office for short terms is democratic, but is quite unpractical alike on technical and psychological grounds. Since it fails to arouse in the employee a proper sense of responsibility, it throws the door open to administrative anarchy. In the ministries of lands under a parliamentary regime, where the whole official apparatus has to suffer from its subordination to the continuous changes in majorities, it is well known that neglect and disorder reign supreme. Where the ministers are changed every few months, every one who attains to power thinks chiefly of making a profitable use of that power while it lasts. Moreover, the confusion of orders and regulations which results from the rapid succession of different persons to command renders control extraordinarily difficult, and when abuses are committed it is easy for those who are guilty to shift the responsibility on to other shoulders. "Rotation in office," as the Americans call it, no doubt corresponds to the pure principle of democracy. Up to a certain point it is adapted to check the formation of a bureaucratic spirit of caste. But this advantage is more than compensated by the exploitive methods of ephemeral leaders, with all their disastrous consequences. On the other hand, one of the great advantages of monarchy is that the hereditary prince, having an eye to the interests of his children and his successors, possesses an objective and permanent interest in his position, and almost always abstains from a policy which would hopelessly impair the vital energies of his country, just as the landed proprietor usually rejects methods of cultivation which, while providing large immediate returns, would sterilize the soil to the detriment of his heirs.

Thus, no less in time of peace than in time of war, the relationships between different organizations demand a certain degree of personal and tactical continuity, for without such continuity the political authority of the organization would be impaired. This is just as true of political parties as it is true of states. In international European politics, England has always been regarded as an untrustworthy ally, for her history shows that no other country has ever been able to confide in agreements concluded with England. The reason is to be found in this, that the foreign policy of the United Kingdom is largely dependent upon the party in power, and party changes occur with considerable rapidity. Similarly, the party that changes its leaders too often runs the risk of finding itself unable to contract useful alliances at an opportune moment. The two gravest defects of genuine democracy, its lack of stability (*perpetuum mobile democraticum*) and its difficulty of mobilization, are dependent on the recognized right of the sovereign masses to take part in the management of their own affairs.

In order to bind the leader to the will of the mass and to reduce him to the level of a simple executive organ of the mass, certain primitive democracies have at all times sought to apply, in addition to the means previously enumerated,[20] measures of moral coercion. In Spain, the patriotic revolutionary Junta of 1808 insisted that thirty proletarians should accompany the general who was to negotiate with the French, and these compelled him, in opposition to his own convictions, to reject all Napoleon's proposals.[21] In modern democratic parties there still prevails the practice, more or less general according to the degree of development these parties have attained, that the rank and file send to the congresses delegates who are fettered by definite instructions, the aim of this being to prevent the delegate from giving upon any decisive question a vote adverse to the opinion of the majority of those whom he represents. This precaution may be efficacious in certain cases, where the questions concerned are simple and clear. But the delegate, since he has no

---

[20] Supra, p. 28.   [21] Roscher, op. cit., p. 392.

freedom of choice, is reduced to the part of puppet, and cannot allow himself to be influenced by the arguments he hears at the congress or by new matters of fact which are brought to light in the course of the debate. But the result is, that not only is all discussion rendered superfluous in advance, but also that the vote itself is often falsified, since it does not correspond to the real opinions of the delegates. Of late fixed instructions have less often been given to the delegate, for it has become manifest that this practice impairs the cohesion so urgently necessary to every party, and provokes perturbations and uncertainties in its leadership.

In proportion as the chiefs become detached from the mass they show themselves more and more inclined, when gaps in their own ranks have to be filled, to effect this, not by way of popular election, but by co-optation, and also to increase their own effectives wherever possible, by creating new posts upon their own initiative. There arises in the leaders a tendency to isolate themselves, to form a sort of cartel, and to surround themselves, as it were, with a wall, within which they will admit those only who are of their own way of thinking. Instead of allowing their successors to be appointed by the choice of the rank and file, the leaders do all in their power to choose these successors for themselves, and to fill up gaps in their own ranks directly or indirectly by the exercise of their own volition.

This is what we see going on to-day in all the working-class organizations which are upon a solid foundation. In a report presented to the seventh congress of Italian labour organizations, held at Modena in 1908, we find it stated that the leaders must recognize capable men, must choose them, and must in general exercise the functions of a government.[22] In England these desiderata have already received a practical application, for in certain cases the new employees of the organization are directly chosen by the old officials.[23] The same thing happens in Germany, where about one-fifth of the trade-union employees are appointed by the central power. Moreover, since the trade-union congresses are composed almost exclusively of employees, the only means of which the individual organized workers can avail themselves for the expression of their personal opinions is to be

[22] Fausto Pagliari, *Le Organizzazioni e i loro Impiegati*, Tip. Coop., Turin, 1908, p. 8.
[23] Sidney and Beatrice Webb, *The History of Trade Unionism*, new edition, Longmans, London, 1907, vol. i, p. 87.

found in contributions to the labour press.[24] In the French labour movement, which claims to be the most revolutionary of all, the secretary of the Confédération Générale du Travail possesses the right of nomination when there is a question of electing new representatives to the executive committee of the federation. He exercises this right by sending to those Bourses du Travail which are not represented on the executive, a list of the comrades whom he considers suitable for this position, recommending the election of these.[25]

In the German socialist party, the individual *Landesvorstände,* or provincial committees, and the central executive claim the right of veto over the selection of candidates. But this right of veto gives them a privilege of an essentially oligarchical character, elevating the committees to the rank of a true government, and depriving the individual branches of one of the fundamental rights of all democracy, the right of individual liberty of action.[26] In Holland, again, the socialist candidatures for parliament must be approved by the party executive, and this executive is as irremovable as that of the German party. It rarely happens that an old member of the executive whose term of office has expired fails to obtain re-election should he desire it. It is in Holland also that we see such conspicuous pluralism among the party officials.

In the nomination of candidates for election we find, in addi-

---

[24] Cf. Paul Kampffmeyer, *Die Entwicklung der deutschen Gewerkschaften,* "Annalen für soziale Politik u. Gesetzg.," vol. i, No. 1, p. 114.

[25] Fernand Pelloutier, *Histoire des Bourses du Travail,* Schleicher Frères, Paris, 1902, p. 150.

[26] W. Heine writes in this connection: "We desire that the people should rule themselves; our party programme demands that in the most important and most difficult problem the people should decide by direct voting and direct legislation; is it right then that in the most immediate and simplest of questions, namely, in what men is the people to put its confidence, the decision of the people should be subject to the goodwill and pleasure of a superior authority? . . . If the party officials are allowed to decide for themselves who is to enter their charmed circle, the danger arises that fresh blood and new ideas will more and more be refused admittance, and that the party will tend to undergo that ossification which is characteristic of all oligarchies and bureaucracies. Further consequences of such a tendency are shown in the slackening of the spirit of initiative and in the decline of interest in the intellectual life of the party, and also in an inclination to an obstinate or unreflective clinging to traditional formulas, in a tendency to stick in a groove. From this point of view, a good bureaucracy is more dangerous than a bad one" (Wolfgang Heine, op. cit., pp. 282, 284).

tion, another grave oligarchical phenomenon, nepotism. The choice of the candidates almost always depends upon a little clique, consisting of the local leaders and their assistants, which suggests suitable names to the rank and file.[27] In many cases the constituency comes to be regarded as a family property.[28] In Italy, although democratic principles are greatly honoured, we not infrequently find that when a representative dies, or can no longer continue in office, the suffrages of the constituency are transferred without question to his son or to his younger brother, so that the position is kept in the family.

Those who love paradox may be inclined to regard this process as the first symptom marking the passage of democracy from a system of plebiscitary Bonapartism to one of hereditary monarchy.

---

[27] "Trois ou quatre personnes au plus rédigent les programmes et choisissent les noms des futurs représentants dans chaque département. Ces personnes font de la politique une carrière: elles veulent surtout et avant tout, je ne dirai pas le pouvoir, mais les places. Ces politiciens trouvent plus commode de se faire agents électoraux pour arriver aux fonctions publiques que de s'y préparer par de longues études." This description of the conditions of French political life is from the pen of Germain, quoted by J. Novicow, *Conscience et Volonté sociales,* Giard et Brière, Paris, 1897, p. 65.

[28] Cf. supra, p. 13.

CHAPTER II

THE FINANCIAL POWER OF THE LEADERS 'AND OF THE PARTY

In the German socialist party desertion and treason on the part of the leaders have been rare. This is conspicuous in contrast with what has happened in the French socialist party, especially as regards the parliamentary group of the latter. The elections of August 20, 1893, sent to the Palais Bourbon six socialist deputies: Paulin Méry, Alphonse Humbert, A. Abel Hovelacque, Alexandre Millerand, Pierre Richard, and Ernest Roche. Of these, one only, the distinguished linguist and anthropologist, Hovelacque, remained faithful to the party to his death; the other five are now declared enemies of the socialist party. The part played by Millerand in socialism, a great one as is well known, came to an end in 1904. In his electoral address of May, 1906, the term "socialist" had passed into the background; he was running in opposition to the official socialist candidate, the sociologist Paul Lafargue, the son-in-law of Marx; his rôle was now that of an anti-collectivist and patriotic bourgeois reformer. The other socialist ex-deputies in the above list had deserted their colours at an even earlier date. The trifling political shock which is associated with the name of General Boulanger sufficed to overthrow the house of cards which represented the socialist convictions of these warriors on behalf of the revolutionary proletariat of France. To-day they are all vowed to the service of the clerico-nationalist reaction. Paulin Méry became one of the Boulangist leaders; in May, 1906, when, in the second ballot, he was opposed to the bourgeois radical, Ferdinand Buisson, the socialists of his constituency unhesitatingly cast their votes in favour of his opponent. At the time of the Dreyfus affair, Alphonse Humbert was one of the most ardent defenders of the general staff of the army. Ernest Roche, at one time a disciple of Auguste Blanqui, and then, in conjunction with Edouard Vaillant, one of the most noted leaders of the Blanquists, is now the lieutenant of Henri Rochefort; in a recent parliamentary election in the seventeenth arrondissement of Paris he was defeated by

the reformist socialist Paul Brousse, although Brousse, the sometime anarchist and theoretical father of the propaganda by deed
in western Europe, had recently forfeited the good-will of the
more revolutionary section of the workers (Brousse, as President
of the Paris municipal council, had received Alfonso XIII as
guest at the Hôtel de Ville, and this conduct was hardly in conformity with socialist principles). It is true that even to-day
Roche still belongs to a *Parti Blanquiste ni Dieu ni Maître* which
announces week by week in the "Intransigeant" meetings of a
more or less private character, but this party is really fictitious,
for though it has a few branches it does not count in political
life; in all practical political questions this petty group works
hand in hand with the antisemites and the nationalists, and in
matters of theory, whenever Roche has occasion to allude to them,
he proclaims himself *le champion incorruptible de la République,
du Socialisme et de la Patrie,* his anti-capitalism being extremely
tame, but his jingoism fanatical.[1]

In contrast with this, the German socialist party shares with
the Italian and the Belgian parties the good fortune of possessing faithful and devoted leaders. The leadership of the German
party has been again and again reinforced by valuable acces-
sions from the other parties of the left, such as August Bebel,
the bourgeois democrat, Max Quarck and Paul Bader, of the
"Frankfurter Zeitung," Paul Göhre and Max Maurenbrecher,
who had previously founded the national socialist party in opposition to the socialists. On the other hand, it has suffered no
extensive losses of significant personalities by desertion to the
bourgeois camp. The only exceptions to this generalization re-
late to leaders of minor importance, such as Max Lorenz,[2] ex-
editor of the "Leipzige Volkszeitung," who subsequently passed
through the gate of national socialism to gain a secure position
as editor of the "Antisozialdemokratische Korrespondenz"; the
young Count Ludwig Reventlow, who in 1906 became a deputy
in the antisemite interest; and a few other academic personalities
of minor importance,[3] besides one or two exceptional converted

---

[1] Cf. Michels, *Die deutsche Sozialdemocratie im internationalen Verbande,* "Arch. f. Sozialw.," vol. xxv, pp. 213 et seq.

[2] Max Lorenz has written a number of small socialist works, and is author
of the reformist book *Die marxistische Sozialdemokratie,* Wiegand, Leipzig,
1896.

[3] Among these may be mentioned: Louis Viereck, formerly an official
in the Prussian service, subsequently socialist deputy to the Reichstag, and

proletarians, such as the basket-maker Fischer.[4] It would not be right to regard as treason in the strict sense of the term a simple passage from the socialist party properly so-called to some other form of militant socialism, such as happened in the case of socialists as fervent and convinced as the deputy Johann Most, the noted binder of Augsburg, and Wilhelm Hasselmann, the chemist, another deputy, who after 1890 broke openly with the party, to adhere first to anti-parliamentary socialism and subsequently to anarchism. To speak of these men as "deserters" would be to identify the notion of desertion of the organized party with desertion of the idea of working-class emancipation. But even if we count as deserters from socialism those who have gone over to the ranks of the anarchists, we are compelled to admit that among the apostates from the German socialist party there has not been one of those who have occupied a leading position in the party.

The fighting proletariat in Germany has hitherto been spared the spectacle of its former representatives seated on the Government benehes surrounded by the enemies of the socialists. There has in Germany been no such figure as Aristide Briand, yesterday advocate of the general strike and counsel for the defence of men prosecuted for anti-militarism, who had expressly declared himself in full sympathy with the anti-militarist theory *plutôt l'insurrection que la guerre*, and to-day, as Minister of Public Instruction, approving no less vigorously and explicitly

---

now correspondent of bourgeois newspapers in New York; Max Pfund, at one time an ardent socialist, author of *Unsere Taktik, ein ehrliches Wort zur Klärung* (Mauerer & Dimmiak, Berlin, 1891—which closes with the words, "Let us see to it that we have a firm standing-ground when the storm begins to rage"), now on the staff of the "Lokal Anzeiger," of Berlin; Dr. Franz Lütgenau, who formerly played a leading part as a socialist in the political life of Westphalia, and was the author of a number of books published by Dietz, and of a work entitled *Darwin und der Staat* (Thomas, Leipzig), but now on the staff of a bourgeois journal at Dortmund; Heinrich Oberwinder, the author, one of the original disciples of Lassalle, but who, during the days of the anti-socialist law was unmasked at Paris as a spy of the German government. (Cf. Franz Mehring, *Geschichte der deutschen Sozialdemokratie*, Dietz, Stuttgart, 1904, 2nd ed., vol. ii, p. 300); Fernand Bueb, of Mülhausen, elected in 1893, when twenty-eight years of age, as socialist deputy to the Reichstag, but who has since deserted the party and disappeared from the political stage.

[4] In order to make a parade of his proletarian origin, Fischer, who has now joined the conservative party, ostentatiously signs his articles "Fischer, the Basket-Maker."

the measures of repression enforced by his colleagues in the Cabinet against anti-militarists. Germany has not known a John Burns, who as a labour leader in 1886 played a prominent part in the organization of huge demonstrations of the unemployed, at which open reference was made to the possible need for destroying the palaces and sacking the shops, and whose activities had led to a panic in the bourgeois world of the English capital, but who a few years later as President of the Local Government Board, when a motion was brought forward in Parliament at the instance of the Labour Representation Committee demanding the intervention of Parliament on behalf of the unemployed, replied that he was neither a public-house politician nor a soft-hearted philanthropist prepared to squander the money of hard-working citizens upon the so-called unemployed, and who advised the workers to save their money in good times and not to spend it upon unworthy objects. Such disillusionments, experienced at the hands of men in whose sincerity and firmness of character the organized workers had an ingenuous confidence, have a politically discouraging and morally enervating effect. They tend to lead the workers to indifferentism, or to one-sided specializations, such as the new unionism, or an exclusive belief in the co-operative movement, or, again, to certain forms of libertarian aspiration, and to alienate them from the thought of political organization, and from a considered and measured parliamentary activity. We see this, above all, in France, where the case of Briand was merely a sequel to that of Millerand, and the case of Millerand a sequel, if you will, to the case of Louis Blanc, and where the great mass of the manual workers are split up into the two sections of those who advocate the most defiant abstentionism and of those whose minds are dominated by the spirit which the French aptly term *jemenfichisme.*[5] The fact that the socialist

---

[5] Quite recently a number of the most eminent socialist leaders in France have passed over into the governmental camp and are thus in violent conflict with their former comrades. Among these may be mentioned René Viviani, now Minister of State; the university professor V. Augagneur, at one time socialist mayor of Lyons and subsequently governor of the Island of Madagascar; Gabriel Deville, disciple of Marx, and one of the founders of the Parti Ouvrier; Alexandre Zévaès, formerly one of the ablest of the Guesdist leaders and at that time a strict Marxist; Joseph Sarraute; and many others. De Pressensé writes very truly, "Combien d'hommes n'a-t-elle pas vus [la classe ouvrière française], qui, après lui avoir prodigué les paroles de révolte, après avoir semé les excitations, après avoir pratiqué sans relâche le verbalisme révolutionnaire, à peine arrivés au pouvoir,

parties of Germany, Italy, and Belgium have hitherto been free from the disturbing and demoralizing effects of such episodes furnishes the chief if not the only reason for the unlimited and often blind confidence which is displayed, as no unprejudiced observer of the members of these parties can fail to notice, in the "tried and trusted" leaders. In Germany, indeed, the authority which this spirit gives to the party leaders, and which continually accentuates the tendency towards centralization, is enormously reinforced by the spirit of organization, by the intense need for guidance, which characterizes the German proletariat, and also by the comparative poverty of the party in individuals of intellectual pre-eminence and of those possessing economic independence. Owing to these exceptional conditions, the leaders are preserved from the disintegrating influence of personal and tactical dissensions, which would otherwise have led them into conflicts with the masses of the party similar to those that have raged with such violence in Italy and in Holland, notwithstanding the stability and the authoritative position of the socialist leaders in these latter countries.

It may be said of the German socialist leaders that they have not yet lost contact with the masses; that there still prevails complete harmony between the form and the content of their tactics even when there should be a conflict between these; that the community of ideas between leaders and led has not yet been broken; and, to sum up, that the executive committee of the party, and also (though perhaps less perfectly) the parliamentary socialist group, still represent the average opinion of the comrades throughout the country. The confidence which the organized German workers give to those that represent them in the complex game of politics is based upon the security which the leaders offer at once from the moral and the political point of view. This security incontrovertibly exists. The manner in which the masses entrust their interests to the leaders is, historically at least, legitimate and explicable. But the causes of the

---

se sont cyniquement retournés contre leur propre passé et contre leurs dupes, leur ont fait un crime d'avoir gardé foi à leurs prédications et se sont faits les ordonnateurs sans merci et sans scrupule des hauts et basses œuvres de la réaction sociale. . . . Il me semble pourtant que rien ne serait plus déraisonnable et plus funeste que de se livrer, pour cette cause, à une apathie sceptique, à un *pococurantisme* gouailleur, qui ferait le jeu de ces viles politiciens au moins autant que le fit jadis la naïve crédulité d'un enthousiasme sans critique" (Francis de Pressensé, *L'Affaire Durant, ou la nouvelle Affaire Dreyfus*, "Le Mouvement Socialiste," xiii, No. 227).

stability of the leaders are naturally, like all causes, complex. Among various explanations, it has been suggested that all the virtue of the German labour leaders lies in the fact that they have never been exposed to serious temptations, so that it resembles that of a young woman who has never been courted. There is a certain element of truth in this explanation, in so far as we have to do with that special political virtue which consists in the faithful defence of the party flag. In a state where parliamentary government does not exist, where the ministers of state are chosen by the sovereign from among the leading officials of the administration without any regard to the parliamentary majority, and where consequently no direct path to office is open to popular representatives, the possibility of intellectual corruption, that is to say of a more or less complete change of front on the part of the socialist leaders under the influence of a desire for ministerial office, is *ipso facto* excluded, just as is excluded an adhesion to the party of bourgeois social reform of the revolutionary socialists who aim at changing the very base of the existing economic order. On the other hand, Arturo Labriola, who has followed the German movement with keen interest and lively sympathy, is undoubtedly right in his caustic prediction that as soon as the day comes when the German Government is willing to afford itself the luxury of a lukewarm liberal ministry, since the socialists are really not difficult to satisfy, the ''reformist infection'' will spread far even in Germany. He adds that the germs of this infection are already widely diffused.[6]

Yet although it is true that the feudal structure of the German Empire, which is still reflected in the laws and in the collective mentality of the country, imposes necessary limits upon the ambition of the labour leaders, it must be admitted that the fact we are now considering does not find an adequate explanation in the mere lack of temptation. Moreover, temptation, in the vulgar and material sense of the term, is no more lacking in Germany than elsewhere. No government, however autocratic, has ever neglected a chance of corrupting the austere virtue of the leaders of any movement dangerous to authority, by the distribution of a portion of those secret service funds which every state has at its disposal, and which have been voted by the popular representatives themselves. Nevertheless, it may be affirmed that the leaders of the German labour movement, even

---

[6] Arturo Labriola, *Riforme e Rivoluzione Sociale,* Soc. Edit. Milan, Milan, 1904, p. 17.

if they do not possess that evangelical morality of which we find
so many examples in the early days of the Italian labour movement, have yet always resisted any attempts to corrupt their integrity by bribes. We need hardly reckon as an exception, the
case which has not yet been fully cleared up of the president of
the Allgemeiner Deutsche Arbeiterverein, Johann Baptist von
Schweitzer, in the year 1872, for it seems probable that the fiery
Bebel, who secured Schweitzer's condemnation and expulsion
from the party, was in reality altogether in the wrong.[7] Even
the subordinates in the leadership of the party, those whom we
may speak of as the non-commissioned officers, have usually
proved altogether inaccessible to the blandishments of the police.
They have sometimes accepted bribes, but always to hand them
over at once to "Vorwärts" or some other socialist paper, in
which there has then appeared an invitation to the owner of the
money to come and claim it personally within a certain number
of days, since if unclaimed it would be handed over to the party
funds.

The unshaken fidelity of the German socialist leaders rests
upon powerful reasons, and some of these are ideal in nature.
The characteristic love of the German for his chosen vocation,
devotion to duty, years of proscription and of persecution shared
with other comrades, the isolation from the bourgeois world of
the workers and their representatives, the invincible conviction
that only a party of a compact and solid structure will be able
to translate into action the lofty aims of socialism, and the consequent aversion for any socialist struggle conducted by free-lances
outside the ranks of the organized party—such are some of the
numerous reasons which have combined to produce in the minds
of the German socialists a love for their organization enabling it
to resist the most violent storms. This attachment to the party,

---

[7] Although, so far as is known, Bebel continued to the end of his life
to maintain the justice of the accusation he brought in 1872 (cf. August
Bebel, *Aus meinem Leben*, Dietz Nachf., Stuttgart, 1911, Part II, p. 130),
the official historian of the party, Franz Mehring (*Geschichte, der deutschen
Sozialdemokratie*, ed. cit., vol. iv, pp. 66 et seq.), takes the opposite view.
Commenting on Schweitzer's declaration after his exclusion from the Verein,
Mehring remarks: "We cannot read without emotion the wise and dig-
nified leave-taking of the man who in difficult times had so firmly steered
the ship of the social democracy, who had rendered so many invaluable
services to the class-conscious proletariat, and who, enmeshed in the consequences of his own best actions, committed more than one unjust action,
but suffered far greater injustice in return."

often manifested by fine and moving actions, certainly represents one of the most solid elements in the foundation upon which has been erected the edifice of German socialism. It enables us to understand the conduct of the socialist leaders during and after numerous crises which, in the view of the profane, would necessarily terminate in the open abandonment of the party by a number of its leaders. It is their love for the party, with which the great majority of the comrades feel themselves to be identified, which has led such men as Eduard Bernstein and Kurt Eisner to retain their membership after violent conflicts which had almost led to their expulsion. It is proper to add that in the course of this struggle these men have always preserved the personal dignity without which a self-respecting man cannot possibly remain among his companions-at-arms.

These ideal motives are reinforced by motives, no less important, of a material order. The practice of paying for the services rendered to the party by its employees creates a bond which many of the comrades hesitate to break, and this for a thousand reasons. The pecuniary remuneration for services to the party which is given by the German social democracy immunizes the party employees against the grosser forms of temptation. Whereas in France, England, Holland, Italy, and elsewhere, socialist propaganda, spoken and written, is effected chiefly by volunteers, in the German socialist party gratuitous propaganda is practically unknown. Elsewhere than in Germany, socialist activity is based upon individual enthusiasm, individual initiative, and individual devotion; but in Germany it reposes upon loyalty, discipline, and the sentiment of duty, encouraged by pecuniary remuneration. In the history of the non-German socialist parties, for example, we find important periodicals, such as the ''Avanguardia Socialista'' of Milan and the ''Nieuwe Tijd'' of Amsterdam, which have been founded by individual initiative, and which are maintained by the political idealism of a few individuals. These continue to carry on their work although the expenses of the venture often exceed the income, and although those who write for the papers in question are unpaid or almost wholly unpaid. In Germany, on the other hand, the ''Vorwärts'' of Berlin, the ''Leipziger Volkszeitung'' and the ''Neue Zeit'' were founded and sustained by the party as a whole, and have a paid editorial staff and paid contributors. It would nevertheless be quite wrong to suppose that socialist propagandists and socialist officials are paid on a scale which enables them with the

hard-earned pence of the workers to lead that luxurious existence which, with an ignorance bordering on impudence, is often
ascribed to them by the ''respectable'' press and the loungers of
the clubs. The life of a socialist journalist is far from resembling that of a spendthrift or a libertine; his day's work is by no
means an easy one, his labours demand an abundance of self-
denial and sacrifice and are nervously exhausting; whilst the
remuneration he receives is a modest one when compared with
the gravity and the difficulty of his task.[8] No one will deny
this who has even an elementary acquaintance with the conditions of work and pay in the socialist press and with the life led
by the employees of the party. Men of the ability and education
of Karl Kautsky, Max Quarck, Adolf Müller, and a hundred
others, would have been able, had they chosen to devote themselves to some other service than that of the workers, to obtain
a material reward much greater than that which they secure in
their present positions.

This reference to the practice of the German socialist party of
remunerating all services rendered was necessary to enable the
reader to understand rightly certain peculiarities of German socialist life. But it must not be supposed that there is no unpaid
socialist work in Germany. In country districts where the organization is still poor, and in the case of small weekly papers whose
financial resources are inconsiderable, much gratuitous work is
done by the socialists. In not a few places, moreover, the local
comrades do not receive pay for any of the speeches they make.
A witness to the idealism which, despite all difficulties, continues
to flourish in the working class is the way in which during elections and at other times many working-class socialists sacrifice
their Sunday rest in order to do propagandist work in the country, vigorously distributing leaflets, electoral addresses, socialist
calendars, etc. This gratuitous work is often carried out, not
only under conditions involving the patient endurance of expo-
sure and privation, but also in face of all kinds of abuse and of
the danger of arrest on the most trivial pretexts, and of attacks
made by excited antisemitic or clerical peasants.

In general, however, the German practice is to pay for all
services to the party, from the most trifling notice contributed to
a newspaper to the lengthiest public discourse. Whilst this deprives the party to a large extent of the spirit of heroism and

---

[8] Cf. pp. 57 et seq.

enthusiasm, and of work done by voluntary and spontaneous collaboration, it gives to the organization a remarkable cohesion, and an authority over the personnel which, though doubtless detracting from its elasticity and its spirit of initiative, and, in essence, tending to impair the very socialist mentality, constitutes none the less one of the most important and indispensable bases of the party life.

Able critics of socialist affairs, such as Ernst Günther, have endeavoured to explain the fact that persons of recognized ability and worth have preferred as a rule to subject themselves to the party-will rather than to break completely with the organization, by the suggestion that had they decided otherwise they would have imperilled their political existence, and would have renounced "the possibility of continuing to represent efficiently the interests of the workers."[9] It is unquestionable that the socialist platform is now the best one from which to advocate the interests of the workers, and is historically the most appropriate, so that the renunciation of this platform almost always involves the loss of the opportunity for defending working-class interests. But it is no less indisputable that "to the average man the close association of his own economic existence with his dependence upon the socialist party seems a sufficient excuse" for the sacrifice of his own convictions in order to remain in a party with which he is in truth no longer in full sympathy.[10]

It has been written:

> Staatserhaltend sind nur jene,
> Die vom Staate viel erhalten.[11]

For all their exaggeration, there is a nucleus of truth in these words, and the criticism applies with equal justice to the party as to the state. The practice of paying for all services rendered, tends in no small degree to reinforce the party bureaucracy and favours centralized power. Financial dependence upon the

---

[9] Ernst Günther, *Die Revisionistiche Bewegung in der deutschen Sozialdemokratie*, Jahrbuch für Gesetzgebung (Schmoller, anno xxx (1906), fasc. 1, p. 253).

[10] Günther, op. cit.

[11] There is a word-play here which renders a literal translation impossible. The general significance is that those only can be counted upon to support the state who receive much at the hands of the state.—Much in the same way as in England the reactionaries are accustomed to say (though here without any intention to gibe) that those only who have a "stake in the country" can be trusted to care for its interests!

party, that is to say upon the leaders who represent the majority, enshackles the organization as with iron chains. The most tenaciously conservative members of the organization are, in fact, those who are most definitely dependent upon it. When this dependence attains to a certain degree of intensity, it exercises a decisive influence upon the mentality. It has been noted that in those countries in which members of parliament are not salaried, but where the party organizations themselves provide for the support of their parliamentary representatives, the deputies have a very strong sense of dependence upon the members of their organizations. Where, on the contrary, members of parliament are remunerated by the state, they feel themselves before all to be parliamentarians, even though they may owe their election exclusively to the socialist party.

It is well known that the numerical strength of the trade unions depends to a very considerable extent upon the economic advantages which the unions offer to their members. The success of the trade-union movement from this point of view has suggested to the German socialists that the socialist party should extend to the rank and file of the membership some of the advantages which have hitherto been the exclusive privilege of the party bureaucracy. Otto Gerisch, treasurer of the party and member of the executive committee, referred to this possibility in a speech on the problem of organization, made at the Bremen Congress of 1904.[12] After quoting facts proving the superiority of the trade-union organization over that of the party, he stated that in his view the real reason of this superiority was to be found in the "accumulation of benefits" which the unions provided for their members. He added that the workers did not prove faithful to their unions until these organizations undertook the practice of mutual aid on the large scale, but that thereafter the membership increased enormously and became far more stable. Continuing this train of thought, he said: "It is characteristic that the Königsberg comrades, who, in view of the advanced position they occupy in the German socialist movement, must certainly be held to possess extensive experience in matters of organization and propaganda, provide subsidies to members of the party to meet funeral expenses.[13] This practice has been

---

[12] *Protokoll über die Verhandlungen des Parteitages der sozialdemokratischen Partei Deutschlands, abgehalten zu Bremen, Sept. 10-24, 1904,* Verlag "Vorwärts," Berlin, p. 272.

[13] A similar institution is found also in Giessen. Here every member of

introduced for a very good reason. We are at a disadvantage in the socialist party as compared with the trade unions, in that we cannot offer any direct advantages to our members. But this will not always be the case." It seems doubtful if these words are to be interpreted as a direct announcement of the intention to introduce a system of mutual life-insurance, or whether Gerisch merely intended a warm recommendation of such a measure. Oda Olberg, who was present at the congress on behalf of the Italian socialist paper "Avanti," interpreted the words in the former sense, and described the speech as a "menace of degeneration." [14] It is certain that in the German socialist party tendencies exist towards laying greater stress upon such material advantages, tendencies which might lead to the transformation of the party organization into a socialistically tinged proletarian assurance society. It is evident that an evolution in this direction would attract to the party hundreds of thousands of new members, so that there would be a considerable accession of strength. At the same time the apparatus of the socialist bureaucracy would be greatly developed. The effects which such an evolution would have upon the real strength of the party vis-à-vis the state, upon its moral impetus, its internal unity, and its tactical cohesion, are questions which cannot be discussed here. For our purpose it has been enough to draw attention to the influence which the practice of paying for services rendered has upon the maintenance and the reinforcement of the organization.

In aristocratic regimes, so long, at least, as the aristocracy retains its essentially plutocratic character, the elected officials are usually unpaid. Their functions are purely honorary, even when they require the whole time of those who undertake them. They are members of the dominant class, are assumed to be rich, to make it a point of honour to spend money for the public good,

---

the local branch of the socialist party pays a monthly subscription of 25 pfennigs. Five pfennigs out of this sum are paid in to a special funeral account, and from this account is made a disbursement of 20 marks for the funeral expenses of every member, or of his wife.

[14] Cf. leading article, *Il Congresso di Brema,* "Avanti," anno viii, No. 2,608. Oda Olberg writes: "Frankly, we cannot conceive a socialist party which attracts and retains its members by offering them economic advantages. We consider that it would be far better to have a handful of devoted comrades who have joined our ranks, not for lucre, but impelled by the socialist faith, ready for every sacrifice, willing to give themselves, rather than a whole army of members who have entered the party regarding

and to occupy, even at considerable pecuniary sacrifice, eminent positions in the service of the state. A similar practice prevails even in modern democracies. The Lord Mayor of London and his colleagues in the other great cities of England are unpaid. The same is true of the Italian Syndics. Inasmuch as the entertainment allowances, etc., are usually altogether inadequate, the holders of such offices must be men of considerable private means to enable them to support the necessary charges, and they must therefore be either wealthy parvenus or men born to wealth. Similar considerations apply to Italian parliamentary representation. In Italy the government opposes the idea of paying salaries to members of parliament, on the ground that it would be improper for the elected of the nation to receive base money for their activities.[15] The consequence is that in Italy, since the Italian socialist party is a poor one, the manual workers are *a priori* excluded from parliament. Among the thirty-six socialist deputies in the Italian chamber during 1909, two only had been manual workers (trade-union leaders). In such conditions it is likely that the party representation in the legislature will be restricted to persons with private means, to those, that is to say, who have time and money which they are able to devote to an unremunerative occupation, and one which demands frequent changes of residence. In France, moreover, where the salaries of the deputies are on a liberal scale, it has been noted that the poorest constituencies are represented in parliament by the richest members.[16]

Even in certain democratic parties the assumption of official

---

it as a mutual aid society.'' This view is estimable from the moral and socialist outlook, but its utterance shows that Oda Olberg has an inadequate understanding of the most conspicuous quality of the masses; unless it be that she has abandoned her Marxism, that after the Blanquist manner she is willing to renounce the democratic criterion of majority rule, and that she looks to find salvation solely from the action of a small but intelligent minority.

[15] Giolitti, replying in the year 1909 to a proposal that the Italian deputies should be salaried, expressed again and again his clear conviction that the payment of members would tend to weaken the repute of parliament throughout the country. In his view, the representative function is a free gift from the people (cf. *Atti del Parlamento Italiano, Camera dei Deputati, sessione 1909*, Tip. della Cam. dei Dep., Rome, 1909, vol. i, pp. 518 and 913).—In the year 1885 Bismarck, àpropos of a paragraph in the Prussian civil code, went so far as to describe the salary paid to the members of the Reichstag as ''a dishonourable gain.''

[16] Eugène Fournière, op. cit., p. 109.

positions in the party may be regarded as an honorary office, especially where the organization is not well supplied with means. Thus there not infrequently arises within the party a peculiar form of financial authority, since the comrades who are better endowed with means, gain and retain influence through the pecuniary services which they render. A plutocratic supremacy of this nature exists in the press of those parties which, lacking means for the independent maintenance of their own organs, are forced to depend upon the pecuniary assistance given by well-to-do comrades. The result, of course, is that these latter, as principal shareholders in the newspaper, possess a natural right of controlling its policy. A typical example of this is found in France, where for a time ''l'Humanité'' was supported by a syndicate of wealthy Jews. Again, in choosing delegates to the party congresses, the preference is often given to those who are able and willing to pay their own travelling expenses. In this way it results that the congresses, which constitute the supreme authority of the party, often come to be chiefly composed, like the parliamentary group in certain countries, of persons who are comparatively well-to-do. This is what happens in Italy, France, Holland, etc.[17] As far as Germany is concerned, this is less likely to occur, partly because very few members of the socialist party are well off, and partly because of the flourishing condition of the party finances. In Germany, therefore, the financial superiority of the rich comrade over the poor one is often replaced by the superiority of the rich branch. It is naturally very difficult for the organizations that are short of money to send delegates to the party congress, especially if this is held in a distant city. Consequently these poor branches, when they are unable to appoint as delegate some one who has the time, the means, and the will to undertake the journey at his own expense, are compelled to abandon the idea of being represented at the congress. It should be added that public opinion within the party has often shown itself strongly adverse to the practice, stigmatizing the delegates who are appointed on these terms as ''mandataries by accommodation,'' and regarding the conferring and the acceptance of such a mandate as a treason to the party and as a form of corruption. At the Bremen congress of 1904, in the case of Fehndrich, it was loudly denounced as a veritable crime.[18] Such

---

[17] As regards France, cf. A. Jobert, *Impressions de Congrès,* ''La Guerre Sociale,'' anno ii, No. 45.

[18] *Protokoll,* pp. 116 et seq., 265 et seq. Cf. also the discussion upon the

accusations are often unjust, for more spirit of sacrifice and love of duty are commonly needed to induce a comrade to attend a congress at his own cost than would be the case if he had a week's holiday at the expense of his local branch.

Nevertheless it remains true that as regards representation at party congresses, the smaller sections are in a position of serious inferiority. Numerous proposals have been made for the remedy of this state of affairs. For instance, in order to realize the democratic postulate of the equal representation of all districts, in the years 1903 and 1904 the section of Marburg proposed that all the costs of delegation should be defrayed by the central treasury. This proposal was not accepted, and consequently another attempt was made to find a remedy, and this has taken the form of uniting numerous local branches into provincial federations. Thus the rules of the provincial federation of Hesse-Nassau contain a clause to the following effect: "Those local branches of the federation which are unable to pay the costs of delegation to the congress will draw lots every year to select one among their number, and the branch thus chosen will have the right to send a delegate to the congress at the expense of the federation." It may be noted in passing that five of the branches out of the ten of which the federation consists have to avail themselves of this privilege.

A party which has a well-filled treasury is in a position, not only to dispense with the material aid of its comparatively affluent members, and thus to prevent the acquirement by these of a preponderant influence in the party, but also to provide itself with a body of officials who are loyal and devoted because they are entirely dependent on the party for their means of subsistence. Before the year 1906, when the payment of members was conceded by the German state, the German socialist party had provided the salaries of its deputies. In this way the party leaders, poor men for the most part, were enabled to enter parliament without being in a position to emancipate themselves from the party, or to detach themselves from the majority of the parliamentary group of socialists—as has happened in France with the formation of the group of "independent socialists." The French socialist party has been forced to recognize the danger involved in the existence of leaders who are not economi-

---

similar case of Lily Braun at the Munich congress of 1902 (*Protokoll*, p. 250).

cally dependent on the party. In those countries in which the representatives of the people are not paid by the government nor salaried by the party, the danger of plutocracy arises from the fact that the members of parliament must necessarily be men of means; but in France such a danger arises in the opposite way, for here not only are the deputies paid, but they are paid at the high rate of £600 a year. Consequently it has occurred to the French socialists to adopt a measure which shall at once reduce the financial supremacy of its representatives at the Palais Bourbon and provide a steady accession to the party funds, and they have decreed that every deputy elected under the ægis of the party must pay over one-fifth of his salary, £120 per annum, to the party treasury. Many of the French socialist deputies, in order to elude this obligation, have simply resigned their membership of the party. Among the causes which in the year 1905 led to the formation of the new parliamentary socialist group, the so-called independent socialists, the chief was certainly the desire to escape this heavy tax, and to preserve intact for themselves the fine round sum paid as salary by the state. Even in the case of the deputies who, in order to preserve their seats, have found it expedient to accept as a matter of principle their liability to the party treasury, the majority have shown little alacrity in the discharge of this liability. Year after year, in fact, at the party congresses, there have been interminable discussions as to the means to be adopted to compel the recalcitrant socialist deputies to discharge their financial obligations. And yet (and here is one of the ironies of history) it has not taken long to discover that to despoil the deputies of a portion of their salary does not after all constitute the most efficacious means of preventing the formation within the party of an oligarchy of plutocrats. From the report made to the congress of Nîmes (1910) by the executive committee it appears that of the 128,000 francs which constitute the party revenue, more than half, 67,250 francs to be precise, was made up by the contributions of the socialist members of parliament.[19] Such a state of affairs is eminently calculated to favour the predominance of the deputies, who become the financial props of the party administration, and thus are persons of importance whom the rank and file must treat with all possible respect.

Speaking generally, when the manual workers become employ-

---

[19] Letter contributed by Grumbach to the "Volksstimme" of Frankfort, March 1, 1910.

ers it is not found that they are easy masters. They are prone to mistrust, and are extremely exacting.[20] Were it not that these employees have as a rule abundant means of escaping from the influence of their many-headed masters, they would be worse treated—so runs the complaint—than by any private employer. In relation to the salaried officials, every member of the organization considers himself a capitalist and behaves accordingly. Moreover, the manual workers often lack any criterion for the appreciation of intellectual labour.

In Rome, many societies for co-operative production make it a principle to pay their commercial and technical managers on the same scale as their manual workers.[21] In Germany, too, for a long time the same tendency prevailed. At the assembly of the Christian miners held at Gelsenkirchen in 1898, the demand found expression that Brust, one of the leaders, should continue manual work as a miner, since otherwise he would forfeit the esteem of his comrades.[22] At the socialist congress held at Berlin in 1892 a motion was discussed for many hours in accordance with which no employee of the party was to be paid a salary exceeding £125 per annum;[23] whilst at the congress of Frankfort in 1894 the proposal to increase the salary of the two party secretaries by £25 had to be withdrawn, since the voting was indecisive, although the ballot was taken several times.[24] For a long time in the German socialist party there continued to prevail the erroneous view that the salaries paid to the party employees, and even the disbursements made to propagandists on account of expenses and time lost, were a sort of gratuity, a "pourboire."[25]

---

[20] Cf. Heinrich Herkner, *Die Arbeiterfrage*, ed. cit., p. 116; Richard Calwer, *Prinzipien und Meinungsfreiheit*, "Soz. Monatsh.," x (xii), fasc. 1.— In an inquiry instituted in Italy by the General Federation of Labour concerning the wages paid to the employees of trade unions, one of the witnesses, when asked, "How are the employees paid in your union?" replied bitterly, "With frequent votes of censure!" (Fausto Pagliari, *Le Organizzazioni e i loro Impiegati*, ed. cit. p. 11).—In England it has been said: "Socialist advocates in England are disgracefully sweated. Heaven help those who throw their bread upon socialist waters; from no mundane source will help come" (S. G. Hobson, *Boodle and Cant*, "International Socialist Review," vol. ii, No. 8, p. 587).

[21] Lamberto Paoletti, *Un Cimitero di Cooperative*, "Giornale degli Economisti," September 1905, p. 266.

[22] Heinrich Herkner, op. cit., p. 114.

[23] *Protokoll*, pp. 116-131.

[24] *Protokoll*, pp. 69 et seq.

[25] Cf. speech by Richard Fischer at the congress of Berlin in 1892, *Protokoll*, p. 127.

In the case of the socialist newspapers, the editor was often worse paid than the business manager and even than the compositors.[26] Matters have changed since then, but there always exists a tendency on the part of the manual workers which induces them to endeavour to keep down the salaries of the party officials to the level of what is paid to a factory hand. A few years ago a trade union passed a motion to the effect that the employees of the union should be paid by the hour, and on the same scale as that which prevailed in the branch of industry to which they belonged as trade unionists. Even now, in fixing the salaries of their own employees, many of the comrades adopt as a principle that the remuneration ought to be less than that which is paid for the same work by capitalist employers.[27] Speaking generally, however, it may be said that the German working class is now accustomed to pay its employees liberally. This improvement is explicable, in part, from the improved financial position of the trade unions and of the socialist party. But there is another reason. The employees have succeeded in withdrawing the question of their salaries from the publicity of the congresses and of reserving the discussion of this question for private committees.

In France, on the other hand, the tendency among the workers to stint their employees has gained ground, especially of late, since the deputies to the Chamber have been allotted salaries of £600 a year. The indignation against the "Quinze Mille" (15,000 francs) has been so great that in many cases the manual workers have been unwilling to pay their employees in the trade unions more than the tenth part of this sum, the modest annual salary of £60.[28] During 1900–1901, the three employees of the Confédération Générale du Travail (the secretary, the treasurer, and the "organizer") received in all only 3,173 francs (i.e., a little over £40 a year each).[29] The two chief employees of the Printers' Federation receive an annual salary of £144

---

[26] Cf. Richard Calwer, *Das Kommunistische Manifest und die heutige Sozialdemokratie*, Günther, Brunswick, 1894, p. 38; also R. Fischer, *Protokoll*, p. 129.

[27] Bernstein, *Arbeiterbewegung*, ed. cit., pp. 142 et seq.

[28] *Enquête sur la crise sindicaliste; réponse de E. Clemczynski*, "Mouvement socialiste," vol. xi, Nos. 215-216, p. 302.

[29] Paul Louis, *Histoire du mouvement syndical en France (1789-1906)*, Alcan, Paris, 1907, p. 244. From March 1901 the salary of the "permanent," Georges Yvetot, was raised to 8 francs a day, £116 a year (Fernand Pelloutier, op. cit., p. 152).

each, whilst the treasurer receives £48 a year. The Metalworkers Federation regards itself as extraordinarily liberal in engaging three employees at a salary of £112 per annum, and (in 1905) seven district secretaries at salaries of £95 each.[30]

In Italy there has not yet come into existence a numerous general staff of employees salaried by the socialist party and the trade-union organizations. This is chiefly explicable by lack of funds. For many years it has been necessary to improvise secretaries, administrators, and treasurers of trade unions and local branches, to find them from day to day by appealing to the goodwill and devotion of the comrades.[31] Before 1905, the Printers' Federation was the only one which had special employees for bookkeeping and for the administration of the funds.[32] Even to-day the life of the labour organizations is extremely rudimentary and is exposed to great vicissitudes. Of late years, indeed, the number of permanent employees of the federations and the Bourses du Travail has undergone a continuous increase, but these employees are still very badly paid. We are told by Rigola that the salary has been raised from 100 lire to 200 lire a month, and that "no self-respecting organization will now offer less." But this increase does not suffice to provide a remedy, for 200 lire will not induce a skilled workman to abandon his trade to become a trade-union leader.[33] Notwithstanding this, if we are to believe the trade unionists, even in Italy some of the trade-union leaders are already manifesting that tendency to grow fat and idle for which the leaders of the rich English labour organizations have sometimes been reproached.

The meagreness of the salaries paid to their employees by the socialist party and the trade unions is not due solely to that employers' arrogance and arbitrariness from which the working class is by no means exempt when it becomes an employer. Where the younger organizations are concerned, the trouble may arise simply from lack of means. Moreover, in paying at a low rate there is a practical end in view, the desire being that the employees should serve for love of the cause, and not with an eye

---

[30] Paul Louis, op. cit., pp. 198-9.

[31] Alessandro Schiavi, *Il Nerbo delle Associazioni operaie*, "Critica Sociale," anno xv, No. 10.

[32] Renato Brocchi, *L'Organizzazione di Resistenza in Italia*, Libr. Editr. Marchigiana, Macerata, 1907, p. 137.

[33] Rinaldo Rigola, *I Funzionari dell' Organizzazione*, "Avanti," anno xiv, No. 341.

to the material advantages attaching to their office. It was hoped that in this way the idealism of the leaders would be artificially fostered, and that it would be possible to prevent them from raising themselves above the social level of their proletarian comrades. During the early and revolutionary period of the labour movement, whether economic or political, such attempts were made in every country of the world. The labour organizations have not always been satisfied with paying their employees on a stingy scale, but members of the party or the union have even been forbidden to accept the money which the state paid to those who became members of parliament. Among the reasons which in the year 1885 induced the socialists of Berlin to abstain from participation in the elections to the Prussian Landtag, the chief was the consideration that the fifteen marks a day which the members of this body receive would tend to lift the socialist members out of their class.[34]

In practice, however, the grudging payment of the leaders which at least in the early days of the trade-union movement was a deliberate policy, has proved to be a very untrustworthy safeguard against possible breaches of duty.

For the great majority of men, idealism alone is an inadequate incentive for the fulfilment of duty. Enthusiasm is not an article which can be kept long in store. Men who will stake their bodies and their lives for a moment, or even for some months in succession, on behalf of a great idea often prove incapable of permanent work in the service of the same idea even when the sacrifices demanded are comparatively trifling. The joy of self-sacrifice is comparable to a fine gold coin which can be spent grandly all at once, whereas if we change it into small coin it dribbles imperceptibly away. Consequently, even in the labour movement, it is necessary that the leaders should receive a prosaic reward in addition to the devotion of their comrades and the satisfaction of a good conscience. Quite early in the his-

---

[34] The following passage may be quoted from the resolution voted in this connection: ''Finally, seeing that every member of the Prussian House of Representatives is paid an allowance of 15 marks a day, we cannot escape recognizing that by participating in the elections we may be opening the way for a renunciation of principles, and may be creating a forcing-house for professional parliamentarians (our principles are sacred to all of us and our representatives are men of honour, but man is a product of circumstances, and it is better to intervene now than when it is too late!)'' (Eduard Bernstein, *Die Geschichte der Berliner Arbeiterbewegung*, Buchhandl. ''Vorwärts,'' Berlin, 1907, vol. ii, p. 160).

tory of the organizations formed by the Italian agricultural workers we find in a manual written for the guidance of these that if the *capolega* or chief of the union is to do his duty it would be well to pay him for his work.[35]

For two additional reasons it is necessary that the employees should be adequately paid. The first of these is a moral one, belonging to the department of socialist ethics. The labourer is worthy of his hire. In Marxist terminology, the worker who does not receive pay correspondent to the social value of his work is being exploited. The other reason belongs to the sphere of practical politics. To pay the leaders poorly as a matter of principle is dangerous precisely because it stakes everything upon the single card of idealism. Eduard Bernstein is right in contending that underpayment leads to corruption and demoralization.[36] The leader who is poorly paid is more likely to succumb to temptation, more likely to betray the party for gain, than one who, being well paid, finds in his occupation a safe and sufficient income. Moreover, the payment of the leaders at a low rate renders difficult the application of another preventive means against the establishment of an oligarchy, for it hinders frequent changes in the personnel of the leading employees, and thus indirectly favours the formation of an oligarchy. In France, where it is still the rule to pay the trade-union leaders very small salaries, there is lacking a new generation of leaders ready to take the place of the old, and for this reason at the trade-union congresses the same members continually appear as delegates.[37]

If, however, the non-payment of the party leaders or their remuneration on a very moderate scale does not afford any safeguard for the observance of democratic principles on the part of the officials, we have on the other hand to remember that an increase in the financial strength of the party, which first renders liberal payment of the officials possible, contributes greatly to nourish the dictatorial appetites of the members of the party bureaucracy, who control the economic forces of the party in virtue of their position as administrators. In the history of Christianity we learn that as the wealth of the Church increased, there increased also the independence of the clergy, of the ecclesiastical employees, vis-à-vis the community. As representa-

---

[35] Egidio Bernaroli, op. cit., p. 27.

[36] Eduard Bernstein, *Die Demokratie in der Sozialdemokratie*, "Sozial. Monatsh.," September 3, 1908, p. 1108.

[37] E. Clemczynski, op. cit., p. 301.

tives of the community they were in charge of the goods. Consequently all those who had need of these goods, or wished in any way to speculate upon them, were dependent upon the clergy. This applied not only to mendicants and to all kinds of receivers of alms, but also to those whose aim it was to swell the ranks of the clergy, or to succeed to the positions of these, all aspirants to sacerdotal honours. For the administration of the funds and for the conduct of affairs, Christianity needed a graded corps of employees. This was the origin of the hierarchy which changed the inner meaning of Christianity and perverted its aims. A similar danger is encountered by all democratic parties which possess an elaborate financial administration.[38] This danger is especially marked in the case of the German socialist party, whose central organization in the year 1908 employed merely in its printing office 298 persons,[39] and all of these, having no share whatever in the net profits, nor any rights in the management of the social property, depend upon the party just as they might depend upon any ordinary private employer. In the hands of the party bureaucracy are the periodical press, the publication and sale of the party literature, and the enrolment of orators in the list of paid propagandists. All these sources of income can at any time be closed to undesirable competitors or to dissatisfied members of the rank and file, and this power is utilized in actual practice.[40] The concentration of power in those

---

[38] This danger has been recognized by Ettore Ciccotti, notwithstanding the optimist tendency of his views on the relationship of the leaders to the masses. Cf. *Psicologia del Movimento socialista*, ed. cit., p. 127.

[39] Eduard Bernstein, *Die Natur und die Wirkungen der capitalistische Wirtschaftsordnung*, Buchhandlung "Vorwärts," Berlin, 1909, p. 12.

[40] During the struggle between the party leaders and the so-called "Jungen," the executive committee forbade the sale in the bookshops of the party of works by Dr. Bruno Wille (youthful writings and poems), since Wille himself belonged to the opposing faction, although the work in question was not written to voice the views of the opposition. In defence of the leaders' action Richard Fischer, a member of the executive, wrote to Wille under date November 6, 1891: "Our party is no mere vague ideal community, but a practical body, with such and such organs. However little we are inclined to exclude from intellectual participation any one from the realm of Cuckoo Cloudland, the party has to take every care that within the framework of the organization its adherents yield to the will of the community in matters of tactics and discipline. One who will not submit himself to these principles of subordination, and who combines with others who are declared to be unworthy to belong to this organization, in order to work against the party, renounces *ipso facto* all claim *to make use of the organs and of the advantages which the organization has created and*

parties which preach the Marxist doctrine is more conspicuous than the concentration of capital predicted by Marx in economic life. For some years past the leaders of the German socialist party have employed numerous methods of oppression, such as the threat to give no aid either in men or money on behalf of the electoral propaganda of a candidate from whose views they dissent, although the local comrades give this candidate their full confidence. It is hardly necessary to say that such a practice as this accords ill with the principles of liberty and fraternity.[41] In this way have come into existence strict relationships of dependence, of hierarchical superiority and inferiority, engendered by the invisible force of the great god Money, and this within the bosom of the working-class party which has taken as its motto Blanqui's phrase, *ni Dieu ni Maître.*

Brief allusion may be made in conclusion to another kind of economic pressure which labour organizations are able to exercise. Publicans whose houses are frequented chiefly or exclusively by members of the working class, or small shopkeepers whose customers consist mainly of working women, are indirectly if not directly dependent, in the economic sense, upon the party and upon the trade union. They are dependent, that is to say, upon the leading personalities in these organizations, who, by declaring a boycott, can involve them in absolute ruin.

---

which it safeguards for its members. One of these organs is our bookselling business, and consequently it was a matter of course that we came to the decision of which you complain'' (Hans Müller, *Der Klassenkampf in der deutschen demokratie,* Verlagsmagazin J. Schabelitz, Zurich, 1892, p. 119). Cf. also a speech made by Von Elm at the Mannheim congress of 1906 (*Protokoll,* p. 300).—The pecuniary effect of such a boycott as that of Wille's book is naturally greater in proportion as all the workers have become accustomed to accept only such intellectual nutriment as has been officially prepared in the party kitchens and is guaranteed as thoroughly wholesome. Above all, then, this applies to Germany.

[41] Wolfgang Heine, op. cit., p. 283.

CHAPTER III

THE LEADERS AND THE PRESS

THE press constitutes a potent instrument for the conquest, the preservation, and the consolidation of power on the part of the leaders. The press is the most suitable means of diffusing the fame of the individual leaders among the masses, for popularizing their names. The labour press, and this applies equally to the trade-union journals and to those which devote themselves predominantly to political ends, is full of panegyrics concerning the personalities of the leaders, of references to their "disinterestedness and self-sacrificingness," to their "ardent idealism, conjoined with a vigorous force of conviction and with invincible tenacity," qualities which, we are told, have alone made it possible for them to create the great working-class organizations.[1] Such flattering phrases as are from time to time used of the socialist leaders by the capitalist press (mostly dictated by motives of electoral opportunism) are complacently reproduced by socialist journals, and whether taken at par value or not they serve, by their diffusion among the socialist rank and file, to increase the prestige of the leaders.[2]

---

[1] Cf. the article entitled *Die Gewerkschaften Deutschlands* in the "Schwäbische Tagwacht," anno xxvii, No. 191 (August 17, 1907).

[2] A typical example of this is furnished by an article *Lob aus gegnerischen Munde* [Praise from the Enemy] which was circulated among the electors of Giessen apropos of an election to the diet, and from which the following passages may be quoted. "Now that the elections to the diet are approaching, we may remind our readers that the activity of our comrades in the Diet of Hesse has been recognized and praised by the leading organ of the national liberals. Six years ago, just before the then elections, an article was published in the 'Kölnische Zeitung,' dealing with the conditions in Hesse and the parties in the diet, judging these last from a thoroughly objective standpoint. The writer, who was obviously well acquainted with his subject, opened by a strongly adverse criticism of the leaders of his own party, the national liberals, who were then predominant in the Hessian diet. Turning them to consider our comrades, he continued: 'The Hessian social democrats in the diet are remarkable men. Not only do they work very hard, indeed harder than all others, in the fulfilment of their parliamentary duties, but they often play a leading

It is true that the press cannot exert the immediate influence which the popular propagandist exercises over his audience in public meetings, debates, and party congresses.[3] In compensation for this defect, however, the circle of influence of the written word is far more extensive. The press can be used with effect to influence public opinion by cultivating a "sensation"— a point in which modern party democracy exhibits a fundamental trait which it shares with Bonapartism. This means is frequently employed by the leaders in order to gain or to retain the sympathy of the masses, and to enable them to keep the guidance of the movement in their own hands. The democratic press

part. Many members of the constitutional parties would do well to take example at the manner in which the socialist locksmith Ulrich of Offenbach performed his duties as secretary of the finance committee, the way in which he examined the demand for universities and schools, showing himself as a rule to be the most zealous and the most friendly to the government of all those who desire to favour a progressive culture. He was supported in this activity by his colleague Dr. David, who, although his views are somewhat more doctrinaire and utopian, none the less greatly excels most of the representatives in point of general culture. Such socialists as these are all the more dangerous because of their moderation, and it is not surprising that they have to be reckoned with.' Again, 'Strongly in contrast with the socialists are the antisemites and the peasant-leagues, for these have always displayed themselves as the bitterest enemies of the government; they are incapable of being influenced by reason, utterly unteachable, rude blusterers, unpractical and barren politicians, insanely particularist, and often positively ludicrous. . . .' '' (''Mitteldeutsche Sonntagszeitung,'' xii, No. 46). The article concludes with a vigorous appeal to the electors to vote for the socialist candidates, because of all the parties the socialist is the one most friendly to the Grand Ducal government!

[3] The powerful stimulus which the personality of Singer exercised over the masses was described by Kurt Eisner in the following terms: ''With a sort of jovial energy and with a never failing sureness of touch he knew how to tame and to lead the rude multitude. . . . Specially remarkable was Singer in the small official speeches, in the 'addresses to the throne' with which he was accustomed to conclude the labours of the 'socialist parliamentary session.' Then it became apparent how importance is conferred upon the individual by the greatness of the cause in which he is as it were rooted. Naturally in such addresses he did not rise above that level of daily commonplace which is appropriate to all official utterances, but he knew so well how to polish his phrases until they shone; his voice, almost completely losing its Berlin twang, then rose to its full strength; pale words and anæmic emotion became transfused with red blood; and he always closed with some word of power, with one of those turns of phrase intermediate between the trivial and the sublime, which are characteristic of the gifted public speaker'' (Kurt Eisner, *Taggeist, Kulturglossen,* Dr. John Edelheim Verlag, Berlin, 1901, pp. 107-108).

is also utilized by the leaders in order to make attacks (more or less masked) upon their adversaries; or to launch grave accusations against persons of note in the world of politics or finance. These attacks may or may not be established upon a sufficient foundation of proof, but at any rate they serve to raise a dust-storm.[4] Sometimes, again, the leaders endeavour to ingratiate themselves with the masses by employing in respect of their capitalist opponents, coarse and insulting language which recalls the proverbial "Billingsgate." All means are good to the popularity-hunter, and he varies them to suit his environment.

The manner in which the leaders make use of the press to secure their domination naturally varies from one country to another in accordance with variation in national customs. Where the party organization and the force at its disposal are still weak, the influence of the leaders is direct and personal. The consequence is that in France, in England, and in Italy, where the popular character still presents a strongly individual stamp, the democratic leader presents himself as personally responsible for what he writes, and signs his articles in full. An article which appears in "Le Socialiste" in Paris will attract attention, not so much on account of its own merits, but because at the foot it displays in large type the signature of a Jules Guesde. The leader imposes his influence upon the masses directly, manifesting his opinion openly, often giving it the form of a decree, published in the most conspicuous part of the paper. From the æsthetic and ethical points of view, this is, moreover, the best form of journalism, for the reader has a right to know the source of the wares which are offered him, and this altogether apart from the consideration that to all public activity there should be applied the fundamental moral principle that each one is responsible to all for his conduct. For the aspirants to leadership, again, the practice of signing newspaper articles has the incontestable advantage that it makes their names known to the

---

[4] In the winter of 1904 "Vorwärts" came out with the sensational news of alleged homosexual misconduct at Capri on the part of Frederick Krupp, of Essen. Shortly afterwards the same journal published details of a plan which the emperor was supposed to have drawn up with his own hand for the construction in Berlin of a fortified castle for defence against the workers. In the winter of 1905, "Avanti" published attacks upon the personal and official honour of Admiral Bettòlo, Minister of Marine—attacks which some years later, when they had attained their end, were withdrawn by the editor-in-chief, Enrico Ferri. Similar examples could be quoted by hundreds from the socialist press.

masses, and this facilitates their gradual rise in the scale of representative honours until they attain to the highest.

In other countries, as for instance in Germany, the faith of the masses in authority is so robust that it does not require to be sustained by the prestige of a few conspicuous individualities. Hence journalism is here almost always anonymous. The individual contributor disappears behind the editorial staff. The journal does not serve to diffuse the writers' names far and wide, and regular readers are often totally ignorant of the individualities of the staff. This explains the comparative unimportance of the personal rôle played by German publicists when compared with those of most other countries; it explains their small part in public life, and the trifling social consideration they enjoy. But this must not be taken to mean that the anonymous press fails to serve the leaders as an instrument of domination. Since the German journalist is identified with the whole editorial staff, and even with the entire party, the result is that his voice appeals to the public with the entire force of this collective authority. His personal ideas thus acquire a prominence and attain an influence which would otherwise be lacking.[5] What the individual member of the staff loses through his anonymity, in respect of direct influence upon the masses, is gained by the journalist leaders as a group. The editorial ''we,'' uttered in the name of a huge party, has a much greater effect than even the most distinguished name. The ''party,'' that is to say the totality of the leaders, is thus endowed with a special sanctity, since the crowd forgets that behind an article which thus presents itself under a collective aspect there is concealed in the great majority of cases but one single individual. In Germany it is not difficult to observe that the anonymous polemical and other articles of ''Vorwärts,'' the central organ of the party, are regarded by the rank and file, and especially in Prussia, as a sort of periodical gospel, as a Bible in halfpenny numbers. It is more especially for the publication of violent personal attacks that anonymous journalism furnishes convenient and almost tempting opportunities, guaranteeing moral and legal impunity. Behind the shelter thus

---

[5] In order to avoid this danger a portion of the German socialist press seeks to render the personality of its writers distinguishable by having the articles signed by one or more initials, whose significance is known at any rate to an inner circle of initiates. Unfortunately this prophylactic measure is not extended to those official journalistic utterances which are apt to contain the most venomous attacks upon certain members of the party.

afforded by anonymity those of base and cowardly nature are apt to lurk in order that they may launch thence in safety their poisoned arrows against their personal or political adversaries. The victim of aggression is thus for four separate reasons placed in a position of inferiority. The rank and file consider the censure which has been expressed against him as having been uttered in the name of a principle or a class, as emanating from a superior and impersonal region, and as consequently of an extremely serious character and practically indelible. On the other hand, the whole editorial staff feels itself responsible for what has been published, for the anonymous article is regarded as published with the unanimous consent of the collectivity; the result is that the whole staff makes common cause with the aggressor, and this renders it almost impossible to secure any reparation for the wrong which has been committed. Further, the person attacked does not know who is the aggressor, whereas if he knew the latter's name he might be able to understand the motives for the attack instead of being forced to fight a shadow. Finally, if he is by chance able to unveil the personality of the aggressor, journalistic etiquette forbids him to undertake his defence on lines directed against the aggressor individually, and he is thus deprived of one of the most efficient methods of defence. It recently happened that a writer in the German socialist press, who had attacked another member of the party, when this latter made a reply which unquestionably demanded a rejoinder, refused to continue the discussion because the person attacked had addressed his reply, not to the editorial staff generally, but "to one single member of that staff," who was in fact the aggressor. The reason given for this refusal was that in thus replying to an individual instead of to the staff the second writer had "infringed the most elementary decencies of party life." [6]

The obliteration of personality in German journalism has favoured the institution, in connection with the socialist press of that country, of what are known as "correspondence bureaux." These organizations, which are managed by some of the writers of the party, transmit every day to the socialist press information relating to special branches, such as foreign politics, cooperative questions, and legislative problems. The bureaux owe their origin in great part to the spirit of intense economy which domi-

---

[6] "Frankfurter Volksstimme," 1909, No. 175.

nates the party press. They confer upon this press a stamp of great uniformity, since dozens of newspapers receive their inspiration from the same source.[7] Further, they insure the supremacy of a small closed group of official journalists over the independent writers—a supremacy which is manifested chiefly in the economic sphere, since those who write for the correspondence bureaux seldom play any notable part in the political life of the party.

In all cases the press remains in the hands of the leaders and is never controlled by the rank and file. There is often intercalated between the leaders and the mass an intermediate stratum of press commissaries who are delegated by the rank and file to exercise a certain supervision over the editorial staff. In the most favourable circumstances, however, these functionaries cannot aspire to more than a very small share of power, and constitute merely a sort of inopportune and untechnical supplementary government. Speaking broadly it may be said that it is the paid leaders who decide all the political questions which have to do with the press.[8]

---

[7] Cf. Heinrich Ströbel, *Ein soziälistisches Echo?*, ''Neue Zeit,'' anno xxvii, vol. ii, No. 45.

[8] Cf. supra, pp. 24, 25, 26, 39-40.

CHAPTER IV

THE POSITION OF THE LEADERS IN RELATION TO THE MASSES IN ACTUAL PRACTICE

In the political organizations of the international proletariat, the highest order of the leaders consists chiefly of members of parliament. In proof of this it suffices to mention the names of a few men who were or are the most distinguished socialist leaders of their day, and at the same time men of note as parliamentarians: Bebel, Jaurès, Guesde, Adler, Vandervelde, Troelstra, Turati, Keir Hardie, Macdonald, Pablo Iglesias. Hyndman is an exception only because he has never succeeded in winning an election. The section of the English party to which he belongs is unrepresented in parliament.

The fact here noted indicates the essentially parliamentary character of the modern socialist parties. The socialist members of parliament are those who have especially distinguished themselves in the party by their competence and by their capacity. But in addition to this superiority, recognized and consecrated by the party itself, there are two reasons for the great authority exercised by the socialist parliamentarian. In the first place, in virtue of his position, he largely escapes the supervision of the rank and file of the party, and even the control of its executive committee. He owes his comparative independence to the fact that the parliamentary representative is elected for a considerable term of years, and can be dispossessed by no one so long as he retains the confidence of the electors. In the second place, and even at the moment of his election, his dependence on the party is but indirect, for his power is derived from the electoral masses, that is to say, in ultimate analysis from an unorganized body. It is true that in certain countries the independence of the party organization thus enjoyed by the parliamentary deputies is subject to limits more or less strict according to the degree of organization and cohesion of the party. But even then the respect and the power enjoyed by the parliamentarians remain unquestioned, since it is they who within the party fill the principal offices, and whose power predominates to a notable degree

in the party executive. This is true, above all, of Germany.[1]
Where the rules forbid the deputy to function also as a member
of the executive committee (in Italy, for example, only one deputy, chosen by the parliamentary group, can sit on the party
executive),[2] much friction is apt to arise between the two groups
of leaders, impairing the authority of both. But, for the reasons
expounded above, the influence of the parliamentary group commonly predominates.

The influence of parliamentarism is particularly great in the
German social democracy. This is clearly shown by the attitude
towards the party commonly assumed by the socialists in parliament. There is no other socialist party in the world in which
the conduct of its representatives in parliament is subject to so
little criticism. The socialist members of the Reichstag frequently make speeches in that body which might be expected to
give rise to the liveliest recriminations, and yet neither in the
party press nor at the congresses is to be heard a word of criticism or of disapproval. During the discussions in the Reichstag
concerning the miners' strike in the basin of the Ruhr (1905),
the deputy Hué spoke of the maximum programme of the party
as "utopian," and in the socialist press there was manifested
no single symptom of revolt. On the first occasion on which the
party departed from its principle of unconditional opposition to
all military expenditure, contenting itself with simple abstention
when the first credit of 1,500,000 marks was voted for the war
against the Hereros, this remarkable innovation, which in every
other socialist party would have unquestionably evoked a storm
from one section of the members, even if there might have been
manifested cheerful approval by another, aroused among the
German socialists no more than a few dispersed and timid protests. Subsequently, at the Bremen congress of 1904, when the
deputies had to give an account of their conduct, very few delegates were found to express disapproval. It is, further, remarkable to what a degree the power of the parliamentary group becomes consolidated as the party increases throughout the country.

---

[1] In France, until 1914, the right of the deputies to enter the executive
committee of the socialist party was restricted by the rules, but in the beginning of that year the restrictions were relaxed, enabling the deputies
to exercise a predominant influence in the councils of the party.

[2] Two deputies may be members of the executive committee if one of these
two is chairman of the central organization, and thus *ex officio* member
of the executive.

In earlier days, far less important questions aroused much more acute struggles between the party and the parliamentary group. To-day, the socialist masses in Germany have accustomed themselves to the idea that the decisive struggle on behalf of the aims they have at heart will be carried out in parliament, and for this reason they scrupulously avoid doing anything which might make difficulties for their parliamentary representatives. This conviction constantly determines the conduct of the masses in relation to their leaders. Hence in many questions the conduct of the parliamentary group is really decisive, *suprema lex*. All vigorous criticism, though made in accordance with the basic principles of socialism, is at once repudiated by the rank and file if it tends to weaken the position of the parliamentary group. Those who, notwithstanding this, venture to voice such criticism are immediately put to silence and are severely stigmatized by the leaders. Two examples may be given in illustration. The "Leipziger Volkszeitung," in the year 1904, in a leading article entitled *The Usury of Bread,* vented its anger in somewhat violent terms upon the political leaders of the capitalist parties. Thereupon in the Reichstag certain orators of the right and of the centre, when Prince Bülow had himself read this article to the house, adducing it as an evil example of journalistic methods, made a great display of indignation against the socialists. When this happened, Bebel, who had hitherto been a declared friend of the "Leipziger Volkszeitung," did not hesitate to repudiate the article in open parliament, though his conduct was here in flagrant contradiction with the best established traditions of democracy, and with the essential principle of party solidarity.[3] At the congress of Bremen in 1904, Georg von Vollmar openly condemned the first attempts at anti-militarism made in Germany by certain members of the party. He did this with the express

---

[3] It is true that the early history of the German socialist party contains one or two precedents for Bebel's action. In 1881, Hasenclever and Blos made use of certain expressions in the Reichstag which amounted to a disavowal of the central party organ of that day, the "Sozialdemokrat." Still better known is the dispute between the parliamentary group and the "Sozialdemokrat" of Zurich apropos of the debate concerning the Steamship Subsidy in 1885, in the course of which the group published a declaration to the effect that the party organ must in no case set itself in opposition to the group, while the group was responsible for the party press: "It is not the journal which has to determine the conduct of the parliamentary group, but the latter which has to control the journal" (Franz Mehring, op. cit., vol. iv, pp. 214 and 267).

approval of most of the delegates and without arousing any disapproval from the others. Yet anti-militarism is a logical consequence of socialism, and for such a party as the socialist, anti-militarist propaganda must surely be a matter of primary importance. Vollmar, however, justified his attitude by remarking that if a systematic anti-militarist propaganda were to be undertaken, the Minister of War would have a pretext ready to his hand for disregarding all the protests and complaints which might be made by the socialist deputies on account of the differential treatment of soldiers known to hold socialist views. If, for example, the party representatives in parliament were to take action against the secret inquiries which the authorities are accustomed to make and to transmit to the district commanders, sending in the names of recruits who before enlistment have been in the habit of frequenting socialist meetings and have even been known as local leaders, the minister could readily reply, and with effect, that socialists, being anti-militarists, are enemies of their country and as such deserve to be handled with all possible rigour. Vollmar concluded by saying: "Anti-militarist propaganda will make it impossible for the socialists in parliament to continue to assert that socialists fulfil their military duties no less patriotically than non-socialists, and that for this reason it is unjust to subject them to exceptional treatment."[4]

It is well known that great efforts have been made by the parliamentary socialist groups in every country to secure for their members *ex-officio* the right to vote at the party congresses. In Germany this right was recognized in 1890 by the congress of Berlin, with the unimportant restriction that in questions concerning their parliamentary activities the rights of the members of the group in congress should be purely deliberative. Despite some opposition, this right was confirmed in the new rules of the party which were passed at the Jena congress in 1905. It is obvious that the deputy, even if he does not as such possess the right to vote, will not find much difficulty in securing delegation to the congress. Auer once said that those deputies who were not thus delegated must be poor fellows indeed.[5] Nevertheless

---

[4] *Protokoll des Parteitags zu Bremen*, p. 186.

[5] "In any case, since, in view of their responsibilities to the party, their presence at the congress may be indispensable, it should not be made necessary for them to go about begging for a mandate" (*Protokoll des Parteitags zu Berlin*, 1890, p. 122).

they have been saved this trifling trouble. Thus the members of the parliamentary group are admitted to an active participation in the most intimate deliberations of the party, not as delegates approved by a vote of the branch to which they belong, but as representatives of the entire electorate of their constituency for the whole period for which they are elected to the legislature. This involves an express recognition of their position as leaders (and a further admission that this leadership owes its origin in part to non-party sources), and obviously raises them to the position of super-comrades independent of the rank and file of the party, or makes them irremovable delegates for so long as they may remain members of the Reichstag. This institution is certainly peculiar to Germany. In other countries identical rules apply for the appointment of all delegates to the congress, whether these may happen to be parliamentary representatives or not.[6] In France and Holland, for instance, the deputies can take part in the congresses, and are able to vote in these only if they are specially delegated for the purpose. In Italy, the members of the executive committee and the members of the parliamentary group cannot speak in the congress unless they are charged by the executive committee to present a report of some kind. In Italy, as in France and Holland, they can vote only when regularly delegated.

Yet in view of their greater competence in various questions, the socialist parliamentary groups consider themselves superior even to the congresses, which are in theory the supreme courts of the party, and they claim an effective autonomy. The members of the parliamentary group obey a natural tendency to restrict more and more the circle of questions which must be submitted to the congress for decision, and to make themselves the sole arbiters of the party destinies. In Germany, many of the socialist deputies put forward a claim in 1903 to decide for themselves, independently of the party congresses, whether the parliamentary group should or should not accept the vice-presidency of the Reichstag for one of its members, and whether, if this post were accepted, the socialist vice-president should conform to the usage attaching to this office, and put in appearances at court.[7]

---

[6] "Avanti," No. 3433. Nevertheless, in these other countries the leading rôles in the socialist congresses are played by the parliamentary representatives.

[7] This claim was endorsed by certain aspirants to parliamentary honours who had recently failed to secure election. Bebel wrote ironically in

In Italy, the socialist and the republican parliamentary groups have secured complete independence of the executives of their respective parties. The socialist group has even been accused at times of accepting deputies who are not even regular members of the party, men who contend that their electors would look askance should they adhere officially to the local socialist organization.

The parliamentary leaders of the socialist as well as those of the capitalist parties assume the right to constitute a closed corporation, cut off from the rest of their party.[8] The parliamentary group of the German socialists has on more than one occasion, and of its own initiative, disavowed the actions of considerable sections of the party. The most notable of such disavowals have been those of the article *The Usury of Bread,* in the "Leipziger Volkszeitung" (1904),[9] and that of the anti-militarist agitation of Karl Liebknecht (1907). In the former instance, the "Leipziger Volkszeitung" could very well console itself for the disapproval of the "fifty-seven comrades" (i.e. the members of the parliamentary group) as that of an infinitesimal minority of the party—in accordance with the historic and typically democratic utterance of the Abbé Sieyès on the eve of the French Revolution, when he said that the rights of the king bore to

this connection: "Remarkable logic! If H. had secured a seat at the last election he would have regarded himself as competent to decide upon this question. But since he has been beaten at the polls he is incompetent. One must therefore be elected deputy in order to secure the necessary mental illumination."

[8] "In this atmosphere of bourgeois parliamentarism, which is so foreign to the essential nature of socialism, the social democracy, involuntarily and unconsciously, has assumed many of the customs of this parliamentarism which harmonize ill with the democratic characteristics of socialism. In the writer's view, the appearance of the parliamentary group as a closed corporation (not merely vis-à-vis the capitalist parties, which is necessary, but also vis-à-vis our own party) is such a development of bourgeois parliamentarism, and may lead to grave inconveniences" (Rosa Luxemburg, *Sozialreform oder Revolution?* Appendix, *Miliz und Militarismus,* ed. of the "Leipziger Volkszeitung," Leipzig, 1899, p. 75).

[9] The declaration made by the party executive in the affair of the "Leipziger Volkszeitung" begins as follows: "On Saturday, the 10th inst., when, after the speech of comrade von Vollmar, the Imperial Chancellor brought up for discussion the subject of the article in the 'Leipziger Volkszeitung' of December 2nd, those members of the parliamentary group who were present agreed to instruct comrade Bebel to state in his speech that the group regretted the publication of this article and repudiated responsibility for it."

those of his subjects the ratio of 1 : 30,000,000. As a matter of pure theory, and considering the democratic principles of the party, the paper here hit the right nail on the head; but in practice its contention had no significance, for to the ineffective right of principle there was opposed the right of the stronger, immanent in the leadership.

The local branches of the party follow their deputies. In the congresses the great majority of the delegates accept as a matter of habit the guidance of the men of note.[10] At the Bremen congress in 1904 the German socialists rejected the idea of the general strike as a general absurdity; at Jena, in 1905, they acclaimed it as an official weapon of the party; at Mannheim, in 1906, they declared it to be utopian. All the individual phases of this zigzag progress were hailed with the conscientious applause of the mass of the delegates in the congress and of the comrades throughout the country, who exhibited on each occasion the same lack of critical faculty and the same unthinking enthusiasm. In France, the little handful of men who constituted the general staff of the French Marxists when these still formed a separate party under the leadership of Jules Guesde was so permeated with the authoritarian spirit that at the party congresses the executive committee (Comité National) was not elected in due form, but was appointed *en bloc* by acclamation; [11]

---

[10] Cramer, deputy to the Hessian diet, in his report concerning a divisional conference in the Grand Duchy, deplores the comparatively slight democratic value which the party congresses have for the mass of the delegates, and how little these assert themselves in opposition to the despotic conduct of the leaders. ''In the press of business'' a proposal sent in before the opening of the session that the conference should last for two days instead of one was completely ignored. ''I feel compelled to say that the propagandist value of the last conference must be regarded as infinitesimal. The work was done in such a hurry, freedom of debate was suppressed so roughly by the chair, and there were so many other disagreeable features, that the conference was in truth a painful spectacle'' (''Mainzer Volkszeitung,'' September 16, 1903).

[11] This practice continues to the present day in the Unified French Socialist party. At the Amiens congress in January 1914, the election of the executive committee (Commission Administrative Permanente) was postponed until the very end of the congress, when a large proportion of the delegates had already left and when those who remained were tired out. The re-election *en bloc* of the executive was then proposed, with the substitution of one name for that of Francis de Pressensé, recently deceased, and the most important administrative act of the congress was thus effected under conditions which made any discussion of the personnel of the executive quite impossible.

it was impossible for the chiefs to conceive that the rank and file of the party could dream of refusing to follow their leaders. Moreover, the congresses were conducted *in camera*.[12] Reports were published in an extremely condensed form so that no one could check the speakers. In the German socialist congresses, and in the reports of these assemblies, it is easy to distinguish between a higher and a lower circle of delegates. The report of what is said by the "ordinary" delegates is greatly abbreviated,[13] whilst the speeches of the big guns are reproduced verbatim. In the party press, too, different measures are applied to the comrades. In the year 1904, when "Vorwärts," then edited by Eisner, did not publish a letter sent by Bebel, the latter moved heaven and earth with his complaints, saying that freedom of opinion was being suppressed in the party and that it was "the most elementary right" for all the comrades to have their letters printed in the party organs. Yet it is hardly possible to ignore that the "right" which Bebel thus invoked is in practice proportional to a comrade's degree of elevation in the party. The excitement over the non-appearance of Bebel's letter shows that his case was an exceptional one.

In the trade-union movement, the authoritative character of the leaders and their tendency to rule democratic organizations on oligarchic lines, are even more pronounced than in the political organizations.[14]

Innumerable facts recorded in the history of trade-union organizations show to what an extent centralized bureaucracy can divert from democracy a primarily democratic working-class movement. In the trade union, it is even easier than in the political labour organization, for the officials to initiate and to pursue a course of action disapproved of by the majority of the workers they are supposed to represent. It suffices here to refer to the two famous decisions of the trade-union congress at Cologne in 1905. In one of these the leaders declared themselves to be

---

[12] Georges Sorel, *Dove va il marxismo?*, "Rivista Critica del Socialismo," i, p. 16 (1889).

[13] Eduard David, *Faktion und Parteitag*, "Vorwärts," anno xxii, No. 131.

[14] "In the socialist party, owing to the nature of the matters with which it has to deal and owing to the characteristics of the political struggle, narrower limits are imposed upon bureaucracy than in the case of the trade-union movement" (Rosa Luxemburg, *Massenstreik, Partei, und Gewerkschaften*, ed. cit., p. 61). This cautious expression of the differences may be accepted.

opposed (in opposition to the views of the majority) to the continued observance of the 1st of May as a general labour demonstration of protest. In the second, the discussion of the general strike was absolutely forbidden. By these and similar occurrences the oligarchical practices of the leaders are sufficiently proved, although some writers continue to dispute the fact.[15]

For a good many years now, the executive committees of the trade-union federations have endeavoured to usurp the exclusive right to decide on behalf of the rank and file the rhythm of the movement for better wages, and consequently the right to decide whether a strike is or is not "legitimate."[16] Since the leaders of the federation are in charge of the funds, which often amount to a considerable sum, the dispute reduces itself in practice to a question as to who is to decide whether a strike shall or shall not be subsidized.[17] This question is one which involves the very life of the democratic right of the organized masses in the trade unions to regulate their own affairs. When the leaders claim that they alone have a right to decide in a matter of such importance, and still more when they already largely possess this right,

---

[15] Heinrich Ströbel, for instance, a writer on the staff of "Vorwärts." "We at least do not believe that the majority of trade-union members favour tactics differing from those pursued by the trade-union officials. Unfortunately the majority of the trade unions, owing to the 'neutrality' which they have observed for some years, have become politically indifferent, and judge the trade-union movement in practice only from the outlook of the petty and immediate interests of their respective trades" (H. Ströbel, *Gewerkschaften und sozialistische Geist*, "Neue Zeit," xxiii, vol. ii, No. 44).

[16] This has recently happened also in Italy (cf. Rinaldo Rigola, *Ventun mesi di Vita della Confederazione del Lavoro*, Tip. Coop., Turin, 1908, pp. 62 et seq.).

[17] In practice, the executive committees have been able, to a large extent, to make good their claim to decide this matter. To-day the decision whether a strike is or is not to take place rarely depends upon local groups, but is in the hands of the central executives. One well acquainted with labour organizations, Otto Geithner of Berlin, a carpenter by trade, quotes the argument employed by the trade-union leaders to justify this tendency, which runs as follows: "Since the executive committees of the unions have to supply the financial means it is necessary that the decision should be in their hands" ("Korrespondenzblatt der Generalkommission der Gewerkschaften Deutschlands," anno vii, No. 28). Geithner makes the apt comment that this seems to imply that the poor officials have to pay the cost of the strike out of their own pockets, that the funds of the union are ends in themselves, and that the movement to secure better wages is an unimportant accessory (Otto Geithner, *zur Taktik der Sozialdemokratie, Betrachtungen eines Lohnarbeiters*, "Neue Zeit," anno xxiii, No. 47).

it is obvious that the most essential democratic principles are gravely infringed. The leaders have openly converted themselves into an oligarchy, leaving to the masses who provide the funds no more than the duty of accepting the decisions of that oligarchy.[18] This abuse of power may perhaps find justification on tactical grounds, the leaders alleging in defence of their procedure the supreme need that a strike should be declared cautiously and in unison. They claim the right to decide the merits of the question on the sole ground that they know better than the workers themselves the conditions of the labour market throughout the country and are consequently more competent to judge the chances of success in the struggle. The trade-union leaders add that since the stoppage of work in a town necessarily impairs the financial strength of the union in that town, and sometimes disturbs the conditions of work of a whole series of organized workers, it is for the leaders to decide when and where a strike should be declared. Thus they consider that their action is justified by the democratic aim of safeguarding the interests of the majority against the impulsive actions of the minority.[19]

---

[18] Some time ago a notice went the rounds of the socialist press in Germany, under the headline *The View Taken by Employers of Trade-union Officials*. This was an extremely characteristic document. It runs as follows: ''The federation of employers in the building trade of Greater Berlin is opposed to the foundation of conciliation boards, but has made a notable proposal in the event of these being instituted by law. The employers demand that in this case it shall be ordained by the law that the officials of the professional associations of the employers and also those of the trade unions shall be eligible for appointment to the boards. It is alleged as a reason that it is much easier and more fruitful to negotiate with the trained employees of the unions than with workers who are still engaged in manual labour and who lack the necessary ability and independence (''Fränkische Tagespost,'' February 26, 1909). Two considerations may be deduced from this notice: 1, that in the view of the more intelligent among the employers the trade-union leader is independent of his union, in other words, that he leads it; 2, that this independence has already become so considerable that the leaders do not hesitate to admit it openly before the led, and even make a parade of their power.—Regarding the omnipotence of the leaders of the English unions cf. Fausto Pagliari: ''In the unions . . . there has come into existence a bureaucracy which is practically irresistible and which rules the organization as an absolute master, and the unity and efficiency of the administration are enhanced by the sacrifice of democratic guarantees and of the education of the rank and file in the methods of trade-union action'' (*L'organizzazione operaia in Europa*, Società Umanitaria, Milan, 1909, 2nd ed., p. 54).

[19] This was the principal argument employed by the German Metalworkers' Federation against the metal-workers' strike at Mannheim in

We are not here concerned, however, with the causation of the oligarchy which prevails in the trade unions. It suffices to point out how little difference exists between the tendencies of proletarian oligarchies and those of such oligarchies as prevail in the life of the state—governments, courts, etc. It is interesting to note that in Germany, as elsewhere, the socialist leaders do not hesitate to admit the existence of a well-developed oligarchy in the trade-union movement; while the leaders of the trade unions, in their turn, draw attention to the existence of an oligarchy in the socialist party; both groups of leaders unite however in declaring that as far as their own organizations are concerned these are quite immune to oligarchical infection.[20]

Nevertheless, the trade-union leaders and the leaders of the socialist party sometimes combine upon a course of action which, were it undertaken by either group of leaders alone, those of the other group would not fail to stigmatize as grossly undemocratic. For example, in the serious question of the 1st of May demonstration, one of primary democratic importance in the year 1908, the executive committee of the socialist party and the general committee of the trade unions issued by common accord an announcement definitely decreeing from above the conduct of the separate political and trade-union organizations. In a question thus profoundly affecting the individual trade unions and local socialist committees, the executives regarded it as quite unnecessary to ask these for their opinion.[21] Such conduct shows how much justification there is for the criticism which each of the two branches of the working-class movement directs against the other. Moreover, the question which has been debated whether the local trades councils might not be directly represented at the trade-union congresses is after all merely one of the enlargement of the oligarchical circle.

Let us next briefly consider the third form of the working-class movement, cooperative organizations, and in particular the

October 1908 (Adolf Weber, *Der Kampf zwischen Kapital und Arbeit,* Mohr, Tübingen, 1910, p. 30).

[20] Cf. articles by K. Kautsky, H. Ströbel, Rosa Luxemburg, Parvus, and Anton Pannekoek, on the one hand, and, on the other, those which have appeared in the trade-union press discussing the eternal politics of the socialist party (for example, those published during the dispute that broke out in December 1905 in the matter of the editorship of "Vorwärts"); here there will be found innumerable documents to sustain what has been said in the text.

[21] "Volksstimme" of Frankfort, anno xix, No. 22, supplement 3.

organizations for cooperative production, as those which in their very nature should incorporate most perfectly the democratic principle.

As far as concerns distributive cooperative societies, it is easy to understand that these cannot be directly governed by the mass of the members. As Kautsky has shown, we are here concerned with an enterprise whose functions are essentially commercial, and therefore outside the competence of the rank and file. For this reason, the principal business activities of these societies must be entrusted to the employees and to a few experts. "Unless we consider buying as cooperation, in which case the customers of an ordinary shopman are also cooperators with the shopman, the members of a cooperative society have nothing more to do with the management than have the shareholders of a limited company; they choose their managing committee, and then leave the machine to run itself, waiting till the end of the year to express their approval or disapproval of the management, and to pocket their dividends." [22] In actual fact, the distributive cooperative societies present in general a monarchical aspect. Read, for example, what was written by a well-disposed critic concerning the cooperative society "Vooruit" of Ghent, which is led by Edouard Anseele, the socialist, and which is definitely socialist in its tendency: "Cette prospérité et cette bonne administration ne vont pas sans quelques sacrifices à la sacrosainte liberté ouvrière. Le 'Vooruit' tout entier porte l'empreinte de la forte personalité qui l'a créé. . . . Une volonté puissante, avide à revendiquer des responsabilités, alors que d'autres reculent sans cesse devant les responsabilités, s'enivre presque toujours d'elle-même. M. Anseele, grand industriel de fait, a volontiers les manières impétueuses, impérieuses et brusques des capitaines d'industrie les plus bourgeois, et le 'Vooruit' n'est rien moins qu'une république anarchique. Il repose plutôt sur le principe d'autorité." [23]

Societies for cooperative production, on the other hand, and especially the smaller of these, offer in theory the best imaginable field for democratic collaboration. They consist of homogeneous elements belonging to the same stratum of the working class, of persons following the same trade, and accustomed to the same manner of life. In so far as the society needs a man-

---

[22] Karl Kautsky, *Konsumvereine und Arbeiterbewegung*, ed. cit., p. 17.
[23] "Pourquoi pas?" Brussels, anno ii, No. 97.

agement, this management can readily be effected by all the members in common, since all possess the same professional competence, and all can lend a hand as advisers and coadjutors. In a political party it is impossible that every member should be engaged in important political work, and it is for this reason that in the political party there necessarily exists a great gulf between the leaders and the rank and file. But in a society for cooperative production, for boot-making for example, all the members are equally competent in the making of boots, the use of tools, and knowledge of the quality of leather. There do not exist among them any essential differences in matters of technical knowledge. Yet despite the fact that the circumstances are thus exceptionally favourable for the constitution of a democratic organism, we cannot as a general rule regard productive cooperatives as models of democratic auto-administration. Rodbertus said on one occasion that when he imagined productive associations to have extended their activities to include all manufacture, commerce, and agriculture, when he conceived all social work to be effected by small cooperative societies in whose management every member had an equal voice, he was unable to avoid the conviction that the economic system would succumb to the cumbrousness of its own machinery.[24] The history of productive cooperation shows that all the societies have been faced with the following dilemma: either they succumb rapidly owing to discord and powerlessness resulting from the fact that too many individuals have the right to interfere in their administration; or else they end by submitting to the will of one or of a few persons, and thus lose their truly cooperative character.[25] In almost all cases, such enterprises owe their origin to the personal initiative of one or a few members. They are sometimes miniature monarchies, being under the dictatorship of the manager, who represents them in all internal and external relations, and upon whose will they depend so absolutely that if he dies or resigns his post they run the risk of perishing.[26] This tendency on

[24] Karl Rodbertus, *Offener Brief an das Komitee des deutschen Arbeitervereins zu Leipzig*, in F. Lassalle's *Politische Reden und Schriften*, ed. cit., vol. ii, p. 9.

[25] Cf. the identical judgment expressed by Frederick van Eeden, the founder and for many years the manager of a cooperative colony in the neighborhood of Amsterdam. His views were expressed in an interview published by the cooperative newspaper ''De Volharding,'' anno v, No. 8.

[26] Lomberto Paoletti, op. cit., pp. 273-274.

the part of the productive cooperative societies is further accentuated by their character as aggregates of individuals whose personal advantages decrease in proportion as the number of the members increases. Thus from their very nature they are subject to the same immutable psychological laws which governed the evolution of the medieval guilds. As they become more prosperous, they become also more exclusive, and tend always to monopolize for the benefit of the existing members the advantages they have been able to secure. For example, by imposing a high entrance-fee they put indirect obstacles in the way of the entry of new members. In some cases they simply refuse to accept new members, or pass a rule establishing a maximum membership. When they have need of more labour-power they supply this need by engaging ordinary wage-labourers. Thus we not infrequently find that a society for cooperative production becomes gradually transformed into a joint-stock company. It even happens occasionally that the cooperative society becomes the private enterprise of the manager. In both these cases Kautsky is right in saying that the social value of the working-class cooperative is then limited to the provision of means for certain proletarians which will enable them to climb out of their own class into a higher.[27] Rodbertus described labour associations as a school for the education of the working class, in which the manual workers could learn administration, discussion, and within limits the art of government.[28] We have seen to how small an extent this statement is applicable.

In the democratic movement the personal factor thus plays a very considerable part. In the smaller associations it is often predominant.[29] In the larger organizations, larger questions commonly lose the personal and petty characteristics which they originally possessed, but all the same the individuals who bring these questions forward, and who in a sense come to personify

---

[27] Karl Kautsky, *Konsumvereine und Arbeiterbewegung*, ed. cit., p. 6.—More recently the socialist professor, Gaetano Salvemini, speaking of the extensive and in many respects noteworthy movement towards cooperative production in Central Italy, has referred to it as a leech applied to the body of the proletariat and as a buttress of the dominant parasitism, and has declared that its aim is to enrich the minority at the expense of the collectivity. (Cf. the series of articles *Cooperative di Lavoro e Movimento socialista*, "Avanti," anno xiv, Nos. 174 et seq.)

[28] Rodbertus, op. cit., p. 9.

[29] This statement is confirmed by the testimony of the German socialist Otto Geithner, who says: "He who like myself has had some experience

them, retain their influence and importance. In England, three or four men, Macdonald, Keir Hardie, Henderson, and Clynes, for instance, enjoy the confidence of the socialist masses so unrestrictedly that, as an able observer declares, it is impossible to exercise an influence upon the rank and file except by influencing these leaders.[30] In Italy, the first among the leaders of the trade-union organizations has affirmed that those only which are headed by a good organizer can continue in existence. "Categories of the most various trades, found in the most diverse environments, have been unable to secure organization and to live through crises, except in so far as they have been able to find first-class men to manage their affairs. Those which have had bad leaders have not succeeded in establishing organizations; or the organizations if formed have proved defective."[31] In Germany, the supreme authority of Bebel was manifested by a thousand signs,[32] from the joy with which he was hailed wherever he went, to the efforts always made in the various congresses by the representatives of different tendencies to win him over to their side. Moreover, the working-class leaders are well aware of their ascendancy over the masses. Sometimes political opportunism leads them to deny it, but more commonly they are extremely proud of it and boast of it. In Italy, and in other countries as well, the socialist leaders have always claimed that the bourgeoisie and the government are greatly indebted to them for having held the masses in check, and as having acted as moderators to the impulsive crowd. This amounts to saying that the socialist leaders claim the merit, and consequently the power, of preventing the social revolution, which, according to them, would, in default of their intervention, have long ago taken place.[33] Disunion in parties, although often evoked by objective necessities,

---

(and I have been an observer of the labour movement for nearly fifteen years), cannot fail to be aware that in small organizations questions of fact are almost always overshadowed by personal considerations, to which an exaggerated importance is attached'' (Discussion in ''Vorwärts,'' anno xxiii, No. 137).

[30] M. Beer's report on the 9th annual congress of the British Labour Party, ''Fränkische Tagespost,'' anno xli, No. 28 (1909).

[31] Rinaldo Rigola, *I Funzionari delle Organizzazioni*, ''Avanti,'' anno xiv, No. 341.

[32] Cf. the excellent description given by Albert Weidner, *Bebel*, ''Der Arme Teufel,'' anno ii, No. 21 (1903).

[33] Cf. the well-known speech of Camillo Prampolini in the Chamber of Deputies March 13, 1902 (Tip. Op., Reggio Emilia, 1902, p. 24); also

is almost always the work of the leaders. The masses never oppose the reconciliation of their chiefs, partly, no doubt, because the differences between the leaders, in so far as they are of an objective character, are for the most part outside the narrow circle of interests and the limited understanding of the rank and file.[34]

The esteem of the leaders for the masses is not as a rule very profound, even though there are some among them who profess great enthusiasm for the masses and repay with interest the honour which these render. In the majority of cases the veneration is a one-sided affair, if only for the reason that the leaders have had an opportunity of learning the miseries of the crowd by first-hand experience. Fournière said that the socialist leaders regarded the crowd, which had entrusted them with the fulfilment of its own aspirations and which consisted of devoted followers, as a passive instrument in their own hands, as a series of ciphers whose only purpose was to increase the value of the little figure standing to the left. "N'en a-t-il qu'un à sa droite, il ne vaut que pour dix; en a-t-il six, il vaut pour un million."[35]

The differences in education and competence which actually exist among the members of the party are reflected in the differences in their functions. It is on the ground of the incompetence of the masses that the leaders justify the exclusion of these from the conduct of affairs. They contend that it would be contrary to the interests of the party if the minority of the comrades who have closely followed and attentively studied the questions under consideration should be overruled by the majority which does not really possess any reasoned opinion of its own upon the matters at issue. This is why the chiefs are opposed to the referendum, at any rate as far as concerns its introduction into party life. "The choice of the right moment for action demands a comprehensive view which only a few individuals in

---

numerous articles and speeches by Filippo Turati, as for example *Il partito socialista e l'attuale momento politico* ("Critica Sociale," Milan, 1902, 3rd edition, p. 15), and his speech to the 7th Italian Socialist Congress at Imola in 1902 (*Rendiconto*, Lib. Soc. Ital., Rome, 1903, p. 54).

[34] Mermeix (*La France socialiste, Notes d'un contemporain*, Fetscherin et Chuit, Paris, 1886 3rd ed., p. 138) wrote as long ago as 1886 with reference to the struggle between the Marxists and the possibilists which occurred in 1875: "Si les chefs pouvaient se donner la main, l'union serait parfaite dans le parti ouvrier." As every one knows, this prophecy was fulfilled in 1904.

[35] E. Fournière, *La sociocratie*, ed. cit., p. 117.

the mass can ever possess, whilst the majority are guided by momentary impressions and currents of feeling. A limited body of officials and confidential advisers, in closed session, where they are removed from the influence of coloured press reports, and where every one can speak without fearing that his words will be bruited in the enemy's camp, is especially likely to attain to an objective judgment." [36]

To justify the substitution of the indirect vote for the direct vote, the leaders invoke, in addition to political motives, the complicated structure of the party organization. Yet for the state organization, which is infinitely more complicated, direct legislation by means of the initiative and the referendum is an integral part of the socialist programme.[37] The antinomy which underlies these different ways of looking at the same thing according as it presents itself in the politics of the state or in those of the party pervades the whole life of the latter.

The working-class leaders sometimes openly avow, with a sincerity verging on cynicism, their own superiority over the troops they command, and may go so far as to declare their firm intention to refuse to these latter any facility for dictating the leaders' conduct. The leaders even reserve to themselves the right of

---

[36] Eduard Bernstein, *Gewerkschaftsdemokratie*, "Sozial. Monatsh.," 1909, p. 86.

[37] Cf., for example, Hans Block, *Ueberspannung der Demokratie*, "Neue Zeit," xxvi, No. 8, p. 266. The author himself sees very clearly how the reasons applied by him to combat democracy within the party are equally applicable against democracy in the state. He therefore takes occasion to cleave democracy in two, and to make a distinction between its application in party life and in the life of the state. He writes: "Our programme, however, demands direct election, rejecting indirect. It also contains the demand for direct legislation by the people through the initiative and the referendum. But elections and votes which concern the life of the state cannot be compared with those which concern party organization. The circumstances are altogether different. In the case of the state, the matters under consideration have taken shape long before the time comes for the vote; the persons involved have already assumed definite positions. The problem is plain and is plainly formulated from the first. Very different is the matter in party life, where even in the last weeks before the annual congress important proposals and recommendations come up for discussion of which an organization which insisted upon employing the ponderous mechanism of the direct vote could not possibly take account" (p. 265).— This distinction is in truth utterly fictitious. It is incomprehensible that the affairs of a party, whose organization when compared with that of the state is small and simple, can be more complicated than those of the state itself, and that therefore a violation of democratic principles can be more readily justified in the case of the party than in the case of the state.

rebelling against the orders they receive. A typical example, among many, is the opinion expressed on this subject by Filippo Turati, an exceptionally intelligent and well-informed man and one of the most influential members of the Italian socialist party, in a labour congress held at Rome in 1908. Referring to the position of the socialist deputy in relation to the socialist masses, he said: "The socialist parliamentary group is always at the disposal of the proletariat, as long as the group is not asked to undertake absurdities." [38] It need hardly be said that in each particular case it is the deputies who have to decide whether the things they are asked to do are or are not "absurd." [39]

---

[38] This speech was made in a Convegno pro Amnistia on March 31, 1908, reported in the Turin "Stampa," xvii, No. 92.

[39] Essentially this view is held also by Eduard Bernstein, who, however, in correspondence with his thoughtful and amiable character, expresses it more mildly, and endeavours to justify it by serious reasons. He tells us that the leader is not the mere mouthpiece of the masses, but has to decide on behalf of the masses what are their true interests. To quote his actual words: "Bebel contends that the leaders should follow the masses. This is not my view. I consider that the so-called 'leaders,' that is to say the confidential agents of the workers, hold the position of experts on behalf of the working class. Unquestionably they must cooperate harmoniously with those from whom they derive their power, but above all they must act in accordance with their own best convictions of what the interests of the working class really demand; when it is needful they must oppose the views of the workers, and make their own opinions prevail. We must not allow ourselves to be carried away by transitory currents. Bebel laughs at the idea of reserving certain questions for the decision of the parliamentary group. But is it not quite right to hold that the deputies, who are always in the Reichstag, can judge certain questions better than those who are not members of this body? Unless it be intended to pass a vote of no-confidence in the group, the question with which we are now concerned can surely be left to its judgment" (Eduard Bernstein, speaking at the socialist party congress, Dresden, 1903, *Protokoll über die Verhandlungen des Parteitages*, Buchh. "Vorwärts," Berlin, 1903, p. 309). Some years earlier Bernstein expressed the view that the control of the masses over their leaders must be restricted to those questions which profoundly concern the interests of the masses and which are not of too specialized a character—but he fails to give us any more precise indication as to the nature of these questions (Eduard Bernstein *Zur Geschichte und Theorie des Sozialismus*, Edelheim, Berlin, 1901, p. 205). Other leaders believe that they can attain the same end, and effect in a less honourable way what in German journalistic language is described as "shepherding the masses." A German trade-union leader has actually declared in writing that the leaders must sometimes say things which are contrary to their own opinions simply because they thus please the masses, "because the masses become wise only after they have burned their own fingers"; and that it is easier for them to act in this way, because "it is always

The accumulation of power in the hands of a restricted number of persons, such as ensues in the labour movement to-day,[40] necessarily gives rise to numerous abuses. The "representative," proud of his indispensability, readily becomes transformed from a servitor of the people into their master.[41] The leaders, who have begun by being under obligations to their subordinates, become in the long run the lords of these: such is the ancient truth which was recognized by Goethe when he made Mephistopheles say that man always allows himself to be ruled by his own creatures. The very party which fights against the usurpations of the constituted authority of the state submits as by natural necessity to the usurpations effected by its own constituted authorities. The masses are far more subject to their leaders than to their governments, and they bear from the former abuses of power which they would never tolerate from the latter.[42] The lower classes sometimes react forcibly against oppression from above, and take bloody reprisals, as happened in the French Jacqueries, in the German Peasants' Wars, in the English revolts under Wat Tyler and Jack Cade, and more recently in the revolts of the Sicilian Fasci in 1893; whereas they do not perceive the tyranny of the leaders they have themselves chosen. If at length the eyes of the masses are opened to the crimes against the democratic ideal which are committed by their party leaders, their astonishment and their stupor are unbounded. If, however, they then rise in rebellion, the nature of their criticisms shows how little they have understood the true character of the problem. Far from recognizing the real fount of the oligarchical evil in the centralization of power within the party, they often consider that the best means of counteracting oligarchy is to intensify this very centralization.[43]

---

within their power as masters to do what their own enlightened intelligence suggests without the masses understanding what they are about" (Tischendörfer in the "Korrespondenzblatt der Generalkommission der Gewerkschaften Deutschlands," quoted by Otto Geithner, *Zur Taktik der Sozialdemokratie*, "Neue Zeit," anno xxiii, vol. ii, p. 657).

[40] Cf. p. 64.

[41] This possibility has been admitted even by Kautsky (Karl Kautsky, *Wahlkreis und Partie*, "Neue Zeit," xxii No. 28, p. 36).

[42] "It is well known that the people finds it far easier to get the better of kings than of legislative assemblies" (Karl Marx, "Neue Rheinische Zeitung," November 11, 1848).

[43] This ineptitude was conspicuously displayed in the debates which took place in Germany concerning the 1st of May demonstrations (see p. 146). Shortly after the official orders upon this subject had been issued, a meet-

ing of the socialist branch of Leipzig, a branch noted for its revolutionary spirit and subject to the influence of Marxist extremists such as Mehring and Lensch, took up a definite position in favour of the 1st of May celebration. In this year (1908) certain concessions had been made by the Leipzig police in the matter of the procession, so that the celebration promised to be more imposing than ever. Consequently in the socialist branch at Leipzig vigorous protests were made against the executive committee of the party, which, in agreement with the executive of the trade-union organizations, had decided that in future the workers who were discharged by their employers in consequence of the 1st of May celebrations should not have any right to out-of-work relief from the central treasury of the socialist party or from that of the general federation of trade unions, but that it would be necessary for special local and voluntary funds to be founded to subsidize the 1st of May manifestants. The resolution passed by the Leipzig socialists, in criticism of this decision, ran as follows: "The Leipzig comrades regard this as an attempt to limit by indirect measures the cessation of work on the 1st of May, and to exercise such an influence upon the trade unions as to lead the individual trade unions to revoke their resolutions in favour of the support of those who are dismissed by their employers because of participation in the celebration. The further attempt to throw upon the local organizations responsibility for and execution of the determinations made by the central organizations is regarded by the Leipzig comrades *as an infringement of the principle of centralization*. The comrades express their profoundest regret that the local branches of the party were not consulted, as were the leaders of the federations, before this decision was arrived at, and they look to the next party congress to regulate the question of the 1st of May demonstration." In this resolution, which in the main is identical with the resolutions adopted by the committees of the party and trade-union branches in Frankfort-on-the-Main, and which was accepted by the committees of the party and trade-union branches in Flensburg, Schleswig ("Volkstimme," Frankfurt a/M. xix, 79), the comrades, revolting against the oligarchico-autocratic consequences of centralization, seriously proposed a more vigorous carrying out of the principle of centralization.

CHAPTER V

THE STRUGGLE BETWEEN THE LEADERS AND THE MASSES

THOSE who defend the arbitrary acts committed by the democracy, point out that the masses have at their disposal means whereby they can react against the violation of their rights. These means consist in the right of controlling and dismissing their leaders. Unquestionably this defence possesses a certain theoretical value, and the authoritarian inclinations of the leaders are in some degree attenuated by these possibilities. In states with a democratic tendency and under a parliamentary regime, to obtain the fall of a detested minister it suffices, in theory, that the people should be weary of him. In the same way, once more in theory, the ill-humour and the opposition of a socialist group or of an election committee is enough to effect the recall of a deputy's mandate, and in the same way the hostility of the majority at the annual congress of trade unions should be enough to secure the dismissal of a secretary. In practice, however, the exercise of this theoretical right is interfered with by the working of the whole series of conservative tendencies to which allusion has previously been made, so that the supremacy of the autonomous and sovereign masses is rendered purely illusory. The dread by which Nietzsche was at one time so greatly disturbed, that every individual might become a functionary of the mass, must be completely dissipated in face of the truth that while all have the right to become functionaries, few only possess the possibility.

With the institution of leadership there simultaneously begins, owing to the long tenure of office, the transformation of the leaders into a closed caste.[1]

Unless, as in France, extreme individualism and fanatical political dogmatism stand in the way, the old leaders present themselves to the masses as a compact phalanx—at any rate whenever the masses are so much aroused as to endanger the position of the leaders.

---

[1] Cf. p. 104.

The election of the delegates to congresses, etc., is sometimes regulated by the leaders by means of special agreements, whereby the masses are in fact excluded from all decisive influence in the management of their affairs. These agreements often assume the aspect of a mutual insurance contract. In the German socialist party, a few years ago, there came into existence in not a few localities a regular system in accordance with which the leaders nominated one another in rotation as delegates to the various party congresses. In the meetings at which the delegates were appointed, one of the big guns would always propose to the comrades the choice as delegate of the leader whose "turn" it was. The comrades rarely revolt against such artifices, and often fail even to perceive them. Thus competition among the leaders is prevented, in this domain at least; and at the same time there is rendered impossible anything more than passive participation of the rank and file in the higher functions of the life of that party which they alone sustain with their subscriptions.[2] Notwithstanding the violence of the intestine struggles which divide the leaders, in all the democracies they manifest vis-à-vis the masses a vigorous solidarity. "Ils conçoivent bien vite la nécessité de s'accorder entre eux, afin que le parti ne puisse pas leur échapper en se divisant."[3] This is true above all of the German social democracy, in which, in consequence of the exceptional solidity of structure which it possesses as compared with all the other socialist parties of the world, conservative tendencies have attained an extreme development.

When there is a struggle between the leaders and the masses, the former are always victorious if only they remain united.[4] At least it rarely happens that the masses succeed in disembarrassing themselves of one of their leaders. At Mannheim, a few years ago, the organized workers did actually dismiss one of their chiefs, but not without arousing intense indignation among the leaders, who described this act of legitimate rebellion as a

---

[2] Similar phenomena have been observed in party life in America (Ostrogorsky, *La Démocratie, etc.*, ed. cit., vol. ii, p. 196).

[3] Antoine Elisée Cherbuliez, *Théorie des Garantis constitutionelles*, Ab. Cherbuliez, Paris, 1838, vol. ii, p. 253.

[4] Domela Nieuwenhuis once compared the organization of the socialist party to a flock of sheep with dogs and shepherds. When any member of the flock endeavours to stray he is immediately driven back by the barking dogs (*Debat tusschen F. Domela Nieuwenhuis en H. Gorter over Sociaal-Demokratie of Anarchisme*, held at Enschedé, October 8, 1904, "Nieuwe Tijd," p. 17).

crime on the part of the rank and file, and were careful to obtain another post for the poor victim of popular anger.[5] In the course of great political agitations and in extensive economic struggles undertaken by the masses against the will of their leaders these soon reacquire the supremacy which they may for a moment have lost. Then it often happens that the leaders, over the heads of the crowd and in opposition to its expressed will, contravening the fundamental principles of democracy and ignoring all the legal, logical, and economic bonds which unite the paid leaders to the paying masses, make peace with the enemy, and order the close of the agitation or the resumption of work. This is what happened in the last Italian general strike, and also in the great strikes at Crimmitschau, Stetten, Mannheim, etc. The masses in such cases are often sulky, but they never rebel, for they lack power to punish the treachery of the chiefs. After holding tumultuous meetings in which they declare their legitimate and statutory displeasure, they never fail to provide their leaders with the democratic fig-leaf of a bill of indemnity. In 1905 the miners of the Ruhr basin were enraged against their leaders when these had taken it upon themselves to declare the great miners' strike at an end. It seemed as if on this occasion the oligarchy was at length to be called to account by the masses.[6] A few weeks

---

[5] Adolf Weber, *Kapital und Arbeit*, ed. cit., p. 380.

[6] Cf. the series of articles *Streikeindrücke*, by Conrad Haenisch, in the "Sächsische Arbeiterzeitung," xvi, Nos. 51-58, and the series in the "Leipziger Volkszeitung," 1905, Nos. 41-44 and 61-63. Haenisch reports: "I shall never forget the moment when it was announced to the rank and file that their leaders had suddenly come to a decision without consulting them. The speech was interrupted by a general shout 'Continue the strike!' and a number of excited miners endeavoured to storm the platform by a side door. Yet it was only a momentary disturbance, for the stewards soon reduced the 'mutineers' to order. But all the more fiercely now flamed the wrath of the masses in the street, who had expected anything rather than such a decision. The cart carrying the 255,000 leaflets announcing the resumption of work, which the committee of seven had had printed the previous day at an ultramontane printer's, was taken by assault. Sachse (socialist deputy, president of the miners' federation, and one of the principal leaders of the strike) was followed to the station by at least 300 desperately raging miners. From the whole of Essen there arose but one cry, 'Treason!' However absurd and unjust this cry may have been, the fact that it was uttered gives us a profound insight into the intensely disturbed popular mind" ("Sachs. Arbz.," xvi, 58). Again: "Old and tried comrades came to the editorial offices at Dortmund, in tears, in an emotional state that I should never have deemed possible to our sober-minded Westphalians, overwhelming us with desperate accusations

later, tranquillity was completely restored, as if it had never been disturbed. The leaders had defied the anger of their followers, and had nevertheless remained in power. In Turin, in October, 1907, on the third day of the general strike, the workers had decided by a large majority that the strike should be continued, but the leaders (the executive committee of the local branch of the party and the committees of the local trade unions) went counter to this decision, which ought to have been valid for them, by issuing a manifesto in which they counselled the strikers to return to work.[7] In the meetings of the party and of the trades council which followed upon these events the breach of discipline was condoned. The rank and file dreaded the resignation of the leaders and the bad appearance which their organizations would have displayed in face of the bourgeoisie when deprived of their best known and most highly esteemed men. Thus the governing bodies of democratic and socialist parties can in case of need act entirely at their own discretion, maintaining a virtual independence of the collectivity they represent, and in practice making themselves omnipotent.[8]

---

which I cannot bring myself to transcribe. The fate of the 255,000 leaflets destroyed by the tumultuous crowd at Essen was shared by innumerable pamphlets of the organization. This may give the reader some idea of the emotions of the organized masses, unaccustomed to discipline! I have said enough, and shall not attempt to describe the scenes of Thursday and Friday at all the mass meetings" ("Leipz. Volksz.," 1905, p. 41).

[7] Whilst the prefect forbade that the decision of the workers to continue the strike should be put into effect, the local authorities, acting on his instructions, did everything they could to secure the adoption of the leaders' proposal that work should be resumed.

[8] It is a remarkable psychological phenomenon that the leaders of great organizations exhibit in private life weaknesses and other deficiencies which are in singular contrast with the qualities of leadership. The great organizer Lassalle perished shamefully through his incapacity for conducting to a happy end an engagement to marry, too lightly undertaken. The domestic relationships of the great majority of the socialist leaders (*nomina sunt odiosa*) are extremely unhappy. The talent for organization and command often becomes transformed into its opposite within the four walls of the house. "Ils semblent incapables de réfléchir et de se conduire dans les circonstances les plus simples, alors qu'ils savaient si bien conduire les autres" (Gustave Le Bon, *Psychologie des Foules*, Alcan, Paris, 1899, p. 110). The marriages contracted by most of the socialist leaders are of a typically bohemian character. Among these leaders those who have been divorced and those who practise the so-called free love constitute a high percentage. A happy and retired family life like that of a few of the most noted among the leaders (Karl Marx, August Bebel, Enrico Ferri) is so exceptional in the case of socialist marriages that the socialists are in the

Such a condition of affairs is essentially oligarchical, and manifold are its consequences in the movements that have been initiated under the banner of democracy. One of the chief of these consists in the daily infringement on the part of the executive of the tactical resolutions whose fulfilment is entrusted to the executive as a sacred charge by the numerous leaders of the second rank who make up the congresses and assemblies of the party;[9] hence arises the practice which becomes continually

habit of trumpeting these exceptions widely, referring to them for propaganda purposes in order to repel the accusation so often levelled that they aim at the disorganization of the family.

[9] The discipline prescribed for the narrower circle of leaders (executives) by the resolutions of the wider circle of leaders (congresses) is very frequently infringed. It was by a breach of discipline that Ulrich was the first socialist to enter the Hessian chamber, for he came forward as a candidate although his party had forbidden any socialist participation in the elections which were effected by a system of indirect suffrage. In many instances the socialists of Bavaria, Würtemberg, and Baden openly disregarded the decisions of the congresses forbiding alliances with the liberals or with the clericals, and in the various diets they often voted the budget although the national congresses had expressly ordained that no support was ever to be given to any ministry. The central executive of the party has also frequently disregarded the decisions of the congresses. For example, this was done in the second ballots for the Reichstag in 1903, when the executive committee decreed that the votes of the socialists might be given to any one who was opposed to restriction of the suffrage, thus violating the resolution of the Munich congress of 1902, which laid down that support at the second ballot given to a bourgeois candidate of the left who was running in opposition to a candidate of the right must depend not only on the candidate's attitude to the question of universal suffrage but also upon his declared opposition to an imperialist colonial policy. Similarly, again, after the congress of Jena (1903), the executive (in accord with the general committee of the trade-union organizations) effected profound modifications in the decision taken at Jena concerning the general strike. In Italy, at the socialist congress of Florence in 1896, it was decreed that no member of the party should under any circumstances fight a duel (cf. Alfredo Angiolini, *Cinquant' Anni di Socialismo in Italia,* Nerbini, Florence, 1904, 2nd ed., p. 346). Notwithstanding this, every year some half dozen of the most conspicuous leaders of the party have sent or accepted challenges. Again, the various votes against freemasonry have had no effect whatever, the socialist freemasons remaining in the party and in their lodges. Even in Germany, where discipline is professedly far more strict, the procedure is extremely lax when authoritative comrades are accused of having transgressed the laws of the party. Thus the parliamentary socialist group of the Grand Duchy of Baden ignoring the decision of the previous national congress of Nuremberg, participated in a vote of confidence in the government (1910). On this occasion the party executive, by failing to censure the group for its action, rendered itself an accessory after the fact. Often

more general of discussing *en petit comité* questions of the greatest importance, and of confronting the party subsequently with
accomplished facts (for example, electoral congresses are not
summoned until *after* the elections, so that the leaders decide on
their sole responsibility what is to be the electoral platform).
Again, there are secret negotiations among different groups of
leaders (as happened in Germany in the case of the 1st of May
demonstration and in that of the general strike), and secret un-
derstandings with the government. Once more, silence is often
maintained by the members of the parliamentary group upon
matters which have been discussed by the group and upon decisions at which they have arrived, and this practice is censured by
members of the executive only when they themselves are kept in
the dark, but is approved by them when it is merely the masses
who are hoodwinked.

There is no indication whatever that the power possessed by
the oligarchy in party life is likely to be overthrown within an
appreciable time. The independence of the leaders increases concurrently with their indispensability. Nay more, the influence
which they exercise and the financial security of their position
become more and more fascinating to the masses, stimulating
the ambition of all the more talented elements to enter the privileged bureaucracy of the labour movement. Thus the rank and
file becomes continually more impotent to provide new and intelligent forces capable of leading the opposition which may be latent among the masses.[10] Even to-day the masses rarely move ex-

---

enough the leaders actually pride themselves on their disregard of the most
elementary principles of democracy. When the socialist group of the
Badenese chamber was reproached for having voted the budget, in defiance
of the rule established at the Nuremberg congress of 1908, the deputy
Ludwig Frank declared: "It would go ill with the party if it lacked
men with the courage to ignore congress resolutions when these are altogether impracticable" (reported in the "Volksstimme," Frankfort, anno
xxi, No. 168). No one can fail to see that this explanation is invalid. It
may well happen that certain resolutions adopted by the congresses are
inopportune, and may be so inopportune that to carry them out would
be an act of madness, or would at least involve serious harm to the party.
But this would merely signify that the delegates responsible for passing such
impossibilist resolutions were characterized by great political immaturity.
He who will not admit this must at least recognize that the frequent infringement by the leaders of the determinations of the party congresses
constitutes a grave lack of democratic sentiment and discipline. *Tertium
non datur.*

[10] Thus Pareto writes: "Si les B [nouvelle élite] prennent peu à peu la
place des A [ancienne élite] par une lente infiltration, et si le mouve-

cept at the command of their leaders. When the rank and file does take action in conflict with the wishes of the chiefs, this is almost always the outcome of a misunderstanding. The miners' strike in the Ruhr basin in 1905 broke out against the desire of the trade-union leaders, and was generally regarded as a spontaneous explosion of the popular will. But it was subsequently proved beyond dispute that for many months the leaders had been stimulating the rank and file, mobilizing them against the coal barons with repeated threats of a strike, so that the mass of the workers, when they entered on the struggle, could not possibly fail to believe that they did so with the full approval of their chiefs.[11]

It cannot be denied that the masses revolt from time to time, but their revolts are always suppressed. It is only when the dominant classes, struck by sudden blindness, pursue a policy which strains social relationships to the breaking-point, that the party masses appear actively on the stage of history and overthrow the power of the oligarchies. Every autonomous movement of the masses signifies a profound discordance with the will of the leaders.[12] Apart from such transient interruptions, the

---

ment de circulation sociale n'est pas interrompu, les C [la masse] sont privés des chefs qui pourraient les pousser à la révolte" (Vilfredo Pareto, *Les Systèmes socialistes*, ed. cit., vol. i, p. 35).

[11] Cf. p. 158, note 6.

[12] The outbreak of the great railway strike in England in August 1911 has been considered by some to have been such a victory on the part of the masses over their leaders. Those who take this view contend that this strike was a sudden transition from the "sluggish and pacific" tactics of the trade unions, whose funds are ample and the "respectability" of whose leaders is indisputable, to a vigorous and revolutionary policy; this change of tactics they suppose to have been due to the impatience of the crowd, rebelling simultaneously against the yoke of the railway companies and that of their own officials. But those who hold such a view have not given due weight to the most conspicuous characteristics of the movement. If ever a strike was conducted by tried and powerful leaders, it was this one. The supreme command of the forces of the "northern army" of the strikers (at the Liverpool headquarters) was in the hands of Tom Mann, one of the boldest and most energetic figures of the modern labour movement, a man who in London in 1889 was one of the leaders of the dockers in their famous and successful strike, and who subsequently, inspired by the sentiment of the class struggle, was an organizer of socialism in Australia. Nay more, the aims of the strike were such that the trade-union leaders were profoundly interested in its success. Not only was their *amour propre* involved, but it was a question of giving a more solid foundation to the economic organization of the workers. If we are to understand the sociology of the English railway strike of 1911, we must not forget that the com-

natural and normal development of the organization will impress upon the most revolutionary of parties an indelible stamp of conservatism.

---

panies were unwilling to meet the representatives of the labour organization and to negotiate with these. But the Amalgamated Society of Railway Servants had unanimously resolved "to give twenty-four hours to the companies to make up their minds that they would at once meet the representatives of the trade unions in order to discuss a basis of agreement." Thus the question was one of recognition of the working-class leaders by the employers' organizations, which amounts to saying that it was one touching the personal interest of the employees of the trade unions. Accounts of the strike written from very various points of view suffice to establish this. Cf., for instance, that of the syndicalist James Barrison in the "Internazionale" of Parma (anno v, No. 18), and that published by the central organ of the Catholic trade unionists of Germany, the "Centralblatt der Christlichen Gewerkschaften Deutschlands" (xi, No. 19).

CHAPTER VI

THE STRUGGLE AMONG THE LEADERS THEMSELVES

The thesis of the unlimited power of the leaders in democratic parties requires, however, a certain limitation. Theoretically the leader is bound by the will of the mass, which has only to give a sign and the leader is forced to withdraw. He can be discharged and replaced at any moment. But in practice, as we have learned, for various reasons the leaders enjoy a high degree of independence. It is none the less true that if the democratic party cannot dispense with autocratic leaders, it is at least able to change these. Consequently the most dangerous defect in a leader is that he should possess too blind a confidence in the masses. The aristocratic leader is more secure than the democratic against surprises at the hands of the rank and file. It is an essential characteristic of democracy that every private carries a marshal's baton in his knapsack. It is true that the mass is always incapable of governing; but it is no less true that each individual in the mass, in so far as he possesses, for good or for ill, the qualities which are requisite to enable him to rise above the crowd, can attain to the grade of leader and become a ruler. Now this ascent of new leaders always involves the danger, for those who are already in possession of power, that they will be forced to surrender their places to the new-comers. The old leader must therefore keep himself in permanent touch with the opinions and feelings of the masses to which he owes his position. Formally, at least, he must act in unison with the crowd, must admit himself to be the instrument of the crowd, must be guided, in appearance at least, by its goodwill and pleasure. Thus it often seems as if the mass really controlled the leaders. But whenever the power of the leaders is seriously threatened, it is in most cases because a new leader or a new group of leaders is on the point of becoming dominant, and is inculcating views opposed to those of the old rulers of the party. It then seems as if the old leaders, unless they are willing to yield to the opinion of the rank and file and to withdraw, must consent to share their power with the new arrivals. If, however, we look more closely into the matter, it is not difficult to see that their submission is in most cases no more than an act of foresight intended to obviate the influence of their younger rivals. The submission of the old leaders is ostensibly an act of homage to the crowd, but in intention it is a means of prophylaxis against the peril by which they are threatened—the formation of a new élite.

The semblance of obedience to the mass which is exhibited by the leaders assumes, in the case of the feebler and the more cunning among them, the form of demagogy. Demagogues are the courtesans of the popular will. Instead of raising the masses to their own level, they debase themselves to the level of the masses. Even for the most honest among them, the secret of success consists in "knowing how to turn the blind impulsiveness of the crowd to the service of their own ripely pondered plans."[1] The stronger leaders brave the tempest, well-knowing that their power may be attacked, but cannot be broken. The weak or the base, on the other hand, give ground when the masses make a vigorous onslaught; their dominion is temporarily impaired or interrupted. But their submission is feigned; they are well aware that if they simply remain glued to their posts, their quality as executants of the will of the masses will before long lead to a restoration of their former dominance. One of the most noted leaders of German socialism said in a critical period of tension between the leaders and the masses, that he must follow the will of the masses in order to guide them.[2] A profound psychological truth is hidden in this sarcasm. He who wishes to command must know how to obey.

It has been affirmed that popular revolutions usually end by destroying their leaders. In proof there have been quoted the names of Rienzi, Masaniello, and Michele di Lando, for Italy, and of Danton and Robespierre, for France. For these and many similar instances the observation is a true one. It would, however, be an error to accuse the crowd of rising against its leaders, and to make the masses responsible for their fall. It is not the masses which have devoured the leaders: the chiefs have devoured one another with the aid of the masses. Typical examples are that of Danton, who was overthrown by Robespierre, and that of Robespierre, who was destroyed by the surviving Dantonists.

---

[1] Kochanowski, *Urzeitklänge, etc.*, ed. cit., p. 10.
[2] "Ich bin ihr Führer, also muss ich ihnen folgen." (Cf. Adolf Weber, *Der Kampf zwischen Kapital u. Arbeit*, ed. cit., p. 369.)

The struggle which arises between the leaders, and their mutual jealousies, induce them to employ active measures and often to have recourse to artifices.[3] Democratic deputies endeavour to disarm their adversaries within the party, and at the same time to acquire a new prestige in the eyes of the masses, by displaying in parliament "a formidable activity on behalf of the common cause." This is regarded at once as a democratic duty and as a measure of personal precaution. Since the great majority of the deputies, electors, and comrades have no precise ideas concerning the functions he exercises, and are continually inclined to accuse him of slackness, the deputy is from time to time forced to recall himself to their memories.[4] It is this need which has given rise to not a few of those speeches to which the Germans give the name of *Dauerreden* (interminable speeches), and it has also been the cause of more than one "scene" in the various parliaments of Austria, France, England, and Italy. It is, in fact, held that the most efficacious means for retaining the attention of the masses and of rendering them proud of their leaders is to be found in the provocation of those personal incidents which are far more interesting to the great public and far more within the scope of its intelligence than a report upon the utilization of water power or upon a commercial treaty with the republic of Argentina. Moreover, it has to be remembered that in many countries, and above all in Italy, such scenes are recorded in the capitalist press with the greatest abundance of detail, whilst serious speeches are summed up in a few lines, and with especial brevity when the speaker is a socialist. Thus even in normal times the oratorical activity of the parliamentary representatives of the democratic parties is considerable. In Italy, the socialist deputies have boasted that between March 25 and July 10, 1909, they spoke in the Chamber 212 times. The figure represents 20.4 per cent. of all the speeches made in parliament during the period, whilst the socialist deputies at this time constituted only 8 per cent. of the members.[5] Such loquacity serves not merely to maintain the prestige of the party in the eyes of

---

[3] Concerning the varied character and the intensity of such activities, the socialist deputy Guido Podrecca has written a charmingly humorous sketch entitled *The Joys of a Deputy* (*Le Gioie del Deputato,* "Avanti," anno xiv, No. 44, Rome, 1910).

[4] Cf. Pio Viazzi, *Le Gioie della Deputazione,* "Rivista Populare," anno xv, No. 11.

[5] Cf. the account given by Oddino Morgari, "Avanti," August 12, 1909.

its opponents, but is also a matter of personal interest to each deputy, being a means to secure his re-election in competition, not only with enemies in other parties, but also with jealous rivals belonging to his own organization.

The differences which lead to struggles between the leaders arise in various ways. Reference has previously been made to the inevitable antagonism between the "great men" who have acquired a reputation in other fields, and who now make adhesion to the party, offering it their services as generals, and the old-established leaders, who have been socialists from the first.[6] Often conflict arises simply between age and youth. Sometimes the struggle depends upon diversity of social origin, as when there is a contest between proletarian leaders and those of bourgeois birth.[7] Sometimes the difference arises from the objective needs of the various branches of activity into which a single movement is subdivided, as when there is a struggle between the political socialist party and the trade-union element, or within the political party between the parliamentary group and the executive. In some cases there is a horizontal stratification, causing a struggle between one stratum of the bureaucracy and another; at other times the stratification is vertical, as when there occurs a conflict between two local or national groups of leaders; between the Bavarian socialists and the Prussian; between those of Frankfort and those of Hanau; between the French followers of Vaillant, Jaurès, and Hervé, and the German adherents of Bebel and von Vollmar (in the anti-militarist discussion at the international congress of Stuttgart). Often enough struggles among the socialists are the outcome of racial differences. The unceasing contests in the international congresses between the German socialists and the French afford in more than one respect a parallel with the Franco-German War of 1870. In these same congresses there participates a third group, misunderstood and heterogeneous, the representatives of English socialism, hostile to all the others and encountering the enmity of all. In most cases, however, the differences between the various groups of leaders depend upon two other categories of motives. Above all there are objective differences and differences of principle in general philosophical views, or at least in the mode in which the proximate social evolution is conceived, and consequent diver-

---

[6] Cf. pp. 74-5.

[7] A special chapter (Part IV, chap. vi) will be devoted to this question.

gences of opinion as to the most desirable tactics: this leads to the manifestation of the various tendencies known as reformist and Marxist, syndicalist and political socialist, and so on. In the second place, we have the struggles that depend on personal reasons: antipathy, envy, jealousy, a reckless attempt to grasp the first positions, demagogy. Enrico Ferri said of his opponent Filippo Turati: "He hates me because he thinks there is not room for two cocks in the same fowl-house."[8] In most cases the two series of motives are somewhat confounded in practice; and in the long run we find that those of the former series tend to be replaced by those of the latter, inasmuch as differences of principle and of the intellectual order soon become personal and lead to a profound hostility between the representatives of the various theories. Conversely it is clear that motives of the second series, since those who are influenced by them are ashamed to display them in their true colours, always endeavour to assume the mantle of theory; personal dislike and personal hostility pompously masquerade as differences of views and tactics.

The oligarchy which issues from democracy is menaced by two grave dangers: the revolt of the masses, and (in intimate relationship with this revolt, of which it is often the result) the transition to a dictatorship when one among the oligarchs succeeds in obtaining supreme power. Of these two dangers, one comes from below, whilst the other arises within the very bosom of the oligarchy: we have rebellion on one side, and usurpation on the other. The consequence is that in all modern popular parties a spirit of genuine fraternity is conspicuously lacking; we do not see sincere and cordial mutual trust; there is a continual latent struggle, a spirit of irritation determined by the reciprocal mistrust of the leaders, and this spirit has become one of the most essential characteristics of every democracy. The mistrust of the leaders is directed above all against those who aspire to command their own organizations. Every oligarchy is full of suspicion towards those who aspire to enter its ranks, regarding them not simply as eventual heirs but as successors who are ready to supplant them without waiting for a natural death. Those who have long been in possession (and this applies just as much to spiritual and psychical possession as to material) are proud of their past, and are therefore inclined to look

---

[8] Speech made by Ferri at Suzzara, reported in "Stampa," anno xlvii, No. 358 (December 27, 1909).

down upon those whose ownership is of more recent date. In certain Sicilian towns, struggles go on between two parties who in popular phrase are ironically termed *i ricchi* and *gli arricchiti* (the wealthy and those who have attained to wealth). The former consists of the old landed gentry; whilst the latter, the parvenus, are merchants, contractors for public works, manufacturers, and the like.[9] A similar struggle makes its appearance in modern democratic parties, although it is not in this case characterized by any flavour of economic distinction. Here also we have a struggle between the *détenteurs d'emploi et les chercheurs d'emploi*, or as the Americans put it, between the "ins" and the "outs." The latter declare war on the former, ostensibly on the ground of eternal principle, but in reality, in most cases, because in such opposition they find the most effective means of forcing their way into the circle of the chiefs. Consequently in meetings they display themselves as implacable theoretical adversaries, "talking big" solely in order to intimidate the accepted leaders, and in order to induce them to surrender a share of the spoil to these turbulent comrades. Often enough, the old leaders resist, and maintain their ground firmly; in such cases their opponents, changing front, abandon the attitude of struggle, and attach themselves to the triumphal car of the men in power, hoping thus to attract favour, and, by a different route, to realize their own ambitions.[10]

The struggle between the old leaders and the aspirants to power constitutes a perpetual menace to freedom of speech and thought. We encounter this menace in every democratic organization in so far as it is well ordered and solidly grounded, and in so far as it is operating in the field of party politics (for in the wider life of the state, in which the various parties are in continual reciprocal concussion, it is necessary to leave intact a certain liberty of movement).[11] The leaders, those who already hold the power of the party in their hands, make no conceal-

---

[9] Giacomo Montalto, *La Questione sociale e il Partito socialista*, Società Editrice Lombarda, Milan 1895, p. 81.—The description of the landed gentry as "the rich" is a striking confirmation of the truth of Sombart's view, that, in the case of a hereditarily gentle class, wealth is a natural attribute, psychologically and socially congenital, qualitative rather than quantitative (cf. Sombart, *Die deutsche Volkswirtschaft, etc.*, ed. cit., p. 542).

[10] Ostrogorsky, *Organisation de la Démocratie*, ed. cit., vol. ii, pp. 203, 206, and 363.

[11] "Experience shows only too clearly that, wherever democracy is tending

ment of their natural inclination to control as strictly as possible the freedom of speech of those of their colleagues from whom they differ.

The consequence is that those in office are great zealots for discipline and subordination, declaring that these qualities are indispensable to the very existence of the party. They go so far as to exercise a censorship over any of their colleagues whom they suspect of rebellious inclinations, forcing them to abandon independent journals, and to publish all their articles in the official organs controlled by the leaders of the majority in the party. The prohibition, in the German socialist party, of collaboration on the part of its members with the capitalist press, is in part due to the same tendency; whilst the demand that the comrades should have nothing to do with periodicals which, though socialist, are founded with private capital and are not subject to the official control of the party executive, arises solely from this suspicion on the part of the leaders.[12]

In the struggle against the young aspirants, the old leader can as a rule count securely upon the support of the masses. The rank and file of the working-class parties have a certain natural distrust of all new-comers who have not been openly protected or introduced into the party by old comrades; and this is above all the case when the new-comer is derived from another social class. Thus the new recruit, before he can come into the open with his new ideas, must submit, if he is not to be exposed to the most violent attacks, to a long period of quarantine. In the German socialist party, this period of quarantine is especially protracted, for the reason that the German party has been longer established than any of the others, and because its leaders therefore enjoy an exceptional prestige. Many of them were among the actual founders of the party, and their personalities have been consecrated by the baptism of fire which they suffered during the enforcement of the anti-socialist laws. A socialist who has had his party card in his pocket for eight or ten years is often regarded in his branch as a "young" member. This tendency is reinforced by the respect for age which is so strong among the Germans, and by the tendency towards hierarchy of

---

to degenerate, freedom of speech and the press are the first to perish" (Roscher, *Politik,* ed. cit., p. 324).

[12] Cf. the discussions of the congresses of the German socialist party at Munich (*Protokoll,* pp. 255 et seq.) and at Dresden (*Protokoll,* pp. 158 et seq.)

which even the democracy has not been able to divest itself. Finally, it may be added that the bureaucracy of the German labour movement, like every strongly developed bureaucracy, tends instinctively towards exclusivism. Consequently in the German social democracy, in contradistinction to other socialist parties which are less solidly organized, we find that not merely the recently enrolled member of the party (the so-called *Fuchs*), but also the ordinary member who does not live in the service and by the service of the party but has preserved his outward independence as a private author or in some other capacity, and has therefore not been incorporated among the cogwheels of the party machine, very rarely succeeds in making his influence felt. There can be no doubt that this fact plays a large part in the causation of that lack of a number of capable young men, displaying fresh energies, and not greatly inferior to the old leaders, a lack which has often been deplored. The annual congresses of the socialist party have even been spoken of as "congresses of the party officials." The criticism is not unjust, for among the delegates to the socialist congresses the percentage of party and trade-union officials is enormous.[13] It is above all in the superior grades of the organization that the tendencies we are here analysing are especially conspicuous. In Germany, the management of the socialist party is not entrusted to young men, as often happens in Italy, or to free publicists, as in France, but to old members, *des anciens,* elderly officials of the party. Moreover, the conservative psychology of the masses supports the aspirations of the old leaders, for it would never occur to the rank and file to entrust the care of their interests to persons belonging to their own proper sphere, that is to say, to those who have no official position in the party and who have not pursued a regular bureaucratic career.[14]

Often the struggle between the old leaders in possession of power and the new aspirants assumes the aspects of a struggle

---

[13] Cf. pp. 120, 127.

[14] In Frankfort-Nordend the list proposed for the election of delegates to the congress of Nuremberg, 1908, drawn up in accordance with the express wishes of the district assemblies of the party, contained, among eleven names, those of eight officials of the labour movement (two socialist journalists, one party secretary, one secretary of trades council, one organizer, one trade-union employee, one insurance-bureau employee, and one cooperative salesman) as compared with three simple wage-earners who were not dependent upon working-class organizations (Frankfort "Volksstimme," Supplement 188, 1908).

between responsible and irresponsible persons.[15] Many criticisms levelled by the latter against the former are beside the mark, because the leaders have grave responsibilities from which the aspirants are free. This freedom gives the aspirants a tactical advantage in their conflict with the old leaders. Moreover, precisely because they are irresponsible, because they do not occupy any official position in the party, the opponents are not subject to that simulacrum of democratic control which must influence the conduct of those in office.

In order to combat the new chiefs, who are still in a minority, the old leaders of the majority instinctively avail themselves of a series of underhand methods through which they often secure victory, or at least notably retard defeat. Among these means, there is one which will have to be more fully discussed in another connection. The leaders of what we may term the "government" arouse in the minds of the masses distrust of the leaders of the "opposition" by labelling them incompetent and profane, terming them spouters, corrupters of the party, demagogues, and humbugs, whilst in the name of the mass and of democracy they describe themselves as exponents of the collective will, and demand the submission of the insubordinate and even of the merely discontented comrades.

In the struggle among the leaders an appeal is often made to loftier motives. When the members of the executive claim the right to intervene in the democratic functions of the individual sections of the organization, they base this claim upon their more comprehensive grasp of all the circumstances of the case, their profounder insight, their superior socialist culture and keener socialist sentiment. They often claim the right of refusing to accept the new elements which the inexpert and ignorant masses desire to associate with them in the leadership, basing their refusal on the ground that it is necessary to sustain the moral and theoretical level of the party. The revolutionary socialists of Germany demand the maintenance of the centralized power of the executive committee as a means of defence against the dangers, which would otherwise become inevitable as the

---

[15] In socialist and trade-union literature this aspect of the problem has often been discussed. Cf. Filippo Turati, *Il Partito socialista e l'attuale Momento politico*, Uffici della "Critica Sociale," Milan, 1901, 3rd ed., p. 19; Paul Kampffmeyer, *Die Entwicklung der deutschen Gewerkschaften*, "Annalen für Soziale Politik und Gesetzgebung," vol. i, fasc. 1, pp. 114 et seq.

party grows, of the predominant influence of new and theoretically untrustworthy elements. The old leaders, it is said, must control the masses, lest these should force undesirable colleagues upon them. Hence they claim that the constituencies must not nominate parliamentary candidates without the previous approval of the party executive.[16]

---

[16] Kautsky defends this claim. "The greater the increase in our voting strength, the greater the dearth of candidates, the more remote from the great centres of economic, political, and intellectual life are many constituencies with socialist majorities, the more essential does it become that the party organizations in the individual constituencies should not possess absolute sovereignty in the choice of candidates, but that the right of selection should be vested in the party as a whole. The best way of securing this is that in the case of candidates for the diet the constituencies should secure the approval of the territorial executive or territorial congress, and in the case of candidates for the Reichstag that of the territorial executive and of the central executive. In 1876 the party congress decided the various candidatures to the Reichstag, in so far as time permitted. But in the case of a number of candidatures it was necessary that the selection should be entrusted to the electoral committee appointed by the congress. It is obvious that there are several different ways in which the party as a whole may exercise a determinative influence in the choice of candidates. Which of these ways is the most practical need not here be discussed. The point of immediate importance is to recognize, in principle, that the selection of a candidate for the Reichstag is a matter which concerns the party as a whole quite as much as it concerns the individual constituency." The expression "the party as a whole" is naturally to be understood as synonymous with "the party executive." Kautsky continues: "Of course the choice of candidates must not be exclusively in the hands of the party executive or of a central electoral committee. The comrades in the constituencies have to shoulder most of the electoral work and it is upon them that success in the election mainly depends. It would certainly be preposterous to force upon them a candidate whom they did not want. But on the other hand the constituency must not have the right to force upon the party a parliamentary representative whom the majority in the party has serious reasons to dislike. The local organizations must choose their own candidates in the first instance. But the candidatures must always be approved by the party as a whole. . . . It may, indeed, sometimes be desirable that the party, or its executive, should itself nominate the candidate. This will be the case especially in those states in which the number of safe constituencies is extremely small. Here the selection of candidates must not be left solely to the play of local influences. The party has a right to demand that in the safe constituencies those candidates shall be run whose presence in parliament is absolutely indispensable. It is owing to the unrestricted autonomy of the constituencies that in Austria such a man as Victor Adler has been excluded from the house of representatives for two parliaments in succession, and it is doubtful if he will secure a seat at the forthcoming elections. But as far as the German Empire is concerned, the number of safe constituencies is so large, that these considera-

The old leaders always endeavour to harness to their own chariot the forces of those new movements which have not yet found powerful leaders, so as to obviate from the first all competition and all possibility of the formation of new and vigorous intellectual currents. In Germany, the leaders of the socialist party and the trade-union leaders at first looked askance at the Young Socialist movement. When, however, they perceived that this movement could not be suppressed, they hastened to place themselves at its head. There was founded for the guidance of the socialist youth a "Central Committee of Young German Workers," comprising four representatives from each of the three parties, that is to say, four from the executive of the socialist party, four from the general committee of trade unions, and four from the Young Socialists (the representatives of the latter being thus outnumbered by two to one).[17] The old leaders endeavour to justify the tutelage thus imposed on the Young Socialists by alleging (with more opportunist zeal than logical acuteness) the incapacity of the youthful masses, if left to their own guidance, of wisely choosing their own leaders and of exercising over these an efficient control.[18]

We have by no means come to an end of our enumeration of the weapons at the disposal of the old leaders in their conflict with the new aspirants to power. Charlemagne effected the final subjugation of the Saxon tribal chiefs by making them counts. In this way he not only increased the brilliancy of their position, but also gave them a restricted share in his own power. This means has been practised again and again in history, where an old ruler has wished to render harmless, insubordinate but influential chiefs, and thus to prevent a rebellion against his own authority. Oligarchies employ this stratagem with just as much success as monarchies. The feudal state of Prussia appointed to the privy council the most defiant among the leaders of its bourgeoisie. At a time when the youthful German bourgeoisie was still filled with a rebellious spirit towards the nobility and towards the traditional authority of the state, this tendency aroused

---

tions hardly apply" (Karl Kautsky, *Wahlkreis und Partei,* "Neue Zeit," xxii, No. 28, p. 36).

[17] "Fränkische Tagespost," anno xxxix, No. 191, Supplement 2.

[18] "The associations of the Young Socialists are impotent vis-à-vis their leaders, lacking the force and adroitness which would enable them to avoid the arbitrary rule of these" (Max Kette, *Die Jugendbewegung,* "Neue Zeit," xxviii, No. 9).

much bitterness. Thus Ludwig Börne wrote in 1830: "Wherever a talented force of opposition has made itself apparent and has secured respect from those in authority, it is chained to the professorial chair, or is controlled by being harnessed to the government. If the governmental ranks are full, so that no place can be found for the new energies, a state livery is at least provided for the authors by giving them titles and orders. In other cases the dangerous elements are isolated from the people by immuring them in some noble's castle or princely court. It is for this reason that nowhere else do we find so many privy councillors as in Germany, where the courts are least inclined to take any one's advice." [19] In the Spanish elections of 1875, we learn that so great was the popular indifference that the government had matters altogether in its own hands, but in order to be secure in any event it thoughtfully selected a certain number of opposition candidates.[20] It seems that things are much the same in Spain even to-day.[21] These tactics are not confined to states that are still permeated by feudal conceptions. Where plutocratic rule is supreme, corruption persists unchanged, and it is only the corrupter who is different. This is plainly shown by Austin Lewis when he writes: "The public ownership contingent in politics being composed of the middle and subjugated class have neither the political ability nor the vital energy necessary for the accomplishment of the task which they have undertaken. The brains of the smaller middle class have already been bought by the greater capitalists. Talent employed in the service of the chiefs of industry and finance can command better prices than can be obtained in the uncertain struggle for economic standing which members of the middle class have to wage. The road to professional and political preferment lies through the preserves of the ruling oligarchy, whose wardens allow no one to pass, save servants in livery. Every material ambition of youth is to be gratified in the service of the oligarchy, which shows, generally, an astuteness in the selection of talent that would do credit to a bureaucrat or a Jesuit.[22]

Of late years the ruling classes in the countries under a demo-

---

[19] Ludwig Börne, *Aus meinem Tagebuche*, Reclam, Leipzig, p. 57.

[20] *Denkwürdigkeiten des Fürsten Hohenlohe*, ed. cit., p. 376.

[21] Nicolas Salmeron y Garçia, *L'état espagnol et la Solidarité catalane*, "Le Courier Européen," iv, No. 23.

[22] Austin Lewis, *The Rise of the American Proletarian*, Charles H. Kerr & Co., Chicago, 1907, pp. 189-190.

cratic regime have hoped to impose obstacles in the way of the
revolutionary labour movement by conceding posts in the ministry to its most conspicuous leaders, thus gaining control over
the revolutionary impulse of the proletariat by allowing its leaders to participate in power, though cautiously and in an extremely restricted measure. The oligarchy which controls the
modern democratic party has often employed the same means
to tame the opposition. If the leaders of the opposition within
the party are dangerous because they have a large following
among the masses, and if they are at the same time few in number, the old party-leaders endeavour to hold them in check and
to neutralize their influence by the conciliatory methods just described. The leaders of the opposition receive high offices and
honours in the party, and are thus rendered innocuous—all the
more so seeing that they are not admitted to the supreme offices,
but are relegated to posts of the second rank which give them
no notable influence, and they are without hope of one day becoming a majority. On the other hand, they divide with their
ancient adversaries the serious weight of responsibility which is
generated by common deliberations and manifestations, so that
their activities become confounded with those of the old leaders.[23]
In order to avoid having to divide their power with new ele-

---

[23] The history of the socialist party alike in Austria and in Germany
affords numerous examples of minorities which were at first pugnacious and
rebellious, but which have allowed themselves to be disarmed in this manner. The leaders of the opposition to the party executive at the Salzburg
congress of the Austrian socialists in 1904, and also those at the Bremen
congress of the German socialists held in the same year, have since then
become members of the superior order of leaders and have been elected
deputies to the parliaments of their respective countries. Simultaneously
they have abandoned their attitude of opposition. The most typical example, however, occurred among the Dutch socialists in the spring of
1909. Here the reformist majority endeavoured to gain control of
the party executive through the criticism which was levelled against the reformists by some of the particularly hardy members of the opposition.
These latter, the so-called Marxist group of the "Niewe Tijd," had their
own organ, an independent and private review; now the reformist leaders
of the party proposed to create a joint review, edited by the party and
therefore subject to the control of the party, on condition that the Marxists
should renounce the "Niewe Tijd." This was an extremely ingenious
scheme for drawing their opponents' teeth. The democratic parties in
America exhibit analogous phenomena. Ostrogorsky writes: "La machine
est prête à tout faire, même à faire aux récalcitrants une place sur le
tiquet" (Ostrogorsky, *Organisation de la Démocratie, etc.*, ed. cit., vol. ii, p.
363).

ments, especially such as are uncongenial by tendency or mental
characteristics, the old leaders tend everywhere with greater or
less success to acquire the right of choosing their own colleagues,
thus depriving the masses of the privilege of appointing the
leaders they themselves prefer.[24]
The path of the new aspirants to power is always beset with
difficulties, bestrewn with obstacles of all kinds, which can be
overcome only by the favour of the mass. Very rarely does the
struggle between the old leaders and the new end in the complete defeat of the former. The result of the process is not so
much a *circulation des élites* as a *réunion des élites*, an amalgam,
that is to say, of the two elements. Those representing the new
tendency, as long as their footing is still insecure, seek all sorts
of side paths in order to avoid being overthrown by the powers-
that-be. They protest that their divergence from the views of
the majority is trifling, contending that they are merely the
logical advocates of the ancient and tried principles of the party,
and express their regret that the old leaders display a lack of
true democratic feeling. Not infrequently it happens that they
avert the blows directed against them by craftily creeping behind the backs of their established and powerful opponents who
are about to annihilate them, solemnly declaring, when wrathful
blows are directed against them, that they are in complete accord with the old leaders and approve of all their actions, so
that the leaders seem to be beating the air. On many occasions
in the recent history of the socialist parties, the reformist minorities, in order to avoid destruction, have bowed themselves beneath the yoke of the so-called revolutionary majorities by voting
(with a fine practical and tactical sense, but with an entire lack
of personal pride and political loyalty) resolutions which were
drafted precisely in order to condemn the political views dear to
the minority.[25] In two cases only does it sometimes happen that

---

[24] The reader's attention may be recalled to what has been said on pp.
103, 104.

[25] At the Dresden congress, 1903, the German reformists found no difficulty
in voting for the so-called "Dresden resolution," which subsequently attained an international status, having been brought forward by the French
Marxists at the international congress of Amsterdam, 1904, where it was
solemnly reconfirmed. It is indisputable that this motion was directed
against the reformists, since it expressly condemns all participation by
socialists in the government. Eleven only among the 268 reformist delegates
had a sense of duty and political honesty or personal rectitude sufficiently
strong to induce them to vote against the resolution. (Cf. the remarks on

the relationships between the two tendencies become strained to the breaking-point. In the first place this may happen when the leaders of one of the two factions possess a profound faith in their own ideas, and are characterized at once by tactical fanaticism and theoretical irreconcilability—or, in other words, when the objective reasons which divide them from their opponents are felt with an unaccustomed force and are professed with an unwonted sincerity. In the second place it may happen when one of the parties, in consequence of offended dignity or reasonable susceptibility, finds it psychologically impossible to continue to live with the other, and to carry on within the confines of the same association a continued struggle for dominion over the masses. The party will then break up into two distinct organisms, and in each of these there will be renewed the oligarchical phenomena we have been describing.

One of the most interesting chapters in the history of the struggles between leaders deals with the measures which these leaders adopt within their own closed corporations in order to maintain discipline—that is to say, in order to preserve the cementing force of the will of the majority. In the struggle which the various groups of leaders carry on for the hegemony of the party, the concept of democracy becomes a lure which all alike employ.

---

this matter of Lily Braun, *Memoiren einer Sozialistin. Kampfjahre,* Langen, Munich, 1911, p. 512). The Austrian socialist, Victor Adler, whose views are most closely akin to the reformists of the German party, wrote in the Viennese ''Arbeiter Zeitung'' concerning the stratagem adopted by the majority of the reformists: ''Secondly, the vote means that those who are termed reformists regard the moment as unfavourable for the decisive and open declaration of their opinions and still more unfavourable for the display of the smallness of their numbers. They are indeed so few that the minority has preferred to hide itself by mingling with the majority'' (from the reprint in the ''Mainzer Volkszeitung,'' 1903, No. 225). A counterpart to this is furnished by the action of the Italian reformists at the socialist congress at Rome, 1906. Here the reformists avoided a defeat only by associating themselves (although their adhesion was repudiated by the majority) with a resolution brought forward by the integralists under the leadership of Ferri, a resolution which was expressly directed against them and which contained various matters irreconcilable with the reformist theory. Thus they met the attack against them by running away. Among the Italian reformists there were not wanting some who regarded this action as inconsistent and politically dishonourable (*Resoconto stenografico del IX Congresso Nazionale a Roma,* 1906, Mongini, Rome, 1907, pp. 275 et seq.). Among those who voted against the resolution were such men as Antonio Graziadei and Alessandro Tasca di Cutò, belonging to the old aristocracy of birth, and perhaps for this reason inclined to take a more elevated view of human dignity.

All means are good for the conquest and preservation of power. It is easy to see this when we read the discussions concerning the system to be employed for the appointment of the party executive. The various tendencies manifested in this connection all aim at the same end, namely, at safeguarding the dominance of some particular group. Thus in France the Guesdists, whose adherents are numerous but who control a small number only of the groups, advocate a system of proportional representation; the Jauressists, on the other hand, who are more influential in respect of groups than of members, and also the Hervéists, oppose proportional representation within the party, for they fear that this would give the Guesdists group too great a facility for the enforcement of its own special methods of action, and they propose to maintain the system of local representation or of representation by delegation.[26]

In the American Congress, each party possesses a special committee which exercises a control over the attendance of its members at the sessions, and which on the occasion of decisive votes issues special summonses or "whips." When an interesting bill is before the house, the party committee also summons a *caucus,* that is to say, a private meeting of the parliamentary group, and this decides how the congressmen are to vote. All members of the party are bound by the decision of such a caucus. Naturally no immediate punishment is possible of those who rebel against the authority of the caucus; but at the next election the independent congressman is sure to lose his seat, for the party-managers at Washington will not fail to report to their colleagues, the bosses of the local constituency, the act of insubordination committed by the congressman concerned. The most vital of all the caucuses is that which precedes the election of the speaker of the congress. The ideas and sympathies of the speaker have a decisive influence upon the composition of the committees and therefore upon the whole course of legislation. For this reason his election is of fundamental importance, and is preceded for several weeks by intrigues and vote-hunting campaigns. Doubtless it is not in every case that the votes are decided in advance at a meeting of the group. Where laws of minor importance are concerned, every member of Congress is free to vote as he pleases. But in times of excitement obedience is exacted, not only to the decisions of the caucus, but also to the authority of the party

---

[26] Cf. the Paris correspondence of "Avanti," anno xv, No. 16.

leaders. This last applies especially to Congress, for in the Senate the members are extremely jealous of their absolute equality. On the other hand, the caucus has an even greater importance in the case of the Senate, for here the groups are smaller and the caucus can therefore function more efficiently. The groups in Congress may number more than two hundred members, whereas those of the Senate rarely exceed fifty.[27]

The parliamentary group of the German social democracy is likewise dominated, as far as its internal structure is concerned, by a most rigorous application of the principle of subordination. The majority of the parliamentary group decides the action of all its members on the various questions submitted to the Reichstag or to the diets, exercising what is known as the *Fraktionszwang* (group coercion). No individual member has the right to independent action. Thus the parliamentary group votes as a single entity, and this not merely in questions of a distinctively socialist bearing, but also in those which are independent of socialist ideas, and which each might decide according to his own personal conceptions. It was very different in the French parliament during the fratricidal struggle between the Jauressists and the Guesdists before the attainment of socialist unity in France, for at that time each deputy used to vote as he pleased. But the German example shows that liberty of opinion no longer exists where the organization demands common action and where it has some force of penetration in political life.

In certain cases, however, all these preventive measures fail of their effect. This happens when the conflict is not simply between a minority and a majority within the group, but between the group and one single member who possesses outside parliament, in certain sections of the party, the full support of the subordinate leaders. When a conflict occurs in such conditions, the deputy, though isolated, is sure of victory. The electors, in fact, usually follow with great docility the oscillations and evolutions of their parliamentary representatives, and they do this even in constituencies where socialist voters predominate. The ministers Briand, Viviani, and Millerand have been expelled from the French socialist party, but the former members of the socialist organizations in their constituencies have remained faithful to these leaders, resigning from the socialist party, and continuing as electors to give the ex-socialists their support. Anal-

---

[27] Bryce, *The American Commonwealth*, abridged ed., Macmillan, New York, 1907, pp. 152-3.

ogous were the cases of John Burns in England (Battersea) and of Enrico Ferri in Italy (Mantua). It was enough in Ferri's case that at an appropriate moment he should reveal a new truth to produce immediately a collective change in the political opinions of an entire region. Having first been, with Ferri, revolutionary and irreconcilable, this region became converted in a single night, always following Ferri, to the principle of class co-operation and of participation in ministerial activity.[28] In Germany, the party executive had to make use of all its authority in order, at the last minute, to induce the comrades of Chemnitz to withdraw their support from their deputy Max Schippel, and those of Mittweida from Otto Göhre, when these two deputies had displayed heterodox leanings.

The tendency of the deputy to set himself above his party is most plainly manifest precisely where the party is strongly organized; especially, therefore, in the modern labour parties; and within these, again, more particularly in the reformist sections. The reformist deputies, as long as they have not upon their side a majority within the party, carry on an unceasing struggle to withdraw themselves from the influence of the party, that is to say, from the mass of the workers who are organized as a party. In this period of their evolution they transfer their dependence upon the organized mass of the local socialist section to the electors of the constituency, who constitute a grey, unorganized, and more or less indifferent mass. Thus from the organized masses, who may be under the influence of their opponents within the party, they appeal to the mass of the electors, with the contention that it is to these latter alone, or at least chiefly, that they have to give an account of their political conduct. It is right to recognize that this appeal to the electorate as the body which has conferred a political mandate is frequently based upon genuinely democratic sentiments and principles. Thus, at the international socialist congress of London (1893), the four French socialist deputies refused to make use of the

---

[28] Cf. a polemic article wherein Giovanni Zibordi gives an account of a visit made by Ferri to Mantua after his political *volte-face*. Zibordi speaks of the ''triumphal tour'' of the adored leader, and deplores how Ferri and Gatti ''passed through the region of Mantua. . . amid the hurrahs of the workers who knew no better, while accompanied by the impotent disdain and grief of the socialists who saw thus installed a dangerous dictatorship, a personal dominion which is the negation of our principles and our methods'' (Giovanni Zibordi, *Quel che succede nel Mantovano*, ''Avanti,'' anno xv, No. 119).

mandates which had been conferred upon them by political or corporative groups, thus defying the rules of admission to the congress. After extremely violent discussions they were ultimately admitted simply as deputies, having raised the question of principle whether an important constituency capable of returning a socialist deputy to the Chamber should not have the same rights which are granted to a local socialist or trade-union branch, especially when it is remembered that such a branch may consist of a mere handful of members.[29] It is true that in certain circumstances a constituency inspired by socialist sentiment, even if it be not socialistically organized, constitutes a better basis, in the democratic sense, for political action than a small socialist branch whose members are mostly petty bourgeois or lawyers;[30] and even if a large local organization exists, the constituency as a whole is a better basis than a badly attended party meeting for the selection of a candidate.[31]

From our study of the intricate struggles which proceed between the leaders of the majority and those of the minority, between the executive organs and the masses, we may draw the following essential conclusions.

Notwithstanding the youth of the international labour movement, the figures of the leaders of that movement are more imposing and more imperious than those displayed in the history of any other social class of modern times. Doubtless the labour movement furnishes certain examples of leaders who have been deposed, who have been abandoned by their adherents. Such cases are, however, rare, and only in exceptional instances do they signify that the masses have been stronger than the leaders. As a rule, they mean merely that a new leader has entered into conflict with the old, and, thanks to the support of the mass,

[29] Hubert Lagardelle, *Les Origines du Syndicalisme en France*, "Mouvement Socialiste," anno xi, Nos. 215-216, p. 249.

[30] It is well to remind English readers that on the Continent, and especially in France and Italy, barristers play a conspicuous part in the oligarchy of socialism, corresponding with that which in England they play in the old political parties.—TRANSLATORS' NOTE.

[31] Rinaldo Rigola, the socialist secretary of the Italian General Confederation of Labour, describes the socialist party as an oligarchy, and therefore contests its right to present candidatures for the elections and to decide the policy of the proletariat. In his view, these functions should rather be allotted to the labour organizations, whose membership is far more extensive and which could constitute themselves into a Labour Party (Rinaldo Rigola, *Discutendo di un Partito del Lavoro*, "Avanti," anno xiv, No. 172).

has prevailed in the struggle, and has been able to dispossess and replace the old leader.[32] The profit for democracy of such a substitution is practically nil.

Whenever the Catholics are in a minority, they become fervent partisans of liberty. In proof of this we need merely refer to the literature issued by the Catholics during the *Kulturkampf* under the Bismarckian regime and during the struggle between Church and State which went on a few years ago in France. In just the same way the leaders of the minority within the socialist party are enthusiastic advocates of liberty. They declaim against the narrowness and the authoritative methods of the dominant group,[33] displaying in their own actions genuine democratic inclinations.[34]

---

[32] Richard Calwer, in a declaration to the socialist press, gives the following account of his dethronement as a party leader: " 'Vorwärts' and the 'Leipziger Volkszeitung' accept as a matter of principle the resolution of the party conference of the third Reichstag-constituency of Brunswick, by which it was decided to repudiate my candidature in future. They do this without reflecting upon the moral poverty which the decision exhibits for the party. The dissatisfaction of the comrades in the constituency with my economic views is supposed to have increased gradually, and at length to have become overwhelming. It is strange that during the entire sixteen years during which I have been a candidate in this constituency there was not until about a year ago the slightest manifestation of dissatisfaction among the comrades in the electorate. Yet never throughout this period have I made any secret of my views. The local comrades have been familiar with them from the first and have never, for this reason, wished to remove their confidence. The alleged divergencies 'in matters of principle' date from no more than a year back, having begun precisely at the moment when comrade Antrick came to Brunswick as secretary. What reasons there were to induce this comrade to attack me 'on principle,' I do not know. In any case, I neither had nor have inclination or time to trouble myself about personal quarrels and to dispute with comrade Antrick" ("Volksstimme," August 15, 1907).

[33] Cf., for example, the pamphlet issued by the displaced members of the staff of "Vorwärts," *Der Vorwärtskonflikt, Gesammelte Aktenstücke* (Birk, Munich 1905), in which we read: "We are not here concerned merely with the moral position of the journalists within the party; the present conflict is a matter of decisive importance to the internal wellbeing of the German labour movement. The question at issue is that of the dignity of all the responsible persons in the confidence of the democracy. What has to be decided is whether a system of absolute publicity is to be replaced by a secret method of jurisdiction; whether open discussion is to yield to the crafty dissemination of suspicions; whether obscure intrigue is to oust comradely confidence; whether blind caprice is to be

---

[34] Cf. p. 18.

As soon as the new leaders have attained their ends, as soon as they have succeeded (in the name of the injured rights of the anonymous masses) in overthrowing the odious tyranny of their predecessors and in attaining to power in their turn, we see them undergo a transformation which renders them in every respect similar to the dethroned tyrants.[35] Such metamorphoses as these are plainly recorded throughout history. In the life of monarchical states, an opposition which is headed by hereditary princes is rarely dangerous to the crown as an institution. In like manner, the opposition of the aspirants to leadership in a political party, directed against the persons or against the system of the old leaders, is seldom dangerous. The revolutionaries of to-day become the reactionaries of to-morrow.

---

more effective than reasoned conviction; whether arbitrary opinion is to be more influential than established fact—whether, in a word, a regime of glib demagogy, of personal ambition, and the most unscrupulous place-hunting, is to be established in the German social democracy!''

---

[35] ''When he has the power in his own hands, he ignores the laws which were made for his restraint'' (Giambattista Casti, *Gli Animali parlanti*, Poema, Tip. Vanelli e Comp., Lugano, 1824, vol. i, p. 30).

CHAPTER VII

BUREAUCRACY. CENTRALIZING AND DECENTRALIZING TENDENCIES.

THE organization of the state needs a numerous and complicated bureaucracy. This is an important factor in the complex of forces of which the politically dominant classes avail themselves to secure their dominion and to enable themselves to keep their hands upon the rudder.

The instinct of self-preservation leads the modern state to assemble and to attach to itself the greatest possible number of interests. This need of the organism of the state increases *pari passu* with an increase among the multitude, of the conviction that the contemporary social order is defective and even irrational—in a word, with the increase of what the authorities are accustomed to term discontent. The state best fulfils the need for securing a large number of defenders by constituting a numerous caste of officials, of persons directly dependent upon the state. This tendency is powerfully reinforced by the tendencies of modern political economy. On the one hand, from the side of the state, there is an enormous supply of official positions. On the other hand, among the citizens, there is an even more extensive demand. This demand is stimulated by the ever-increasing precariousness in the position of the middle classes (the smaller manufacturers and traders, independent artizans, farmers, etc.) since there have come into existence expropriative capitalism on the grand scale, on the one hand, and the organized working classes on the other—for both these movements, whether they wish it or not, combine to injure the middle classes. All those whose material existence is thus threatened by modern economic developments endeavour to find safe situations for their sons, to secure for these a social position which shall shelter them from the play of economic forces. Employment under the state, with the important right to a pension which attaches to such employment, seems created expressly for their needs. The immeasurable demand for situations which results from these conditions, a demand which is always greater than the supply, creates the so-called "intellectual proletariat." The numbers of this body are subject to great fluctuations. From time to time the state, embarrassed by the increasing demand for positions in its service, is forced to open the sluices of its bureaucratic canals in order to admit thousands of new postulants and thus to transform these from dangerous adversaries into zealous defenders and partisans. There are two classes of intellectuals. One consists of those who have succeeded in securing a post at the manger of the state, whilst the other consists of those who, as Scipio Sighele puts it, have assaulted the fortress without being able to force their way in.[1] The former may be compared to an army of slaves who are always ready, in part from class egoism, in part for personal motives (the fear of losing their own situations), to undertake the defence of the state which provides them with bread. They do this whatever may be the question concerning which the state has been attacked and must therefore be regarded as the most faithful of its supporters. The latter, on the other hand, are sworn enemies of the state. They are those eternally restless spirits who lead the bourgeois opposition and in part also assume the leadership of the revolutionary parties of the proletariat. It is true that the state bureaucracy does not in general expand as rapidly as do the discontented elements of the middle class. None the less, the bureaucracy continually increases. It comes to assume the form of an endless screw. It grows ever less and less compatible with the general welfare. And yet this bureaucratic machinery remains essential. Through it alone can be satisfied the claim of the educated members of the population for secure positions. It is further a means of self-defence for the state. As the late Amilcare Puviani of the University of Perugia, the political economist to whom we are indebted for an important work upon the legend of the state, expresses it, the mechanism of bureaucracy is the outcome of a protective reaction of a right of property whose legal basis is weak, and is an antidote to the awakening of the public conscience.[2]

The political party possesses many of these traits in common with the state. Thus the party in which the circle of the *élite* is unduly restricted, or in which, in other words, the oligarchy is composed of too small a number of individuals, runs the risk of

[1] Scipio Sighele, *L'Intelligenza della Folla*, Bocca, Turin, 1903, p. 160.
[2] Amilcare Puviani, *Teoria della Illusione finanziaria*, R. Sandron, Milan-Naples-Palermo, 1903, pp. 258 et seq.

being swept away by the masses in a moment of democratic effervescence. Hence the modern party, like the modern state, endeavours to give to its own organization the widest possible base, and to attach to itself in financial bonds the largest possible number of individuals.[3] Thus arises the need for a strong bureaucracy, and these tendencies are reinforced by the increase in the tasks [4] imposed by modern organization.[5]

As the party bureaucracy increases, two elements which constitute the essential pillars of every socialist conception undergo an inevitable weakening: an understanding of the wider and more ideal cultural aims of socialism, and an understanding of the international multiplicity of its manifestations. Mechanism becomes an end in itself. The capacity for an accurate grasp of the peculiarities and the conditions of existence of the labour movement in other countries diminishes in proportion as the individual national organizations are fully developed. This is plain from a study of the mutual international criticisms of the socialist press. In the days of the so-called "socialism of the émigrés," the socialists devoted themselves to an elevated policy of principles, inspired by the classical criteria of internationalism. Almost every one of them was, if the term may be used, a specialist in this more general and comprehensive domain. The whole course of their lives, the brisk exchange of ideas on unoccupied evenings, the continued rubbing of shoulders between men of the most different tongues, the enforced isolation from the bourgeois world of their respective countries, and the utter impossibility of any "practical" action, all contributed to this result. But in proportion as, in their own country, paths of activity were opened for the socialists, at first for agitation and soon afterwards for positive and constructive work, the more did a recognition of the demands of the everyday life of the party divert

---

[3] The governing body of Tammany in New York consists of four hundred persons. The influence of this political association is concentrated in a sub-committee of thirty persons, the so-called Organization Committee (Ostrogorsky, *La Démocratie etc.*, ed. cit., vol. ii, p. 199).

[4] Cf. pp. 33 et seq.

[5] Inquiries made by Lask have shown how deeply rooted in the psychology of the workers is the desire to enter the class of those who receive pensions. A very large number of proletarians, when asked what they wished to do with their sons, replied: "To find them employment which would give right to a pension." Doubtless this longing is the outcome of the serious lack of stability characteristic of the social and economic conditions of the workers (Georg v. Schulze-Gaevernitz, *Nochmals: "Marx oder Kant?," "Archiv für Sozialwiss.,"* xxx, fasc. 2, p. 520).

their attention from immortal principles. Their vision gained in precision but lost in extent. The more cotton-spinners, boot and shoe operatives, or brush-makers the labour leader could gain each month for his union, the better versed he was in the tedious subtleties of insurance against accident and illness, the greater the industry he could display in the specialized questions of factory inspection and of arbitration in trade disputes, the better acquainted he might be with the system of checking the amount of individual purchases in co-operative stores and with the methods for the control of the consumption of municipal gas, the more difficult was it for him to retain a general interest in the labour movement, even in the narrowest sense of this term. As the outcome of inevitable psychophysiological laws, he could find little time and was likely to have little inclination for the study of the great problems of the philosophy of history, and all the more falsified consequently would become his judgment of international questions. At the same time he would incline more and more to regard every one as an "incompetent," an "outsider," an "unprofessional," who might wish to judge questions from some higher outlook than the purely technical; he would incline to deny the good sense and even the socialism of all who might desire to fight upon another ground and by other means than those familiar to him within his narrow sphere as a specialist. This tendency towards an exclusive and all-absorbing specialization, towards the renunciation of all far-reaching outlooks, is a general characteristic of modern evolution. With the continuous increase in the acquirements of scientific research, the polyhistor is becoming extinct. His place is taken by the writer of monographs. The universal zoologist no longer exists, and we have instead ornithologists and entomologists; and indeed the last become further subdivided into lepidopterists, coleopterists, myrmecologists.

To some of the "non-commissioned officers" who occupy the inferior grades of the party bureaucracy may be aptly applied what Alfred Webber said of bureaucracy in general at the congress of the *Verein für Sozialpolitik* held at Vienna in 1909.[6]

---

[6] Cf. *Protokoll*, pp. 283 et seq.—The Dutch Christian socialist S. J. Visser has made a scientific attempt to defend the bureaucracy which would be installed by the socialist state, basing this defence upon the dangers inherent in private bureaucracy; but his defence must be considered a complete failure (S. J. Visser, *Over Socialisme*, M. Nyhoff's Gravenhage. See Chap. II, "Functionnarisme en Démokratie," pp. 116-165).

Bureaucracy is the sworn enemy of individual liberty, and of all bold initiative in matters of internal policy. The dependence upon superior authorities characteristic of the average employee suppresses individuality and gives to the society in which employees predominate a narrow petty-bourgeois and philistine stamp. The bureaucratic spirit corrupts character and engenders moral poverty. In every bureaucracy we may observe place-hunting, a mania for promotion, and obsequiousness towards those upon whom promotion depends; there is arrogance towards inferiors and servility towards superiors. Wolfgang Heine, who in the German socialist party is one of the boldest defenders of the personal and intellectual liberty of the members, who is always in the breach to denounce "the tendency to bureaucracy and the suppression of individuality," goes so far, in his struggle against the socialist bureaucracy, as to refer to the awful example of the Prussian state. It is true, he says, that Prussia is governed in accordance with homogeneous principles and by a bureaucracy which must be considered as a model of its kind; but it is no less true that the Prussian state, precisely because of its bureaucratic characteristics, and notwithstanding its external successes, is essentially retrogressive. If Prussia does produce any distinguished personalities, it is unable to tolerate their existence, so that Prussian politics tend more and more to degenerate into a spiritless and mechanical regime, displaying a lively hostility to all true progress.[7] We may even say that the more conspicuously a bureaucracy is distinguished by its zeal, by its sense of duty, and by its devotion, the more also will it show itself to be petty, narrow, rigid, and illiberal.

Like every centralizing system, bureaucracy finds its justification in the fact of experience that a certain administrative unity is essential to the rapid and efficient conduct of affairs. A great many functions, such as the carrying out of important statistical inquiries, can never be satisfactorily effected in a federal system.

The outward form of the dominion exercised by the leaders over the rank and file of the socialist party has undergone numerous changes *pari passu* with changes in the historical evolution of the labour movement.

In Germany, the authority of the leaders, in conformity with the characteristics of the nation and with the insufficient education of the masses, was at first displayed in a monarchical form;

---

[7] Wolfgang Heine *Demokratische Randbemerkungen zum Fall Göhre,* "Soz. Monatsh.," viii (x), fasc. 4.

there was a dictatorship. The first labour organization on German soil was the *Allgemeiner Deutscher Arbeiterverein* of Ferdinand Lassalle. This organization was founded in 1873 and lasted until 1875, when it became fused with the internationalist and Marxist section of German socialism, the "Eisenachers." The personal creation of a man of extraordinary force of character, it received even in its smallest details the stamp of his personality. It has been contended that Lassalle's association was founded upon the model of the *Nationalverein,* a German national league which was extremely influential at that epoch. This may be true in respect of the base of the Arbeiterverein, but is certainly not true of its summit. The Arbeiterverein, like the Nationalverein, was a unitary society whose members were dispersed throughout Germany and did not form any properly organized local branches. The membership was not local but national, each member being directly dependent upon the central organization. But whereas in the Nationalverein the central executive was a committee of several members, the Arbeiterverein was autocratically ruled by a single individual, Ferdinand Lassalle, who exercised, as did his successor Johann Baptist von Schweitzer, as president of the party of German workers, a power comparable with that of the doge of the Venetian Republic, and indeed a power even more unrestricted, since the president's power was not, as was that of the doge, subject to any kind of control through oligarchical institutions. The president was an absolute monarch, and at his own discretion nominated his subordinate officials, his plenipotentiaries, and even his successor. He commanded, and it was for the others to obey. This structure of the organization was not the outcome merely of the personal qualities of Lassalle, of his insatiable greed for power, and of that egocentric character [8] which made him, despite his genius, so poor a judge of men; it corresponded also to his theoretical view

---

[8] Already in his student career Lassalle displayed a thoroughly imperious and egoistic character. In Berlin he offered a distant relative, a young man of slender means, the privilege of sharing a dwelling whose cost was beyond his own purse, but in which he had a great desire to live. Subsequently he boasted of having found a "sort of valet" in this unlucky youth. He threatened the young man (who was as far as his means permitted paying his share towards the expenses of the joint establishment) that he would evict him without ceremony if he should prove lazy or ill-behaved, or should in any way provoke Lassalle's displeasure. (Cf. a letter from Lassalle to his father, dated Berlin, April 24, 1844. *Intime Briefe Ferdinand Lassalles an Eltern u. Schwester,* Buchhandlung "Vorwärts," Berlin, 1905, p. 23.)

of the aim of all party organization. In his famous speech at Ronsdorf he said: "Wherever I have been I have heard from the workers expressions of opinion which may be summarized as follows: 'We must forge our wills into a single hammer, and place this hammer in the hands of a man in whose intelligence, character, and goodwill we have the necessary confidence, so that he can use this hammer to strike with!' . . . The two contrasts which our statesmen have hitherto believed incapable of being united, freedom and authority, whose union they have regarded as the philosopher's stone—these contrasts are most intimately united in our Verein, which thus represents in miniature the coming social order!"[9] Thus in the eyes of the president his dictatorship was not simply a sad necessity temporarily forced upon a fighting organization,[10] but dictatorship was the ultimate aim of the labour movement.[11] In the days of Lassalle, the labour movement in Germany was still weak, and, like a little boy, was still urgently in need of paternal guidance. When the father came to die he made testamentary arrangements for the provision of a guardian (for the German labour movement could still be an object of testamentary depositions). After Lassalle's death, the decisive executive power, the quintessence (if the term be permitted) of the structure of the young labour movement, continued to rest at the almost absolute disposal of a single individual, Schweitzer.[12] This authoritative tendency was an outcome, not so much of the historical necessity of the moment, as of the traditions and of the racial peculiarities of the German stock. With the lapse of time this characteristic has been notably attenuated by theoretical and practical democracy, and by the varying necessities of the case; above all, by the appearance of a typically southern socialism, less rigid than that of Prussia and of Saxony, and jealous of its own autonomy. But the tendency has not disappeared, nor can it disappear.

Whilst there was thus forming in Germany the massive organization of the followers of Lassalle, the leaders of the International Association adopted a different form of organization. The International Workingmen's Association was characterized by

---

[9] Ferdinand Lassalle, *Die Agitation des Allgemeinen Deutschen Arbeitervereins u. das Versprechen des Königs von Preussen*, ed. cit., p. 40.
[10] Cf. pp. 41 et seq.
[11] Cf. Gustav Mayer, *J. B. von Schweitzer, etc.*, ed. cit., p. 256.
[12] Cf. also Hermann Oncken, *Lassalle*, Frommann (E. Hauff), Stuttgart, 1904, p. 397.

mutual jealousy on the part of the various national sections, and this was a potent obstacle in the way of any tendency towards dictatorship. Thus there came into existence in London the General Council, the supreme authority of the International, consisting of a handful of members belonging to the different countries represented in the organization. But the powers of this executive were in many respects hardly less restricted than those of the president of the Allgemeiner Deutscher Arbeiterverein. The General Council forbade the associations which were affiliated to it to elect presidents, regarding this as contrary to democratic principles.[13] Yet as far as concerned itself, it proudly asserted, through the mouth of the most conspicuous among its members, that the working class had now discovered a "common leadership."[14] It nominated from among its own members the officers necessary for the general conduct of its business, such as the treasurer, the general secretary, and the corresponding secretaries for the different countries,[15] nor did it hesitate, on occasions, to allot several offices to the same individual. Engels, though a German, was for some time secretary for four different countries—Spain, Italy, Portugal, and Denmark.[16] It may be added that the secretariat carried with it important prerogatives, such as the right of recognizing newly constituted sections, the right to grant or refuse pecuniary subsidies, and the adjustment of disputes among the comrades.[17] It is unquestionable that for several years the General Council was subject, in respect of all its most significant practical and theoretical manifestations, to the iron will of one single man, Karl Marx.[18] The conflict in the

---

[13] Cf. *Compte-Rendu du 4e Congrès International tenu à Bâle en sept. 1869,* D. Brismée, Brussels, 1869, p. 172.

[14] (Marx), *L'Alliance de la Démocratie Socialiste et l'Association Int. des Travailleurs,* Rapports et Documents, London-Hamburg, 1873, p. 25.

[15] Karl Stegmann and C. Hugo (H. Lindemann), *Handbuch des Socialismus,* J. Schabelitz, Zurich, 1897, p. 342.

[16] Letter from F. Engels to Sorge, March 17, 1872 (*Briefe u. Auszüge aus Briefen von Joh. Phil. Becker, Jos. Dietzgen, Fried. Engels, Karl Marx, u. A. an F. A. Sorge u. A.,* Dietz Nachf., Stuttgart, 1906, p. 54).

[17] *Compte-Rendu du 4e Congrès,* p. 172.

[18] "A provisional General Council was elected, and the soul of this body, as of all subsequent General Councils down to the Hague congress of 1872, was Marx himself. Their history is related elsewhere. In this place it suffices to say that Marx edited almost all the documents issued by the General Council, from the inaugural address of 1864 down to the address dealing with the civil war in France in 1871" (Stegmann u. Hugo, *op. cit.,* p. 500).

General Council between the oligarchy *de jure* and the monarchy *de facto* was the inner cause of the rapid decline of the Old International. The General Council and especially Marx were accused of being the negation of socialism because, it was said, in their disastrous greed for power, they had introduced the principle of authority into the politics of the workers.[19] At first these accusations were directed from without, coming from the groups that were not represented on the General Council: the accusers were Bakunin, the Italians, and the Jurassians. The General Council, however, easily got the upper hand. At the Hague congress in 1872, the "authoritarians," making use of means characteristic of their own tendencies (the hunting of votes, the calling of the congress in a town which was little accessible to some of the opponents and quite inaccessible to others),[20] obtained a complete victory over the anti-authoritarians. Before long, however, voices were raised within the Council itself to censure the spirit of autocracy. Marx was abandoned by most of his old friends. The French Blanquists ostentatiously separated themselves from him when he had arbitrarily transferred the General Council to New York. The two influential leaders of the English trade unions who were members of the General Council, Odger and Lucraft, quarrelled with Marx because they had not been consulted about the manifesto in favour of the Paris Commune to which their signatures were attached. The German refugees in England, Jung and Eccarius, declared that it was impossible to work with persons as dictatorial as Marx and Engels. Thus the oligarchs destroyed the larval monarchy.

In 1889 the so-called New International was founded. The socialist parties of the various countries agreed to undertake

---

[19] James Guillaume, *L'Internationale, Documents et Souvenirs*, Cornély, Paris, 1907 vol. ii.

[20] *Idem*, p. 327; cf. also a letter from Marx to Sorge, dated London, June 21, 1872, in which Marx begs Sorge to send him a number of blank voting cards for certain friends in America whom he mentions by name (*Briefe u. Auszüge aus Briefen*, ed. cit., p. 33).—The locale of the congress was a convenient one for the English, the French, and the Germans, who were on the whole favourable to the General Council, but extremely inconvenient for the Swiss, the Spaniards, and the Italians, who were on the side of Bakunin. Bakunin himself, who was living in Switzerland, was unable to attend the congress, for to reach The Hague he must have crossed Germany or France, and in both these countries he was liable to immediate arrest.

common deliberations, and to meet from time to time in congresses for this purpose. Therewith the "idea of internationalism" (to quote a phrase employed by Jaeckh) underwent a transformation. The Old International had worked along the lines of the greatest possible centralization of the international proletariat, "so that it might be possible, at any place at which the economic class-struggle became especially active, to throw there immediately into the scale the organized power of the working class."[21] The New International, on the other hand, took the form of an extremely lax system, a union of elements which were strangers one to another; these elements were national organizations of a very rigid form, each confined within the limits of its own state. In other words, the New International is a confederation of autonomous states, and lacks any unitary and homogeneous organization.[22] The Old International was an individual dictatorship, masquerading as an oligarchy. The New International may be compared to the old States General of the Netherlands; it is a federal republic, consisting of several independent oligarchies. The General Council of London was all-powerful. The modern Sécrétariat Socialiste International, whose seat is in Brussels, is nothing but an office for the exchange of letters, devoid of all authority. It is true that the international socialist congresses have sometimes furnished an opportunity for thoroughly self-conscious and vigorous national oligarchies to attempt usurpations in the international field. Thus, in particular, the German social democracy, when forced upon the defensive at the Stuttgart congress of 1907, endeavoured, and not without success, to impose upon the other socialist parties its own particular tactics, the verbal revolutionarism which had originated in the peculiar conditions of Germany.[23] The international unification of tactics has always been limited by the varying needs of the different national oligarchies. In other words, whilst national supremacies are still possible in the con-

---

[21] Cf. Gustav Jaeckh, *Die Internationale*, Leipz. Buchdr. Akt. Ges., Leipzig, 1904, p. 218.

[22] Cf. speech by Wilhelm Liebknecht to the Int. Cong. Paris, 1889 (*Protokoll*, deutsche Uebersetzung, Wörlein, Nuremberg, 1890, p. 7).

[23] Cf. R. Michels, *Die deutsche Sozialdemokratie im Internationalen Verbande*, "Arch. für Sozialwiss.," anno 1907). This is a detailed study of the conditions of fact and the complex of causes which rendered it possible for the German party to exercise such a pressure upon the other parties in the International; it deals also with the subsequent decline of its hegemony.

temporary socialist International, it is no longer possible for the socialist party of one country to exercise a true hegemony over the other national parties. The dread of being dominated increases in each national party in proportion as it becomes firmly established, consolidating its own existence and rendering itself independent of other socialist parties. International concentration is checked by the competition of the various national concentrations. Each national party stands on guard to prevent the others from extending their sphere of influence.[24] The result is that the international efficiency of the resolutions voted at the international congresses is almost insignificant. At the international socialist congress of Amsterdam, in 1904, the Belgian Anseele made it clear that he would not regard himself as bound by an international vote forbidding socialists to participate in bourgeois governments.[25] Thus, again, Vollmar, with the approval of the Germans, speaking at the international socialist congress at Stuttgart in 1907, repudiated any interference on the part of the French in the military policy of the German socialists, protesting in advance against any international resolution regulating the conduct of the socialists of all countries in case of war.[26] Considered from close at hand the international German principalities of the eighteenth century, consisting of nobles, ecclesiastics, and a few burgomasters, assemblies whose chief preoccupation was to avoid yielding to the prince a jot of their "freedoms," that is to say of their peculiar privileges. In just the same way, the various national socialist parties, in their international congresses, defend with the most jealous care all their prerogatives and their national particularism, being all determined to yield not an inch of ground in favour of His Majesty the International.[27]

---

[24] Eduard Bernstein expressed himself similarly as long ago as 1893. Cf. *Zur Geschichte u. Theorie des Sozialismus*, Edelheim, Berlin-Berne, 1901, p. 143.

[25] Cf. speech by Edouard Anseele, *Protokoll des internat. Soz. Congress, 1904*, "Vorwärts," Berlin, 1904, pp. 47-9.

[26] Cf. speech by Georg von Vollmar, *Protokoll des internaz. Soz. Congress, 1907*, "Vorwärts," Berlin, 1907, p. 93.

[27] Hence all coherency of tactics is lacking to international socialism, so that alike theoretically and practically every national "section" works in accordance with its own will and pleasure. One advocates protection, another free trade; one adheres to the *Kulturkampf*, whilst others agitate for the repeal of the laws against the Jesuits. (Cf. R. Michels, *Le Incoerenze internazionali nel Socialismo contemporaneo*, "Riforma Sociale," xiii, fasc. 8.)

The national oligarchies are willing to recognize the authority of international resolutions only when by an appeal to the authority of the International they can quell a troublesome faction in their own party. Sometimes the leaders of the minority secure an international bull to authenticate the purity of their socialist sentiments as contrasted with the majority, whom they accuse of heresy. Sometimes, on the other hand, it is the leaders of the majority who endeavour, on the international field, to gain a victory over the leaders of the minority, whom they have been unable to subdue within the limits of their national organization. A typical example of the former case is furnished by the action of the Guesdist minority, at the congress of Amsterdam in 1904, which endeavoured to discredit in the opinion of the International the ideas of their great cousin Jaurès in matters of internal policy. The manœuvre proved effective, for the Guesdists succeeded in attaching Jaurès to their chariot, and in holding him prisoner within the serried ranks of the unified French party.[28] An example of the second mode of action is afforded by the conduct of the Italian and German socialist parties in appealing to the decisions of the international congresses (Paris, 1889; Zurich, 1893; London, 1895) in order to get rid of their anti-parliamentary and anarchist factions.

Side by side with this international decentralization, we see to-day a vigorous national centralization. Certain limitations, however, must be imposed on this generalization.

In the modern labour movement, within the limits of the national organizations, we see decentralizing as well as centralizing tendencies at work. The idea of decentralization makes continuous progress, together with a revolt against the supreme authority of the central executive. But it would be a serious error to imagine that such centrifugal movements are the outcome of the democratic tendencies of the masses, or that these are ripe for independence. Their causation is really of an opposite character. The decentralization is the work of a compact minority of leaders who, when forced to subordinate themselves in the central executive of the party as a whole, prefer to withdraw to their own local spheres of action (minor state, province, or commune). A group of leaders which finds itself in a minority has no love for strong national centralization. Being unable to rule the whole country, it prefers to rule at home, considering it better

---

[28] Cf. the explanations of Bebel at the German congress of Bremen, 1904 (*Protokoll*, Berlin, 1904, p. 308).

to reign in hell than serve in heaven. Vollmar, for example, who in his own land possesses so great an influence that he has been called the uncrowned king of Bavaria, cannot consent to play second fiddle in the German national organization. He would rather be first in Munich than second in Berlin!

The rallying cry of the majority is centralization, while that of the minority is autonomy. Those of the minority, in order to gain their ends, are forced to carry on a struggle which often assumes the aspect of a genuine fight for liberty, and this is reflected in the terminology of the leaders, who declare themselves to be waging war against the new tyranny. When the leaders of the minority feel themselves exceptionally strong, they push their audacity to the point of attempting to deny the right to existence of the majority, as impersonated in the central executive. At the Italian socialist congress held at Imola in 1902, the leader of the Italian reformists, Filippo Turati, joined with his friends in putting forward a formal proposal to suppress the central executive. It was necessary, he said, to substitute for this obsolete, dictatorial, and decrepit institution the complete autonomy of the local organizations, or at least to replace it by a purely administrative and executive organism consisting of three specialist employees. He added that it was a form of jacobinism to wish to govern the whole party from above. The opponents of this democratic conception rejoined with an effective argument when they pointed out that if the central executive were abolished, the parliamentary deputies would remain the sole and uncontrolled masters of the party. Consequently, whenever it became necessary to take action upon some urgent question, when time was lacking to make a direct reference to the party as a whole, it would be the parliamentary group, deriving its authority not from the party but from the electorate, which would decide upon the line of conduct to be pursued.[29] If we accept the hypothesis that a true democracy may exist within the party, the tendency to the subdivision of powers is unquestionably anti-democratic, while centralization is, on the other hand, the best way of giving incontestable validity to the will of the masses. From this point of view, Enrico Ferri was perfectly right when he told the reformists that the proposed abo-

---

[29] Such was the view put forward by Ferri, Longobardi, and others. When a vote was taken, the numbers were equal, and the central executive was retained (*Rendiconto del VII Congresso Nazionale del P. S. I., Imola, Settembre, 1902*, Libr. Soc. Ital., Rome, 1903, p. 79).

lition of the central executive would be equivalent to the suppression of the sovereignty of the members in general, since the executive is the legitimate expression of the mass-will, and derives its rights from the party congresses.[30]

This decentralizing movement which manifests itself within the various national socialist parties does not conflict with the essential principle of oligarchy. The minority in opposition, which has been thus careful to withdraw itself from the control of the central executive, proceeds within its own sphere of dominion to constitute itself into a centralized power no less unrestricted than the one against which it has been fighting. Thus such movements as we have been considering represent no more than an attempt to effect a partition of authority, and to split up the great oligarchies into a number of smaller oligarchies. In France and in Italy every socialist deputy endeavours to become as independent as possible of the central executive of his party, making himself supreme in his local organization. A similar process may be observed in Germany, where the persistence of numerous petty states, mutually independent, and each governed by its own parliament, has hitherto prevented the constitutional and administrative unification of the party throughout the country, and has greatly favoured decentralizing tendencies.[31] In consequence of this state of affairs we find in Germany that all the parties in the separate states, from Bavaria to Hesse, desire autonomy, independence of the central executive in Berlin. But this does not prevent each one of them from exercising a centralized authority within its own domain.

The decentralizing currents in German socialism, and more particularly those of the German south, are adverse to centralization only as far as concerns the central executive of Berlin, whilst within their own spheres they resist federalism with the utmost emphasis.[32] Their opposition to the centralization in Berlin

---

[30] *Idem*, p. 79.

[31] Certain theorists cover these decentralizing tendencies with the mantle of science. Cf. Arthur Schulz, *Oekonomische und politische Entwicklungstendenzen in Deutschland*, Birth, Munich, 1909, p. 95. The sub-title of this interesting work is *Ein Versuch die Autonomieforderung der suddeutschen sozialdemokratischen Landesorganisationen theoretisch zu Begründen.* Thus the work is in effect an attempt to provide a theoretical foundation for the claims to autonomy advanced by the socialist organizations in the various states of southern Germany.

[32] This was pointed out by Adolf Braun at the Bavarian socialist congress held at Schweinfurt in 1906.

takes the form of a desire in the local parties to retain financial independence of the central treasury. At the Schweinfurt congress in 1906, Ehrhart, socialist deputy to the Bavarian diet, said: "It comes to this, the central executive has the management of the money which goes to Berlin, but it is for us to decide how we shall spend the money which is kept here."[33] Hugo Lindemann of Würtemberg, one of the most ardent adversaries of the Prussianization of the party and an advocate of federalism, has declared that it is undesirable to deplete the local finances of the South German states in favour of the central treasury in Berlin, where the executive is always inclined to a policy of hoarding money for its own sake.[34]

The struggles within the modern democratic parties over this problem of centralization versus decentralization are of great scientific importance from several points of view. It would be wrong to deny that the advocates of both tendencies bring forward a notable array of theoretical considerations, and occasionally make valid appeals to moral conceptions. We have, however, to disabuse our minds of the idea that the struggle is really one for or against oligarchy, for or against popular sovereignty or the sovereignty of the party masses. The tendency to decentralization of the party rule, the opposition to international centralization (to the far-reaching authority of international bureaux, committees, congresses), or to national centralization (to the authority of the party executives), has nothing to do with the desire for more individual liberty.

The democratic tendency may be justified by practical reasons, and in particular by differences in the economic or social situation of the working classes in the various districts, or by other local peculiarities. The tendencies to local, provincial, or regional autonomy are in fact the outcome of effective and ineradicable differences of environment. In Germany, the socialists of the south feel themselves to be divided as by an ocean from their comrades of the north. They claim the right of self-government and participation in government because they live in countries where parliamentarism already possesses a glorious history dating from more than a century back, whereas Prussia is still thoroughly imbued with the authoritarian and feudal spirit. They claim it also because in the south agriculture is

---

[33] "Volksstimme" of Frankfort, March 6, 1906.
[34] Hugo Lindemann, *Centralismus u. Föderalismus in der Sozialdemokratie,* "Soz. Monatsh.," viii (x), No. 4.

carried on mainly under a system of petty proprietorship, whereas in the central and eastern provinces of Germany large landed estates predominate. The result is that class differences, with their consequent differences of mental outlook, are less conspicuous in the south than in the north, so that the opposition to the socialists is of a different character in the two regions. In the struggles between the northern and the southern leaders within the socialist party, struggles which are often lively and at times extremely violent, each section levels the same accusation against the other, declaring it to belong to a country in which civilization is comparatively backward and where theoretical conceptions are obsolete. The socialists of the north contend that those of the south are still living in a petty bourgeois, pacific, countrified environment, whereas they themselves, in the land of large-scale manufacture, represent the future. The men of the south proudly reply that it is they who live in conditions to which their comrades of the north have yet to attain, by abolishing the large landed estates and by suppressing the class of junkers.[35]

Similar environmental differences divide the Italian socialists. Here also the socialists of the south demand complete autonomy, contending that the theoretical basis of socialism in the south is different from that in the north. They say that in the former kingdom of Naples the actual conditions of production and distribution are not such as to establish a sharp distinction between the two classes which according to classical socialism exist everywhere in strife. Consequently the introduction into this region of the Marxist revolutionary propaganda would marshal against socialism, not the great and medium landowners alone, but also the petty proprietors.[36] Whilst the socialists of the plain of the Po fiercely oppose a duty upon grain because this would increase the cost of living for the labouring masses agglomerated in great cities, the socialists of the south have on several occasions declared in favour of the existing protectionist system, because its suppression would bring about a crisis in production in a region where proletarians and employers all alike live by agriculture.[37]

---

[35] Arthur Schulz, *Oekonomische u. Politische Entwicklungstendenzen,* ed. cit., pp. 11, 25, 67.

[36] Francesco Ciccotti, *Socialismo e Cooperativismo agricolo nell' Italia Meridionale,* Nerbini, Florence, 1900, p. 8.

[37] Cf. a speech by Gaetano Salvemini at the socialist congress of Florence, September 21, 1908 (*Resoconto,* p. 122).

Again, in the north, where manufacturing industry is dominant, the socialists disapproved of the Tripolitan campaign, whereas in the south, where they are for the most part agriculturists, an enthusiastic sentiment in favour of territorial expansion prevailed. In addition to these reasons, which may be termed intrinsic because they derive from the objective differences between the north and the south, we find that an opposition between the socialists of the two areas arises from the attitude of the government in the respective regions. The Italian Government is double-faced, being liberal in the north, but often very much the reverse in the south, for here it is largely in the hands of local coteries which, in a region where the voters are scattered, become the sole arbiters in times of election. In the year 1902, when Giolitti was in power, this duplex attitude of the government gave rise to a serious difference within the socialist party, for the socialists of the north did not disguise their ardent desire to participate in government, whilst those of the south (although their tendencies were rather reformist than revolutionary) attacked the government fiercely.[38]

Thus, as has been shown at length, the various tendencies towards decentralization which manifest themselves in almost all the national parties, whilst they suffice to prevent the formation of a single gigantic oligarchy, result merely in the creation of a number of smaller oligarchies, each of which is no less powerful within its own sphere. The dominance of oligarchy in party life remains unchallenged.

---

[38] Cf. Alessandro Tasca di Cutò, *Dell' Opera antisociale del Ministero nel Mezzogiorno*, and *Sincerita*, "Avanti," December 4 and 11, 1902.

PART THREE

THE EXERCISE OF POWER AND ITS PSYCHOLOGICAL REACTION UPON THE LEADERS

CHAPTER I

PSYCHOLOGICAL METAMORPHOSIS OF THE LEADERS

THE apathy of the masses and their need for guidance has as its counterpart in the leaders a natural greed for power. Thus the development of the democratic oligarchy is accelerated by the general characteristics of human nature. What was initiated by the need for organization, administration, and strategy is completed by psychological determinism.

The average leader of the working-class parties is morally not lower, but on the whole higher, in quality than the average leader of the other parties.[1] This has sometimes been unreservedly admitted by the declared adversaries of socialism.[2] Yet it cannot be denied that the permanent exercise of leadership exerts upon the moral character of the leaders an influence which is essentially pernicious. Yet this also, from a certain point of view, is perhaps good. The bitter words which La Bruyère applied to the great men of the court of Louis XIV, that the imitative mania and veneration exhibited towards them by the masses would have grown into an absolute idolatry, if it had occurred to any of them to be simply good men as well as great ones—these words, *mutatis mutandis*, could be applied with equal truth to the leaders of the vast democratic movements of our own days.[3]

In the majority of instances, and above all at the opening of his career, the leader is sincerely convinced of the excellence of the principles he advocates. Le Bon writes with good reason: "Le meneur a d'abord été le plus souvent un mené. Il a lui-

---

[1] For documentary proof of this assertion as far as the Italian labour movement is concerned cf. R. Michels, *Il Proletariato e la Borghesia nel Movimento socialista Italiano*, Bocca, Turin, 1908, pp. 28-58, 68-76, 106-14, 265-391; also R. Michels, *Der ethische Faktor in der Parteipolitik Italiens,* "Zeitschrift für Politik," vol. iii, fasc. 1, pp. 56-91.

[2] Vilfredo Pareto, *Les Systèmes socialistes*, ed. cit., vol. i, p. 61; W. Sombart, *Dennoch! zur Theorie u. Geschichte der gewerkschaftlichen Arbeiterbewegung*, Fischer, Jena, 1900, p. 107.

[3] La Bruyère, *Caractères*, Penaud, Paris, p. 156.

même été hypnotisé par l'idée dont il est ensuite devenu l'apôtre."[4] In many cases the leader, at first no more than a single molecule of the mass, has become detached from this involuntarily, without asking whither his instinctive action was leading him, without any personal motive whatever. He has been pushed forward by a clearer vision, by a profounder sentiment, and by a more ardent desire for the general good; he has been inspired by the elasticity and seriousness of his character and by his warm sympathy for his fellows.[5] It is obvious that this will be true above all where the leader does not find already established a solid organization capable of offering remunerative employment, but where his first step must be to found his own party. But this must not be taken to mean that wherever a well-organized party already exists the leader seeks at the outset to gratify his personal interests.

It is by no means always by deliberate desire that people become officers of the masses. Using familiar French terms, we may express this more clearly by saying that not every *arrivé* was at first an *arriviste*. But he who has once attained to power will not readily be induced to return to the comparatively obscure position which he formerly occupied.[6] The abandonment of a public position obtained at the cost of great efforts and after many years of struggle is a luxury which only a "grand seigneur" or a man exceptionally endowed with the spirit of self-sacrifice can afford. Such self-denial is too hard for the average man.

The consciousness of power always produces vanity, an undue belief in personal greatness. The desire to dominate, for good or for evil, is universal.[7] These are elementary psychological facts. In the leader, the consciousness of his personal worth,[8]

---

[4] Gustave le Bon, *Psychologie des Foules,* ed. cit., p. 106. Cf. also S. G. Hobson, *Boodle and Cant,* "International Socialist Review," Chicago, 1902, ii, No. 8, p. 585.

[5] Ettore Ciccotti, *Montecitorio,* ed. cit., p. 54.

[6] Pio Viazzi, one of the most trusted deputies in the Italian Chamber, a member of the republican party, has declared that any one who has once been elected to parliament will henceforward do all he can to secure reelection (Pio Viazzi, *Le Gioie della Deputazione,* "Rivista Populare," anno xv, No. 9).

[7] "L'amour de la puissance ainsi que l'amour de l'indépendance et de la liberté, sont des passions inhérentes à l'homme" (Holbach, *Systèmes sociales, ou Principes naturelles de la Morale et de la Politique,* Niogret, Paris, 1822, vol. i, p. 196).

[8] "Beyond question individuality is indispensable wherever it is requi-

and of the need which the mass feels for guidance, combine to induce in his mind a recognition of his own superiority (real or supposed), and awake, in addition, that spirit of command which exists in the germ in every man born of woman.[9] We see from this that every human power seeks to enlarge its prerogatives. He who has acquired power will almost always endeavour to consolidate it and to extend it, to multiply the ramparts which defend his position, and to withdraw himself from the control of the masses. Bakunin, the founder of anarchizing socialism, contended that the possession of power transformed into a tyrant even the most devoted friend of liberty.[10] It is certain that the exercise of power produces a profound and ineffaceable change in the character. This is admirably described by Alphonse Daudet when he writes: "Bien vite, s'il s'agit de l'affreuse politique, nos qualités tournent au pire: l'enthousiasme devient hypocrisie; l'éloquence, faconde et boniment; le scepticisme léger, escroquerie; l'amour de ce qui brille, fureur du lucre et du luxe à tout prix; la sociabilité, le besoin de plaire, se font lâcheté, faiblesse, et palinodie."[11] To retain their influence over the masses

---

site to incite deliberately to conscious acts of volition. Man derives pleasure from the expression of his individuality in the activities which, thanks to it, are brought to pass. We should none of us be willing to exchange our own individualities for those of others, just as we should be unwilling to change our physiognomy. This inclination results in part from habit, but in part from self-love. The individual is used to his own defects and would not like to be deprived of his merits" (Eduard von Hartmann, *Gedanken über Individualismus,* "Türmer-Jahrbuch," Stuttgart, 1903, p. 215).

[9] Cf. the psychological reflections of Ugo Foscolo on the evolution of Napoleon I, *Ultime Lettere di Giacopo Ortio,* Perino, Rome, 1892, p. 143.

[10] Bakunin, *Il Socialismo e Mazzini,* F. Serantoni, Rome-Florence, 1905, p. 22.—Similarly Herzen writes: "Donnez à Proudhon le portefeuille des finances, ou faites-le président, et il sera une espèce de Bonaparte" (Alexandre Herzen, *De l'autre Rive,* Geneva, 1871, 3rd ed., p. 186).—Shelley's lines on this subject are singularly apposite:—

"... The man
Of virtuous soul commands not, nor obeys.
Power, like a desolating pestilence,
Pollutes whate'er it touches; and obedience,
Bane of all genius, virtue, freedom, truth,
Makes slaves of men, and, of the human frame,
A mechanized automaton."

—*Queen Mab,* § iii, ll. 174-80.

[11] Léon Daudet, *Alphonse Daudet,* ed. cit., p. 179.

the leaders study men, note their weaknesses and their passions, and endeavour to turn these to their own advantage.[12]

When the leaders are not persons of means and when they have no other source of income, they hold firmly to their positions for economic reasons, coming to regard the functions they exercise as theirs by inalienable right. Especially is this true of manual workers who, since becoming leaders, have lost aptitude for their former occupation. For them, the loss of their positions would be a financial disaster, and in most cases it would be altogether impossible for them to return to their old way of life.[13] They have been spoiled for any other work than that of propaganda.[14] Their hands have lost the callosities of the manual toiler, and are likely to suffer only from writer's cramp.

Those leaders, again, who are refugees from the bourgeoisie are used up after having devoted a few years to the service of the socialist party. It was as youthful enthusiasts that they joined the organized workers and soon attained to dominant positions. The life they then had to lead, however great may have been its advantages in certain respects, was one full of fatigue and hardship, and, like all careers in which fame can be acquired, was extremely exhausting to the nervous system. Such men grow old before their time. What are they to do? They have become estranged from their original profession, which is altogether out of relation with their chosen vocation of professional politician. A barrister, indeed, can continue to practise his profession, and may even devote almost all his time to it, without being forced to abandon the party. The political struggle and the life of the lawyer have more than one point of contact, for is not the political struggle a continuous act of advocacy? The barrister who plays a leading part in public life will find many opportunities for the gratification of his love of oratory and argument, and will have no lack of chances for the display of the power of his lungs and the expressiveness of his

---

[12] Ostrogorsky, *La Démocratie, etc.*, ed. cit., ii, p. 344.

[13] Cf. Part IV, chap. v.

[14] This is not merely true of "those lazy fellows who are good for nothing more than the parrot-like repetition of a few phrases culled from the party literature, and of those whose only equipment is to have a voice like that of a bull," from whose influence Sombart would like to see the workers freed, and for whose eradication he recommends, in especial, attention to the practical work of the trade unions (Werner Sombart, *Dennoch!*, ed. cit., p. 91)—but it applies with equal force to the trade-union officials destined to replace the type to which he objects.

gestures. It is very different with men of science. These, if they play an active part in the life of the party, be it as journalists, as propagandists, or as parliamentary deputies, find that their scientific faculties undergo a slow but progressive atrophy. Having become absorbed in the daily political round, they are dead for their discipline, for they no longer have time for the serious study of scientific problems and for the continuous development of their intellectual faculties.

There are, however, additional reasons for the mental transformation which the leaders undergo as the years pass.

As far as concerns the leaders of bourgeois origin in the working-class parties, it may be said that they have adhered to the cause of the proletariat either on moral grounds, or from enthusiasm, or from scientific conviction.[15] They crossed the Rubicon when they were still young students, still full of optimism and juvenile ardour. Having gone over to the other side of the barricade to lead the enemies of the class from which they sprang, they have fought and worked, now suffering defeats and now gaining victories. Youth has fled; their best years have been passed in the service of the party or of the ideal. They are ageing, and with the passing of youth, their ideals have also passed, dispersed by the contrarieties of daily struggles, often, too, expelled by newly acquired experiences which conflict with the old beliefs. Thus it has come to pass that many of the leaders are inwardly estranged from the essential content of socialism. Some of them carry on a difficult internal struggle against their own scepticism; others have returned, consciously or unconsciously, to the ideals of their pre-socialist youth.

Yet for those who have been thus disillusioned, no backward path is open. They are enchained by their own past. They have a family, and this family must be fed. Moreover, regard for their political good name makes them feel it essential to persevere in the old round. They thus remain outwardly faithful to the cause to which they have sacrificed the best years of their life. But, renouncing idealism, they have become opportunists. These former believers, these sometime altruists, whose fervent hearts aspired only to give themselves freely, have been transformed into sceptics and egoists whose actions are guided solely by cold calculation.

As we have previously seen, these new elements do not join the

---

[15] Cf. Part IV, chap. ii.

party with the declared or even the subconscious aim of attaining one day to leadership; their only motives have been the spirit of sacrifice and the love of battle. Visionaries, they see a brother in every comrade and a step towards the ideal in every party meeting.[16] Since, however, in virtue of their superiority (in part congenital and in part acquired), they have become leaders, they are in the course of years enslaved by all the appetites which arise from the possession of power, and in the end are not to be distinguished from those among their colleagues who became socialists from ambition, from those who have from the first deliberately regarded the masses as no more than an instrument which they might utilize towards the attainment of their own personal ambitions.

It cannot be denied that the factor of individuality plays its part in all this, for different individualities react differently to the same environment. Just as women and girls in similar erotic situations act differently in accordance with their varying degrees of congenital sexual irritability and with the differences that have been induced in them by moral education, remaining immaculate, becoming demi-vierges, or yielding to advances, so also the specific qualities of the leaders, in so far as these are acquired and not immanent, manifest themselves differently in different individuals in face of the numerous temptations to which they are exposed in party life.[17] The sense of satiety which arises in those who have attained their end varies greatly in intensity from person to person. There are similar variations in adaptability to a new and anti-democratic environment, or to

---

[16] This may be seen in the accounts which many socialists have given of their first adhesion to the party. For instance: "And from these assemblies come forth the new converts from the bourgeoisie, freed from their last doubts, having attained to a new state of mind, to a peace hitherto unknown; the younger men full of thoughts unfamiliar to their heedless youth; the older ones rejuvenated in heart and spirit; all filled with a profound sense of complacency, as if in the meeting they have attended there had not been talk merely, but action, labour for the good of the world, dispersing for the future the blessed seed of truth, benevolence, and justice" (Edmondo de Amicis, *Le Discordie socialiste*, "Avanti," anno viii, No. 2665, 1907). As regards Holland, F. Domela Nieuwenhuis writes in similar terms in *Van Christen Tot Anarchist*, ed. cit., p. 100. As Turati well expresses it, this is "the golden age, the age of apostolic, pure, and immaculate spirits" (Filippo Turati, *Il Partito socialista italiano*, ed. cit., p. 10).

[17] This is admitted by Arturo Labriola, *Riforme e Rivoluzione sociale*, ed. cit., p. 225.

an environment hostile to the ideas which the individual has at heart. Some socialists, for instance, are so greatly intimidated by the parliamentary milieu that they are ashamed in that milieu to make use of the expressions "class struggle" and "collectivism,"[18] although it is to the unwearying insistence upon these ideas that they owe their present position. Others among their comrades find amid all the circumstances of their new life that right feeling and that old courage of conviction which cannot be prescribed by any formal rules. It is absurd to maintain, as does Giuseppe Prezzolini, that in the parliamentary atmosphere it is as impossible for a deputy to preserve his socialist purity as it would be for a Joseph to remain chaste while frequently visiting brothels.[19] Such a view is false, if only for the reason that here, as in all social phenomena, we have to consider the personal as well as the environmental factor. It is nevertheless true that in the course of party evolution, as the led becomes a subordinate leader, and from that a leader of the first rank, he himself undergoes a mental evolution, which often effects a complete transformation in his personality.[20] When this happens, the leader often sees in his own transformation nothing more than a reflex of a transformation in the surrounding world. The times have changed, he tells us, and consequently a new tactic and a new theory are necessary. A greater maturity of judgment corresponds to the greater maturity of the new age. The reformist and revisionist theory in the international socialist party is largely the outcome of the psychological need to furnish an explanation and an excuse for the metamorphosis which has taken place in the leaders. A few years ago, one of the leaders of the Italian clericals, after declaring that triumphant reform-

---

[18] Cf. Ettore Ciccotti, *Psicologia del Movimento socialista*, ed. cit., p. 292.

[19] G. Prezzolini, *La Teoria sindacalista*, Perrella, Naples, 1909, p. 65.

[20] At the German socialist congress of Frankfort (1894) it was above all the present leaders of the great German trade unions, such as Bömelburg, Legien, and Timm, who contended that the salaries of the employees of the labour movement should be restricted to a very moderate figure (*Protokoll*, p. 69). In the seventies, Eugène Fournière actively opposed Louis Blanc, the former maintaining the socialist principle that the socialist deputies ought to pay over to the party treasury the whole of the 9,000 francs which was at that time the deputy's salary (Jean Allemane, *Le Socialisme en France*, Imp. Ouvière, rue St. Sauveur, Paris, 1900, p. 7). Thirty years later, this same Fournière, now himself a deputy, when a party congress decided that a portion of the salary of the socialist deputies (meanwhile increased to 15,000 francs) must be paid over to the party treasury, declared that he could not spare any of it.

ism, having an evolutionary and legalist character, was in these respects preferable to strict syndicalism, went on to say that in his view the basis of reformist socialism was still the materialist conception of man, of life, and of history, but further corrupted by contact with the utilitarian and Epicurean spirit of the free-thinking bourgeoisie, and that it was consequently even more profoundly anti-Christian than the ideas of the ultra-revolutionists.[21] There is a kernel of truth in this idea. However much we are forced to recognize that reformism sometimes manifests itself as a sane rebellion against the *apriorism* of orthodox Marxist dogma, and as a scientific reaction against the phraseology of pseudo-revolutionary stump-orators, it is nevertheless incontestable that reformism has a logical and causal connection with the insipid and blasé sciolism and with the decadent tendencies which are so plainly manifest in a large section of the modern bourgeois literary world. In many instances, in fact, reformism is no more than the theoretical expression of the scepticism of the disillusioned, of the outwearied, of those who have lost their faith; it is the socialism of non-socialists with a socialist past.

It is above all the sudden passage from opposition to participation in power which exercises a powerful influence on the mentality of the leaders. It is evident that in a period of proscriptions and persecutions of the new doctrine and its advocates on the part of society and of the state, the morality of the party-leaders will maintain itself at a much higher level than in a period of triumph and of peace, if only for the reason that in the former conditions those of egotistic temperament and those inspired by narrow personal ambition will hold aloof from the party since they have no desire for the martyr's crown.[22] These considerations apply, not merely to the old leaders who have been members of the party during its days of tribulation, and whose qualities, if not completely corrupted by the sun of governmental

---

[21] Filippo Meda, *Il Partito socialista in Italia dell' Internazionale al Riformismo,* Lib. ed. Florentina, Florence, 1909, p. 46.

[22] In troublous times the socialists are glad to avail themselves of references to the high ethical qualities of their leaders as a means of agitation. A pamphlet issued in 1894 by the Rhenish socialist Wilhelm Gewehr, *Warum der Kampf gegen die Sozialdemokratie?* (Grimpe, Elberfeld, p. 32), closes with the words: ''Let him who has honourable and loyal intentions towards the poor place himself on the side of the socialists, who are fighting and sacrificing themselves on behalf of the ideal!'' In times of struggle such utterances have no ludicrous flavour.—Regarding Italian conditions, **cf. R.** Michels, *Der ethische Faktor, etc.,* ed. cit., pp. 68 et seq.

favour (so as to lead them to abandon the cause of the proletariat), are yet so greatly changed as to render them almost unrecognizable by the masses; but it is equally true of the new
leaders who do not put in an appearance until the sun has begun
to shine upon the party.

As long as the struggle on behalf of the oppressed brings
to those engaged in it nothing more than a crown of thorns,
those members of the bourgeoisie who adhere to socialism must
fulfil functions in the party exacting great personal disinterestedness. Bourgeois adherents do not become a danger to
socialism until the labour movement, abandoning its principles,
enters the slippery paths of a policy of compromise.

At the international congress of Amsterdam, Bebel exclaimed
with perfect truth, in answer to Jaurès: "When a socialist
party forms an alliance with a section of the bourgeoisie, and
institutes a policy of co-operation with the government, not only
does it repel its own best militants, driving them into the ranks
of the anarchists, or into isolated action, but it also attracts to
itself a swarm of bourgeois of very dubious value." [23] In Italy,
during the period of persecutions, all scientific investigators
bore striking witness to the high moral qualities of the socialist
leaders. No sooner, however, had the socialist party (towards
1900) begun to display friendship for the government than
voices were heard on all hands deploring a deterioration in the
composition of the party, and denouncing the numerous elements
entering the party simply because they regarded it as the best
means by which they could secure a share in the loaves and
fishes of public administration.[24]

Wherever the socialists have gained control of the munici-

---

[23] From the report in "Het Volk," v, No. 1341. In the German *Protokoll* (which, be it remarked in passing, is extremely inadequate) this
passage is not reported. Bebel's observation is in flat contradiction with
what he has frequently said in the Reichstag, that in his view the carrying
of socialism into effect after the victory would be greatly facilitated by
the inevitable adhesion to the various branches of the new administration
of numerous competent elements from the official bureaucracy. (Cf.
August Bebel, *Zukunftstaat und Sozialdemokratie*, p. 13; speech in Reichstag, February 3, 1893.)

[24] Cf. R. Michels, *Il Proletariato e la Borghesia, etc.*, ed. cit., p. 348;
Romeo Soldi, *Die politische Lage in Italien*, "Neue Zeit," xxi, No. 30, p.
116; Giovanni Lerda, *Sull' Organizzazione politica del Partito socialista
italiano*, a report to the Italian socialist congress of 1902, Coop. Tip.-Ed.,
Imola, 1902, p. 10; Filippo Turati, *Il Partito socialista e l'attuale Momento
politico*, "Critica Sociale," Milan, 3rd ed., 1901.

palities, wherever they run people's banks and distributive co-operative societies, wherever they have remunerative posts at their disposal, we cannot fail to observe a notable decline in their moral level, and to see that the ignorant and the self-seeking now constitute the majority among them.

CHAPTER II

BONAPARTIST IDEOLOGY

NAPOLEON I, as head of the state, desired to be regarded as the chosen of the people. In his public activities, the emperor boasted that he owed his power to the French people alone. After the battle of the Pyramids, when his glory began to attain its acme, the general imperiously demanded that there should be conferred on him the title of *premier représentant du peuple,* although hitherto the style of "popular representative" had been exclusively reserved for members of the legislative bodies.[1] Later, when by a plebiscite he had been raised to the throne of France, he declared that he considered his power to repose exclusively upon the masses.[2] The Bonapartist interpretation of popular sovereignty was a personal dictatorship conferred by the people in accordance with constitutional rules.[3]

The Cæsarism of Napoleon III was founded in still greater measure upon the principle of popular sovereignty. In his letter to the National Assembly written from London on May 24, 1848, the pretender to the crown recognized the French Republic which was the issue of the February revolution and was founded upon universal suffrage. At the same time he claimed for himself, and at the expense of the exiled king Louis Philippe, a hereditary right to insurrection and to the throne. This recognition and this claim were derived by him from the same principle. With simultaneous pride and humility he wrote: "En présence d'un

---

[1] Louis Napoléon Bonaparte, *Idées napoléoniennes,* 1839, Italian ed., Pelazza, Turin, 1852, p. 74.

[2] *Ibid.,* p. 119.

[3] At times, indeed, a casuistical significance was given to the term "popular sovereignty" which deprived it of all practical meaning. Thus in St. Helena Napoleon said: "Le premier devoir du prince est de faire ce que veut le peuple; mais ce que veut le peuple n'est presque jamais ce qu'il dit; sa volonté, ses besoins doivent se trouver moins dans sa bouche que dans le cœur du prince" (Emmanuel Augustin Dieudonné Las Cases, *Mémorial de Ste-Hélène,* Paris, 1821, vol. ii, p. 82). This note is often sounded in the public utterances of modern party leaders (cf. pp. 152, 153).

roi élu par deux cents députés, je pouvais me rappeler être l'héritier d'un empire fondé sur l'assentiment de quatre millions de français; en présence de la souveraineté nationale (résultante du suffrage universel), je ne peux et ne veux revendiquer que mes droits de citoyen français."[4] But Napoleon III did not merely recognize in popular sovereignty the source of his power, he further made that sovereignty the theoretical basis of all his practical activities. He made himself popular in France by declaring that he regarded himself as merely the executive organ of the collective will manifested in the elections, and that he was entirely at the disposition of that will, prepared in all things to accept its decisions.[5] With great shrewdness, he continually repeated that he was no more than an instrument, a creature of the masses. While still president he declared in a speech that he was prepared as circumstances might dictate either for *abnégation* or for *persévérance,* or, in other words, that he was ready to go or to remain.[6] It was the pure Bonapartist spirit which was expressed by Ollivier, the keeper of the seals, when in the Chamber, in one of the stormy sittings of the summer of 1870, he declared: "Nous vous appartenons; vous nous reprendrez quand vous voudrez, nous serons toujours là pour subir vos reproches et vos anathèmes."[7]

Bonapartism recognized the validity of the popular will to such an extreme degree as to concede to that will the right of self-destruction: popular sovereignty could suppress itself. Yet if we look at the matter from a purely human point of view, popular sovereignty is inalienable. Moreover, if we think of succeeding generations, it seems illogical and unjust that those of this generation should claim the moral right of renouncing on behalf of their descendants. Consequently the democrats of the Napoleonic epoch insisted most energetically that the power of popular sovereignty was limited to this extent, that it did not carry with it any right of abdication.[8] Bonapartism is the theory of individual dominion originating in the collective will, but

---

[4] Eugène Tenot, *Paris en Décembre 1851. Etudes historiques sur le Coup d'Etat,* Le Chevalier, Paris, 1868, p. 10.

[5] Victor Hugo, *Napoléon le Petit,* Jeffs, London, 1852, p. 54.

[6] E. Tenot, *Paris en Décembre 1851,* ed. cit., p. 26.

[7] Garnier Pagès, *L'Opposition et l'Empire. Dernière Séance du Corps Législatif, 1870.* Bibl. Démocratique, Paris, 1872, p. 157.

[8] G. B. A. Godin, *La Souveraineté et les Droits du Peuple,* Bibl. Dém., Paris, 1874, pp. 115 et seq.

tending to emancipate itself of that will and to become sovereign
in its turn. In its democratic past it finds a shield against the
dangers which may threaten its anti-democratic present.[9] In
Bonapartism, the rule of Cæsar (as was said by a wit of the last
years of the second empire) becomes a regular organ of the popular sovereignty. "Il sera la démocratie personnifiée, la nation
faite homme."[10] It is the synthesis of two antagonistic concepts, democracy and autocracy.[11]

---

[9] Emile Littré, in his *Dictionnaire de la Langue française* (Hachette,
Paris, 1863), under the word *Césarisme*, speaks of "princes portés au gouvernement par la démocratie, mais revêtus d'un pouvoir absolu" (vol. i,
p. 534).

[10] Cf. Edouard Laboulaye, *Paris en Amérique*, Charpentier, Paris, 1869,
24th ed., p. 381.—The Bonapartist conception of popular sovereignty is
not democratic, while, on the other hand, it in no way corresponds with the
political conception of legitimate monarchy. Jurieu, a Protestant pastor,
endeavoured in the seventeenth century to find a theoretic foundation for
absolute monarchy in popular sovereignty, but without success. Bossuet,
the greatest writer on the idea of the state in the days of Louis XIV,
paraphrased the ideas of Jurieu in the following ironical sentences: "Le
peuple fait les souverains et donne la souveraineté: donc le peuple possède
la souveraineté et la possède dans un degré plus éminent; car celui qui communique doit posséder ce qu'il communique, d'une manière plus parfaite,
et quoiqu'un peuple qui a fait un souverain ne puisse plus exercer la souveraineté par lui-même, c'est pourtant la souveraineté du peuple qui est
exercée par le souverain; et l'exercice de la souveraineté, qui se fait par
un seul, n'empêche pas que la souveraineté ne soit dans le peuple comme
dans sa source, et comme dans son premier sujet" (Bossuet, *Cinquième
Avertissement aux Protestants sur les Lettres de M. Jurieu contre l'Histoire
des Variations*, Œuvres, Paris, 1743, vol. iv, p. 280).—Only in quite recent
times, in which, as we have seen, certain opportunists have endeavoured to
justify monarchy from a democratic standpoint, has the attempt of Julieu
been revived, although in a somewhat different form. In Germany, Friedrich Naumann issued the watchword "Democracy and Emperordom"
(*Demokratie und Kaisertum*). In Italy, Ettore Sacchi, the leader of
the bourgeois-radical party, has based his acceptance of the monarchy upon
the opinion that (in Italy) it is a democratic institution, in the first place
because it has been expressly sanctioned by the people, and in the second
place because the monarchy is now tacitly accepted by all (Giuseppe Rensi,
Gli, "Ancien Régime" e la Democrazia diretta, Colombi, Belinzona, 1902,
p. 7). It may, however, be pointed out that in the plebiscite of 1861, in
which the people who had been freed from their princes declared themselves
in favour of the rule of the House of Savoy, the question had really been

---

[11] Hohenlohe relates that in 1874, when he was ambassador in Paris, some
one said to him that the Frenchman is *démocrate* and *authoritaire*. Consequently the empire was the best form of government for the French and
was the hope of the future, for this form of government satisfied both
these popular needs (*Denkwürdigkeiten*, ed. cit., vol. ii, p. 126). Napo-

Once elected, the chosen of the people can no longer be opposed in any way. He personifies the majority, and all resistance to his will is antidemocratic. The leader of such a democracy is irremovable, for the nation, having once spoken, cannot contradict itself.[12] He is, moreover, infallible, for "l'Elu de six millions de suffrages exécute les volontés du peuple, il ne les trahi pas." It is reasonable and necessary that the adversaries of the government should be exterminated in the name of popular sovereignty, for the chosen of the people acts within his rights as representative òf the collective will, established in his position by a spontaneous decision.[13] It is the electors themselves, we are assured, who demand from the chosen of the people that he

---

put in such a way as to leave no other choice, for the alternatives proposed were the kingdom versus nothing at all. Further, if we were to accept the principle that tacit endurance signifies approval, every political situation would, apart from open rebellion of the ruled, be established upon a granite foundation of democracy. But such an idea of democracy is illogical, as false as is the logic of those bad governments which, as Macaulay says in one of his speeches, justify themselves by appealing to the aphorism: if the people is unruly, it is not ripe for liberty; while if it is quiet, it does not desire liberty.

---

leon III admirably characterized the nature of Bonapartism when he declared of his system that it was based on democracy, since all its powers were conferred by the people, whilst in organization it was hierarchical, since such an organization was essential to stimulate the capacities slumbering in the various degrees of society (*Idées Napoléoniennes*, ed. cit., p. 83).

[12] In the time of Napoleon I a subtle distinction was made between the terms *émaner* and *resider*. In 1814, Count Molé remarked to the emperor that in the declaration of the Council there were certain dangerous words which recalled nothing so much as the principles of 1793: "Elle commence par 'toute souveraineté réside dans le peuple.' Avec ce principe le peuple peut changer de gouvernement et de monarque tous les jours; il donne et retire à son gré la couronne, il pourra la refuser à votre fils; encore, s'il y avait *émane;* on pourrait dire qu'en déléguant à jamais à un homme et à sa race la souveraineté il aliène le droit de la lui retirer, mais *réside* ne laisse pas de bornes à l'instabilité des institutions et du trône." —"Votre observation est très juste, j'en suis frappé," replied the emperor (Comte Molé, *Les Cent-Jours*, Documents inédits, "Revue de la Révolution," 1888, vol. xi, p. 95).

[13] Such were the expressions used by Louis Napoleon in a speech at Lyons, immediately after he had been elected Life-President of the Republic (E. Tenot, *Paris en Décembre 1851*, ed. cit., p. 26).—When he first assumed the presidency in December 1848, Louis Napoleon, speaking to the Chamber, solemnly enunciated the principle: "Je verrai des ennemis de la Patrie dans tous ceux qui tenteraient de changer par des voies illégales ce que la France entière a établi" (V. Hugo, *Napoléon le Petit*, ed. cit., p. 16).

should use severe repressive measures, should employ force, should concentrate all authority in his own hands.[14] One of the consequences of the theory of the popular will being subsumed in the supreme executive is that the elements which intervene between the latter and the former, the public officials, that is to say, must be kept in a state of the strictest possible dependence upon the central authority, which, in its turn, depends upon the people.[15] The least manifestation of liberty on the part of the bureaucracy would be tantamount to a rebellion against the sovereignty of the citizens. The most characteristic feature of this view is the idea that the power of the chief of the state rests exclusively upon the direct will of the nation. Bonapartism does not recognise any intermediate links. The *coup d'état* of December 2, 1851, was represented as an emancipation of the people from the yoke of parliament, and as having for its necessary corollary a plebiscite. Victor Hugo compared the relationship between the parliament and the ministry under Napoleon III to the relationship between master and servants, the master (the ministry) being appointed by the emperor, and the servants (the parliament) being elected by the people.[16] This affirmation, though incontestable in fact, is theoretically inexact. In theory, every act of Bonapartism was perfectly legitimate, even if it led to the shedding of the blood of the citizens. The plebiscite was a purifying bath which gave legitimate sanction to every illegality. Napoleon III, when he received the formal announcement of his triumph in the plebiscite, declared that if in the *coup d'état* he had infringed the laws it was only in order to reenter the paths of legality: "Je ne suis sorti de la légalité que pour rentrer dans le droit." He was granted absolution by seven million votes.[17] This sanction by plebiscite, three times repeated by the French people, and given to the illegal government of the third Napoleon—confirmed as it was by innumerable and noisy demonstrations of popular sympathy —gave to accommodating republicans a ready pretext for passing from the side of the opposition to that of the monarchy. Was

---

[14] Napoleon III maintained that it was only on account of the democratic instincts of the first Napoleon that the emperor had not abolished the legislative bodies. The people would have had no objection to their abolition (*Idées Napoléoniennes,* ed. cit., p. 71).

[15] *Ibid.,* p. 38.

[16] V. Hugo, *Napoléon le Petit,* ed. cit., pp. 79, 80.

[17] E. Tenot, *Paris en Décembre, 1851,* ed. cit., pp. 206, 207.

not this plebiscitary Cæsarism established upon the same foundation as the republic of their dreams? Emile Ollivier divided the forms of government into the two great categories of personal and national government. The ruler in the case of a national government is no more than "un délégué de la nation pour l'exercice des droits sociaux."[18] In this manner his republican conscience was tranquillized and his conversion to Bonapartism could present itself as logical and in conformity with his principles.

The history of modern democratic and revolutionary parties and trade unions exhibits phenomena similar to those we have been analysing. The reasons are not far to seek. In democratic crowds, Bonapartism finds an eminently favourable soil, for it gives the masses the illusion of being masters of their masters; moreover, by introducing the practice of delegation it gives this illusion a legal colour which is pleasing to those who are struggling for their "rights." Delegation, and the abdication by the people of the direct exercise of power, are accomplished in strict accordance with all the rules, by a deliberate act of the popular will, and without that metaphysical divine intervention vaunted on its own behalf by the detested hereditary and legitimate monarchy. The chosen of the people thus seems to be invested in his functions by a spontaneous act of the popular will; he appears to be the creature of the people. This way of looking at the relations between the masses and the leaders is agreeable to the *amour propre* of every citizen, who says to himself: "Without me he would not be what he is; I have elected him; he belongs to me."

There is another reason, at once psychological and historical, why the masses accept without protest a certain degree of tyranny on the part of their elected leaders: it is because the crowd submits to domination more readily when each one of its units shares the possibility of approximating to power, and even of acquiring some power for himself. The bourgeois and the French peasants in the middle of the nineteenth century, imbued with democratic ideas, detested legitimate monarchy, but they gladly gave their votes to the third Napoleon, remembering how readily many of their fathers had become great dignitaries under his glorious uncle.[19]

---

[18] Emile Ollivier, *Le 19 janvier. Compte Rendu aux Electeurs de la III⁰ Circonscription de la Seine,* Paris, 1869, 7th ed. p. 119.
[19] Alexandre Herzen, *De l'autre Rive,* Geneva, 1871, 3rd ed., p. 119.—In

Similarly in the case of political parties, the weight of an oligarchy is rarely felt when the rights of the masses are codified, and when each member may in the abstract participate in power. In virtue of the democratic nature of his election, the leader of a democratic organization has more right than the born leader of the aristocracy to regard himself as the emanation of the collective will, and therefore to demand obedience and submission to his personal will. As a socialist newspaper puts it: "The party executive is the authority imposed by the party as a whole and thus incorporating the party authority. The first demand of democratic discipline is respect for the executive."[20] The absolute obedience which the organized mass owes to its leaders is the outcome of the democratic relationships existing between the leaders and the mass, and is merely the collective submission to the collective will.[21]

The leaders themselves, whenever they are reproached for an anti-democratic attitude, appeal to the mass-will from which their power is derived by election, saying: "Since the masses have elected us and re-elected us as leaders, we are the legitimate expression of their will and act only as their representatives."[22] It was a tenet of the old aristocracy that to disobey the orders of the monarch was to sin against God. In modern democracy it is held that no one may disobey the orders of the oligarchs, for in so doing the people sin against themselves, defying their own will spontaneously transferred by them to their representatives,[23] and thus infringing democratic principle. In

---

the light comedy *Le Gamin de Paris* by Bayard and Vanderburgh the words of the general typify the rôle of Napoleonism among the French common people: "Nous étions des enfants de Paris . . . des imprimeurs . . . des fils de charrons, nous avions du cœur . . . nous voulions faire notre chemin . . . nous serions peutêtre restés en route . . . sans l'Empereur! . . . qui s'est trouvé là . . . qui nous a emportés dans son tourbillon. . . . La chance était tout!" (Velhagen, Bielefeld, 1861, 4th ed., p. 77).

[20] "Düsseldorfer Volkszeitung," November 13, 1905.

[21] This idea is admirably expressed by Rienzi (Van Kol), *Socialisme et Liberté*, ed. cit., p. 249.

[22] This argument is repeatedly employed by socialist speakers. Their reasoning is that the very fact that the leaders are still leaders proves that they have the support of the masses—otherwise they would not be where they are. (Cf. Karl Legien's speech at the socialist congress of Jena (Protokoll, "Vorwärts," Berlin, 1905, p. 265); also P. J. Troelstra, *Inzake Partijleiding. Toelichtingen en Gegevens*, ed. cit., p. 97.)

[23] During the second empire the like reasoning was applied to defend

democracies, the leaders base their right to command upon the democratic omnipotence of the masses. Every employee of the party owes his post to his comrades, and is entirely dependent upon their goodwill. We may thus say that in a democracy each individual himself issues, though indirectly, the orders which come to him from above.[24] Thus the reasoning by which the leaders' claim to obedience is defended and explained is, in theory, clear and unanswerable. In practice, however, the election of the leaders, and above all their re-election, is effected by such methods and under the influence of suggestions and other methods of coercion so powerful that the freedom of choice of the masses is considerably impaired.[25] In the history of party life it is undeniable that the democratic system is reduced, in ultimate analysis, to the right of the masses, at stated intervals, to choose masters to whom in the interim they owe unconditional obedience.

Under these conditions, there develops everywhere in the leaders, alike in the democratic political parties and in the trade unions, the same habit of thought. They demand that the masses should not merely render obedience, but that they should blindly and without murmuring carry out the orders which they, the leaders, issue deliberately and with full understanding of the circumstances. To the leaders it is altogether inconceivable that the actions of the supreme authority can be subjected to criticism, for they are intimately convinced that they stand above criticism, that is to say above the party. Engels, who was endowed with an extremely keen sense of the essence of democracy, regarded it as deplorable that the leaders of the German socialist party could not accustom themselves to the idea that the mere fact of being installed in office did not give them the right to be treated with more respect than any other comrade.[26]

---

the plebiscitary emperordom. For instance, Edmond About, one of the few distinguished democratic writers who had gone over to the Napoleonic camp, wrote: ''Ce n'est pas obéir que de se conformer aux lois qu'on a faites, de remplir ses engagements envers les chefs qu'on a choisis: c'est se commander à soi-même'' (Edmond About, *Le Progrès*, Hachette, Paris, 1864, p. 67).

[24] We owe to Georges Sorel the rediscovery of the relationships between democracy in general and absolutism, and their point of intersection in centralization. Cf., for instance, his *Les Illusions du Progrès*, Rivière, Paris, 1908, pp. 9 et seq.

[25] Cf. pp. 156 et seq.

[26] F. Engels, in a letter dated March 21, 1891; also Karl Marx, in a let-

It is especially exasperating to the leaders when the comrades are not content with mere criticism, but act in opposition to the leaders' advice.[27] When they speak of their differences with those whom they regard as inferiors in education and intelligence, they are unable to restrain their moral indignation at such a profound lack of discipline.[28] When the masses "kick against the advice of the leaders they have themselves chosen," they are accused of a great lack of tact and of intelligence. In the conference of trade-union executives held from February 19 to 23, 1906—a conference which marks an important stage in the history of the German labour movement—Paul Müller, employee of a trade union, complained bitterly that his revolutionary comrades of the socialist party were endeavouring "to estrange the members of the unions from the leaders they had chosen for themselves. They have been directly incited to rebellion. They have been openly urged to breaches of discipline. What other expressions can be used when in meetings we are told that the members ought to fight against their leaders?"[29]

---

ter dated September 19, 1879 (*Briefe u. Auszüge aus Briefen*, etc., ed. cit., pp. 361 and 166).

[27] Sometimes the members of the rank and file are officially exhorted to respect the authority of their elected representatives. In a Belgian trade-union journal we read among the "Ten Commandments" drawn up for the organized workers the following admonitions: "1. De la propagande tu feras, pour grouper les indifférents; 2. Aux assemblés tu assisteras, pour devenir intelligent; 3. Ta cotisation tu payeras, tous les mois régulièrement; 4. *Dans les cabarets tu ne critiqueras, ce qui n'arrive que trop souvent*" ("Journal des Correspondances," Organe officiel des Syndicats affiliés à la Commission Syndicale, Brussels, 1905, ii, No. 9).

[28] Here is a typical example. The socialist leaders of Chemnitz in Saxony had proposed to raise the price of subscription to the local organ of the party, but the majority of the socialist assembly of the constituency rejected this proposition. Here are the remarks upon the subject made by one of the leaders: "An increase in the monthly price of subscription by 10 pfennig would have saved the situation. But the great moment did not find those ready to seize it. Neither the detailed report of the business manager, Comrade Landgraf, nor yet the magnificent expositions of Comrades Noske and Heldt, of Zeisig and Riemann, the members of the press committee, and others, who in the course of many years' active work have acquired a profound knowledge of journalistic enterprise, sufficed to convince the majority of the assembly that it was absolutely essential to increase the monthly subscription by 10 pfennig. The leaders had to submit to the indignity of seeing their proposal voted down" ("Volksstimme" of Frankfort, anno xxi, No. 37).

[29] *Partei u. Gewerkschaften*, textual reprint from the §§ P. and G. of the *Protokoll*, p. 4.

Whenever a new current of opposition manifests itself within the party, the leaders immediately endeavour to discredit it with the charge of demagogy. If those of the comrades who are discontented with the leaders make a direct appeal to the masses, this appeal—however lofty may be its motives, however sincere the convictions of those who make it, however much they may be justified by a reference to fundamental democratic rights—is repudiated as inexpedient, and is even censured as a wicked attempt to break up the party, and as the work of vulgar intriguers.[30] We have to remember, in this connection, that the leaders, who hold in their hands all the mechanism of power, have the advantage of being able to assume an aureole of legality, whereas the masses, or the subordinate leaders who are in rebellion, can always be placed in an unfavourable light of illegality. The magic phrase with which the leaders invariably succeed in stifling embarrassing opposition in the germ is "the general interest." In such circumstances they exhibit a notable fondness for arguments drawn from the military sphere. They maintain, for instance, that, if only for tactical reasons, and in order to maintain a necessary cohesion in face of the enemy, the members of the party must never refuse to repose perfect confidence in the leaders they have freely chosen for themselves. It is in Germany, above all, that in the trade-union organizations the authoritarian spirit is developed with especial force, and that the leaders are prone to attribute to their adversaries the "criminal intention" of attempting "to dissolve trade-union discipline."[31] Even the socialist leaders make similar charges against their opponents. If we translate such an accusation from the language of the trade-union leaders into that of government officials, the charge becomes one of "inciting to revolt against constituted authority." If the critics are not officials of the party, if they are mere sympathizers or friends, they are then in the eyes of the attacked leaders intrusive and incompetent persons, without any right whatever to form an opinion on the matter. "On no account must the faith of the people be disturbed! Such is the principle in accordance with which all

---

[30] Cf. pp. 171, 172.

[31] At the conference of the trade-union executives, February 19 to 23, 1906, Rexhäuser said: "The poison which spreads in this way through the masses corrodes everything, and when one day you want to unite for some decisive action, you find that discipline has gone to the devil, and that the rank and file will not obey their leaders" (*Protokoll*, pp. 23-4).

lively criticism of the objective errors of the movement are stigmatized as an attack on the movement itself, whilst the elements of opposition within the party are habitually execrated as enemies who wish to destroy the party.''[32]

The general conduct of the leaders of democratic parties and the phraseology typically employed by them (of which our examples might be multiplied a hundredfold) suffice to illustrate how fatal is the transition from an authority derived from ''the favour of the people'' to a right based upon ''the grace of God'' —in a word, to the system which in French history we know by the name of Bonapartism. A right of sovereignty born of the plebiscite soon becomes a permanent and inviolable dominion.

---

[32] Rosa Luxemburg, writing of the trade-union leaders in *Massenstreik, Partei u. Gewerkschaften,* ed. cit., p. 61.

CHAPTER III

IDENTIFICATION OF THE PARTY WITH THE LEADER
("LE PARTI C'EST MOI")

WE have shown that in their struggle against their enemies within the party the leaders of the labour movement pursue a tactic and adopt an attitude differing very little from those of the "bourgeois" government in its struggle with "subversive" elements. The terminology which the powers-that-be employ is, *mutatis mutandis,* identical in the two cases. The same accusations are launched against the rebels, and the same arguments are utilized in defence of the established order: in one case an appeal is made for the preservation of the state; in the other, for that of the party. In both cases, also, there is the same confusion of ideas when the attempt is made to define the relationships between thing and person, individual and collectivity. The authoritarian spirit of the official representatives of the German socialist party (a spirit which necessarily characterizes every strong organization) exhibits several striking analogies with the authoritarian spirit of the official representatives of the German empire. On the one side we have William II, who advises the "malcontents," that is to say those of his subjects who do not consider that all is for the best in the best of all possible empires, to shake the dust off their feet and go elsewhere. On the other side we have Bebel, exclaiming that it is time to have done once for all with the eternal discontents and sowings of discord within the party, and expressing the opinion that the opposition, if it is unable to express itself as satisfied with the conduct of affairs by the executive, had better "clear out."[1] Between these two attitudes, can we find any difference other than that which separates a voluntary organization (the party), to which one is free to adhere or not as one pleases, from a coercive organization (the state), to which all must belong by the fact of birth?[2]

---

[1] August Bebel, speech to the Dresden congress, *Protokoll,* p. 308.

[2] In the text, the writer has repeatedly mentioned the name of Bebel

It may perhaps be said that there is not a single party leader who fails to think and to act, and who, if he has a lively temperament and a frank character, fails to speak, after the example of Le Roi Soleil, and to say *Le Parti c'est moi*.[3]

---

when he has wished to illustrate by typical examples the conduct of the leaders towards the masses. Yet it would be erroneous to regard Bebel as a typical leader. He was raised above the average of leaders, not only by his great intellectual gifts, but also by his profound sincerity, the outcome of a strong and healthy temperament, which often led him to say things openly which others would have left unsaid and to do things openly which others would have left concealed. It was for this reason that "Kaiser Bebel" was frequently exposed to the suspicion of being exceptionally autocratic in his conduct and undemocratic in his sentiments. Nevertheless, a thorough analysis of Bebel's character and of his conduct on various memorable occasions would establish that, side by side with a marked tendency to self-assertion and a taste for the intrinsic forms of rule, he exhibited strong democratic leanings, which distinguished him from the average of his colleagues, just as much as he was distinguished from them by the frankness with which he always displayed his dictatorial temperament. This is not the place for such an analysis, but the writer felt it was necessary to guard against a false interpretation of his references to Bebel by a brief allusion to the complexity of character of this remarkable man. In ultimate analysis, Bebel was no more than a representative of his party, but he was one in whom the individual note was never suppressed by the exigencies of leadership or of demagogy.

[3] We learn this from a study of all the great party leaders. As regards Marx, cf. Michels, *Storia del Marxismo in Italia*, Bocca, Turin, 1909, pp. 19 et seq.—As regards Lassalle, cf. Julius Vahlteich, *Ferdinand Lassalle*, ed. cit., pp. 42 et seq.—Liebknecht's official biographer tells us that he was not always able, owing to his strong and lively individuality, to distinguish between persons and things (Kurt Eisner, *Wilhelm Liebknecht*, "Vorwärts," Berlin, 1906, 2nd ed., p. 100).—Of Bebel, von Gerlach, one of his admirers, wrote: "He lives only for the party, identifying himself fully with the party. This is his strength, but often also it is his weakness. Just as Bismarck regarded every attack upon Bismarck as an attack upon the well-being of the German empire, so Bebel sees in every attack upon Bebel an attack upon the party interests. Thus his intervention is extraordinarily weighty, but often it is extremely unjust. Very rarely has he been fair to his opponents, and least of all to his opponents within the party. . . . He always regards himself as the guardian of the party interests, and his personal adversaries as the enemies of the party. His subjectivity is really terrible" (Helmuth von Gerlach, *August Bebel. Ein biographische Essay*, Albert Langen, Munich, 1909, pp. 59, 60). Cf. also the speech against Bebel delivered by Vollmar at the Dresden congress, 1903 (*Protokoll*, pp. 321 et seq.).—Vollmar's speech reminds us of Zibordi's bitter criticism of Enrico Ferri: "This man speaks of himself, of himself, of himself; of his mother, his wife, his children, always with reference to himself; of his own talents, of his own career, of his enemies, of his forecasts, of his goodness, of his health. The workers, socialism,

The bureaucrat identifies himself completely with the organization, confounding his own interests with its interests. All objective criticism of the party is taken by him as a personal affront. This is the cause of the obvious incapacity of all party leaders to take a serene and just view of hostile criticism.[4] The leader declares himself personally offended, doing this partly in good faith, but in part deliberately, in order to shift the battleground, so that he can present himself as the harmless object of an unwarrantable attack, and arouse in the minds of the masses towards his opponents in matters of theory that antipathy which is always felt for those whose actions are dictated by personal rancour.[5] If, on the other hand, the leader is attacked personally, his first care is to make it appear that the attack is directed against the party as a whole. He does this not only on diplomatic grounds, in order to secure for himself the support of the party and to overwhelm the aggressor with the weight of numbers, but also because he quite ingenuously takes the part

proletarian politics, the nation, are always discussed by him as centering in his own personality'' (G. Zibordi, *La "Tournée" oratoria di E. Ferri,* ''Secolo,'' April 25, 1911). Yet this way of speaking must not be attributed to personal vanity; it is rather the inevitable consequence of Ferri's absolute conviction of his sovereign power over the masses.

[4] Here are typical examples. The leaders of the Italian socialists in the early part of 1870, well-to-do idealists ready for sacrifice and for martyrdom, derived for the most part from the upper bourgeois and aristocratic circles, were described by Marx as a crowd of rascally students seeking careers in the International. The reason for this outburst of spleen was that the Italians had without exception supported Bakunin and opposed Marx (cf. R. Michels, *Proletariato e Borghesia,* ed. cit., pp. 63-76). Engels, again, speaking of the opposition within the party, of the group known as *die Jungen,* to which Hans Müller, Paul Ernst, Bruno Wille, Paul Kampffmeyer, O. E. Hartleben, etc., belonged, qualified them in the following terms: ''Unquestionably there are some among them in the pay of the police; others are masked anarchists who wish to make recruits from among our ranks; the rest are blockheads, students swollen with conceit, would-be candidates, and self-seekers of all kinds'' (*Briefe u. Auszüge,* ed. cit., p. 370).

[5] In a polemic against the Marxists of the party, the trade-union leader H. Jochade writes: ''We have to ask ourselves seriously what is the meaning of this new campaign. Is it dictated by the love of scandal, by the excess of zeal of a few quill-drivers, or have malice and cunning anything to do with the matter? There can be no doubt that all these influences are at work in originating the attack upon the trade-union employees'' (*Krieg gegen die Gewerkschaftsbeamten,* ''Korrespondenzblatt der Generalkommission der Gewerkschaften Deutschlands,'' anno xviii, No. 51, December 19, 1908, p. 810).

for the whole. This is frequently the outcome, not merely of blind fanaticism, but of firm conviction. According to Netchajeff, the revolutionary has the right of exploiting, deceiving, robbing, and in case of need utterly ruining, all those who do not agree unconditionally with his methods and his aims, for he need consider them as nothing more than *chair à conspiration*. His sole objective must be to ensure the triumph of his essentially individual ideas, without any respect for persons—*La Révolution c'est moi!* Bakunin uttered a sound criticism of this mode of reasoning when he said that its hidden source was to be found in Netchajeff's unconscious but detestable ambition.[6]

The despotism of the leaders does not arise solely from a vulgar lust of power or from uncontrolled egoism, but is often the outcome of a profound and sincere conviction of their own value and of the services which they have rendered to the common cause. The bureaucracy which is most faithful and most efficient in the discharge of its duties is also the most dictatorial. To quote Wolfgang Heine: "The objection is invalid that the incorruptibility and efficiency of our party officials, and their love for the great cause, would suffice to raise a barrier against the development of autocracy within the party. The very opposite is true. Officials of high technical efficiency who unselfishly aim at the general good, like those whom we are fortunate enough to possess in the party, are more than all others inclined, being well aware of the importance of their own services, to regard as inalterable laws whatever seems to them right and proper, to suppress conflicting tendencies on the ground of the general interest, and thus to impose restraints upon the healthy progress of the party."[7] Similarly, where we have to do with excellent and incorruptible state officials like those of the German empire, the megalomaniac substitution of thing for person is partly due to the upright consciences of the officials and to their great devotion to duty.[8] Among the members of such a

---

[6] James Guillaume, *L'Internationale*, ed. cit., vol. ii, p. 62.

[7] W. Heine, *Demokratische Randbemerkungen zum Fall Göhre*, "Soz. Monatsh.," viii (x), fasc. iv, p. 284.

[8] "The [Prussian] state tends to become a republic of official employees, in which the employees are the only fully qualified citizens, whilst all others, notwithstanding the apparent possession of constitutional rights, exist simply in order to be ruled and to provide the cost of working the governmental machine. The danger is not lessened by the fact that the bureaucracy does not merely make a profession of working for the general good, but is honestly convinced that it is endeavouring to secure it. Every official

bureaucracy, there is hardly one who does not feel that a pin-prick directed against his own person is a crime committed against the whole state. It is for the same reason that they all hold together *comme les doigts de la main.* Each one of them regards himself as an impersonation of a portion of the whole state, and feels that this portion will suffer if the authority of any other portion is impaired.[9] Further, the bureaucrat is apt to imagine that he knows the needs of the masses better than these do themselves,[10] an opinion which may be sound enough in individual instances, but which for the most part is no more than a form of megalomania. Undoubtedly the party official is less exposed than the state official to the danger of becoming fossilized, for in most cases he has work as a public speaker, and in this way he maintains a certain degree of contact with the masses. On the other hand, the applause which he seeks and receives on these occasions cannot fail to stimulate his personal vanity.

When in any organization the oligarchy has attained an advanced stage of development, the leaders begin to identify with themselves, not merely the party institutions, but even the party property, this phenomenon being common both to the party and to the state. In the conflict between the leaders and the rank and file of the German trade unions regarding the right to strike, the leaders have more than once maintained that the decision in this matter is morally and legally reserved for themselves, because it is they who provide the financial resources which enable the workers to remain on strike.[11] This view is no more than the ultimate consequence of that oligarchical mode of thought which inevitably leads to a complete forgetfulness of true democratic principles. In Genoa, one of the labour leaders, whose influence had increased *pari passu* with the growing strength of the organized proletariat of the city, and who, en-

---

who seeks to maintain his own power persuades himself that he does this for the benefit of the ruled'' (W. Heine, *Die Beamten Republik,* ''März,'' anno iii, fasc. 21, p. 175).

    [9] Edmond About, *Le Progrès,* Hachette, Paris, 1864, p. 232.

    [10] Max Weber, for instance, in a discussion upon municipal enterprise at the Vienna congress of the Verein für Sozialpolitik declared: ''I should think myself a very poor bureaucrat indeed, if I did not believe myself to know better than these blockheads what is really good for them'' (*Protokoll,* p. 285).

    [11] Cf. ''Korrespondenzblatt der Gewerkschaften Deutschlands,'' anno vii, No. 28.

joying the unrestricted confidence of his comrades, had acquired
the most various powers and had filled numerous positions in
the party, regarded himself as justified, when as a representative of the workers he made contracts with capitalists and concluded similar affairs, in feathering his own nest in addition to
looking after the workers' interests.[12]

---

[12] This was the barrister, Gino Murialdi, who in youth had made many
sacrifices for the movement. He was in receipt of a regular salary from
the trade unions and cooperative societies, but this did not prevent him
from accepting money from the employers when he was negotiating with
them as the workers' representative. When taken to task on this account,
he said that by his exertions he had obtained such brilliant advantages for
the workers, that he saw no reason why he should not secure for himself
a little extra profit at the cost of the employers. Murialdi's actions led
to a violent quarrel between him and the other leaders in Genoa, and ultimately caused his expulsion from the socialist party. Cf. ''Avanti,'' anno
xiii (1909), Nos. 1 and 24.

PART FOUR

SOCIAL ANALYSIS OF LEADERSHIP

CHAPTER I

INTRODUCTORY. THE CLASS STRUGGLE AND ITS DISINTEGRATING INFLUENCE UPON THE BOURGEOISIE

THE masses are not easily stirred. Great events pass before their eyes and revolutions are accomplished in economic life without their minds' undergoing profound modifications. Very slowly do they react to the influence of new conditions.

For decades, and even for centuries, the masses continue to endure passively outworn political conditions which greatly impede legal and moral progress.[1] Countries which from the economic point of view are fairly well advanced, often continue to endure for lengthy periods a political and constitutional regime which derives from an earlier economic phase. This is especially noteworthy in Germany, where an aristocratic and feudal form of government, the outcome of economic conditions which the country has outlived, has not yet been able to adapt itself to an economic development of the most advanced capitalist character.

These historical phenomena, which at first sight appear paradoxical, arise from causes of two different orders. In the first place it may happen that classes or sub-classes representing an extinct economic form may survive from a time in which they were the authentic exponents of the then dominant economic relationships; they have been able to save from the wreck a sufficiency of moral prestige and effective political force to maintain their dominion in the new phase of economic and civil development, and to do this even in opposition to the expressed will of the majority of the people. These classes succeed in maintain-

---

[1] "Unreflectingly, sometimes with a sigh, but often without a thought of the possibility of better things, the nations have borne for centuries, and continue to bear, all the burdens and all the shames imposed upon them by tyranny, like the lower animals, who with satisfaction and even gratitude accept a bare subsistence, from the hand of the master to whom they belong, and who makes use of them and chastises them at his will" (Carl von Rotteck, *Allgemeine Geschichte, etc.*, ed. cit., p. 81).

ing themselves in power by the strength of their own political energy and with the assistance of numerous elements essentially foreign to themselves, but which they can turn to their own advantage by suggestive influences. Most commonly, however, we find that the classes representing a past economic order continue to maintain their social predominance only because the classes representing the present or future economy have as yet failed to become aware of their strength, of their political and economic importance, and of the wrongs which they suffer at the hands of society. Moreover, a sense of fatalism and a sad conviction of impotence exercise a paralysing influence in social life. As long as an oppressed class is influenced by this fatalistic spirit, as long as it has failed to develop an adequate sense of social injustice, it is incapable of aspiring towards emancipation. It is not the simple *existence* of oppressive conditions, but it is the *recognition of these conditions by the oppressed*, which in the course of history has constituted the prime factor of class struggles.[2]

The mere existence of the modern proletariat does not suffice *per se* to produce a "social problem." The class struggle, if it is not to remain a nebulous theory, in which the energy is for ever latent, requires to be animated by class consciousness.

It is the involuntary work of the bourgeoisie to arouse in the proletariat that class consciousness which is necessarily directed against the bourgeoisie itself. History is full of such ironies. It is the tragical destiny of the bourgeoisie to be instructor of the class which from the economic and social point of view is its own deadly enemy. As Karl Marx showed in his *Communist Manifesto,* the principal reason for this is found in the unceasing struggle which the bourgeoisie is forced to carry on "at once with the aristocracy, with those sections of its own class whose interests are opposed to industrial progress, and with the bourgeoisie of all foreign countries." Unable to carry on this struggle effectively by its own unaided powers, the bourgeoisie is continually forced "to appeal to the proletariat, to demand its aid, and thus to launch the proletariat into the political mêlée, thus putting into the hands of the proletariat a weapon which

---

[2] This is now generally recognized, as, for instance, even by so guarded a writer as Johannes Conrad in his *Grundriss zum Studium der politischen Oekonomie,* Part II, *Volkswirtschaftspolitik,* Fischer, Jena, 1898, 2nd ed., p. 48.

the latter will turn against the bourgeoisie itself.[3] Under yet another aspect the bourgeoisie appears as the instructor, as the fencing-master of the working class. Through its daily contact with the proletariat there results the detachment from its own body of a small number of persons who devote their energies to the service of the working classes, in order to inflame these for the struggle against the existing order, to make them feel and understand the deficiencies of the prevailing economic and social regime. It is true that the number of those who are detached from the bourgeoisie to adhere to the cause of the proletariat is never great. But those who thus devote themselves are among the best of the bourgeoisie; they may, in a sense, be regarded as supermen, raised above the average of their class, it may be by love of their neighbours, it may be by compassion, it may be by moral indignation against social injustice or by a profound theoretical understanding of the forces at work in society, or, finally, by a greater energy and logical coherence in the translation of their principles into practice. In any case, they are exceptional individualities, these bourgeois who, deserting the class in which they were born, give a deliberate direction to the instincts still slumbering in the proletariat, and thus hasten the emancipation of the proletarian class as a whole.

The proletarian mass is at first aware by instinct alone of the oppression by which it is burdened, for it entirely lacks the instruction which might give a clue to the understanding of that historical process which is in appearance so confused and labyrinthine. It would seem to be a psychologico-historical law that any class which has been enervated and led to despair in itself through prolonged lack of education and through deprivation of political rights, cannot attain to the possibility of energetic action until it has received instruction concerning its ethical rights and politico-economical powers, not alone from members of its own class, but also from those who belong to what in vulgar parlance are termed a "higher" class. Great class-movements have hitherto been initiated in history solely by the simple reflection: it is not we alone, belonging to the masses without education and without legal rights, who believe ourselves to be oppressed, but that belief as to our condition is shared by those who have a better knowledge of the social mechanism and who are therefore

---

[3] Karl Marx, *The Communist Manifesto*, "Vorwärts," Berlin, 1901, 6th ed., p. 16.

better able to judge; since the cultured people of the upper classes have also conceived the ideal of our emancipation, that ideal is not a mere chimera.[4]

The socialist theory has arisen out of the reflections of philosophers, economists, sociologists, and historians. In the socialist programmes of the different countries, every word represents a synthesis of the work of numerous learned men.[5] The fathers of modern socialism were with few exceptions men of science primarily, and in the second place only were they politicians in the strict sense of the term. It is true that before the days of such men there were spontaneous proletarian movements initiated by an instinctive aspiration towards a higher intellectual and economic standard of life. But these movements manifest themselves rather as the mechanical outcome of an unreflecting though legitimate discontent, than as the consequence of a genuine sentiment of revolt inspired by a clear consciousness of oppression. It was only when science placed itself at the service of the working class that the *proletarian* movement became transformed into a *socialist* movement, and that instinctive, unconscious, and aimless rebellion was replaced by conscious aspiration, comparatively clear, and strictly directed towards a well-defined end.

Similar phenomena are apparent in all earlier class struggles. Every great class-movement in history has arisen upon the instigation, with the co-operation, and under the leadership of men sprung from the very class against which the movement was directed. Spartacus, who urged the slaves to revolt on behalf of their freedom, was, it is true, of servile origin, but he was a freedman, a Thracian property-owner. Thomas Münzer, to whose agitation the Thuringian Peasants' War was largely due,

---

[4] This sequence of ideas is so obvious that its recognition has been general. Otto von Leixner, for instance, notwithstanding the superficiality of his studies, refers to it in his psychological sketches upon the labour movement in Berlin. (Cf. *Soziale Briefe aus Berlin*, 1888-91, Pfeilstücker, Berlin, 1891, p. 147.)

[5] This is admitted even by the opponents of socialism. Oldenberg, for instance, writes: "From the historical point of view, socialism is an idealist fantasy, mechanically transplanted into the heads of the proletarian masses from the highest spheres of philosophical and scientific thought. It is from the outset a misalliance, described by Lassalle as 'the alliance between science and the workers'" (Karl Oldenberg, *Die Ziele der deutschen Sozialdemokratie* in *Evangelisch-soziale Zeitfragen*, Grunow, Leipzig, 1891, p. 58).

was not a peasant but a man of learning. Florian Geier was a knight. The most distinguished leaders of the movement for the emancipation of the *tiers état* at the outset of the French Revolution, Lafayette, Mirabeau, Roland, and Sieyès, belonged to the privileged classes, and Philippe-Egalité, the regicide, was even a member of the royal house. The history of the modern labour movement furnishes no exception to this rule. When the German historian, Theodor Lindner, affirms [6] that the contemporary socialist movement is always "called to life" by non-workers, we must indeed criticize the statement, which recalls to our mind the working of the necromancer's magic wand: "Let there be a labour movement! And there was a labour movement." Lindner's statement is likewise inexact and incomplete, because it fails to recognize that this "calling to life" cannot produce something out of nothing, and that it cannot be the work of one of those famous "great men" whom a certain school of historians make the corner-stone of their theory of historical causation—for the coming into existence of the labour movement necessarily presupposes a given degree of social and economic development, without which no movement can be initiated. But Lindner's view, though badly formulated, is to this extent true, that the heralds of the modern labour movement are chiefly derived from the "cultured classes." [7] The great precursors of political socialism and leading representatives of philosophical socialism, Saint-Simon, Fourier, and Owen; the founders of political socialism, Louis Blanc, Blanqui, and Lassalle; the fathers of economic and scientific socialism, Marx, Engels, and Rodbertus, were all bourgeois intellectuals. Of comparatively trifling importance in the international field, alike in respect of theory and of practice, were Wilhelm Weitling, the tailor's apprentice, and Pierre Leroux, the self-taught philosopher. It is only Proudhon, the working printer, a solitary figure, who attains to a position of superb grandeur in this field. Even among the great orators who during recent years have been devoted to the cause of labour, ex-bourgeois constitute the great majority, while men of working-class origin are altogether exceptional. Pages could be filled with the names of leading socialist politi-

---

[6] Theodor Lindner, *Geschichtsphilosophie*, Cotta, Stuttgart, 1904, 2nd ed., p. 132.

[7] This was pointed out by Heinrich von Sybel as long ago as 1872. Cf. *Die Lehren des heutigen Sozialismus u. Kommunismus*, M. Cohen, Bonn, 1872, p. 91.

cians sprung from the bourgeoisie, whereas in a single breath we could complete the list of political leaders of truly working-class origin whose names will be immortalized in the history of their class. We have Bénoît Malon, August Bebel, and Eduard Anseele; but not one of these, although they are great practical leaders of the working class and potent organizers, is numbered among the creative theorists of socialism.

The presence of bourgeois elements in the proletarian movement organized to form a political party is a historical fact, and one which may be noted wherever the political movement of the international working class is attentively observed.[8] This phenomenon reproduces itself wherever the socialist tree throws out new branches, as may be seen, for example, in Japan and Brazil.[9]

Moreover, this phenomenon must be considered as a logical consequence of historical evolution. Nay more, it has been

---

[8] In studies relating to individual countries this has been made almost everywhere apparent. Regarding Italy, cf. Michels, *Proletariato e Borghesia nel Movimento Socialista Italiano*, ed. cit., pp. 19-118. Regarding England, cf. Eduard Bernstein, *Die Arbeiterbewegung*, ed. cit., p. 144; W. E. H. Lecky, *Democracy and Liberty*, Longmans, London, 1899, vol. ii, p. 370. Regarding Russia, cf. *Eine geheime Denkschrift über die nihilistischen Umtriebe vom Jahre 1875*, compiled from the official reports of the Russian Minister of Justice, Count von der Pahlen, ''Deutsche Rundschau,'' anno vii (1881), fasc. 9; and from the revolutionary side, *Bericht an den Internationalen Sozialistischen Congress in Paris, 1900, Ueber die russische Sozialdemokratische Bewegung, Geschrieben im Auftrage des Bundes russischer Sozialdemokraten von der Redaktion der Rabotscheje Djelo*, by Boris Kricewski, in which we are told that ''the propagandist group of the Russian social democracy during the years 1890-5 consisted almost exclusively of intellectuals (p. 5). Regarding France, Mermeix, *La France socialiste, Notes d'un Contemporain*, Fetscherin and Chuit, Paris, 1886, 3rd ed., p. 52. In Holland, the bourgeois elements in the socialist party are so numerous, that the adversaries of socialism have taken advantage of the fact to coin a nickname for the party. Its official name is Sociaal-Demokratische Arbeiders Partij, known for short as S.D.A.P. In the nickname, the initials are expanded into Studenten Dominees en Advokaten Partij. (Cf. Schaper, *Op. de Bres. Alfabetisch Strijdschrift voor de Sociaal-Demokratie*, Stuffers, The Hague, 1905, p. 23.)

[9] Regarding the origin of socialism in Japan, see the study by Gustav Eckstein, *Die Arbeiterbewegung im modernen Japan*, ''Neue Zeit,'' anno xxii, vol. i, pp. 667 et seq.—In Brazil, at the second congress of the Socialist Workers of Brazil held at Sao Paulo in 1902, where the party first became firmly organized and established its programme, of the seven persons constituting the party executive, no less than three bore the title of ''Doctor.'' (Cf. Paul Löbe, *Die sozialistische Partei Brasiliens*, ''Neue Zeit,'' anno xx, vol. ii, p. 529.) As far as the writer is aware, the two members of the executive of Italian origin were also intellectuals.

shown that not merely the presence of ex-bourgeois in the party of the fighting proletariat, but further the leading rôle which these play in the movement for proletarian enfranchisement, is the outcome of historical necessity.

The question might arise, and it has in fact been mooted, whether the presence of a large number of bourgeois refugees among the proletarian militants does not give the lie to the theory of the class struggle. In other words, we have to ask whether the desired future social order in which all class distinctions are to be abolished (for this is the common aim, more or less distinctly formulated, of all socialists and other advanced reformers, ethical culturists, anarchists, neo-Christians, etc.) may not come to be realized by a gradual psychical transformation of the bourgeoisie, which will become increasingly aware of the injustice of its peculiar economic and social privileges. This consideration naturally leads us to ask whether the sharp line of cleavage which exists on the political field between class-parties representing class-interests is really necessary, or whether it is not a sort of cruel sport, and therefore useless and injurious. Rudolph Penzig, editor of "Ethische Kultur," in a controversy with the present writer, went so far as to claim that the deserters from the bourgeoisie to the socialist ranks were "precursors." [10] Now this expression logically involves the belief that these bourgeois pioneers will be followed by the whole mass of the bourgeoisie, who will thus come over to the camp of those who economically and socially are their moral enemies. We might be inclined to speak of this as a theory of hara-kiri, did we not know that hara-kiri is not usually practised as a deliberate voluntary act, but is effected in obedience to orders from above, to coercion from without. Let us briefly examine the soundness of the theory in question.

The socialist poet Edmondo de Amicis enumerates the factors which he regards as working most effectively for the ultimate victory of socialism. There is the general sense of weariness which, in his opinion, follows a great industrial crisis, and the utter disgust felt by the possessing classes with the unending struggle; there is the anxiety felt by these same classes to avoid at all costs a revolution in which they are destined to perish miserably, overcome by fire and sword; there is, finally, the indefi-

---

[10] Rudolph Penzig, *Die Unvernunft des Klassenkampfes*, written in answer to R. Michels, *Endziel, Intransigenz, Ethik*, "Ethische Kultur," December 26, 1903, xii, No. 52.

nite need, with which the bourgeoisie is also affected, for rejuve-
nation and idealism, and for avoiding "the horror of living amid
the ruins of an expiring world."[11] A similar train of thought
was expressed fifty years earlier by Heinrich Heine, who lacked
to make him a fighter for socialism merely the courage to give
open expression to his political ideas. In his letters from Paris
upon politics, art, and national life he writes, under date June
15, 1843: "I wish here to draw especial attention to the point
that for communism it is an incalculable advantage that the enemy against which the communists contend has, despite all his
power, no firm moral standing. Modern society defends itself
simply because it must do so, without any belief in its own
rights, and even without any self-respect, just like that ancient
society which crumbled to ruin at the coming of the carpenter's
son."[12]

In many respects, the views of these two poets may be accepted. And yet it seems more than questionable whether a dy-
ing bourgeois society would not defend itself to the last, and
endeavour to maintain by force of arms, if need be, its property
and its prerogatives, however greatly these might be undermined
and threatened, in the hope that the final victory of the proletariat might at least be postponed. Unquestionably, too, Heine's
opinion in 1843 that in the bourgeoisie of his day there was a
widespread lack of confidence, is open to criticism, seeing that,
as we all know, the bourgeois resistance is to this day animated
by a vigorous belief in his own rectitude. But the fundamental
thought of de Amicis and Heine is so far sound, in that a society
which lacks a lively faith in its own rights is already in its
political death-agony. A capacity for the tough and persevering
defence of privilege presupposes in the privileged class the existence of certain qualities, and in especial of a relentless energy,
which might thrive, indeed, in association with cruelty and un-
conscientiousness, but which is enormously more prosperous if
based upon a vigorous faith in its own rectitude. As Pareto has
said,[13] the permeation of a dominant class by humanitarian
ideas, which lead that class to doubt its own moral right to existence, demoralizes its members and makes them inapt for defence.
The same law operates likewise where men are absolutely con-

---

[11] Edmondo de Amicis, *Lotte civili*, Nerbini, Florence, 1899, p. 294.
[12] Heinrich Heine, *Lutetia* in *Sämtliche Werke*, Hoffmann u. Kampe,
Hamburg, 1890, x, p. 93.
[13] Vilfredo Pareto, *Les Systèmes socialistes*, ed. cit., vol. i, pp. 37 and 57.

vinced of their sacred right to existence. It is equally valid of
national aggregates. Where a nation lacks the sense of such a
right, decadence and ruin inevitably ensue. We may regard it
as an established historical law that races, legal systems, institutions, and social classes, are inevitably doomed to destruction
from the moment they or those who represent them have lost
faith in their own future. The Poles, widely dispersed, and dis-
membered among three separate powers, have preserved their
nationality and their faith in themselves and in their rights. No
power in the world, not to mention the Prusso-Russian micro-
cosm, can annihilate the Polish people whilst their brains still
cherish the consciousness of their right to national existence.
The Wends, on the other hand, a Slav people like the Poles,
owing to the nature of the historical epoch in which they were
subdued and to the peculiar circumstances under which this
historical occurrence took place, did not succeed in retaining intact the consciousness of their national existence—if they ever
possessed one. Even where, as in the Spreewald, they have retained their language, they have been thoroughly absorbed into
the German system, and are in our day, as Wends, completely
expunged from the history of civilization. Although they in-
habit quite a large area of Germany, they have in many cases
so utterly lost all sense of their Slav origin as to have become
the most ardent Pan-Germanists, although they are in reality
Germans only in virtue of the legal fiction of the state and of
the customs and speech which have been imposed upon them by
their ancient conquerors.

No social struggle in history has ever been permanently won
unless the vanquished has as a preliminary measure been morally weakened. The French Revolution was rendered possible
only because the ardent pre-revolutionary writers, Voltaire,
D'Alembert, Rousseau, Holbach, Diderot, etc., who made so
plainly manifest the "immorality" of the economic privileges
possessed by the ruling classes of the old regime, had already
demoralized (in the psychological sense of the word) a conspicuous portion of the nobility and the clergy. Louis Blanc remarked, apropos of the French Revolution: "Sortie vibrante de
l'Encyclopédie, ce grand laboratoire des idées du XVIIIe siècle,
elle n'avait plus en 1789, qu'à prendre matériellement possession
d'un domaine déjà conquis moralement." [14] The unification of

---

[14] Louis Blanc, *Organisation du Travail*, Camille, Paris, 1845, 4th ed., p.
xiii.

Italy, previously broken up into seven states, was effected with a minimal shedding of blood (if we except the deaths that resulted in the struggle against foreigners), and after the foundation of the kingdom there was hardly a single inhabitant of the peninsula who shed any tears over the fate of the fallen dynasties, this attitude of mind forming a strong contrast to what happened in Germany in the corresponding historical period. The reason for the difference was that in Italy the unification of minds had long preceded the unification of administration.[15] In the war of secession in the United States of America, it was not merely the armed strength of the Northern states which decided the issue, but also the consciousness of moral error which towards the end of the war began to spread among a large number of the slave-owners of the Southern states.[16] Examples of this nature could be multiplied at will.

The aim of agitation is to shake the opponent's self-confidence, to convince adversaries of the higher validity of our own arguments. Socialism can least of all afford to underrate the enormous force of rhetoric, the compelling power of persuasion, for it is to these means that socialism owes its great successes. But the force of persuasion has a natural limit imposed by social relationships. Where it is used to influence the convictions of the popular masses or of social classes to induce them to take part in a movement which is directed towards their own liberation, it is easy, under normal conditions, to attain to positive results. But attempts at persuasion fail miserably, as we learn again and again from the history of social struggles, when they are addressed to privileged classes, in order to induce these to

---

[15] In the Pontifical State, even in the last years of its existence, a petition of the Jewish community against the severity of the taxation imposed upon them was rejected on the express ground that the Jews deserved to be specially taxed because they had killed the Saviour of mankind. At popular festivals the Jews had to furnish a pig, which for the enjoyment of the people was rolled down from the Testaccio; until Clement IX graciously modified the observance, it had been a Jew and not a pig! Notwithstanding these practices, which bear witness to the contempt felt for the Jews, the Romans, immediately after the incorporation of the Pontifical State into the kingdom of Italy, elected a considerable number of their Jewish fellow-citizens as municipal councillors, provincial councillors, and parliamentary deputies. ''The revolution which had taken place in opinion was sufficient to remove all obstacles'' (Aristide Gabelli, *Roma e i Romani*, ''Nuova Antologia,'' anno xvi, p. 420).

[16] Woodrow Wilson, *A History of the American People*, Harper, New York and London, 1903, vol. iv, p. 311.

abandon, to their own disadvantage, as a class and as individuals, the leading positions they occupy in society.

The individual human being is not an economic automaton. His life consists of a perennial conflict between his financial needs and the interests which bind him to a given class or caste, on the one hand, and, on the other, those tendencies which are outside class considerations, outside the orbit of social struggles, and which may arouse in his mind passions capable of diverting him from a purely economic path, attracting him within the sphere of influence of some ideal sun, leading him to act in ways more consonant with his own individual character. But all this applies only to the individual human being. The mass, if we leave out of consideration certain pathological influences to which it is exposed, and which may lead its members into activities conflicting with purely material advantage, is unquestionably an economic automaton. The common manifestations of its members are stamped with the seal of the economic interests of the mass, just as the individual sheep of a flock bear the mark of their owner. Consequently the seal need not necessarily be useful to the individual who bears it, nor correspondent with his ends; any more than is the imprint upon the back of the sheep, which often consigns the animal to slaughter. But in the human herd the economic imprint extends its influence into the physical life. The kind of work and of interests imposed by economic conditions makes spirit and body alike dependent on occupation.

It is doubtless true that the socialist doctrine has won over many children of bourgeois families, penetrating their minds so profoundly as to lead them to abandon everything else—to leave father and mother, friends and relatives, social position and respect. Without regret and without hesitation they have consecrated their lives to the emancipation of humanity as conceived by socialism. But we have here to do with isolated instances only, and not with compact groups representing an entire economic class. The class to which the deserters belong is no wise weakened by the desertion. A class considered as a whole never spontaneously surrenders its position of advantage. It never recognizes any moral reason sufficiently powerful to compel it to abdicate in favour of its "poorer brethren." Such action is prevented, if by nothing else, by class egoism,[17] a natural attri-

---

[17] From class egoism arises the only form of solidarity known to us in

bute of the proletarian as of other social classes, with the difference that, in the case of the proletariat, class egoism comes in ultimate analysis to coincide—*in abstracto,* at least—with the ideal of a humanity knowing nothing of classes.[18] It will not be denied that in the various strata of the dominant and possessing classes there are considerable differences in the extent to which this class egoism is developed. There are certain representatives of landed property, and above all the Prussian junkers, who bluntly declare even to-day that we should treat as criminals or lunatics all who claim political, economic, or social rights by which their own class-privileges are endangered. There are other classes in modern society less hostile to reforms and less crassly egoistic than the numerically small class of the Prussian junkers; but these too are not accessible to considerations of social justice, except in so far as no sensible injury is offered to their instinctive class-interests.[19] The proletariat is therefore

addition to the coercive (that of the state, the army, etc.). Collective life arises only out of the need for defence against common enemies. (Cf. Michels, *La Solidarité en Allemagne,* a report to the International Congress of Sociology held at Berne, August, 1909, and published in ''Annales de l'Institut International de Sociologie,'' Giard et Brière, Paris, 1910, vol. xii.)—At the same time it is unquestionable that with increasing class consciousness the social sentiment becomes narrowed in all classes, and that the morality of conduct towards the members of other classes diminishes, whilst morality towards other members of the same class is enhanced. This was pointed out quite recently by one of the Dutch socialists, amid storms of dissent from bourgeois and even from socialist moralists (Herman Gorter, *Het Historisch Materialisme, Voor Arbeiders verklaard,* ''De Tribune,'' Amsterdam, 1909, p. 72).

[18] ''All earlier classes which attained to dominion endeavoured to secure the position they had conquered by subjecting the whole of society to the conditions of their system of exploitation. The proletariat, on the other hand, can effect a conquest of the social productive forces only by abolishing the existing mode of appropriation and therewith all previously existing modes of appropriation. Proletarians have no property of their own to safeguard'' (Marx, *Communist Manifesto,* ed. cit., p. 17).

[19] It is by this that firm and unalterable limits are imposed upon so-called social reforms. The Prussian conservatives, constituting the party of the great landed proprietors, favoured laws for the protection of the workers until they perceived that an increase in the number of manufacturing operatives was leading to a dearth of labour in the rural districts. Thenceforward they showed themselves hostile to all measures for the improvement of the condition of the industrial workers. (Cf. the brief but brilliant essay by the Baroness Elisabeth von Richthofen, at one time factory inspector at Heidelberg, *Ueber die historische Wandlung in der Stellung der autoritären Parteien zur Arbeiterschutzgesetzgebung, und die Motive dieser Wandlungen,* Rossler, Heidelberg, 1901.)

perfectly logical in constituting itself into a class party, and in considering that the struggle against the bourgeoisie in all its gradations, viewed as a single class, is the only possible means of realizing a social order in which knowledge, health, and property shall not be, as they are to-day, the monopolies of a minority.

There is no contradiction whatever between the necessity which leads the proletariat to fight the bourgeoisie on the lines of the class struggle and the necessity which leads it to lay so much stress upon the general principle of human rights. Unquestionably, in pursuit of the conquest of power, persuasion is an excellent means to employ, for, as has already been pointed out, a class which has been convinced even against its will that its adversary's ideal is based upon better reasons than its own and is inspired by loftier moral aims, will certainly lack force to continue the struggle; it will have lost that faith in its own rights which alone confers upon resistance a moral justification. Persuasion, however, does not suffice, for a class, even if partially paralysed by its recognition of the fact that the right of the hostile class is superior to its own, would none the less, hypnotized by its own class egoism, continue the struggle, and would in the end yield to the force, not of words, but of facts. The writer believes that all these considerations suffice to establish as an axiom that the entrance of bourgeois elements into the ranks of the workers organized as a class party is determined mainly by psychological motives, and that it represents a process of spontaneous selection. It must be regarded as a logical consequence of the historical phase of development through which we are now passing, but in view of the special conditions which induce it there is no reason to interpret it as a preliminary symptom of a spontaneous and general dissolution of the bourgeoisie. To sum up, the issue of the struggle which is proceeding between the two great classes representing conflicting economic interests cannot possibly be decided by the passage of individual or isolated molecules from one side to the other.

CHAPTER II

ANALYSIS OF THE BOURGEOIS ELEMENTS IN THE SOCIALIST LEADERSHIP

SOCIALIST leaders, considered in respect of their social origin, may be divided into two classes, those who belong primarily to the proletariat, and those derived from the bourgeoisie, or rather from the intellectual stratum of the bourgeoisie. The lower middle class, that of the petty bourgeois, the minor agriculturists, independent artisans, and shopkeepers, have furnished no more than an insignificant contingent of socialist leaders. In the most favourable conditions, the representatives of this lower middle class follow the labour movement as sympathetic onlookers, and at times actually join its ranks. Hardly ever do they become numbered among its leaders.

Of these two classes of leaders, the ex-bourgeois, although at the outset they were naturally opposed to socialism, prove themselves on the average to be animated by a more fervent idealism than the leaders of proletarian origin. The difference is readily explained on psychological grounds. In most cases the proletarian does not need to attain to socialism by a gradual evolutionary process; he is, so to speak, born a socialist, born a member of the party—at least, this happens often enough, although it does not apply to all strata of the proletariat and to all places. In the countries where capitalist development is of long standing, there exists in certain working-class milieux and even in entire categories of workers a genuine socialist tradition. The son inherits the class spirit of the father, and he doubtless from the grandfather. With them, socialism is "in the blood." To this it must be added that actual economic relationships (with the class struggle inseparable from these, in which every individual, however refractory he may be to socialist theory, is forced to participate) compel the proletarian to join the labour party. Socialism, far from being in opposition to his class sentiment, constitutes its plainest and most conspicuous expression. The proletarian, the wage-earner, the enrolled member of the party, is a socialist on the ground of direct personal interest. Adhesion to socialism may cause him grave material damage, such as the loss of his employment, and may even make it impossible for him to gain his bread. Yet his socialist views are the spontaneous outcome of his class egoism, and he endures the hardships to which they may lead all the more cheerfully because he is suffering for the common cause. He is comforted by the more or less explicit recognition or gratitude of his comrades. The action of the socialist proletarian is a class action, and in many cases it may notably favour the immediate interests of the individual.[1]

Very different is the case of socialists of bourgeois origin. Hardly any of these are born in a socialist milieu. On the contrary, in their families the tradition is definitely hostile to the workers, or at least full of disdain for the aspirations of modern socialism. Among the bourgeois, just as much as among the proletarians, the son inherits the spirit of the father, but in this case it is the class spirit of the bourgeoisie. The young bourgeois has "in the blood" not socialism, but the capitalist mentality in one of its numerous varieties, and he inherits in addition an intellectualism which makes him proud of his supposed superiority. We have further, on the one hand, to take into account the economic conditions in which the bourgeois child is born and grows to maturity, and on the other the education which he receives at school, all of which predisposes him to feel nothing but aversion for the struggles of a working class pursuing socialist aspirations. In his economic environment he learns to tremble for his wealth, to tremble when he thinks of the shock his class will one day have to sustain when attacked by the organized masses of the *quatrième état*. Thus his class egoism becomes more acute, and is even transformed into an implacable hatred. His education, based upon official science, contributes to confirm and to strengthen his sentiments as a member of the master class. The influence which the school and the domestic environment exercise upon the youthful scion of the bourgeoisie is of such potency that even when his parents are themselves socialist sympathizers and on moral and intellectual grounds devoted to the cause of the workers, it most commonly happens that his bourgeois instincts gain the upper hand over the socialist traditions of his family. We learn from actual

---

[1] Cf. Part IV, chap. iv.

experience that it is very rare for the children of socialists, when they have received the education of intellectuals, to follow in their parents' footsteps. The cases of the children of Marx, Longuet, Liebknecht, and Molkenbuhr, remain altogether exceptional. It cannot be doubted that the rarity of such instances is due to the methods of education which usually prevail in a socialist family, methods which have nothing in common with socialism. Even when it is otherwise, when the immediate family environment is not opposed to the development of the socialist consciousness, the young man of bourgeois origin is strongly influenced by the milieu in which he is brought up. Even after he has joined the socialist party, he will retain a certain solidarity with the class from which he has sprung; for example, in his relations with the servants in his household he will remain always an employer, an "exploiter," in the sociological if not in the coarser sense of the latter term. For the bourgeois, adhesion to socialism signifies an estrangement from his own class, in most cases extensive social and ideal injury, and often actual material loss. In the case of the petty bourgeois, the evolution towards socialism may occur peacefully, for by his intellectual and social conditions the petty bourgeois is closely approximated to the proletarian, and above all to the better paid manual worker, from whom he is in many cases separated by purely imaginary barriers composed of all kinds of class prejudices. But the wealthier the family to which the bourgeois belongs, the more strongly it is attached to its family traditions, the higher the social position that it occupies, the more difficult is it for him, and the more painful, to break with his surroundings, and to adhere to the labour movement.

For the son of a wealthy capitalist, of an official in the higher ranks, or for a member of the old-established landed aristocracy, to join the socialists is to provoke a catastrophe.[2] He is free to give himself up to vague and harmless humanitarian dreams, and even in private conversation to speak of himself as a "socialist." But as soon as he displays the intention of becoming an active member of the socialist party, of undertaking public work on its behalf, of enrolling himself as an actual member of the "rebel" army, the deserter from the bourgeoisie is regarded

---

[2] Cf., for example, the first volume of *Memoiren einer Sozialistin*, by Lily Braun, the daughter of the German general von Kretschmann (Langen, Munich, 1909), where we find an admirable description of the conditions to which reference has been made in the text.

by his own class as either a knave or a fool. His social prestige falls below zero, and so great is the hostility displayed towards him that he is obliged to break off all relations with his family. The most intimate ties are abruptly severed. His relatives turn their backs upon him. He has burned his boats and broken with the past.

What are the motives which may lead the intellectual to desert the bourgeoisie and to adhere to the party of the workers? Among those who do this we may distinguish two fundamental types.

There is first of all the man of science. The ends which he pursues are of an objective character, but to the vulgar these seem at first sight devoid of practical utility, and even fantastical and extravagant. The stimulus which drives him is idealistic in this sense, that he is capable of sacrificing all other goods to science and its gains. In thus acting, he obeys the powerful impulse of his egoism, though it is an egoism ennobled. Scientific coherency is an inborn need of his nature. Psychology teaches us that in human beings every free exercise of faculty produces a sentiment of pleasure. Consequently the sacrifices which the socialist man of science makes for the party serve to increase the sum of his personal satisfaction. Notwithstanding all the material injuries he will suffer as a bourgeois in joining the socialist party, he will have gained a greater inward content and will have a more tranquil conscience. In some cases, too, his sentiments will take the form of an ambition to render signal services to the cause. In his case, of course, this ambition is very different from the grosser ambition of those who look merely for an increase in personal well-being—for a career, wealth, and the like.

The second category consists of those who are inspired with an intense sentimental attachment to socialism, who burn, so to speak, with the sacred fire. Such a man usually becomes a socialist when he is quite young, before material considerations and precautions have erected a barrier in the way of obedience to the impulses of his sanguine and enthusiastic temperament. He is inspired with the ardour of the neophyte and the need for devoting himself to the service of his kind.[3] The principal mo-

---

[3] There are numerous Italian novels describing the conversion of the young man of family to the principles of modern socialism, and in these the conversion is always attributed to sentiments of generosity and compassion. Cf. Edmondo de Amicis, *Lotte civili* (Nerbini, Florence, 1899),

tives which animate him are a noble disdain for injustice and a
love for the weak and the poor, a delight in self-sacrifice for the
realization of great ideas, for these are motives which often give
courage and love of battle to the most timid and inert charac-
ters.[4] With all this, there is usually found in the socialist en-
thusiast of bourgeois origin a considerable dose of optimism, a
tendency to overestimate the significance of the moral forces of

and especially the admirable sketch in this volume (pp. 53 et seq.) entitled
A una Signora; G. B. Bianchi (pseudonym of the psychiatrist Pietro
Petrazzani) in his romance of Emilian life *Il primo Maggio* (La Poligra-
fica, Milan, 1901); Vincenzo Vacirca in his novel *L'Apostata* (''Parola dei
Socialisti,'' Ravenna, 1905).—In the best-known Dutch socialist novel,
entitled *Barthold Meryan,* by Baroness Cornelie Huygens (Van Kampen,
5th ed.), the hero is a young bourgeois intellectual inspired by a lofty spirit
of self-denial.—To the same motive has been attributed the adhesion to
socialism comparatively late in life of the Swedish poet Gustaf af Geijerstam. Under date July 11, 1910, the ''Frankfurter Zeitung'' writes as
follows: ''What, then, were the motives that led Geijerstam, a man of
thoroughly conservative spirit, and proud of his rank, into the socialist
camp? On the one hand, unquestionably there were operative the influences of Strindberg's circle, to which Geijerstam belonged in his youth;
but his principal reason was his tenderness of conscience. There has been
a general awakening of the social conscience in all countries, but in Sweden
and in the work of Geijerstam this awakening attained its climax.''—The
generous impulse of the receptive youthful mind is often extremely strong.
It is true that sometimes the direction of this impulse becomes transferred
to some smaller but nearer goal which has nothing in common with the original aim. Read, for example, the description given in his *Tagebuch* (Langen, Munich, 1907) by Otto Erich Hartleben of his own development, a description in which he confesses himself with perfect frankness. ''For a
long period in my life I was ashamed of my natural love of pleasure. I
was never indeed a Christian, but I sometimes believed it to be my duty
to become a socialist, and regarded it as essential to devote my energies
to the service of some good cause. I have put all this behind me. I have
learned that one is one's own good cause, and I now endeavour to employ
my energies in my own service'' (p. 228). This is termed by Hartleben the
''inner evolution towards the ultimate acquirement of a joyful faith in one-
self.''

''As you see, I have the physique neither of an athlete nor of a lion.
In the moral sphere, too, I lack the qualities of the fighter. In the bottom
of my soul I love peace and quietness, and I should remain utterly inactive
if it were not that the socialist faith forces me in spite of myself to take
part in the struggles of our time—that faith which inculcates a profound
hatred of injustice and privilege, a no less strong conviction that they
must be abolished, and an irresistible desire to do all that we can to attain
this end.'' Such are the confessions of Camillo Prampolini, one of the
most distinguished figures of modern Italian socialism. (Cf. his *Resistete
agli Arbitrii!* [*Cosa avrei detto ai giurati*], Libreria Gavagnani e Pagliani,
Modena, 1900, p. 11)

the movement, and sometimes an excessive faith in his own self-abnegation, with a false mode of conceiving the rhythm of evolution, the nearness of the final victory, and the ease with which it will be attained. The socialist faith is also in many cases nourished by æsthetic sensibilities. Those endowed with poetical aptitudes and with a fervent imagination can more readily and intuitively grasp the extent and the depth of human suffering; moreover, the greater their own social distance from the imagined objects, the more are they able to give their fancies free rein.[5] It is for this reason that among the ranks of those who are fighting for the emancipation of labour we find so many poets and imaginative writers, and so many persons of fiery, impassioned, and impulsive dispositions.[6]

The question arises, which category is the more numerous, that of those who become socialists from reasoned conviction, or that of those who are guided by sentimental considerations. It is probable that among those who become socialists in youth the sentimentalists predominate,[7] whereas among those who go over to socialism when they have attained maturity, the change is usually dictated by scientific conviction. But in most cases mixed motives are at work. Very numerous, in fact, are the bourgeois who have always given a moral approval to socialism, who have held that it is the only solution of the social problem which conforms to the demands of justice, but who do not make their effective adhesion to the doctrine until they acquire the conviction (which at times seizes them quite unexpectedly) that the aspirations of their heart are not merely just and beautiful, but also realizable in practice.[8] Thus the socialist views of these

---

[5] Cf. also Ettore Ciccotti, *Psicologia del Movimento Socialista*, ed. cit., pp. 45-6 and 85.

[6] A few only of the most notable of such persons, who are or who have been active workers on behalf of socialism, may be mentioned here: William Morris, Bernard Shaw, H. G. Wells, Jack London, George D. Herron, Upton Sinclair; J. B. Clément, Clovis Hugues, Anatole France, Jules Destrée; Cornelie Huygens, Hermann Gorter, Henriette Roland-Holst; Georg Herwegh, Wilhelm Holzamer, Karl Henkell, Emil Rosenow; Edmondo de Amicis, Mario Rapisardi, Diego Garoglio, Angelo Cabrini, G. Romualdi, Virgilio Brocchi, Tomaso Monicelli; Maxim Gorki; Gustav af Geijerstam.

[7] Such is also the opinion of Hubert Lagardelle, as expressed in his pamphlet *Les Intellectuels devant le Socialisme*, "Cahiers de la Quinzaine," Paris, 1900, p. 57.

[8] "Take the case of an idealist who aims in theory at the triumph of good, but who through insufficient knowledge of the real state of affairs arrives at theoretical conclusions and advocates practical expedients which

persons are a synthesis of sentiment and science. In 1894, an inquiry was made as to the attitude towards socialism of the most distinguished Italian artists and men of learning. They were asked whether their sympathy with socialist aims, their indifference to socialism, or their hostility to the doctrine, was the outcome of a concrete investigation of socialist problems, or whether their feelings were of a purely sentimental character. The majority of those who replied declared that their attitude towards socialism was the outcome of a psychical predisposition, reinforced by objective convictions.[9] A similar answer might

---

tend to consecrate the triumph of evil. Can we say here that he is guided by the suggestions of personal interest? Where does self-interest come in? The suggestions at work arise from errors of the intelligence. Similarly the increase in the number of thinkers and idealists who in critical periods devote themselves to the service of the revolutionary classes, may in part, and in the case of many of them, be due to the conscious or unconscious suggestions of self-interest; but to a large extent, and in many, this action is determined by the influence of ideal aspirations which at one time they believed incapable of realization, but which now, under the new conditions, they regard as realizable. . . . To the historian of the social movement, these psychological distinctions may appear of secondary importance; not so to the moralist'' (Benedetto Croce, *Materialismo storico ed Economia marxistica. Saggi Critici*, Remo Sandron, Milan-Palermo, 1900, p. 57). Bernstein gives a similar analysis of the motives which influence the various adherents to socialism, but touches on the question rather lightly (E. Bernstein, *Zur Geschichte u. Theorie des Sozialismus*, Dümmler, Berlin, 1904, 4th ed., vol. iii, pp. 42 et seq.).

[9] *Il Socialismo giudicato da Letterati, Artisti e Scienziati italiani.* Inchiesta, con Prefazione di Gustavo Macchi, Carlo Aliprandi, Milan, 1895.— Gustavo Macchi, who was himself at one time a member of the International, enquired of twenty-one socialists belonging without exception to cultured circles, for what reason they had become socialists. Nine declared that they had taken this step solely on ethical grounds, many of them adding that their socialist convictions had been subsequently reinforced by scientific studies; four stated that they had been turned towards socialism by the ''simultaneous'' influence of sentimental and scientific considerations; one (the novelist Giovanni Cena) said simply that he was himself a child of the proletariat; another (the poet Diego Garoglio) said that he had received the first impulse towards socialism through observing the life-activities of his father, who was a judge, but that he had in part been influenced by Christian considerations; Enrico Ferri's answer displayed the influence of mixed motives (''humanitarian sentiment by predisposition, progressively reinforced by a study of the question, leading finally to a profound scientific conviction''); five only claimed to have attained to socialist convictions chiefly or exclusively upon scientific grounds. Among the members of this last group one, Arturo Graf, declared that his adhesion to socialism was solely the outcome of study and conviction, in conflict with various opposing conditions, and in especial with his per-

doubtless be given by the Marxists, notwithstanding their superb disdain for all ideology and sentimental compassion, and notwithstanding the materialism with which they love to dress their windows. In so far as they are not completely absorbed in party life, or rather so long as they have not been completely overpowered by the ties of party life, they display a strictness of principle which is essentially idealist.[10]

Not all those, indeed, who sympathize with socialism or have a rational conviction of the truth of socialist principles become effective members of the socialist party. Many feel a strange repugnance at the idea of intimate association with the unknown crowd, or they experience an æsthetic disgust at the thought of close contact with persons who are not always clean or sweet-smelling.[11] Still more numerous are those held back by laziness or by an exaggerated fondness for a quiet life, or, again, by the more or less justified fear that open adhesion to the party will react unfavourably upon their economic position. Sometimes the impulse to join the party is given by some external circumstance, insignificant in itself, but sufficient to give the last impetus to resolution: it may be a striking instance of social injustice which stirs a collective emotion; it may be some personal wrong inflicted upon the would-be socialist himself or upon one of those dear to him,[12] when a sudden explosion of egoism finishes the slow work of altruistic tendencies. In other cases it is a necessity of fate, or the outcome of the ill-will and stupidity of human beings, which forces the man who has been a

---

sonal inclinations, with his tastes, and his mode of life; another, Olindo Malagodi, now editor of the "Tribuna," said that towards socialism he was "normally sympathetic" but "pathologically indifferent"; a third, Giovanni Lerda, made the sound observation that those who become socialists exclusively from sentimental reasons and without any scientific understanding of the doctrine are undesirable adherents; Filippo Turati eluded the question with the remark that he had never found it possible "to separate sentiment from reason."

[10] "Ils ont gardé la fidélité au but proposé, la fidélité quand même, sans se soucier des difficultés du chemin à parcourir.—'En avant! advienne que pourra'—disent les *matérialistes* ayant les yeux constamment fixé sur leur idéal supérieur. Ce n'est plus l'idéalisme verbal, enivrant et stérile. C'est l'idéalism en action. C'est la vie quotidienne élargie, agrandie, éclairée par une conception supérieure" (Charles Rappoport, *La Philosophie de l'Histoire comme Science de l'Evolution*, Jacques, Paris, 1903, p. v).

[11] The present writer has frequently heard people say: "I have every sympathy with socialism—if only there were not any socialists!"

[12] Ettore Ciccotti, *Psicologia del Movimento socialista*, ed. cit., p. 47.

secret socialist to cross the Rubicon, almost by inadvertence. For example, something may happen which discredits him in the eyes of the members of his own class, displaying to all the socialist ideas which he has hitherto jealously concealed. Many a person does not join the party of the workers until, after some imprudent manifestation of his own, an enemy has denounced him in the bourgeois press, thus placing him in a dilemma: he must either make a shameful retreat, at the cost of a humiliating retraction, or else must make public acknowledgment of the ideas which he has hitherto held secret.[13] Such persons become members of the socialist party as young women sometimes become mothers, without having desired it. The Russian nihilist Netchajeff made the idea of unmasking these timid revolutionary-minded persons the basis of a scheme of revolutionary agitation. He contended that it was the revolutionist's duty to compromise all those who, whilst they shared most of his ideas, did not as yet share them all; in this way he would force them to break definitely with the enemy, and would gain them over completely to the "sacred cause."[14]

It has often been asserted that the receptivity to socialist ideas varies in the different liberal professions. It is said that the speculative sciences (in the strictest sense of the term), such as philosophy, history, political economy, theology, and jurisprudence, are so profoundly imbued with the spirit of the past that those engaged in their study are refractory *a priori* to the reception of all subversive ideas. In the legal profession, in particular, it is contended there is inculcated a love of order, an attachment to the thing which is, a sacred respect for form, a slowness of procedure, and, if you will, a certain narrowness of view, which are all supposed to constitute natural correctives to the errors inherent in democracy.[15] In a general sense, we

---

[13] "An article in a newspaper may be for you, as bourgeois, a sentence of death. Do you regard this as a small matter? Once compromised, you will find yourself quite alone; you will suddenly become aware that no one will have anything more to do with you. You may be clever, and handsome, talented and free-handed, cheerful and helpful; but once thoroughly compromised you have become a social leper; everyone who sits beside you in a public place, who walks with you in the street, who talks with you in a restaurant, will become compromised in his turn, and for this reason carefully avoids you" (Max Tobler, *Ihr, die Ihr den Weg finden sollt!,* "Polis," anno ii, No. 1, p. 10).

[14] James Guillaume, *L'Internationale, etc.,* ed. cit., vol. ii, p. 62.

[15] Roscher, *Politik,* ed. cit., p. 385.

are told, the deductive and abstract sciences are authoritative and aristocratic in spirit, and those who pursue these paths of study incline to reactionary and doctrinaire views. Those, on the other hand, engaged in the study of the experimental and inductive sciences are led to employ their faculties of observation, which conduct them gradually to wider and wider generalizations, and they must thus be easy to win over to the cause of progress.[16] The doctor, above all, whose profession is a continued struggle against human misery, must carry in his mind the germs of the socialist conception.[17]

An analysis of the professions of the intellectuals belonging to the various socialist parties does not confirm this theory. It is in Italy and France alone that we find a considerable number of medical men in the socialist ranks, and even here they are less numerous than the devotees of pure science, and conspicuously less numerous than the lawyers.[18] In Germany, the relations between the socialist workers and those medical men who are least well-to-do (the doctors of the insurance-bureaux) are far from cordial. To sum up, it may be said in general terms that the doctor's attitude towards socialism is colder and more hostile than that of the abstract philosopher or the barrister. One reason for this may perhaps be that among doctors, more than among other intellectuals, there prevails, and has prevailed for the past forty years, a materialistically conceived and rigidly held Darwinism and Haeckelism. A supplementary cause may be found in the cynicism, often pushed to an ego centric extreme, by which many doctors are affected, as a natural reaction against the smell of the mortuary which attends their life-work and as

---

[16] Michael Bakunin, *Les Endormeurs*, Imp. Jean Alemane, Paris, 1900, p. 11.—Ettore Ciccotti, *Psichol. del Mov. Soc.*, ed. cit., p. 51.

[17] Ciccotti, *ibid.* p. 52.

[18] In the parliamentary socialist group in Germany and Holland, although there will be found a fair number of lawyers, there are no medical men nor any men engaged in the study of natural science. The Italian socialist group, indeed, contained in 1904 four medical men, but at the same time there were seventeen lawyers; moreover, among the four doctors, two were engaged in university teaching, and were thus theorists rather than practitioners. (Cf. detailed examination by Michels, *Proletariato e Borghesia,* ed. cit., pp. 90 et seq.) The French parliamentary group of the *Socialistes Unifiés* contained in the year 1910: manual workers and employees (for the most part employees of trade unions), 31; small farmers, 7; schoolmasters, 3; manufacturers and shopkeepers, 5; university professors, 8; journalists, 7; engineers, 1; chemists, 1; barristers, 7; doctors and pharmacists, 6 ("L'Humanité," June 1, 1910).

an outcome of their experience of the wickedness, the stupidity, and the frailty of the human material with which their practice brings them in contact.

In certain Protestant countries, in Holland, Switzerland, Great Britain, and America, we find a considerable number of the clergy among the socialists (but this is not the case in Germany, where the state is vigilant and powerful whilst the Lutheran Church is strict and intolerant). These ministers, we are told, make their adhesion to socialism on account of an elevated sense of duty towards their neighbour,[19] but perhaps in addition there is operative the need which is no less strong in the preacher than in the popular orator, to be listened to, followed, and admired by the crowd—it is of little importance whether by believers or unbelievers.

Here some reference may be made to the abundance of Jews among the leaders of the socialist and revolutionary parties. Specific racial qualities make the Jew a born leader of the masses, a born organizer and propagandist. First among these qualities comes that sectarian fanaticism which, like an infection, can be communicated to the masses with astonishing frequency; next we have an invincible self-confidence (which in Jewish racial history is most characteristically displayed in the lives of the prophets); there are remarkable oratorical and dialectical aptitudes, a still more remarkable ambition, an irresistible need to figure in the lime-light, and last but not least an almost unlimited power of adaptation. There has not during the last seventy-five years been any new current agitating the popular political life in which Jews have failed to play an eminent part. Not a few such movements must be distinctively considered as their work. Jews organize the revolution; and Jews organize the resistance of the state and of society against the subversive forces. Socialism and conservatism have been forged by Jewish hands and are impregnated with the Jewish spirit. In Germany, for example, we see on the one side Marx and Lassalle fanning the flames of revolution, and on the other, after 1848, Julius Stahl working as the brilliant theorist of the feudal reaction. In England, the Jew Disraeli reorganized the forces of the conservative party. We find Jews at the head of the movements which marshal against one another the nationalities

---

[19] Cf. the interesting study, detailed and well-furnished with evidence by Karl Vorländer, *Sozialdemokratische Pfarrer*, ''Archiv für Sozialwiss.,'' vol. xxx, fasc. 2.

animated by a reciprocal hate. At Venice, it was Daniel Manin who raised the standard of liberty against the Austrians. During the Franco-German war, the work of national defence was organized by Gambetta. In England, Disraeli was the inventor of the watchword "the integrity of the British Empire," whilst in Germany, the Jews Eduard Simson, Bamberger, and Lasker, were the leading champions of that nationalist liberalism which played so important a part in the foundation of the empire. In Austria, Jews constitute the advance-guard of almost all the strongly nationalist parties. Among the German Bohemians, the Italian irredentists, the Polish nationalists, and in especial among the Magyars, the most fanatical are persons of Jewish race. The Jews, in fact, are capable of organizing every kind of movement; even among the leaders of antisemitism there are not wanting persons of Jewish descent.

The adaptability and the intellectual vivacity of the Jews do not, however, suffice to explain the quantitative and qualitative predominance of persons of Hebrew race in the party of the workers. In Germany, above all, the influence of Jews has been conspicuous in the labour movement. The two first great leaders, Ferdinand Lassalle and Karl Marx, were Jews, and so was their contemporary Moses Hess. The first distinguished politician of the old school to join the socialists, Johann Jacoby, was a Jew. Such also was Karl Höchberg, the idealist, son of a rich merchant in Frankfort-on-the-Main, founder of the first socialist review published in the German language. Paul Singer, who was almost invariably chairman of the German socialist congresses, was a Jew. Among the eighty-one socialist deputies sent to the Reichstag in the penultimate general election, there were nine Jews, and this figure is an extremely high one when compared with the percentage of Jews among the population of Germany, and also with the total number of Jewish workers and with the number of Jewish members of the socialist party. Four of the nine were still orthodox Jews (Stadthagen, Singer, Wurm, and Haase). In various capacities, Jews have rendered inestimable services to the party: Eduard Bernstein, Heinrich Braun, Jakob Stern, Simon Katzenstein, and Bruno Schönlank, as theorists; Gradnauer, Eisner, and Josef Bloch, the editor of the "Sozialistische Monatshefte," as journalists; Hugo Heimann, in the field of municipal politics; Leo Arons, as a specialist in electoral affairs; Ludwig Frank, as organizer of the socialist youth. In Austria, the predominance of Jews in the socialist movement is conspicuous; it suffices to mention the names of Victor Adler, Ellenbogen, Fritz Austerlitz, Max Adler, F. Hertz, Therese Schlesinger-Eckstein, Dr. Diamand, Adolf Braun, etc. In America we have Morris Hillquit, A. M. Simons, M. Untermann. In Holland, we have Henri Polak, the leader of the diamond workers, D. J. Wijnkoop, the independent Marxist, and M. Mendels. In Italy, Elia Musatti, Claudio Treves, G. E. Modigliani, Riccardo and Adolfo Momigliano, R. L. Foà, and the man of science Cesare Lombroso. Even in France, although here the rôle of the Jews is less conspicuous, we may mention the names of Paul Louis, Edgard Milhaud, and the shareholders of "l'Humanité" in 1904. The first congress of the Parti Ouvrier in 1879 was rendered possible by the liberal financial support of Isaac Adolphe Crémieux, who had been governor of Algeria under Gambetta.[20]

In many countries, in Russia and Roumania for instance, but above all in Hungary and in Poland, the leadership of the working-class parties (the Russian Revolutionary Party excepted) is almost exclusively in the hands of Jews, as is plainly apparent from an examination of the personality of the delegates to the international congresses. Besides, there is a great spontaneous export from Russia of Jewish proletarian leaders to foreign socialist parties: Rosa Luxemburg and Dr. Israel Helphant (Parvus) have gone to Germany; Charles Rappoport to France; Anna Kulishoff and Angelica Balabanoff to Italy; the brothers Reichesberg to Switzerland; M. Beer and Theodor Rothstein to England. Finally, to bring this long enumeration to a close, it may be mentioned that among the most distinguished leaders of the German anarchists there are many Jews, such as Gustav Landauer, Siegfried Nacht, Pierre Ramus, Senna Hoj (Johannes Holzmann).

The origin of this predominant position (which, be it noted, must in no sense be regarded as an indication of "Judaization," as a symptom of dependence of the party upon the money of Jewish capitalist comrades) is to be found, as far at least as concerns Germany and the countries of eastern Europe, in the peculiar position which the Jews have occupied and in many respects still occupy. The legal emancipation of the Jews has not here been followed by their social and moral emancipation. In large sections of the German people a hatred of the Jews and

---

[20] Mermeix, *La France Socialiste*, ed. cit., p. 69.

the spirit of the Jew-baiter still prevail, and contempt for the Jews is a permanent feeling. The Jew's chances in public life are injuriously affected; he is practically excluded from the judicial profession, from a military career, and from official employment. Yet everywhere in the Jewish race there continues to prevail an ancient and justified spirit of rebellion against the wrongs from which it suffers, and this sentiment, idealist in its origin, animating the members of an impassioned race, becomes in them more easily than in those of Germanic blood transformed into a disinterested abhorrence of injustice in general and elevated into a revolutionary impulse towards a grandly conceived world-amelioration.[21]

Even when they are rich, the Jews constitute, at least in eastern Europe, a category of persons who are excluded from the social advantages which the prevailing political, economic, and intellectual system ensures for the corresponding portion of the Gentile population. Society, in the narrower sense of the term, is distrustful of them, and public opinion is unfavourable to them. Besides the sentiment which is naturally aroused in their minds by this injustice, they are often affected by that cosmopolitan tendency which has been highly developed in the Jews by the historical experiences of the race, and these combine to push them into the arms of the working-class party. It is owing to these tendencies that the Jews, guided in part by reason and in part by sentimental considerations, so readily disregard the barriers which the bourgeoisie endeavours to erect against the rising flood of the revolution by the accusation that its advocates are *des sans patrie.*

For all these reasons, the Jewish intelligence is apt to find a shorter road to socialism than the Gentile, but this does not diminish the obligations of the socialist party to the Jewish intellectuals. Only to the intellectuals, indeed, for the Jews who

---

[21] Liebknecht declared in a speech: "Slavery does not merely demoralize; it illuminates the mind, elevates the strong, creates idealists and rebels. Thus we find that in the more powerful and nobler natures among the Jews a sense of freedom and justice has been inspired by their unworthy situation and a revolutionary spirit has been cultivated. The result is that there is proportionately a much larger amount of idealism among Jews than among non-Jews" (Wilhelm Liebknecht, *Ueber den Kölner Parteitag mit besonderer Berucksichtigung der Gewerkschaftsbewegung*, Buchdruckerei Volkswacht, Bielefeld, 1893, p. 33).—Regarding the revolutionary-idealist-fanatical tendencies of Judaism, see also the brilliant analysis by Guglielmo Ferrero in *L'Europa giovane*, Treves, Milan, 1897, pp. 358 et seq.

belong to the wealthy trading and manufacturing classes and also the members of the Jewish petty bourgeoisie, whilst often voting socialist in the elections, steadily refuse to join the socialist party. Here the interests of class prevail over those of race. It is very different with the Jewish intellectuals, and a statistical enquiry would certainly show that not less than 2 to 3 per cent. of these are members of the socialist party. If the socialist party has always manifested an unhesitating resistance to antisemite sentiment, this is due not merely to the theoretical socialist aversion for all "nationalism" and all racial prejudices, but also to the consciousness of all that the party owes to the Jewish intellectuals.

"Antisemite socialism" made its first appearance about 1870. Eugen Dühring, at that time *Privatdozent* at the University of Berlin, inaugurated a crusade in favour of a "German" socialism as opposed to the "Jewish" socialism of Marx and his collaborators.[22] This movement was inspired by patriotic motives, for Dühring held that the victory of Marxian socialism could not fail to result in the complete subordination of the people to the state, to the advantage of the prominent Jews and their acolytes.[23] Towards 1875, Dühring became the centre of a small group of Berlinese socialists of which Johann Most and the Jew Eduard Bernstein were members. The influence of this group, however, did not survive the great polemic which Dühring had to sustain with Friedrich Engels, the spiritual brother of "Marx the Jew."[24] Dühring's influence upon the socialist masses in fact declined in proportion as his antisemitism became accentuated, and towards 1878 it was extinct. In 1894 another attempt was made to give socialism an antisemite tendency. This was the work of Richard Calwer, another socialist of strongly nationalist views, at that time on the staff of the "Braunschweiger Volksfreund." "For every good Jewish writer," he declared, "there will be found at least half a dozen who are altogether worthless, but who possess an extraordinary power of self-assertion and an inexhaustible flow of words, but no real understanding of socialism."[25] Calwer's campaign had, however, no better

---

[22] Cf. Eugen Dühring, *Kritische Geschichte der Nationalœkonomie u. der Sozialismus*, Th. Grieben, Berlin, 1871, pp. 589 et seq.

[23] Eugen Dühring, *Sache, Leben u. Feinde*, Carlsruhe, 1882, p. 207.

[24] Cf. Engels' work, *Herrn Eugen Dührings Umwälzung der Wissenschaft*, first published in 1877 in the Leipzig "Vorwärts."

[25] R. Calwer, *Das Kommunistische Manifest*, ed. cit., p. 41.

success than that of Dühring. A year before, when petty bourgeois antisemitism was spreading through the country as an
anti-capitalist movement which was forming itself into a political party and making victims everywhere, the Cologne congress
(October 1893) took up a definite position towards this new political movement. Bebel's report (which in antisemite circles
had been anticipated with satisfaction), although far from exhaustive, was inspired throughout by a sentiment friendly towards the Jews. Bebel said: ''The Jewish student is as a rule
industrious during the greater part of his university career,
whereas the 'Germanic' student most commonly spends his time
in the drinking-bars and restaurants, in the fencing-schools, or
in other places which I will not here more particularly specify
(laughter).'' [26] Wilhelm Liebknecht, in his well-known speech
at Bielefeld,[27] notably reinforced the impression hostile to antisemitism produced by the congress. Since that time (if we except certain observations made at the Lübeck congress in 1901 by
the barrister Wolfgang Heine in a polemic against Parvus and
Rosa Luxemburg [28]—remarks that were maladroit rather than
expressions of principle, and at the worst foolish reminiscences
of a youth passed as a leader in the *Verein deutscher Studenten*)
the German socialists have remained immune to the virus of
race hatred, and have shown themselves quite unconcerned when
ignorant opponents have endeavoured to arouse popular prejudice against them by speaking of them as a party of ''Jews and
their satellites.'' [29]

We may now add certain observations upon the frequent adhesion to socialism of members of the plutocracy, an adhesion
which at first sight seems so strange. Certain persons of a gentle
and charitable disposition, abundantly furnished with everything
that can satisfy their desires, are sometimes inspired by the
need of undertaking propagandist activities. They wish, for
example, to make their neighbours share in the well-being which
they themselves enjoy. These are the rich philanthropists. In
most cases their conduct is the outcome of hypersensitiveness or

[26] *Protokoll*, p. 234.
[27] Quoted above, p. 261.
[28] *Protokoll*, p. 195.
[29] At election times the German antisemites make it a regular practice
to exploit the barbarous race-prejudices with which the common people
are still animated, endeavouring in this way to render suspect as a Jew,
or at least as a protégé of the Jews, every socialist candidate whose name
might suggest a Jewish origin, such as David, or even Auer.

sentimentalism; they cannot endure the sufferings of others, not so much because they experience a genuine pity for the sufferers, but because the sight of pain arouses pain in themselves and shocks their æsthetic sense. They thus resemble the majority of human beings, who cannot bear to see pigeons slaughtered but whose sentiments in this respect do not impair their relish for a pigeon-pie.

In the sick brains of certain persons whose wealth is exceeded only by their love of paradox, there has originated the fantastic belief that in view of the imminence of the revolution they can preserve their fortunes from the confiscatory fury of the revolutionists only by making profession of the socialist faith, and by thus gaining the powerful and useful friendship of its leaders. It is this ingenuous belief which has thrown them into the arms of the socialists. Others, again, among the rich, hasten to enrol themselves as members of the socialist party, in the dread lest their lives should be threatened through the exasperation of the poor.[30] More frequently, however, as has been well shown by Bernard Shaw, the rich man is drawn towards socialism because he finds the greatest possible difficulty in procuring for himself any new pleasures. He begins to feel a disgust for the bourgeois world, and in the end this may stifle his class consciousness, or at least may suppress the instinct which has hitherto led him to fight for self-preservation against the proletariat.[31]

It is a very striking phenomenon how large is the percentage of Jewish *rentiers* who become members of the socialist party.[32] In part this may be due to the racial characteristics of the Jew to which reference has already been made. In part, however, it is the outcome of the psychological peculiarities of the wealthy man afflicted with satiety. In certain cases, again, the strongly developed love of acquisition characteristic of the Jews affords the explanation, where the possibility has been recognized of making a clever investment of capital even in working-class undertakings.

---

[30] "'O riches, une solidarité de céleste origine vous enchaîne à leur misère [la misère des prolétaires] par la peur, et vous lie par votre intérêt même à leur délivrance future'' (Louis Blanc, *Organisation du Travail*, ed. cit., p. 25).

[31] Bernard Shaw, *Socialism for Millionaires*, Fabian Society, London, 1901.

[32] This fact has been noted by various writers, among others by G. Sorel, *Illusions du Progrès*, ed cit., pp. 206 et seq., and Domela Nieuwenhuis, *Van Christen*, etc., ed. cit., p. 322.

It may, however, be said without fear of error that the great majority of young bourgeois who come over to socialism do so, to quote an expression used by Felice Momigliano, in perfect sincerity and inspired by ardent goodwill. They seek neither popular approbation, nor wealth, nor distinctions, nor well-paid positions. They think merely that a man must set himself right with his own conscience and must affirm his faith in action.[33]

These men, again, may be classed in two distinct categories. We have, on the one hand, the loving apostles of wide sympathies, who wish to embrace the whole of humanity in their ideal. On the other hand we have the zealots, fierce, rigid, austere, and uncompromising.[34]

But among the socialists of bourgeois origin we find other and less agreeable elements. Above all there are those who make a profession of discontent, the neurasthenics and the *mauvais coucheurs*. Yet more numerous are the malcontents from personal motives, the charlatans, and the ambitious. Many hate the authority of the state because it is inaccessible to them.[35] It is the old story of the fox and the grapes. They are animated by jealousy, by the unassuaged thirst for power; their feelings resemble those of the younger sons of great families who are inspired with hatred and envy towards their richer and more fortunate brothers. They are animated by a pride which makes them prefer the position of chief in proletarian Gaul to that of subordinate in aristocratic Rome.

There are yet other types somewhat similar to those just enumerated. First of all, there are the eccentrics. It seems natural that those whose position is low should attempt to storm the heights. But there are some whose position is lofty and who yet experience an irresistible need to descend from the heights, where they feel that their movements are restricted, and who believe that by descending they will gain greater liberty. They seek "sincerity"; they endeavour to dis-

---

[33] Momigliano, in an article which appeared in the "Ragione" of Rome, reprinted in "Cœnobium," anno iv, fasc. i, p. 139.

[34] "Le mépris et les persécutions ne les touchent pas, ou ne font que les exciter d'avantage. Intérêt personnel, famille, tout est sacrifié. L'instinct de la conservation lui-même est annullé chez eux, au point que la seule récompense qu'ils solicitent souvent est de devenir des martyrs" (Gustave le Bon, *Psychologie des Foules*, ed. cit., p. 106).

[35] Cf. Jules Destrée, *Révolution verbale et Révolution pratique*, "Le Peuple," Brussels, 1902, p. 51; also Giorgio Arcoleo, *Forme vecchie, Idee nuove*, Laterza, Bari, 1909, p. 196.

cover "the people" of whom they have an ideal in their minds; they are idealists to the verge of lunacy.

There may be added all those disillusioned and dissatisfied persons who have not succeeded in gaining the attention of the bourgeoisie to an extent proportionate to their own conception of their genius. Such persons throw themselves on the neck of the proletariat,[36] in most cases with the vague and instinctive hope of attaining a speedier success in view of the deficient culture of the working classes, of gaining a place in the limelight and playing a leading part. They are visionaries, geniuses misunderstood, apostates of all kinds, literary bohemians, the unrecognized inventors of various social panaceas, *ratés, rapins, cabotins,* quack-salvers at the fair, clowns—all persons who are not thinking of educating the masses but of cultivating their own egos.

The numerical increase of the party, which is associated with an increasing prestige (in the popular esteem, at least, if not in the official world), exercises a great force of attraction. In such countries as Germany, above all, where the gregarious spirit is highly developed, small parties are condemned to a stinted and rickety existence.[37] But numerous bourgeois believe that they will "find in the great socialist party what they have not been able to find in the bourgeois parties," a suitable platform for political activity upon a vast scale.[38] For this reason, and above all when the party passes from opposition to governmental collaboration,[39] there results a great increase in the number of those who regard the party as a mere means to their own ends, as a pedestal from whose elevation they can better satisfy their ambition and their vanity, those who regard success not as a goal to be attained for the good of the cause, or as the reward for arduous service in pursuit of ideal aims, but one coveted on its own account for the enlargement of their own personalities. As Arcoleo has well expressed it, we dread the triumph of such persons as if it were the unchaining of hungry wild beasts, but on closer examination we discover that after all they are no more than greedy molluscs, harmless on the whole.[40] These consider-

---

[36] Cf. Giuseppe Prezzolini *La Teoria sindacalista,* ed. cit., p. 90.

[37] Cf. letter published by Fr. Naumann apropos of the dissolution of the *Nationalsozialer Verein* after the elections of 1904.

[38] August Bebel, *Ein Nachwort zur Vizepräsidentenfrage u. Verwandtem,* loc. cit., "Neue Zeit," 1903 (Separatabzug), pp. 20, 21.

[39] Cf. also the considerations to which reference has been made on pp. 212-214.

[40] G. Arcoleo, *Forme Vecchie, Idee Nuove,* ed. cit., p. 80.

ations apply to petty affairs as well as to great ones. Whenever the party of the workers founds a cooperative society or a people's bank which offers to intellectuals an assured subsistence and an influential position, there flock to the scene numerous professional socialists who are equally devoid of true socialist knowledge and genuine socialist sentiment. In democracy as elsewhere success signifies the death of idealism.

CHAPTER III

SOCIAL CHANGES RESULTING FROM ORGANIZATION

THE social changes which organization produces among the
proletarian elements, and the alterations which are effected in
the proletarian movement through the influx of those new influences which the organization attracts within its orbit, may be
summed up in the comprehensive customary term of the *embourgeoisement* of working-class parties. This embourgeoisement is
the outcome of three very different orders of phenomena: (1)
the adhesion of petty bourgeois to the proletarian parties; (2)
labour organization as the creator of new petty bourgeois strata;
(3) capitalist defence as the creator of new petty bourgeois
strata.

1. *The Adhesion of Petty Bourgeois to the Proletarian Parties.*

For motives predominantly electoral, the party of the workers
seeks support from the petty bourgeois elements of society, and
this gives rise to more or less extensive reactions upon the party
itself. The labour party becomes the party of the "people." Its
appeals are no longer addressed simply to the manual workers,
but to "all producers," to the "entire working population,"
these phrases being applied to all the classes and all the strata
of society except the idlers who live upon the income from in-
vestments.[1] Both the friends and the enemies of the socialist
party have frequently pointed out that the petty bourgeois
members tend more and more to predominate over the manual
workers. During the struggles which occurred during the early
part of 1890 in the German socialist party against the so-called
"youths," the assertion that during recent years a complete
transposition of power had occurred within the party aroused a
veritable tempest. On one side it was maintained that the proletarian elements were to an increasing extent being thrust into

---

[1] Cf. p. 16.

the background by the petty bourgeois. The other faction repudiated this accusation as a "calumny." One of the best established generalizations which we obtain from the study of history is this, that political parties, even when they are the advocates of moral and social ideas of profound import, find it very difficult to tolerate the utterance of inconvenient truths. We have seen that the most unprejudiced enquiries are apt to be regarded as the outcome of a vicious tendency to fault-finding. The truth is, however, that an objective and searching discussion of the question leads us to recognize the wrongheadedness at once of those who are content flatly to deny the embourgeoisement of the socialist party and also of those who are content to sing the praises of the great socialist petty bourgeois party. Neither view is sound. The processes at work are too complex for solution by easy phrase-making.

It may sometimes happen (although statistical proof of this is lacking) that in South Germany in certain socialist branches, and still more in certain party congresses, the petty bourgeoisie, though not numerically predominant, can yet exercise a preponderant influence. It may even be admitted that under certain conditions the strength of the petty bourgeois elements and the respect which is paid to them may at times compromise the proletarian essence of the party. Even so rigid a Marxist as Karl Kautsky is of opinion that the attitude of socialists towards distributive cooperative societies must depend mainly upon their attitude towards the minor distributive trade in general, so that, "on political grounds," socialists must oppose the foundation of cooperative societies wherever, as often happens, small traders offer a favourable recruiting-ground for socialism.[2]

Wherever it has been possible to analyse the composition of the socialist party, and to ascertain the classes and the professions of its adherents, it has generally been found that the bourgeois and petty bourgeois elements, although well represented, are far from being numerically preponderant. The official statistics of the Italian socialist party present the following figures:— Industrial workers, 42.27%; agricultural labourers, 14.99%; peasant proprietors, 6.1%; independent artisans, 14.92%; employees, 3.3%; property owners, 4.89%; students and members of the liberal professions, 3.8%.[3] As regards the German social-

---

[2] Karl Kautsky, *Der Parteitag von Hannover,* "Neue Zeit," anno xviii, No. 1.

[3] Michels, *Proletariato e Borghesia, etc.,* ed. cit., p. 136.

ist party, the writer has shown elsewhere [4] that in all the branches the proportion of proletarians is yet greater than in Italy, ranging from 77.4% to 94.7%. It may even be said, with Blank, that if there is a party in which the proletarian element predominates, it is the German socialist party—not indeed in respect of its voting strength,[5] but pre-eminently in respect of its inscribed membership. It is this social homogeneity which renders the socialist party so great an electoral force, giving to it a cohesion unknown to the other political parties, and especially to the other parties of the left. German liberalism has always been (at any rate since the unification of the empire) a multi-coloured admixture of classes, united not so much by economic needs as by common ideal aims. Socialism, on the other hand, derives its human materials from the only class which presents those economic, social, and numerical conditions requisite to furnish the greatest possible vigour for the struggle to overthrow the old world and to instal a new one in its place. Blind indeed must be he who fails to recognize that the spring which feeds the socialist party in Germany, a spring which shows no signs of running dry, is the proletariat, the class of wage-labourers.

We must therefore accept with all reserve the statements of those anarchizing socialists and bourgeois radicals who accuse the socialist party of "embourgeoisement" because it contains a certain number of small manufacturers and small traders. The embourgeoisement of the party is an unquestionable fact, but its causes will be found in a process very different from the entry into the organizations of the fighting proletariat of a few hundred members of the middle class. The chief of these causes is the metamorphosis which takes place in the leaders of working-class origin, with the resulting embourgeoisement of the whole atmosphere in which the political activities of the party are carried on.[6]

---

[4] Michels, *Die deutsche Sozialdemokratie. Parteimitgliedschaft u. soziale Zusammensetzung,* "Archiv f. Sozialwiss.," vol. xxiii, pp. 471-559.

[5] R. Blank, *Die sociale Zusammensetzung der sozialdemokratischen Wählerschaft Deutschlands,* "Archiv f. Sozialwiss.," vol. xx, fasc. 3; but the author is wrong in drawing the conclusion (p. 535) "that the German social democracy is not a class party in respect of composition." He should have said, "In respect of the composition of the socialist electorate."

[6] Parvus writes: "There is a confusion between two distinct things: the petty bourgeois existences which are created by the party movement, and the entrance of petty bourgeois elements into the party. These should

2. *Labour Organization as the Creator of New Petty Bourgeois Strata.*

The class struggle, through the action of the organs whereby it is carried out, induces modifications and social metamorphoses in the party which has come into existence to organize and control the struggle. Certain groups of individuals, numerically insignificant but qualitatively of great importance, are withdrawn from the proletarian class and raised to bourgeois dignity.

Where, as in Italy, the party of the workers contains a considerable proportion of bourgeois, most of the posts which the party has at its disposal are in the hands of intellectuals. In England, on the other hand, and still more in Germany, it is otherwise, for here the demand on the part of the socialist movement for employees is met chiefly by a supply of persons from the rank and file. In these countries the party leadership is mainly in the hands of the workers, as is shown by the following table:—

SOCIALIST GROUP IN THE REICHSTAG, 1903-6.

By Origin.		By Profession.	
I. Intellectuals and Bourgeois..	13	I. Professional men	17
	—		—
II. Petty Bourgeois............	15	II. Independent means........	2
	—	Manufacturers	1
		Publishers	2
			—
		Bourgeois	5
III. Proletarians:		III. Petty Bourgeois:	
Textile	3	Innkeepers	6
Tobacco	8	Independent artisans and	
Printing	7	working employers	6
Tailoring	3	Small shopkeepers	3
Glass-blowing	2	Small manufacturers	5
Masonry	1	Owners of printing works.	4
Lithography	1		—
Basket-work	1	*Petty bourgeois*	24
Glove-making	1		

be separately considered'' (Parvus, *Die Gewerkschaften und die Sozialdemokratie Kritischer Bericht über die Lager u. die Aufgaben der deutschen Arbeiterbewegung*, ''Sächs. Arbeiterzeitung,'' Dresden, 1896, 2nd ed., p. 65).

III. Proletarians (*continued*):

Saddlery	1		
Stone-cutting	1		
Turning	1		
Carpet-weaving	1		
Bootmaking	1		
Wood-working	10	IV. Employees in the labour	
Bookbinding	1	movement	35
Mining	2		
Metallurgy	6		
Brush-making	1		
Pottery	1		

Manual workers....... 53

By Origin.		By Profession.	
	%		%
13 intellectuals and bourgeois	= 16.05	17 professional men	= 20.99
15 petty bourgeois	= 18.52	5 bourgeois	= 6.17
54 proletarians (*skilled workers*)	= 65.43	24 petty bourgeois	= 29.63
		35 employees	= 43.21

Consequently an entry into the party hierarchy becomes an aim of proletarian ambition.

An ex-member of the German socialist party who some years ago, having entered the service of one of the bourgeois parties, amused himself by caricaturing his former comrades, declared that the whole party organization with all its various degrees of propagandist activity was "cut upon the military model," and that the members were "promoted by seniority." [7] There is at least this much truth in Abel's assertion, that to every member of the party the possibility of gradual advance remains open, and that each may hope, should circumstances prove exceptionally favourable, to scale the olympian heights of a seat in the Reichstag.

Proletarian leaders of the socialist parties and of the trade unions are an indirect product of the great industry. At the dawn of the capitalist era certain workers, more intelligent and more ambitious than their fellows, succeeded, through indefatigable exertions and thanks to favourable circumstances, in raising themselves to the employing class. To-day, however, in view of the concentration of enterprise and wealth and of the high cost of production, such a transformation can be observed only in

---

[7] Abel, quoted by "Vorwärts," August 5, 1904.

certain parts of North and South America (which explains, it may be mentioned in passing, the insignificant development of socialism in the New World). As far as Europe is concerned, where there is no longer any virgin soil to exploit, the "self-made man" has become a prehistoric figure. Thus it is natural that enlightened workmen should seek some compensation for the lost paradise of their dreams. Numerous are to-day the workers whose energies and aptitudes are not fully utilized in the narrow circle of their professional occupations, often utterly uninteresting and demanding purely mechanical labour.[8] It is chiefly in the modern labour movement that such men now seek and obtain the opportunity of improving their situation, an opportunity which industry no longer offers. The movement represents for them a new and loftier mode of life, and offers at the same time a new branch of employment, with a chance, which continually increases as the organization grows, that they will be able to secure a rise in the social scale. There can be no doubt that the socialist party, with its posts of honour, which are almost always salaried, exercises a potent stimulus upon active-minded youths of the working class from the very outset of their adhesion to its ranks. Those who are keen in political matters, and also those among the workers who possess talent as writers or speakers, cannot fail to experience the magnetic influence of a party which offers so rich a field for the use and development of their talents. Consequently we must accept as a logical truth what was pointed out by Guglielmo Ferrero, that whilst the adhesion of anyone of proletarian origin to the socialist party always presupposes a certain minimum of special aptitudes and favourable circumstances, yet such adhesion must be considered desirable and advantageous, not only upon ideal grounds and from motives of class egoism, but also for speculative reasons of personal egoism. For an intelligent German workman there is hardly any other way which offers him such rapid opportunities of "improving his condition" as service in the socialist army.[9] One of the first persons to recognize the bearing of these possibilities, and to utilize them, with considerable partisan exaggeration, for his own peculiar political ends, was Prince Bismarck. During the violent struggle between the government and

---

[8] Heinrich Herkner, *Die Arbeiterfrage*, ed. cit., p. 186; as regards Italy, Angelo Mosso, *Vita moderna degli Italiani*, Treves, Milan, 1906, pp. 249, 262-3.

[9] Guglielmo Ferrero, *L'Europa giovane*, ed. cit., pp. 72 et seq.

the socialist party he declared: "The position of socialist agitator has to-day become a regular industry, just like any other. A man becomes an agitator or a popular orator as in former days he became a smith or a carpenter. One who adopts this new occupation is often much better off than if he had kept at his old work, gaining a more agreeable and freer life, one which in certain circles brings him more respect."[10] The allusion to the agreeable and free life of the socialist agitator recalls a phrase used by William II, who, apropos of the Krupp affair, spoke of the "safe ambush" from which socialist editors could shoot their carefully aimed arrows of calumny. The emperor's criticism is unjust, for the socialist editor who departs from the truth is always exposed to the risk of prosecution and punishment. Bismarck hit the right nail on the head.

A gigantic and magnificently organized party like the German socialist party has need of a no less gigantic apparatus of editors, secretaries, bookkeepers, and numerous other employees, whose sole task is to serve this colossal machine. *Mutatis mutandis* the same is true of the other great branch of the working-class movement, the trade-union organizations. Now, for the reasons that have previously been discussed, there are available for the service of the German labour movement no more than a very small number of refugees from the bourgeoisie. It is for this reason that most of the posts are filled by men of working-class origin, who by zeal and by study have succeeded in gaining the confidence of their comrades. It may, then, be said that there exists a proletarian *élite* which arises spontaneously by a process of natural selection within the socialist party, and that its members come to perform functions altogether different from those which they originally exercised. To make use of a phrase which is convenient and comprehensible despite its lack of scientific precision, we may say that such men have abandoned manual work to become brain-workers. For those who make such a change considerable advantages accrue, altogether independent of the advantages which attach *per se* to mental work when compared to manual. The manual worker who has become an official of the socialist party is no longer in a position of strictly personal and purely mercenary dependence upon his employer or upon the manager of the factory; he has become a free man,

---

[10] Speech in the Reichstag, October 9, 1878. Cf. *Fürst Bismarck's Reden, mit verbind geschichtlicher Darstellung von Philipp Stein*, Reclam, Leipzig, vol. viii, p. 110.

engaged in intellectual work on behalf of an impersonal enterprise. Moreover, he is bound to this enterprise, not solely by his strongest material interests, but also by the powerful ties of the ideal and of solidarity in the struggle. And notwithstanding certain exceptions which may confuse the minds of the profane, he is treated far more humanely than by any private employer. In relation to the party the employee is not a simple wage-earner, but rather a profit-sharing associate—not, of course, a profit-sharer in the industrial sense, since the party is not a commercial undertaking for the earning of dividends, but a profit-sharer in the ideal sense. It is not suggested that the party employee earns his bread in the most pleasant way in the world. On the contrary, as has been said in earlier chapters,[11] the daily bread, which with rare exceptions is not unduly plentiful, must be earned by the fulfilment of an enormous amount of labour, prematurely exhausting health and energy. Nevertheless the ex-manual worker can live with dignity and comparative ease. Since he has a fixed salary, his position is more secure, and though outwardly more stormy, it is inwardly more tranquil, than that of the ordinary wage-earner. Should he be imprisoned, the party cares for him and his dependents, and the more often he is prosecuted the better become his chances of rapid advancement in his career of socialist official with all the advantages attaching to the position.

We may here consider the interesting question, What is the numerical ratio between the socialist bureaucracy and the organized masses; how many comrades are there for each party official? If we include in the term "official" all the mandataries of the party in the communes, etc., most of whom are unpaid, we sometimes attain to surprising results. For example, the socialist organization of the grand duchy of Baden, with a membership(1905) of 7,332, had more than 1,000 municipal councillors.[12] According to these figures, every seventh member of the Badenese party had the honour of being a party representative. This example, however, was quoted by the executive in its report to the congress of Jena precisely on account of its abnormality. Even though it may not be unique in southern Germany, it does not in truth bear upon the question we are now considering, which is the numerical relation between the enrolled

---

[11] Cf. pp. 57, 115.
[12] *Protokoll d. Verhandl. d. Parteitags zu Jena*, 1905, p. 16.

membership and the party employees in the strict sense of the term, considered as a group of persons permanently and directly engaged in the service of the collectivity. The following figures give some idea of this ratio. According to a notice which in 1904 went the round of the German socialist press,[13] the party at that time employed, in addition to 1,476 persons engaged in the party printing establishment (about two-thirds of whom enjoyed the benefits of the eight-hour day, whilst many also had the right to regular holidays), 329 individuals working on the editorial staff and as delivery agents. The daily socialist press had in 1909 a circulation of one million, whilst the trade-union journals, weekly for the most part, had a far higher circulation.[14] Alike in the trade unions and in the socialist party the number of paid employees is rapidly increasing. The first regularly appointed and paid leaders in the European labour movement were the officials nominated in 1840 by the English Ironfounders' Society. To-day in the trade-union organizations of the United Kingdom there are more than one thousand salaried employees.[15] In Germany, in the year 1898, the number of trade-union officials was 104; in 1904 it was 677, of whom 100 belonged to the metal-workers and 70 to the bricklayers and masons' union. This increase in the officialdom is accelerated, not merely by the steady increase in the membership, but also by the increasing complexity of the benefits offered by the organizations. Almost every meeting of the central executive discusses and determines upon the appointment of new officials, rendered essential by the further differentiation of the trade-union functions.[16] There are always found advocates for the creation of fresh specialized posts in the labour movement, to fulfil various technical offices, to keep abreast of new discoveries and advances in methods of manufacture, to check the returns made by factory employers, to act as economists and compile trade statistics.[17]

For some years past the same tendency has been manifest in the German socialist party. According to the report of the executive for the year 1909, very many district organizations now employ salaried secretaries. The number of district secretaries

[13] "Mitteldeutsche Sonntagszeitung," xi, No. 14.

[14] Karl Kautsky, *Der Weg zur Macht*, "Vorwärts," Berlin, 1909, p. 56.

[15] Fausto Pagliari, *Le Organ. e i loro Impiegati*, ed. cit., pp. 8-9.

[16] Ernst Deinhardt, *Das Beamtenelement im den deutschen Gewerkschaften*, "Sozial Monatsh.," ix (xi), fasc. 12, p. 1019.

[17] Adolph Braun, *Gewerkschaftliche Verfassungsfragen*, "Neue Zeit," xxix, No. 89.

is 43, whilst in a single year the number of secretaries of constituencies increased from 41 to 62.[18] There is a mutual aid society for officials of the socialist party and of the trade unions, and its membership continually increases. In 1902 it had 433 members; in 1905, 1,095; in 1907, 1,871; and in 1909, 2,474. But there must be officials who are not members of the society.[19]

When he abandons manual work for intellectual, the worker undergoes another transformation which involves his whole existence. He gradually leaves the proletariat to become a member of the petty bourgeois class. At first, as we have seen, there is no more than a change in his professional and economic situation. The salaries paid by the party, although modest, are distinctly greater than the average wage which the worker gained before his entry into the socialist bureaucracy, and are calculated to enable the recipients to lead a petty bourgeois life. In one of the German socialist congresses, Wilhelm Liebknecht apostrophized the other leaders in the following terms: "You are for the most part aristocrats among the workers—aristocrats, I mean, in respect of income. The workers in the Erzgebirge or the weavers of Silesia would regard the salaries you earn as the income of a Crœsus." [20] It is true, at least in the majority of cases, that the career of the party or trade-union employee does not positively transform the ex-manual worker into a capitalist.[21] Yet this career effects a notable elevation of the worker above the class to which he primarily belonged,[22] and in Germany there

---

[18] *Protokoll d. Ver. d. Parteitags zu Leipzig*, "Vorwärts," Berlin, 1909, p. 20.—Similar phenomena may be observed in Italy, cf. *supra*, p. 125.

[19] Adolf Weber, *Kapital und Arbeit*, ed. cit., p. 389.

[20] *Protokoll des Parteitags zu Berlin*, 1892, p. 122.

[21] It may be noted that the bourgeois aspect of certain positions to which the former manual worker attains, thanks to the party, is apparent rather than real. Thus, certain German socialist leaders are described as being by civil status "owners of printing works," when they are in reality no more than the *legal* proprietors of undertakings belonging to the party, and receive, in addition to the salary properly payable for the work in which they are engaged, no more than a percentage on the profits of the undertaking.

[22] It is obvious that those proletarians who have become members of the Reichstag, and whose speeches display a technical knowledge of working-class life, cannot remain manual workers. It is impossible to be working as a bricklayer at three o'clock and at four to give a speech in parliament upon stock-exchange legislation. Parliamentary life requires study and expert knowledge, and the work of party leadership involves a man's whole activities. For economic reasons, too, it is impossible for the parliamentary representative to remain in the working class. The attempt to combine

is applied to the existence led by such persons the sociologically precise term of *gehobene Arbeiterexistenz* (a working-class life on a higher scale). Karl Marx himself did not hesitate to classify the working-class leaders under two heads, as *höherklassige* (workers of a superior class, intellectual workers) and *Arbeiter* (manual workers properly speaking).[23] As we shall show in fuller detail in a subsequent chapter,[24] the manual worker of former days becomes a petty bourgeois or even a bourgeois. In addition to this metamorphosis, and despite his frequent contact with the mass of the workers, he undergoes a profound psychological transformation. The paid official, living at a higher social level, will not always possess the moral strength to resist the seductions of his new environment. His political and social education will seldom suffice to immunize him against the new influences. August Bebel repeatedly drew the attention of the party to the dangers by which the leaders were beset, the risks to their class purity and to their unity of thought. The proletarian party-officials, he said, are "persons whose life has become established upon a comparatively stable basis."[25]

A closer examination will show that the phenomenon here considered has a profound social significance, and that neither within nor without the party has it hitherto received the attention it deserves. For the German workers, the labour movement has an importance analogous to that of the Catholic Church for certain fractions of the petty bourgeoisie and of the rural population. In both cases we have an organization which furnishes opportunities to the most intelligent members of certain classes to secure a rise in the social scale. In the Church, the peasant's son will often succeed in achieving social advance, whose equivalent in all the other liberal professions has remained the monopoly of members of the aristocracy of birth or of wealth. No one of peasant birth becomes a general or a prefect, but not a few peasants become bishops. Pope Pius X was of peasant origin. Now that which the Church offers to peasants and to petty

---

manual labour with parliamentary has always failed. Until a few years ago, until June, 1906, in the Badenese diet there was a member who was still engaged as a factory hand, but one day his employer said that he really could not any longer find employment for a representative of the people.

[23] Karl Marx, *Briefe u. Auszuge, etc.*, ed. cit., p. 159.

[24] Part IV, chap. v.

[25] August Bebel, speaking at the Dresden congress, 1903. *Protokoll über die Verhandlungen des Parteitags*, "Vorwärts," Berlin, 1903, p. 230.

bourgeois, namely, a facility for ascent in the social scale, is offered to intelligent manual workers by the socialist party.

As a source of social transformations the socialist party has many affinities with another institution, namely, the Prussian military organization. The son of a bourgeois family who adopts a permanent military career becomes a stranger to his own class. Should he attain to high rank, he will receive a title from the emperor. He loses his bourgeois characteristics and adopts the usages and opinions of his new feudal environment. It is true that these military officers are only manifesting the tendency to the attainment of ''gentility'' in which the whole bourgeoisie is involved,[26] but in their case this process is greatly accelerated, and is effected with a full consciousness of its consequences. Every year hundreds of young men from the upper and middle strata of the bourgeois class become officers in the army, simply from the desire to secure a higher position and more social consideration.[27] In the socialist party a similar effect is often the result of necessity, the individual's social metamorphosis taking place independently of the will. But the general results are similar.

Thus the socialist party gives a lift to certain strata of the working class. The more extensive and the more complicated its bureaucratic mechanism, the more numerous are those raised by this machine above their original social position. It is the involuntary task of the socialist party to remove from the proletariat, to deproletarianize, some of the most capable and best informed of its members. Now, according to the materialist conception of history, the social and economic metamorphosis gradually involves a metamorphosis in the realm of ideas.[28] The consequence is that in many of the ex-workers this embourgeoisement is very rapidly effected. Naturally the change is less speedy in proportion as socialist theory is more deeply rooted in the mind of the individual. Numerous are those manual workers who, having attained a higher social and economic situation, none the less remain throughout their lives profoundly attached

---

[26] Franz Mehring: ''It is distressing that at a time when the army cannot exist without bourgeois money and bourgeois intelligence, the bourgeois youth should have no higher ambition than to force his way into the feudal caste'' (*Der Krieg gegen die Troddeln,* ''Leipziger Volkszeitung,'' xi, No. 4).

[27] Cf. *supra,* p. 14.

[28] Cf. August Bebel's speech to the Dresden congress to which reference has already been made (*Protokoll,* loc. cit.).

to the socialist cause. In this case, however, the ex-manual worker is, just like the ex-bourgeois socialist, an "ideologue," since his mentality does not correspond to his position in society. Sometimes, again, the psychological metamorphosis we are considering is, as it were, inhibited by a tenacious and vigorous hereditary socialist mentality: 'here we see the children and grandchildren following their parents as whole-hearted combatants on behalf of the labour party, notwithstanding the elevated position to which they have attained. Experience shows, however, that such cases are exceptional. Even when the deproletarianized socialist remains a sincere advocate of proletarian emancipation, and grows grey in his position of socialist editor or deputy, his children, sons as well as daughters, are thoroughgoing members of the higher social class into which they have been removed by the improvement in their father's social position, and this not merely in the material sense, but in respect of their ideas, so that it becomes impossible to distinguish them from their fellow-bourgeois.[29] In most cases the only bond which remains to attach the father to the working class, his faith in the politico-social dogma of socialism, is slackened in the son to become an absolute indifference and sometimes an open hostility to socialism. To sum up, it may be said that these former working-class people, considered as families and not as individuals, are absorbed sooner or later into the new bourgeois environment. The children receive a bourgeois education; they attend better schools than those to which their father had access;[30] their interests are bourgeois and they very rarely recall the revolutionary and anti-bourgeois derivation of their own entrance into the bourgeoisie. The working-class families which have been raised by the revolutionary workers to a higher social position, for the

[29] It need hardly be said that this phenomenon is not universal. We observe certain cases in which the children of ex-manual workers who have become officials of the socialist party either desire of their own initiative to become ordinary wage-earners or are forced to do so by the insufficiency of their father's salary, which, especially when the family is a large one, does not suffice to give the children an education "suitable to their new status." There are certain socialist deputies and journalists whose sons have to earn their living as factory hands and whose daughters are ballet-dancers.

[30] A German trade-union employee whose education had been greatly inferior to that of his colleagues, and who, as he himself put it, had never attained to any ease in the right use of the dative and accusative cases, said to me about his son: "I shall be able to send him to the Realgymnasium. My means will run to that now!"

purpose of a more effective struggle against the bourgeoisie, thus come before long to be fused with the bourgeoisie.[31]

Reference has previously been made to a similar phenomenon in the case of the families of working-class leaders who are refugees from the class of bourgeois intellectuals.[32] The final result is the same, the only difference being that the children of the ex-manual workers forget their class of origin, whilst the children of the bourgeois intellectuals recall it. The result is that in the history of the labour movement we may observe a similar irony to that which may be seen in the history of the bourgeois resistance to the workers. The bourgeoisie has not been able to prevent a number of the best instructed, most capable, and most adroit among its elements from placing themselves at the head of the mortal enemies of the bourgeoisie; it is often these ex-bourgeois who stimulate the proletarians to resistance and organize them for the struggle. The proletariat suffers a similar fate. In the severe struggle it has undertaken for the expropriation of the expropriators, it elevates from the depths of its own class those who have the finest intelligences and the keenest vision, by serious collective sacrifices gives them the pen to use in place of ruder tools, and in doing so it throws into the arms of the enemy those who have been selected with the express purpose of fighting the privileged class. If the chosen combatants do not themselves go over to the enemy, their children at least will do so. This is indeed a tragical destiny: ex-bourgeois on the one side, and ex-manual workers on the other. The imposing politi-

---

[31] It is by no means uncommon to find that the sons of noted socialist leaders, when they do not avoid all political activity and exhibit a disinclination to the discussion of political problems, frequently display themselves in public as the most violent opponents of socialism. Among such opponents, in Germany, we have a son of the socialist deputy Karl Ulrich (who was a metal-worker before he entered the party bureaucracy); a son of the late socialist leader Wilhelm Bracke, the barrister Bracke of Breslau, who belongs to the extreme right and is a member of the Reichsverband zur Bekämpfung der Sozialdemokratie (anti-socialist league); and there are other instances. Sometimes it is doubtless the outcome of unhappy family relationships that the children of socialists follow other paths than the fathers: the bourgeois family of the socialist leader persists in its old anti-socialist views, in which the pater-familias has been unable to effect any change. The wife and daughter of Jean Jaurès, the anti-clerical, for example, are strict Catholics. The daughter for a long time cherished the idea of entering a convent, hoping by this sacrifice to avert God's anger which would otherwise be visited upon her father on account of his political activities.

[32] Cf. *supra,* p. 250.

cal contest between the classes representing respectively capital and labour ends, however paradoxical this may appear, in a manner analogous with that which in the sphere of economic competition is determined through the operation of supply and demand, speculation, personal adroitness, etc.—in a social exchange among the classes. It is hardly necessary to repeat that this interchange of the ripples on the surface of the waves does not weaken, and far less annul, the profundity of social antagonisms. It is obvious that the process of social exchange can on either side affect no more than infinitesimal minorities. But it affects the most influential, and herein lies its sociological importance. It affects the self-made leaders.

3. *Capitalist Defence as the Creator of New Petty Bourgeois Strata.*

The embourgeoisement of certain strata of the working-class party has other factors in addition to the influence of the bureaucratic apparatus of the socialist party, the trade unions, and the cooperative societies. This development, which is a necessary characteristic of every movement towards emancipation, is to a certain extent paralleled by the constitution of a petty bourgeoisie of strongly proletarian characteristics, itself also developed from below upwards, itself also an accessory phenomenon of the struggle of the organized workers for social emancipation, but which takes place outside the various forms of socialist organization. We allude to those proletarian elements which become particularly numerous in times of crisis, when the labour organizations are still weak and persecuted, as was the case in Germany during the days of the anti-socialist law. At such times numerous proletarians are victimized, it may be on account of their passive fidelity to party or trade union, it may be because their attitude is frankly socialist and "subversive." Forced by necessity, these victims of capitalist reprisals have no other resource than to adopt some form of independent enterprise. Abandoning their ancient handicraft, they open a small shop, fruit and vegetables, stationery, grocery, or tobacco; they become pedlars, keep a coffee-stall, or the like.[33] In most cases

---

[33] Richard Calwer (*Das kommunistische Manifest, etc.*, ed. cit., pp. 8 et seq.) inveighs with especial vigour against these petty bourgeois socialists. He makes the caustic observation: "To-day a man's every need, from clothing to cigars, can be supplied at petty bourgeois socialist establishments." No doubt he is aiming also at the cooperatives.

their ancient associates support them with admirable solidarity, regarding it as a duty to assist these unfortunate comrades by giving them their custom. It sometimes happens that some of these new petty bourgeois find their way definitely into the middle class. Thus capitalist resistance has automatically created new strata of petty bourgeois.

In addition to these victims of the struggle for proletarian emancipation, there are not a few workers who leave their class, not from necessity, but influenced to a large extent by the love of speculation and the desire to improve their social position. Thus there has come into existence a whole army of ex-proletarians, petty bourgeois and small shopkeepers, who all claim, in virtue of a superior moral right, that the comrades must support them by dealing exclusively at their establishments. The mode of life of these small traders often reduces them, despite all their good wishes, to the level of social parasites; their command of capital being extremely small, the goods they offer to their customers, that is to say to the organized workers, are both bad and dear.

Still more important in German socialism is the rôle of those who are termed *Parteibudiger*, that is to say tavern-keepers who are members of the party. During the prevalence of the anti-socialist law their political mission was of incontestable importance. In many small towns the tavern-keepers belonging to the party still exercise multifarious and important functions. It is in their houses that the executive committee meets; often these are the only places where socialist and trade-union journals are found on the tables; and in many cases, since the owners of other halls are hostile or timid, it is here alone that public meetings can be held. In a word, they are necessary instruments in the local socialist struggle.[34] In the more important centres, however, these places, with their unhygienic environment, become a veritable curse to the party. It may be added that the brutal struggle for existence leads the petty bourgeois

---

[34] We owe to the pens of foreign observers some vigorous descriptions of the life of these *Parteikneipen*, a life not devoid of psychological interest. Among these we may refer to *La Démocratie socialiste allemande*, by Edgard Milhaud, professor of political economy at the University of Geneva, a French socialist (pp. 148 et seq.); also to the work of Otto Von Leixner, which dates back to the days of the anti-socialist law (*Soziale Briefe*, ed. cit., p. 325)—but this writer of feuilletons gives us a picture which is too highly coloured.

tavern-keepers to exercise improper pressure upon the socialist organizations. They enjoy a considerable influence among the comrades, and this pressure is commonly exerted in a manner directly injurious to the interests of the proletariat. The attempts which have been made in Germany, especially since 1890, to induce the workers to abandon the unwholesome rooms of the old taverns and to frequent the great modern establishments with fine airy halls, have led, as was inevitable, to "a vigorous opposition" on the part of the socialist tavern-keepers.[35] For many years the members of the party whose living is made by the sale of drink have energetically resisted the foundation of "People's Houses"; notwithstanding the sympathy for such institutions they may theoretically possess, they dread this new form of competition, and act in accordance with their immediate personal interests. In most cases their opposition has proved ineffectual.[36] Not always, however. Even to-day there exist German towns with from twenty thousand to thirty thousand inhabitants in which the existence of a *Parteikneipe* (which despite its name of "Party tavern" is the exclusive property of some individual member of the party) has proved an insuperable obstacle in the way of the local labour organizations when they have desired to build a place of their own, or even to obtain from other and non-socialist innkeepers the use of a more commodious hall for their meetings.

For an additional reason, these socialist taverns are calamitous in their influence upon the party, in that they oppose a potent obstacle to the extension of the temperance movement which has been initiated during recent years.[37] It is no secret in socialist

---

[35] R. Calwer, op. cit., p. 9.

[36] The "Korrespondenzblatt" of the General Committee published in 1906 (No. 29) statistics regarding the activity of *Gewerkschaftskartelle* (Trades' Councils), from which we cull the following details. A *Gewerkschaftshaus* (an establishment belonging to the trade unions) exists in the following localities: Berlin, Brunswick, Breslau, Cassel, Charlottenburg, Cologne, Dresden, Elberfeld, Feuerbach, Frankfort-on-the-Main, Hanau, Heidelberg, Kiel, Leipzig, Liegnitz, Mannheim, Mühlhausen in Thuringia, Offenbach-on-the Main, Plauen in Vogtland, Solingen, Stettin, Stralsund, Stuttgart, Treves, Wilhelmshaven, and Zittau. Even when these places, which are often called "People's Houses," are not the exclusive property of the Trades Councils, they owe their existence in great part to the local trade unions, and in some cases also to the socialist party. It should be observed that the productive and distributive cooperative societies, being in Germany strictly neutral in political matters, play no part in these undertakings.

[37] To the delegates at the socialist congress of Jena was given a number

circles that long before the congress of Essen (1907) the party
would have declared openly against alcoholism, and that after
this congress it would have applied its decisions with greater
vigour, had not the party leaders been restrained by the fear

---

of ''Der abstinente Arbeiter,'' the official organ of the League of Abstinent
Workers, edited by Georg Davidsohn, from which the following passage may
be quoted: ''The Socialist Publicans' Association of Berlin has been asked
on two occasions whether its members desired a conference upon the subject of public-house reform. No answer was ever received!—Comrade M.
subsequently enquired on three separate occasions whether the Association
would not like to take part in such a conference, imagining that he had
to deal with impartial and objective-minded comrades, who would no longer
continue to ignore a question so closely touching their own interests, unless
they wished grave misunderstandings to arise between two organizations
within the framework of the party. But again no answer was received!

''The president of the Charlottenburg section of the League of Free Publicans was in favour of discussion of the subject, but the meeting refused
to consider it! Do the dealers in alcohol then imagine that they can in this
way prevent the spread of the teetotal movement, that they can set back the
hands of the world's clock? This is as little possible to them as it is to
others, and if they continue to shut their eyes to the forward movement,
it is they alone who will have to pay the price.

''A most serious incident, which throws a strong light upon the pernicious
influence exercised upon the life of our party by certain socialist publicans,
may be described in a few plain words. On August 22nd was held in Berlin
the party meeting to decide upon the subjects for discussion at the Jena
congress. In the fourth electoral district of Berlin our comrades had been
engaged in an excellent work of preparation, distributing among those
present at the meeting about 600 leaflets and a number of pamphlets upon
the drink question. Here could be observed a thing which three years ago
would have seemed barely conceivable. On almost every table were bottles
of seltzer water and the waiters could hardly get around fast enough to
supply the demand for this beverage. The sentiment of the meeting, therefore, could not fail to be favourable to our two proposals (one presented
by district 167A, whilst the other was backed by numerous signatures just
obtained from among those present at the meeting) to have the alcohol
question placed upon the agenda of the next congress. But who can count
upon fortune! One proposal after another was read and discussed, without
any mention being made of ours. I had already risen to propose our
motion. All of a sudden, however, the chairman, a publican, declared that
the discussion of the proposals was concluded and that the delegates to
the congress were now to be elected! I demanded that our proposals should
be read. But the chairman ruled that it was 'too late' and the names of
delegates were already being sent in. Our proposals, which were differentiated from the others by being printed in a larger format, had (both of
them as luck would have it!) been 'by an oversight' slipped beneath a
newspaper, so that the chairman and his two assessors (all of whom had
read the proposals before the meeting was opened) had overlooked them
and forgotten them! In answer to my remonstrances the chairman promised
that he would endeavour to bring the matter up for discussion after the

that the measures recommended, and even a simple temperance propaganda, would react injuriously upon the interests of an influential category of the members of the party.

It is impossible to determine with any accuracy the number of individuals who have become independent petty bourgeois as the outcome of the struggles of the workers and the political reprisals of the employers. Tobacconists, grocers, etc., elude statistical investigation. The only definite information we possess relates to tavern-keepers. In the parliamentary group we find that in 1892, of 35 socialist deputies, 4 were publicans (11.4%); in 1903, of 58 socialist deputies, 5 were publicans (8.6%); and in 1906, of 81 socialist deputies, 6 were publicans (7.4%). In the local socialist sections, the proportion of tavern-keepers is considerable. At Leipzig, in 1887, there were 30 *Parteikneipen.* In 1900, among the socialist branches of the Leipzig country districts with 4,855 members there were 84 restaurant-keepers and publicans (1.7%); in Leipzig city, where the socialists numbered 1,681, there were in 1900, 47 tavern-keepers, and in 1905, 63 (3.4%). Offenbach, in 1905, 1,668 members, 74 publicans and 2 retailers of bottled beer (4.6%). Munich, in 1906, 6,704 members; milk-retailers, tobacconists, sellers of cheese, etc., and publicans (wine merchants not included), 369 (5.5%). Frankfort-on-the-Main, in 1906, 2,620 members, 25 publicans (12 retailers of bottled beer and tobacconists excluded —approximately 1%). Marburg, in 1906, 114 members, 2 publicans (1.8%). Reinickendorf-Ost, near Berlin, in 1906, 303 members, 18 tavern- and restaurant-keepers (5.9%). These figures serve to show that in certain towns there is a socialist publican for every twenty members. Since the socialist publican depends mainly upon socialist customers, it follows that these twenty comrades must provide the chief financial resources of the enterprise.

The best proof of the numerical strength and the importance

---

delegates had been elected. But in the circumstances this was impossible; it was already after midnight, so that when the election was over, and even before the chairman could close the meeting, the comrades were all streaming out of the door. The only thing the chairman could answer to our complaints was: 'Oh, well, such proposals have been brought forward in vain year after year; they would have been rejected again as usual.' Such are the arguments used by a comrade who occupies a position of trust in the labour movement. What a perspective does this open when we remember that, at any rate here in East Berlin, the majority of our party officials are publicans!'' (Anno iii, No. 18.)

of this category of the members of the party is that they have founded at Berlin a powerful association, the Berlin League of Socialist Publicans and Innkeepers. It must not be forgotten that this association has largely come into existence from the consideration that the socialist publicans have other political tasks to fulfil from those which devolve upon their "bourgeois" colleagues, nor can it be denied that its members constitute a category of chosen socialists of tried fidelity, who have rendered important services to the party in its political campaigns and agitations, and whose socialist clientèle is actuated by a high spirit of solidarity in giving these comrades its custom. It is inevitable, however, that the existence of such an organization, which represents peculiar economic interests, should in certain cases involve inconveniences, not merely for its competitors, the bourgeois publicans, but also for the socialist comrades, and that it should tend to assume the aspect of a party within the party. In the summer of 1906, the increase in the cost of production of beer, which resulted from new taxation by which the breweries were especially hard hit, led the publicans to raise the price to the consumers. Thereupon the German workers in a great many towns protested most energetically, and declared what was known as the "beer war," boycotting certain breweries and the publicans who had raised the price—an agitation which led certain foreign socialists to observe sarcastically that you may take anything from the German worker except his beer. In this struggle, which was in many places conducted with great obstinacy, the organized workers encountered resistance from a notable proportion of socialist publicans. These, adopting a tactical outlook estranged from socialist principles, endeavoured to alarm the comrades by insisting upon the dangers of their campaign, and by predicting that if the consumers should succeed in forcing the producers to bear the new taxes, the government, delighted to find that these taxes were not pressing upon the masses of the people but were borne only by a restricted class of brewers and factory owners, would hasten to introduce new and yet heavier taxation, which could not fail to affect the consumers.

To sum up, it may be said that the petty bourgeois of proletarian origin, although the conditions of their life are not as a rule notably better than those of the proletarian strata from which they derive, constitute in more than one respect, on account of the particular interests they represent, a serious ob-

stacle to the forward march of the working-class legions. Moreover, it has to be remembered that the influence of this new
stratum impresses upon the party from the mental point of view
(in consequence of the new place which these elements occupy
in the general economic process) a markedly petty bourgeois
stamp.

CHAPTER IV

THE NEED FOR THE DIFFERENTIATION OF THE WORKING CLASS

EVERY individual member of the working class cherishes the hope of rising into a higher social sphere which will guarantee to him a better and less restricted existence. The workman's ideal is to become a petty bourgeois.[1] To non-initiates and to superficial observers the working-class members of the socialist parties seem always to be petty bourgeois. The proletariat has not been able to emancipate itself psychically from the social environment in which it lives. For example, the German worker, as his wages have increased, has acquired the disease which is in the blood of the German petty bourgeoisie, the club-mania. In every large town, and not a few small ones, there is a swarm of working-class societies: gymnastic clubs, choral societies, dramatic societies; even smokers' clubs, bowling clubs, rowing clubs, athletic clubs—all sorts of associations whose essentially petty bourgeois character is not destroyed by the fact that they sail under socialist colours. A bowling club remains a bowling club even if it assumes the pompous name of "Sons of Freedom Bowling Club."

Just as little as the bourgeoisie can the socialist workers be regarded as a great homogeneous grey mass, although this consideration does not modify the fact that since proletarians all live by the sale of their only commodity, labour, the organized socialist workers are, at least in theory, conscious of their own unity in their common opposition to the owners of the means of production and to the governmental representatives of these.

---

[1] According to Tullio Rossi Doria (*Le Forze Democratiche ed il Programma socialista,* "Avanti," anno xiv, No. 30), every struggle for higher wages has the same end in view. But as a rule the struggle for higher wages is carried out by a trade union, and the aim of the trade unions is to secure a better position for the manual workers, not to make them petty bourgeois. The organized workers as a whole desire to live like the petty bourgeois, but not to fulfil the economic function of these. They wish to remain manual workers.

Yet it cannot be denied that the actual system of manufacture which unites under the same roof all the different categories of workers employed in a modern establishment for the production of railway-carriages, for instance, does not serve to overthrow the barriers which separate the various sub-classes of workers.[2] Nor is it less true, looking at the matter from the other side, that there exists among the workers the sense of a need for differentiation which will readily escape those who do not come in personal contact with them. The kind of work, the rate of wages, differences of race and climate, produce numerous shades of difference alike in the mode of life and in the tastes of the workers. As early as 1860 it was said: "Entre ouvriers il y a des catégories et un classement aristocratique. Les imprimeurs prennent la tête; les chiffonniers, les vidangeurs, les égoutiers ferment la marche."[3] Between the compositor and the casual labourer in the same country there exist differences in respect of culture and of social and economic status more pronounced than those between the compositor in one country and the small manufacturer in another.[4] The discrepancy between the different categories of workers is plainly displayed even in the trade-union movement. We know, for example, that the policy of the compositors' unions in Germany, France, and Italy differs from that of the other unions, and also from that of the socialist party, exhibiting a tendency towards the right, being more opportunist and more accommodating. In Germany, the compositors' union has for its president a Rexhäuser, and in France a Keufer. We observe, too, in the conduct of the diamond-workers in Holland and in Belgium the same unsocialistic, unproletarian, and particularist tendencies. The aristocratic elements of the working class, the best paid, those who approximate most closely to the bourgeoisie, pursue tactics of their own. In the active work of the labour movement, the division of the organized masses into different social strata is often plainly manifest. Working-class history abounds in examples showing how certain fractions or categories of the proletariat have, under the influence of interests peculiar to their sub-class, detached themselves

---

[2] Rudolf Broda and Julius Deutsch, *Das moderne Proletariat*, Reimer, Berlin, 1910, p. 73.

[3] Edmond About, *Le Progrès*, ed. cit., pp. 51-2.

[4] Cf. the interesting communication upon the increasing differentiation of the working classes made by Hermann Herkner to the congress of the Verein für Sozialpolitik held at Nuremberg in 1911 (*Protokoll*, pp. 122 et seq.).

from the great army of labour and made common cause with the bourgeoisie. Thus it happens, generally speaking, that the workers in armaments factories have little sympathy with anti-militarist views. In the London congress of the Independent Labour Party in 1910, the Woolwich delegate, largely representing the view of the employees at Woolwich arsenal, expressed strong dissent from the opinion of those delegates who had brought forward a resolution in favour of a restriction of armaments and of compulsory arbitration in international disputes.[5] Again, the check which was sustained at Venice by the general strike of protest against the Tripolitan campaign was due to the opposition of a section of the arsenal workers.[6] The very fact that the cessation of work on May 1st is but a partial demonstration renders it possible to divide the workers into two classes. One consists of those who, thanks to better conditions of life and other favourable circumstances, "can allow themselves the luxury" of celebrating the 1st of May; the other comprises those who by poverty or ill-fortune are compelled to remain at work.[7]

---

[5] "Volksstimme," 1910, No. 76, fourth supplement.

[6] Exaggeration must be avoided here, and it is desirable to point out that in the election of March 1912 in the Venetian constituency in which the arsenal is situated, notwithstanding all kinds of adverse pressure, two thousand electors expressed their definite disapproval of the African campaign by voting for the intransigeant socialist Musatti ("Avanti," anno xvi, No. 85).

[7] The phrase quoted in the text is used by a correspondent of the "Volksstimme," of Frankfort (*Die Maifeier am ersten Maisonntag*, Manifest-Nummer, 1910, seventh supplement). The same article shows from how distinctively capitalist an outlook the better-paid workers regard the May Day celebration. We read as follows: "Now a few words upon the pecuniary and principal question. By my occupation and as son of a socialist publican I have come much in contact with working-class circles, and have questioned a great many working men (many of them organized both politically and industrially, and some of them earning as much as 45s. a week) as to their attitude towards the May Day celebration. I am convinced that notwithstanding all their idealism and willingness for self-sacrifice, the more intelligent workers are disinclined to lose a day's wages on behalf of May Day. The pecuniary sacrifice has no adequate relationship to any practical or ideal aim! It would even seem that the better-paid workers would be foolish to abstain from work on the 1st of May; for one who has a daily earning of six or seven shillings will, notwithstanding any subsidy he may receive from the union, have to sacrifice a great deal more (including what he will lose by being locked out!) than one who earns no more than three or four shillings a day. The money devoted by the trade unions to the payment of subsidies could be far better employed in giving a more brilliant and imposing form to the May Day celebration."—The

The need for differentiation is manifested still more clearly when we consider more extended groups of workers. The difference between skilled and unskilled workers is primarily and predominantly economic, and displays itself in a difference of working conditions. As time passes, this difference becomes transformed into a veritable class distinction. The skilled and better paid workers hold aloof from the unskilled and worse paid workers. The former are always organized, while the latter remain "free" labourers; and the fierce economic and social struggles which occur between the two groups constitute one of the most interesting phenomena of modern social history. This struggle, which by the physiologist Angelo Mosso is termed *ergomachia*, the struggle for the feeding-ground,[8] is waged with ever-increasing intensity. The organized workers demand from the unorganized the strictest solidarity, and insist that the latter should abandon work whenever they themselves are in conflict with the employers. When this demand is not immediately complied with, they insult the unorganized workers by the use of opprobrious names which have found a place in scientific terminology. In France, in the days of Louis Philippe, they were called *bourmont* and *ragusa*. At the present day they are in Germany termed *Streikbrecher;* in Italy, *krumiri;* in England, *blacklegs;* in America, *scabs;* in Hainault, *gambes de bos;* in France, *jaunes, renards,* or *bédouins;*[9] in Holland, *onderkruipers;* and so on. It is incontestable that the grievances of the organized workers against the unorganized are largely justified. On the other hand, it cannot be denied that in the working class this ergomachia is not essentially the outcome of differences between the well-disposed workers and the ill-disposed, as masters and men naïvely believe, of course inverting the rôles. For the socialists, in fact, the strikers are always heroes and the strike-breakers are always villains; whilst for the employers the strike-breakers are honest and hardworking fellows, whilst the strikers are idle good-for-nothings. In reality, ergomachia does not consist of a struggle between two categories distinguished by ethical

---

writer in the "Volksstimme" alludes here to the proposal to abandon the idea of abstaining from work on May 1st, and to celebrate the occasion in the evening by a great festival.

[8] Angelo Mosso, *Vita moderna degli Italiani*, ed. cit., p. 178.

[9] Similarly in Italy, towards 1890, the term *beduini* was employed. Cf. Sombart, *Studien zur Entwicklungsgeschichte des italienischen Proletariats,* "Archiv für Soz. Gesetzg. u. Statistik," vol. vi, p. 235.

characteristics, but is for the most part a war between the better-paid workers and the poorer strata of the proletariat. The latter, from the economic aspect, consist of those who are still economically unripe for a struggle with the employers to secure higher wages. We often hear the most poverty-stricken workers, conscious of their inferiority, contend that their wages are high enough, whilst the better paid and organized workers declare that the unorganized are working at starvation rates. One of the most indefatigable of French socialist women [10] has well said: "On est presque tenté d'excuser les trahisons de ces supplanteurs, quand on a vu, de ses propres yeux vu, tout le tragique du problème des sans-travail en Angleterre. Dans les grands ports du sud ou de l'ouest, on voit rangés, le long d'un mur de quaie, des milliers et des milliers d'affamés, à la figure hâve, grelottants, qui espérent se faire embaucher comme débardeurs. Il en faut quelques dizaines. Quand les portes s'ouvrent, c'est une terrible ruée, une véritable bataille. Récemment, un de ces hommes, les côtes pressés, mourut étouffé dans la mêlée." The organized workers, on their side, do not consider themselves obliged to exhibit solidarity towards the unorganized, even when they are all sharing a common poverty during crises of unemployment. The German trades councils often demand that the subsidies which (in accordance with the so-called Strasburg system) are provided in certain large towns from the public funds to render assistance in cases of unemployment, should be reserved for the organized workers, declaring that the unorganized have no claim to assistance.[11]

The more fortunate workers do not only follow their natural inclination to fight by all available means against their less well-to-do comrades, who, by accepting lower wages, threaten the higher standard of life of the organized workers—using in the struggle, as always happens when economic interests conflict, methods which disregard every ethical principle. They also endeavour to hold themselves completely aloof. The union button is often, as it were, a patent of nobility which distinguishes

---

[10] Madame Sorgue, *Retour d'Angleterre*, "La Société Nouvelle," xvi, No. 8, p. 197.

[11] The reader will find a more copious and more detailed study of this matter in an essay compiled by the present writer in collaboration with his wife. Michels, *Das Problem der Arbeitslosigkeit und ihre Bekämpfung durch die deutschen freien Gewerkschaften*, "Archiv f. Sozialw.," xxxi, September 2, 1910, pp. 479-81.

its wearer from the plebs. This happens even when the unorganized workers would like nothing better than to make common cause with the organized. In almost all the large British and American trade unions there is manifest a tendency to corporatism, to the formation of sharply distinguished workingclass aristocracies.[12] The trade unions, having become rich and powerful, no longer seek to enlarge their membership, but endeavour rather to restrict it by imposing a high entrance fee, by demanding a certificate of prolonged apprenticeship, and by other similar means, all deliberately introduced in order to retain certain privileges in their own hands at the expense of other workers following the same occupation. The anti-alien movement is the outcome of the same professional egoism, and is especially conspicuous among the Americans and Australians, who insist upon legislation to forbid the immigration of foreign workers.[13] The trade unions in such cases adopt a frankly "nationalist" policy. In order to keep out the "undesirables" they do not hesitate to appeal for aid to the "class-state," and they exercise upon the government a pressure which may lead their country to the verge of war with the labour-exporting land.[14] In Europe, too, we may observe, although here to a less degree, the formation within the labour movement of closed groups and coteries (and it is in this that the tendency to oligarchy consists), which arise in direct conflict with the theoretical principles of socialism. The workers employed at the Naples arsenal, who recently demanded of the government that "a third of the new places to be filled should be allotted to the sons of existing employees who are following their fathers' trade," [15] are in sentiment by no means so remote from the world of our day as might at first be imagined. As has been well said, "la

---

[12] Cf., inter alia, Daniel De Leon, *The Burning Question of Trades Unionism*, Labour News Co., New York, 1906, p. 13.

[13] This phenomenon has recently been well expounded by an Italian political economist, a member of the Conservative party—Giuseppe Prato, *Il Protezzionismo operaio e l'Esclusione del Lavoro straniero*, Soc. Tip-Editr. Nazionale, Turin, 1910. This work, however, exhibits a certain tendency to over-statement, and inclines to ignore the opposing ideological and socialist tendencies which are to-day manifest among the organized workers of continental Europe.

[14] The American labour organizations have played a notable part in producing tension between the United States and Japan, a tension which, a few years ago, nearly culminated in war.

[15] Angelo Mosso, *Vita moderna degli Italiani*, ed. cit., p. 191.

lutte de classe a pour objectif de faire monter la classe inférieure au niveau de la supérieure, c'est ainsi que les révolutions réussissent souvent, non à démocratiser les eugéniques, mais à eugéniser les démocrats.'' [16]

The policy of social reform, which finds its most definite expression in labour legislation, does not entail the same advantages for all sections of the working class. For example, the law which raises the minimum age of the factory worker will have varying effects according as may vary the power of the labour organizations, the rate of wages, the conditions of the labour market, etc., in the different branches of industry or agriculture. Thus in certain categories of workers the effect of the law will be a transient depression of the standard of life, whilst in other cases it will lead to a permanent elevation in that standard.[17] There results an even greater accentuation of the differentiation which the proletarian groupings already present as the outcome of national, local, and technical differences.

To sum up, it may be affirmed that in the contemporary working class there is already manifest a horizontal stratification. Within the *quatrième état* we see already the movements of the embryonic *cinquième état*. One of the greatest dangers to the socialist movement, and one which must not be lightly disregarded as impossible, is that gradually there may come into existence a number of different strata of workers, as the outcome of the influence of a general increase of social wealth, in conjunction with the efforts made by the workers themselves to elevate their standard of life; this may in many cases enable them to secure a position in which, though they may not completely lose the common human feeling of never being able to get enough, from which even millionaires are not altogether exempt, they will become so far personally satisfied as to be gradually estranged from the ardent revolutionary aspirations of the masses towards a social system utterly different from our own—

---

[16] Cf. Raoul de La Gracerie, *Les Luttes Sociales,* ''Annales de l'Institut intern. de Sociologie,'' vol. xi, p. 185.

[17] It is for this reason that in debates concerning the beneficial or injurious character of laws for the protection of labour and for the improvement of housing conditions, it is altogether erroneous to answer the questions involved with a simple yes or no. In Italy, in especial, the dispute has been conducted from a restricted outlook, although with great ardour and brilliancy of thought. Cf., for example, the polemic in the review ''Il Socialismo'' during the year 1907 between Gina Lombroso and Tullio Rossi Doria.

aspirations born of privation.[18] Thus the working class will become severed into two unequal parts, subject to perpetual fluctuations in their respective size.

---

[18] "The more the personal well-being of the workman increases, the more harshly practical does he tend to become. Whilst still paying his theoretical tribute to the imperishable memory of Marx, what really interests him is to give a more vigorous support to his union" (F. Naumann, *Das Schicksal des Marxismus*, "Die Hilfe," xiv, No. 41).

CHAPTER V

LABOUR LEADERS OF PROLETARIAN ORIGIN

ATTEMPTS have not been lacking to solve the insoluble problem, how to obviate the leaders' dominion over the led. Among such attempts, there is one which is made with especial frequency, and which is advocated with considerable heat, to exclude all intellectuals from leadership in the working-class movement. This proposal reflects the dislike of the intellectuals which, in varying degrees, has been manifested in all countries and at all times. It culminates in the artificial creation of authenticated working-class leaders, and is based upon certain general socialist dogmas, mutilated or imperfectly understood, or interpreted with undue strictness—on an appeal, for instance, to the principle enunciated at the constitutive congress of the first International held at Geneva in 1866, that the emancipation of the workers can be effected only by the workers themselves.

Above all, however, such proposals are based upon an alleged greater kinship between the leaders of proletarian origin and the proletarians they lead. The leaders who have themselves been manual workers are, we are told, more closely allied to the masses in their mode of thought, understand the workers better, experience the same needs as these, and are animated by the same desires. There is a certain amount of truth in this, inasmuch as the ex-worker can not only speak with more authority than the intellectual upon technical questions relating to his former occupation, but has a knowledge of the psychology and of the material details of working-class life derived from personal experience. It is unquestionably true that in the leaders of proletarian origin, as compared with the intellectuals, we see conspicuously exhibited the advantages of leadership as well as the disadvantages, since the proletarian commonly possesses a more precise understanding of the psychology of the masses, knows better how to deal with the workers. From this circumstance the deduction is sometimes made that the ex-worker, when he has become immersed in the duties of political leadership, will

continue to preserve a steady and secure contact with the rank
and file, that he will choose the most practicable routes, and that
his own proletarian experiences will afford a certain safeguard
against his conducting the masses into regions and by-paths from
which they are by nature totally estranged.[1]

The central feature of the syndicalist theory is found in the
demand for direct action on the part of the trade union, enfran-
chised from the tutelage of socialist leaders predominantly bourgeois in origin, the union being self-sufficient and responsible to
itself alone.   Direct action means that the proletariat is to pursue its aims without the intermediation of parliamentary representation.   Syndicalism is described as the apotheosis of proletarian autonomy.   Everything is to be effected by the energy,
initiative, and courage of individual workers.   The organized
proletariat is to consist of an army of *franc-tireurs*, disembar-
rassed of the impotent general staff of effete socialist bureau-
crats, unhampered, autonomous, and sovereign.[2]   Passing, however, from fiction to fact, we find that the most substantial difference between syndicalism and political socialism, apart from
questions of tactics, is to be found in a difference of social origin in the leaders of the respective tendencies.   The trade union
is governed by persons who have themselves been workers, and
from this the advocates of syndicalism infer, by a bold logical
leap, that the policy of the leaders of working-class origin must
necessarily coincide with the policy of the proletariat.[3]

The syndicalist leaders are to be, both in the intellectual and
moral sense, chosen manual workers.[4]   The leader of working-
class origin is regarded as the Messiah who will cure all the ills
of proletarian organization; he is, in any case, the best of all
possible leaders.[5]

---

[1] It was this consideration which led the Milanese labour party, in the
year 1882 and subsequently, to decide that it would accept as members
none but manual workers.   (Cf. Michels, *Eine exklusivistische Arbeiterpartei in Italien im Jahre, 1882*, ''Archiv für Sozialismus,'' Karl Grünberg,
Vienna, anno i, fasc. 2, pp. 291 et seq.

[2] Edouard Berth, *Les nouveaux Aspects du Socialisme*, Rivière, Paris,
1908, p. 30.

[3] Emile Pouget, *Le Parti du Travail*, Bibl. Syndicaliste, Paris, No. 3,
p. 12.

[4] Fernand Pelloutier, *Histoire des Bourses du Travail*, ed. cit., p. 86.

[5] Among the great majority of the revisionist and reformist socialists we
find a similar tendency to overestimate the importance of leaders of working-
class origin.

It is hardly necessary to point out that it is an illusion to imagine that by entrusting its affairs to proletarian leaders the proletariat will control these affairs more directly than if the leaders are lawyers or doctors. In both cases, all action is effected through intermediaries. In the modern labour movement it is impossible for the leader to remain in actual fact a manual worker. Directly a trade union selects one of the comrades in the factory to minister regularly to the collective interests in return for a definite salary, this comrade is, consciously or not, lifted out of the working class into a new class, that of the salaried employees.[6] The proletarian leader has ceased to be a manual worker, not solely in the material sense, but psychologically and economically as well. It is not merely that he has ceased to quarry stones or to sole shoes, but that he has become an intermediary just as much as his colleagues in leadership, the lawyer and the doctor. In other words, as delegate and representative, the leader of proletarian origin is subject to exactly the same oligarchical tendencies as is the bourgeois refugee who has become a labour leader. The manual worker of former days is henceforward a *déclassé*.

Among all the leaders of the working class, it is the trade-union leaders who have been most sympatheticaly treated in the literature of the social sciences. This is very natural. Books are written by men of science and men of letters. Such persons are, as a rule, more favourably disposed towards the leaders of the trade-union movement than towards the leaders of the political labour movement, for the former do not, as do so often the latter, encroach upon the writer's field of activity, nor disturb his circle of ideas with new and intrusive theories. It is for this reason that often in the same learned volume we find praise of the trade-union leader side by side with blame of the socialist leader.

It has been claimed that service as buffers between employers and employed has led in the leaders to the development of admirable and precious qualities; adroitness and scrupulousness, patience and energy, firmness of character and personal honesty. It has even been asserted that they are persons of an exceptionally chaste life, and this characteristic has been attributed to the comparative absence of sexual desires which, in accordance with the law of psychological compensation discovered by Guglielmo Ferrero, is supposed to characterize all persons exceptionally de-

---

[6] Cf. *supra*, p. 277, note 22.

voted to duty.[7] Two qualities in which most of the trade-union leaders unquestionably excel are objective gravity and individual good sense (often united with a lack of interest in and understanding of wider problems), derived from the exceptionally keen sense they have of direct personal responsibility, and in part perhaps from the dry and predominantly technical and administrative quality of their occupations.[8] The trade-union leaders have been deliberately contrasted with the verbal revolutionists who guide the political labour movement, men of the type of the loquacious Rabagas in Sardou's play, and, not without exaggeration, there has been ascribed to the former a sound political sense which is supposed to be lacking in the latter—an insight into the extraordinary complexity of social and economic life and a keen understanding of the politically practicable.[9] The nucleus of truth which such observations contain is that the trade-union leaders (leaving out of consideration for the

---

[7] Arturo Salucci, *La Teoria dello Sciopero*, Libr. Moderna, Genoa, 1902, p. 151. Salucci goes so far as to affirm that while the trade-union leaders marry quite young, marriage is for them not so much a union for sexual purposes as a matter of ''comfort to them in their lives of continual agitation.'' The analyses produced by many authors of the psychology of trade-union leaders remind us at times of the reports of travellers in foreign lands, who tell us of human beings altogether different from those with whom we are acquainted, and even of actions which appear utterly opposed to nature. Herein we have a criterion which leads us to doubt the trustworthiness of such reports, even when they are not adorned with stories of matters demonstrably false, as of dragons, centaurs, and other mythical monsters. (Cf. David Hume, *Enquiries Concerning the Human Understanding*, ed. Clar. Press, edited by Selby-Bigge, Oxford, 1902, p. 84). The exaggeration which is so often manifested in the enumeration and description of the good qualities of the trade-union leaders can be explained on political grounds. It arises from the satisfaction felt in bourgeois circles with the practical tendencies of these leaders, and from the hope that is placed in them by the opponents of revolutionary socialism.

[8] Even the opponents of such men in the labour movement do not deny what is said in the text. For instance, Ernesto Cesare Longobardi, in an article criticizing the tactics of the Italian General Confederation of Labour, admits that the members of the executive committee of this body display technical competence, familiarity with the problems of working-class life, and unremitting industry (*La Crisi nelle Organizzazioni operaie*, ''Il Viandante,'' anno i, No. 29).

[9] Werner Sombart, *Dennoch! Aus Theorie u. Geschichte der Gewerkschaftlichen Arbeiterbewegung*, Fischer, Jena, 1900, pp. 90-1; Salucci, *La Teoria dello Sciopero*, ed. cit., p. 152; Herkner, *Die Arbeiterfrage*, ed. cit., p. 156; Sidney and Beatrice Webb, *Industrial Democracy*, ed. cit., p. 152; Paul de Rousiers, *Le Trade-unionisme en Angleterre*, Colin, Paris, 1897, p. 368; Eduard Bernstein, *Die Arbeiterbewegung*, ed. cit., p. 147.

present those of syndicalist tendency) differ in many respects from the leaders of political socialism.

Among the trade-union leaders themselves, however, there are great differences, corresponding to the different phases of the trade-union movement. The qualities requisite for the leadership of an organization whose finances are still weak, and which devotes itself chiefly to propaganda and strikes, must necessarily differ from those requisite for the leadership of a trade union supplying an abundance of solid benefits and aiming above all at peaceful practical results. In the former case the chief requisites are enthusiasm and the talents of the preacher. The work of the organizer is closely analogous to that of the rebel or the apostle. According to certain critics, these qualities may well be associated, above all in the early days of the proletarian movement, with the crassest ignorance.[10] During this period, propaganda is chiefly romantic and sentimental, and its objective is moral rather than material. Very different is it when the movement is more advanced. The great complexity of the duties which the trade union has now to fulfil and the increasing importance assumed in the life of the union by financial, technical, and administrative questions, render it necessary that the agitator should give place to the employee equipped with technical knowledge. The commercial traveller in the class struggle is replaced by the strict and prosaic bureaucrat, the fervent idealist by the cold materialist, the democrat whose convictions are (at least in theory) absolutely firm by the conscious autocrat. Oratorical activity passes into the background, for administrative aptitudes are now of the first importance. Consequently, in this new period, while the leadership of the movement is less noisy, less brilliant, and less glorious, it is of a far more solid character, established upon a much sounder practical competence. The leaders are now differentiated from the mass of their followers, not only by their personal qualities as specialists endowed with insight and mastery of routine, but in addition by the barrier of the rules and regulations which guide their own actions and with the aid of which they control the rank and file. The rules of the German federation of metal-workers occupy forty-seven printed pages and are divided into thirty-nine paragraphs, each consisting of from ten to twelve sections.[11] Where

---

[10] Fausto Pagliari, *Le Organizzazioni e i loro Impiegati*, ed. cit., p. 6.

[11] Herkner, *Die Arbeiterfrage*, ed. cit., p. 116.—It may be noted that the abundance of rules and regulations is one of the historical causes of the

is the workman who would not lose himself in such a labyrinth? The modern trade-union official, above all if he directs a federation, must have precise knowledge of a given branch of industry, and must know how at any moment to form a sound estimate of the comparative forces of his own organization and the adversaries'.

He must be equally well acquainted with the technical and with the economic side of the industry. He must know the cost of manufacture of the commodities concerned, the source and cost of the raw materials, the state of the markets, the wages and conditions of the workers in different regions. He must possess the talents at once of a general and those of a diplomatist.[12]

These excellent qualities of the trade-union leader are not always compatible with the democratic regime, and indeed they often conflict unmistakably with the conditions of this regime.

It is especially in the ex-manual worker that the love of power manifests itself with the greatest intensity. Having just succeeded in throwing off the chains he wore as a wage-labourer and a vassal of capital, he is least of all disposed to indue new chains which will bind him as a slave of the masses. Like all freedmen, he has a certain tendency to abuse his newly acquired freedom—a tendency to libertinage. In all countries we learn from experience that the working-class leader of proletarian origin is apt to be capricious and despotic. He is extremely loath to tolerate contradiction. This trait is doubtless partly dependent upon his character as parvenu, for it is in the nature of the parvenu to maintain his authority with extreme jealousy, to regard all criticism as an attempt to humiliate him and to diminish his importance, as a deliberate and ill-natured allusion to his past. Just as the converted Jew dislikes references to his Hebrew birth, so also the labour leader of proletarian origin

---

distance which has been established between the class of employees and the mass. Colbert tells us that the French bureaucracy was born out of the mania for codification. "Son oppression devint inquiète, diffuse, minutieuse, et se perdit dans une telle génération de règlements que, par exemple, le seul code des marchands de bois de Paris égale en volume tout le Corps du Droit Romain" (Lémontey, *Essai sur l'Etablissement monarchique de Louis XIV*, ed. cit., p. 339).—Enough has been said to enable us to judge the value of the opinion sometimes expressed (cf. Octors, *De Catechismus van den Werkman*, ed. cit., p. 21) that the problem of trade-union organization is so simple that any workman can master it.

[12] C. Pagliari, *Le Organizzazioni, etc.*, ed. cit., p. 7.

dislikes any references to his state of dependence and his position as an employee.

Nor must it be forgotten that, like all self-made men, the trade-union leader is intensely vain. Although he commonly possesses extensive knowledge of material details, he lacks general culture and a wide philosophical view,[13] and is devoid of the secure self-confidence of the born leader; for these reasons he is apt to show himself less resistant than he should be towards the interested and amiable advances of bourgeois notables. In a letter to Sorge, Engels wrote of England:[14] "The most repulsive thing in this country is the bourgeois 'respectability' which has invaded the very blood and bone of the workers. The organization of society into firmly established hierarchical gradations, in which each one has his proper pride, but also an inborn respect for his 'betters' and 'superiors,' is taken so much as a matter of course, is so ancient and traditional, that it is comparatively easy for the bourgeois to play the part of seducers. For example, I am by no means sure that John Burns is not prouder in the depths of his soul of his popularity with Cardinal Manning, the Lord Mayor, and the bourgeoisie in general, than of his popularity among his own class. Even Tom Mann, whom I regard as the best of these leaders of working-class origin, is glad to talk of how he went to lunch with the Lord Mayor."

In Germany, one of the few "class-conscious" German workers who have come into personal contact with William II did not venture in the royal presence to give expression to his convictions or to manifest his fidelity to the principles of

---

[13] The twilight of culture which has been dispersed through the proletariat through the participation of modern workers in politics and in intellectual discussions bearing upon political life, often produces in the minds of such persons an attitude which Sombart rather unhappily terms "dogmatism" (Werner Sombart, *Das Proletariat*, Rütten u. Loening, Frankfort-on-the Main, 1906, p. 84), but one which is certainly not apt to contribute to freedom of the spirit. It is very natural that this should be so. The share of culture which the modern working man has won for himself at an incredible cost of physical and mental energy necessarily seems to him (who lacks leisure and adequate preliminary knowledge to make a good use of what he has learned, and who lacks the ability to control the accuracy of his own mental acquirements) a *noli me tangere*, an invaluable treasure, which must be relentlessly and zealously guarded against all criticism (his own or another's) precisely because it has been won by so much labour.

[14] *Briefe und Auszüge, etc.*, ed. cit., pp. 324-5.

his party.[15] There already exists in the proletariat an extensive stratum consisting of the directors of cooperative societies, the secretaries of trade unions, the trusted leaders of various organizations, whose psychology is entirely modelled upon that of the bourgeois classes with whom they associate.[16]

The new environment exercises a potent influence upon the ex-manual worker. His manners become gentler and more refined.[17] In his daily association with persons of the highest birth he learns the usages of good society and endeavours to assimilate them. Not infrequently the working-class deputies endeavour to mask the change which has occurred. The socialist leaders, and the same is true of the democratic-Christians and the trade-union leaders, if of working-class origin, when speaking to the masses like to describe themselves as working men. By laying stress upon their origin, upon the characteristics they share with the rank and file, they ensure a good reception and inspire affection and confidence. During the elections of 1848 in France it was the mode for candidates to speak of themselves as *ouvriers*. This was not simply a title of honour, but also a title which helped to success. No less than twenty-one of these *ouvriers* thus secured election. The real signification of

[15] "Arbeiterzeitung" of Dortmund, September 16, 1903: "In the year 1900, the representatives of the Imperial Insurance Institute were commanded to an audience at the court, on the occasion of the inauguration of the new administrative building in Berlin. The stucco-worker Buchholz, well known in trade-union circles, was present with his colleagues. Buchholz, who was wearing the iron cross, attracted the personal attention of William II. The king was apparently aware of Buchholz's position as a socialist, and said: 'I believe the socialists are all opponents of the monarchy?' Buchholz promptly answered: 'No, Your Majesty, not all!'"

[16] The princes of the *ancien régime*, being profound psychologists, knew better than the socialists of to-day how to value at its worth the influence of environment upon personality. In the political testament of Augustus II of Saxony, King of Poland, we find a remarkable passage in which he recommended his successor to change ambassadors frequently, for they were apt to accommodate themselves to the interests of the court to which they were accredited, and to allow themselves to be overcome by the influences of their new environment (Paul Haake, *Ein Politisches Testament König Augusts der Starken*, "Historische Zeitschrift," lxxxvii, fasc. 1, p. 7).

[17] "Among the fifty-eight socialist deputies, there are at least thirty who come from the factory or the workshop and whose natural temperamental energy has never been chastened by the discipline of the drawing-room; it should certainly give occasion for astonishment to the bourgeois that they are almost invariably well-behaved, that they hardly ever break the conventions" (Maximilian Harden, "Zukunft," anno x, No. 2, December 6, 1902).

this title may be learned from a study of the list of candidates presented by the modern socialist party in France, Italy, and elsewhere; here we find that a master-tinsmith (a man who keeps a shop and is therefore a petty bourgeois) describes himself as a "tinker," and so on. It even happens that the same candidate will describe himself as a workman in an electoral address intended for working-class readers, and as an employer in an appeal to the bourgeoisie. When they have entered Parliament, some of the ex-manual workers continue, more or less ostentatiously, to differentiate themselves by their dress from their bourgeois colleagues. But it is not by such external signs of a proletarian origin that they can hope to prevent the internal change, which was described by Jaurès (before his own adhesion to socialism) in the following terms: "Les députés ouvriers qui arrivent au Parlement s'embourgeoisent vite, au mauvais sens du mot; ils perdent leur sève et leur énergie première, et il ne leur reste plus qu'une sorte de sentimentalité de tribune." [18]

Inspired with a foolish self-satisfaction, the ex-worker is apt to take pleasure in his new environment, and he tends to become indifferent and even hostile to all progressive aspirations in the democratic sense. He accommodates himself to the existing order, and ultimately, weary of the struggle, becomes even reconciled to that order.[19] What interest for them has now the dogma of the social revolution? Their own social revolution has already been effected. At bottom, all the thoughts of these leaders are concentrated upon the single hope that there shall long continue to exist a proletariat to choose them as its delegates and to provide them with a livelihood.[20] Consequently

---

[18] Jean Jaurès, "Dépêche de Toulouse," November 12, 1887.

[19] Max Weber, a few years ago, advised the German princes, if they wished to appease their terrors of socialism, to spend a day on the platform at a socialist congress, so that they might convince themselves that in the whole crowd of assembled revolutionists "the dominant type of expression was that of the petty bourgeois, of the self-satisfied innkeeper," and that there was no trace of genuine revolutionary enthusiasm (Max Weber's speech at the Magdeburg congress of the Verein für Sozialpolitik, stenographic report of the sitting, October 2, 1907).

[20] Madeleine Pelletier (*La Fin du Guesdisme*, "Guerre Sociale," iii, No. 4), writing of the evolution of the French labour leaders, says: "Mais l'âge, la maladie, étaient venus et l'anénergie avec eux. Autour du Maître s'étaient formés des centaines d'élèves que la lutte des classes avaient fait députés, conseillers généraux et municipaux, maires, secrétaires de mairie et qui, enchantés de l'aubaine, songeaient, sans

they contend that what is above all necessary is to organize, to organize unceasingly, and that the cause of the workers will not gain the victory until the last worker has been enrolled in the organization. Like all the *beati possidentes*, they are poor fighters. They incline, as in England, to a theory in accordance with which the workers and the capitalists are to be united in a kind of league, and to share, although still unequally, in the profits of a common enterprise. Thus the wages of the labourers become dependent upon the returns of the business. This doctrine, based upon the principle of what is known as the sliding-scale, throws a veil over all existing class-antagonisms and impresses upon labour organizations a purely mercantile and technical stamp. If a struggle becomes inevitable, the leader undertakes prolonged negotiations with the enemy; the more protracted these negotiations, the more often is his name repeated in the newspapers and by the public. If he continues to express "reasonable opinions," he may be sure of securing at once the praise of his opponents and (in most cases) the admiring gratitude of the crowd.

Personal egoism, pusillanimity, and baseness are often associated with a fund of good sense and wide knowledge, and so intimately associated that a distinction of the good qualities from the bad becomes a difficult matter. The hotheads, who are not lacking among the labour leaders of proletarian origin, become cool. They have acquired a conscientious conviction that it would be a mistake to pursue an aggressive policy, which would in their view not merely fail to bring any profit, but would endanger the results hitherto attained. Thus in most cases two orders of motives are in operation, the egoistic and the objective, working hand in hand. The resultant of these influences is that state of comparative calm proper to the labour leader, regarding which an employee of one of the trade unions has expressed himself with great frankness: "It is no matter for reproach, but is perfectly comprehensible, that when we were all still working at the bench and had to get along as best we could with our small wages, we had a keener personal interest in a speedy change of the existing social order than we have in our present conditions." [21] Such a state of mind will

---

oser l'avouer, que le besoin d'une révolution sociale ne se faisait plus aussi vivement son tir qu'au temps où ils gagnaient cent sous par jour."

[21] Kloth, leader of the bookbinders' union, speaking at the conference of the trade-union executives in Berlin, 1906 (*Protokoll*, p. 10). In the

be yet further reinforced if the former manual worker should be, as he often is, engaged in journalistic work. Although in most cases he will with admirable diligence have amassed a considerable amount of knowledge, he has not had the necessary preliminary training to enable him to assemble, re-elaborate, and assimilate the elements of his knowledge to constitute a scientific doctrine, or even to create for himself a system of directive ideas. Consequently his personal inclinations towards quietism cannot be neutralized, as unquestionably happens in the case of many Marxists, by the preponderant energy of a comprehensive theory. Marx long ago recognized this defect in proletarian leaders, saying: "When the workers abandon manual labour to become professional writers, they almost always make a mess of the theoretical side." [22]

We see, then, that the substitution of leaders of proletarian origin for those of bourgeois origin offers the working-class movement no guarantee, either in theory or in practice, against the political or moral infidelity of the leaders. In 1848, when the elections ordered by the provisional government took place in France, eleven of the deputies who entered the Chamber were members of the working class. No less than ten of these promptly abandoned the labour programme on the strength of which they had been elected.[23] A yet more charactertistic example is furnished by the history of the leaders of the Italian branch of the International (1868-79). Here the leaders, who were for the most part derived from the bourgeoisie and the nobility, nearly all showed themselves to be persons of distinguished worth. The only two exceptions were men of working-class origin. Stefano Caporusso, who spoke of himself as "the model workingman," embezzled the funds of the socialist group of Naples, of which he was the president; while Carlo Terzaghi, president of the section of Turin, turned out to be a police spy and was expelled from the party.[24] Speaking generally, we learn from the history of the labour movement that a socialist party is exposed to the influence of the political en-

---

Protokoll it is here noted that there were vigorous cries of objection, and also the remark, "What you say applies still more to the employees of the socialist party." (Cf. *supra*, p. 146.)

[22] Letter to Sorge, October 19, 1877, *Briefe u. Auszüge, etc.*, ed. cit., p. 159.

[23] Arthur Arnould, *Histoire populaire et parlementaire de la Commune de Paris*, Kistemaeckers, Brussels, 1878, vol. ii, p. 43.

[24] Cf. Michels, *Proletariato et Borghesia, etc.*, ed. cit., pp. 72 et seq.

vironment in proportion to the degree in which it is genuinely proletarian in character. The first deputy of the Italian socialist party (which at that time consisted exclusively of manual workers), Antonio Maffi, a type-founder, elected to parliament in 1882, speedily joined one of the bourgeois sections of the left, declaring that his election as a working man did not make it necessary for him to set himself in opposition to the other classes of society.[25] In France, the two men who under the Second Empire had been the leaders of the Proudhonists, Henri Louis Tolain, the engraver, and Fribourg, the compositor, and who at the first international congress in Geneva (1866) had urgently advocated an addition to the rules to effect the exclusion of all intellectuals and bourgeois from the organization, when the Commune was declared in 1871 ranged themselves on the side of Thiers, and were therefore expelled from the International as traitors. It may be added that Tolain ended his career as a senator under the conservative republic. Odger, the English labour leader, a member of the general council of the International, abandoned this body after the insurrection in Paris. It is true that he was in part influenced in this direction by his objection to the dictatorial methods of Marx. But Marx could rejoin, not without reason, that Odger had wished merely to make use of the International to acquire the confidence of the masses, and that he was ready to turn his back upon socialism as soon as it seemed to him an obstacle to his political career. A similar case was that of Lucraft, also on the general council of the International, who secured an appointment as school inspector under the British government.[26] In a word, it may said that when the forces of the workers are led against the bourgeoisie by men of working-class origin, the attack is always less vigorous and conducted in a way less accordant with the alleged aims of the movement than when the leaders of the workers spring from some other class. A French critic, referring to the political conduct of the working-class leaders of the proletariat, declares that alike intellectually and morally they are inferior to the leaders of bourgeois origin, lacking the education and the culture which these possess. The same writer declares that the behaviour of many of the leaders of working-class origin cannot fail to contribute to the intensive

---

[25] Alfredo Angiolini, *Cinquent'anni di Socialismo in Italia*, ed. cit., pp. 180–6.

[26] G. Jaeckh, *Die Internationale*, ed. cit., p. 152.

culture of anti-parliamentarist tendencies. "Après le règne de la féodalité, nous avons eu le règne de la bourgeoisie. Après le bourgeois, aurons-nous le contremaître?—Notre ennemi, c'est notre maître, a dit La Fontaine. Mais le maître le plus redoutable, c'est celui qui sort de nos rangs et qui, à force de mensonges et de roublardises, a su s'élever jusqu'au pouvoir." [27]

It was hoped that the energetic entry of the proletariat upon the world-stage would have an ethically regenerative influence, that the new elements would exercise a continuous and unwearied control over the public authorities, and that (endowed with a keen sense of responsibility) they would strictly control the working of their own organizations. These anticipations have been disappointed by the oligarchical tendencies of the workers themselves. As Cesare Lombroso pointed out without contradiction in an article published in the central organ of the Italian socialist party, the more the proletariat approximates to the possession of the power and the wealth of the bourgeoisie, the more does it adopt all the vices of its opponent and the more does it become an instrument of corruption. "Then there arise all those subdivisions of our so-called popular parties, which have all the vices of the bourgeois parties, which claim and often possess a prestige among the people, and which easily become the tools of governmental corruption sailing under liberal colours in their name." [28] We have sufficient examples in European history, even in that of very recent date, of the manner in which the artificial attempt to retain the party leadership in proletarian hands has led to a political misoneism against which the organized workers of all countries have every reason to be on their guard. The complaint so frequently voiced by the rank and file of the socialists that almost all the defects of the movement arise from the flooding of the proletarian party with bourgeois elements are merely the outcome of ignorance of the historical characteristics of the period through which we are now passing.

[27] Flax (Victor Méric), *Coutant* (d'Ivry), "Hommes du Jour," Paris, 908, No. 32.

[28] Cesare Lombroso, *I Frutti di un Voto,* "Avanti," No. 2987 (April 27, 1905). The criminologist Raffaele Garofalo prophesies that the proletariat will follow in the footsteps of the bourgeoisie, "that *tiers état* which was to substitute its youthful energies for a decadent and degenerate aristocracy," but which instead of doing this "has displayed a hundred-fold the defects and the corruption of its predecessors" (Garofalo, *La Superstizione socialista,* Turin, 1894, p. 178).

The leaders of the democratic parties do not present everywhere the same type, for the complex of tendencies by which they are influenced necessarily varies in accordance with environment, national character, climate, historical tradition, etc. The United States of America is the land of the almighty dollar. In no other country in the world does public life seem to be dominated to the same extent by the thirst for gold. The unrestricted power of capital necessarily involves corruption. In America, however, this corruption is not merely exhibited upon a gigantic scale, but, if we are to believe American critics, has become a recognized institution.[29] Whilst in Europe such corruption gives rise to censure and anger, in America it is treated with indifference or arouses no more than an indulgent smile. Lecky declares that if we were to judge the Americans solely by the manner in which they conduct themselves in public life, our judgments would be extremely unfavourable—and unjust.[30]

We cannot wonder, then, that North America should be preeminently the country in which the aristocratic tendencies of the labour leaders, fostered by an environment often permeated, as has just been explained, by a gross and unrefined materialism,

---

[29] The extent to which, in the States, corruption has progressed among the representatives of the people would seem to be displayed by a news-item recently circulated in the principal European papers. In this we were told that a society had been formed in Washington, known as the "Private Secretaries' Union," which was to protect its members against being plundered by the American popular representatives. The members of the House of Representatives are paid, in addition to their salary of $7,500 a year, a sum of $1,500 for a secretary. The congressmen receive this supplement personally, but must furnish documentary proof that the amount is paid over to a secretary. Many of these statesmen, being of a thrifty disposition, engage a shorthand writer for the session at a fee of $500, and pocket the balance. Others install relatives of their own as private secretaries, so that all the money shall be kept in the family. Another arrangement is for five of the congressmen to combine to employ a common secretary, who receives $3,000 a year, but each of the five employers clears $900 by the transaction. Thus there are numerous variations, but in any case the private secretary fails to secure all the fruits of his labour.

[30] W. E. H. Lecky, *Democracy and Liberty*, ed. cit., vol. i, pp. 113–14. According to Robert Clarkson Brooks (*Corruption in American Politics and Life*, Dodd Mead & Co., New York, 1910, p. 54), the corruption existing in the States is merely the expression of the higher moral level of public life: "If monarchies are less corrupt than democracies, it is also true that monarchies do not repose so much faith in the fundamental honesty of their citizens as do democracies."

should have developed freely and upon a gigantic scale. The leaders of the American proletariat have merely followed the lead of the capitalism by which the life of their country is dominated. The consequence is that their party life has also become essentially plutocratic.[31] When they have secured an improved rate of wages and similar advantages, the officials of the trade unions, wearing evening dress, meet the employers in sumptuous banquets. At congresses it is the custom to offer foreign delegates, and even their wives, valuable gifts, jewellery, etc. The special services of the leaders are rewarded by increases of salary, which sometimes attain considerable figures. We learn from indisputable authority that many of the labour leaders, and especially of the trade-union leaders, regard their positions simply as a means for personal advancement. According to the testimony of the well-informed, the American working class has hitherto produced few leaders of whom it has any reason to be proud. Many of them shamelessly and unscrupulously exploit for personal ends the posts which they have secured through the confidence of their fellow-workmen. Taken as a whole, the American labour leaders have been described as "stupid and cupid."[32] We owe to Gaylord Wilshire, himself also an American and a socialist, the following unflattering picture of the socialist leader: "He is a man who often expresses a social dissatisfaction based upon personal failure. He is very apt to be loud rather than profound. He is, as a rule, not an educated man, and his demands and urgings are based too often on ignorance."[33] Intelligent and honest workmen are consequently repelled from the labour organizations or induced to follow false paths. We have even been told that not a few labour leaders are altogether in the hands of the capitalists. Being uneducated parvenus, they are extremely sensible to flattery,[34] but this seems to be among the least of their defects. In many cases they are no more than paid servants of capital. The "Union Officer" then becomes a

---

[31] In 1909 the congress of the American labour organizations made a special grant of $4,000 each to Gompers, Morrison, and Mitchell, who had been condemned by the Supreme Court for offences connected with the labour movement.

[32] Austin Lewis, *The Rise of the American Proletariat*, ed. cit., p. 200.

[33] Gaylord Wilshire, *Wilshire Editorials*, Wilshire Book Co., New York, 1906, p. 140.

[34] Austin Lewis, op. cit., p. 202.

"boss" in the hands of the enemy, a "scab" or, to use a still more significant American expression, "a labour lieutenant of the capitalist class."[35] It is from the socialists themselves that we learn almost incredible details regarding certain categories of American workers who have achieved a privileged position, but who are utterly devoid of moral sense. Among the best organized unions there are some which enter into regular treaties with the capitalists in their respective branches of industry in order to exploit the consumer and to effect with the capitalist a friendly division of the spoil.[36] In other cases, the leaders of a federation of trade unions, bribed by one group of employers, will organize strikes among the employees of another group. On the other hand, many strikes which are progressing favourably for the workers come abruptly to an end because the employers have made it worth the leaders' while to call the strike off. The absence of socialist tendencies among the American workers, their lack of class consciousness, have been noted with admiration by distinguished writers and leading members of the employing class, who praise these workers for their exceptional intelligence, and hold them up as examples to the degenerate and lazy European working men.[37] Yet these same intelligent American workers are led by the nose by such men as we have been describing, and appear to be the only ones who fail to notice the misdeeds of the labour leaders. Indeed, they favour these misdeeds by refusing to work at the same bench with those of their comrades who, more perspicacious than themselves, have attracted the enmity of the leaders by discovering and unmasking the frauds of the latter.[38]

The history of the organized working class in North America certainly rivals, in respect of the frequent occurrence of corruption, the history of a part of the capitalist class in the same country. A historian of the American labour movement exclaims: "It is in both cases a sordid and dreary tale and, in the case of organized labour, is unrelieved to a disappointing degree by the heroism and sentiment which have played such

---

[35] Daniel De Leon, *The Burning Question of Trades-Unionism*, ed. cit., pp. 10–12, 41–43.

[36] George D. Herron, *The Day of Judgment*, Kerr, Chicago, 1904, p. 17. —See also Werner Sombart, *Warum gibt es in den Vereinigten Staaten keinen Sozialismus?*, ed. cit., p. 33.

[37] Cf., for example, E. Cauderlier, *L'Evolution économique du XIX siècle*, Brussels, 1903, p. 209.

[38] De Leon, ed. cit., p. 12.

a conspicuous part in the labour movements of other countries. The cynicism of a civilization based on cash seems to have found its way into the bones of both capitalist and proletarian.[39] The American labour movement is the purest in respect of its proletarian composition and is at the same time the richest in examples of social perversion. Side by side with the vulgar and interested corruption to which we have referred, there exists, indeed, a corruption which arises from idealism, and the latter must not be confused with the former. It sometimes happens that the leader allows himself to be induced by pecuniary considerations to attack a given party, the money being furnished by other parties or by the government. That he should do this presupposes, indeed, that his point of view regarding money is *non olet;* but he acts as he does exclusively in the interest of his party, and not a penny of the money he receives goes into his own pocket. An American political economist has justly pointed out that such corruption sometimes involves a heroic capacity for self-sacrifice on the part of the leader who, to secure advantages for the party with the foreign money, faces the fiercest attacks and the worst suspicions, and even, if need be, accepts his own political annihilation. He offers up his honour to the party, the greatest sacrifice that a man of honour can make.[40] Of this kind, for example, is the corruption of which the leaders of the political labour movement have frequently been accused by the liberals, namely, when they have accepted money from the conservatives or from the government in order to fight liberals or radicals. There are not a few instances of this kind in the history of the international labour movement. Thus, in England, during the general election of 1885, the leaders of the Social Democratic Federation, in order to run two candidates in metropolitan constituencies, accepted money from the tory party, whose aim it was to split the votes of its opponents, and thus to secure the defeat of the liberal candidates;[41] the sum payable in this case was determined by the number of votes given to the socialist candidate, £8 for every vote.[42] Similarly, Constantino

---

[39] Austin Lewis, op. cit., p. 196.

[40] Robert Clarkson Brooks, op. cit., pp. 65 et seq.

[41] Stegmann and Hugo [Lindemann], *Handbuch des Soz.*, ed. cit., p. 180.

[42] Bernard Shaw, *The Fabian Society: What it has done: How it has done it,* Fabian Society, Lond., 1892, p. 6.

Lazzari, leader of the Milanese labour party, accepted from the government the sum of 500 lire to carry on an electoral struggle against the bourgeois radicals.[43] In Germany, the conduct of Schweitzer during the last years in which he was president of the Allgemeine Deutsche Arbeiterverein, conduct which led to accusations of corruption in which Bebel joined, appears to have been dictated by similar considerations. Such at least is the impression produced by a perusal of the various references to the matter made by Gustav Mayer.[44] In none of these cases is it fair to accuse the party leaders of personal corruption, since the money was not accepted for personal ends but for the supposed advantage of the party. Whether such procedures are politically wise, whether they make for the general advance of political morality, are different questions. Indubitably their influence on the mentality of the masses is not educational in a good sense. They are, moreover, especially dangerous to the leaders' own morale. Corruption for honourable motives is likely to be succeeded by corruption for dishonourable. If the method were to be accepted as a regular and legitimate element of party politics, it would be easy for able but unscrupulous leaders to put a portion of the price of corruption into their own pockets, and yet to remain more "useful" to the party than their disinterested and conscientious colleagues.[45] This would be the beginning of the end, and would open the door to plutocracy in the party.

It cannot be said that the English labour leaders are in these respects greatly superior to the American, although in England, perhaps, corruption assumes a more subtle and less obvious form. At the Amsterdam congress (1906) Bebel related in a private conversation what Marx and Engels had said to him once in London: "English socialism would certainly be far more advanced than it is to-day had not the capitalists been clever enough to check the movement by corrupting its leaders."[46] Hyndman, the leader of the English Marxists, a man of bourgeois origin who sacrificed a diplomatic career for the sake

---

[43] Alfredo Angiolini, *Cinquant'anni di Socialismo in Italia*, Nerbini, Florence, 1900, 1st ed., p. 135.

[44] Gustav Mayer, *J. B. Schweitzer*, ed. cit., pp. 129, 161, 181, 195, 321, 379.

[45] Cf. also R. C. Brooks, op. cit., p. 66: and *supra*, note 12, p. 231.

[46] Daniel De Leon, *Flashlights of the Amsterdam Congress*, Labour News Co., New York, 1906, p. 41.

of socialism, relates in his memoirs that many of the working-class leaders, and among these the most energetic and the most gifted, after having acquired a genuine political culture with the aid of socialists of bourgeois origin, have not hesitated to sell this new acquirement to the bourgeoisie. Nor do the workers themselves complain of this, for, full of admiration for what they call the cleverness of their leaders, they have by their votes rendered possible the gradual rise of these in public life.[47] Another writer well acquainted with the English labour movement declares: "A prominent labour leader remarked recently that the labour movement was a charnel-house of broken reputations. That puts it too strongly, but, in essence, how true!"[48]

Thus in the United States, and also, though to a less degree, in England, there exists a peculiar category of working-class leaders of proletarian origin. Among these there are unquestionably to be found many men of strong character, and many who are uninfluenced by selfish considerations, although but few who take lofty views, who are endowed with a fine theoretical insight, or capacity for coherent political work and the avoidance of opportunities for error. Most of them are excellent organizers and technicians. But apart from these somewhat exceptional categories, there can be no doubt that many of the labour leaders are half-educated and arrogant egoists. We might almost imagine that Diderot had a premonition of such individuals when he made his ambitious Parisian beggar, Lumpazius, say: "Je serai comme tous les gueux revêtus. Je serai le plus insolent maroufle qu'on eût encore vu."[49]

---

[47] H. M. Hyndman, *The Record of an Adventurous Life*, Macmillan, London, 1911, p. 433.

[48] S. G. Hobson, *Boodle and Cant*, loc. cit., p. 588.

[49] Diderot, *Le Neveu de Rameau*, Delarue, Paris, 1877, p. 44.

CHAPTER VI

INTELLECTUALS, AND THE NEED FOR THEM IN THE WORKING-CLASS PARTIES

IN the early days of the labour movement the bourgeois intellectuals who adhered to the cause of the workers were regarded by these with profound esteem; but as the movement matured the attitude of the proletariat became transformed into one of undue criticism. This antipathy on the part of the rank and file of the socialists is based upon false presuppositions, and proceeds from two antithetical points of view. Some, like the group of the "Neue Zeit" and the "Leipzige Volkszeitung" in Germany, with the support of the revolutionary-minded workers of Berlin, of the two Saxonies, and of Rhenish Westphalia, persisting in the maintenance of intransigent revolutionary conceptions, think themselves justified in accusing the intellectuals of a tendency to "take the edge off" the labour movement, to "water it down," to give it "bourgeois" characteristics, to rob it of proletarian virility, and to inspire it with an opportunist spirit of compromise. The others, the reformists, the revisionists, who find inconvenient the continued reminder *principiis obsta!* with which they are assailed by the revolutionists, in their turn attack the intellectuals,[1] regarding them as meddlesome intruders, fossilized professors, and so on, as persons who are utterly devoid of any sound ideas of the labour movement and of its necessities, disturbing its normal course with their ideas of the study. Thus whilst the first group of critics regard the intellectuals as being for the most part reformists, bourgeois-minded socialists of the extreme right, the other group of critics classes the intellectuals as ultra-revolutionary, as anarchizing socialists of

---

[1] Sometimes, even, when these belong to their own tendency. Thus Eduard Bernstein was attacked by the German trade-union leaders at the trade-union congress of Cologne on account of his theory of the general strike, being treated as an incompetent and uninvited intruder.

the extreme left. In Italy, towards 1902, the intellectuals found themselves placed between two fires. On one side the reformists claimed to represent the healthy proletarian energy of the economic organizations of the peasants as against the *circoletti ambiziosetti* ("the self-seeking petty circles"—i.e. socialist groups in the towns), which were composed for the most part, so they affirmed, of bourgeois and petty bourgeois. On the other side, the revolutionists of the "Avanguardia Socialista" group entered the lists against the employees and the bourgeois leaders, in the name of the class-conscious proletariat of industrial workers. Thus by both factions alike the intellectuals were treated as scapegoats and made responsible for all the mistakes and sins of the party.[2] But both sides are wrong. Above all it is hardly possible to imagine the reasons which would induce refugees from the bourgeoisie to adhere to the extreme right wing of the working-class party. It is rather the adverse thesis which might be sustained by psychological and historical arguments which are good but not decisive.

1. Let us first consider the psychological arguments. Kautsky, referring to a period when "even by educated persons socialism was stigmatized as criminal or insane" (a period which Kautsky wrongly imagines to have passed away), makes the judicious observation that the bourgeois who adheres to the socialist cause needs more firmness of character, stronger revolutionary passion, and greater force of conviction, than the proletarian who takes a similar step.[3] The violent internal and external struggles, the days full of bitterness and the nights without sleep during which his socialist faith has ripened, have combined to produce in the socialist of bourgeois origin, especially if he be derived from the higher circles of the bourgeoisie, an ardour and a tenacity which are rarely encountered among proletarian socialists. He has broken completely with the bourgeois world, and henceforward confronts it as a mortal enemy, as one irreconcilable *a priori*. The consequence is that, in the struggle with the bourgeoisie, the socialist

---

[2] Cf. Michels, *Il Proletariato, etc.*, ed. cit., pp. 357 et seq. Cf. also, as regards France, the articles of Charles Rappoport in the "Neue Zeit" during the years 1909–10–11.

[3] Karl Kautsky, *Die Soziale Revolution.* 1. *Sozialreform u. Soziale Revolution,* "Vorwärts," Berlin, 1902, p. 27; also *Republik u. Sozialdemocratie in Frankreich,* "Neue Zeit," xxiii, No. 11, p. 333.

intellectual will incline towards the most revolutionary tendencies.[4]

There is, however, another reason which leads the ex-bourgeois to make common cause with the intransigent socialists, and this is his knowledge of history and his intimate acquaintance with the nature of the bourgeoisie. To the proletarian socialist it is often difficult to form any precise idea of the power of his adversaries and to learn the nature of the means at their disposal for the struggle.[5] Often, too, he is inspired with an ingenuous admiration for the benevolent attempts at social reform patronized by certain strata of the bourgeoisie. Faced by the more or less serious or more or less deceitful offer of panaceas, he is often in the position of the peasant at the fair who listens open-mouthed while the quack vaunts the miraculous virtue of his remedies.[6] Conversely the socialist of bourgeois origin will interpret more precisely the efforts made by the bourgeoisie to put the labour movement to sleep. His experience as a bourgeois will enable him to penetrate more easily the real motives of the different proceedings of the enemy. That which to his proletarian comrade seems a chivalrous act and proof of a conciliatory spirit, he will recognize as an act of base flattery, performed for the purposes of corruption. That which a proletarian socialist considers a great step forward towards the end, will appear to the bourgeois socialist as an infinitesimal advance along the infinitely extended road of the class struggle.

The difference of intellectual level between those who advocate the same idea, dependent upon their respective derivation from a proletarian or a bourgeois environment, must necessarily reflect itself in the manner in which they represent this idea in the face of non-socialists, and in the tactics they employ towards

---

[4] Cf. *supra*, pp. 251 et seq.

[5] Augusto Novelli, the dramatist, at one time a compositor in his native city of Florence, was for years an active member of the socialist party. In one of his comedies, a workman is asked what he and his comrades have done for their defence in a struggle with their employer in which they are engaged. The workman replies that a mixed committee has been chosen to represent the views of the strikers, a committee of workers and intellectuals. The questioner exclaims: "But why mixed? Could you not settle the matter yourselves?" To which the other replies: "We need a man with some intelligence or else we are likely to be humbugged" (A. Novelli, *La Chiocciola*, L'Elzeviriana, Florence, 1901, p. 117).

[6] Cf. *supra*, pp. 303, 308-9, 312.

adversaries and sympathizers. The psychological process which goes on in the socialists of these two categories rests upon a logical foundation. The proletarian adherent of the party who remains a simple member of the rank and file attentively follows the progress made in all fields by the idea on behalf of which he is an enthusiastic fighter; he notes the growth of the party, and experiences in his own person the increase in wages secured in the struggle with the employers; besides being a member of the party, he belongs to his trade union, and often to a cooperative society as well. His experience in these various organizations induces a feeling of comparative content. He regards social evolution in a rosy light, and easily comes to take an optimistic view of the distance which his class has to traverse in order to attain to the fulfilment of its historic mission. Ultimately social progress is regarded by him as a continuous rectilinear movement. It appears incredible, even impossible, that the proletariat should suffer reverses and disasters; when they actually occur, they seem to him merely transient phenomena. This state of mind renders him generous and considerate even towards his adversaries, and he is far from disinclined to accept the idea of peace with the enemy and of class collaboration. It need hardly be said that this disposition is yet more accentuated among those proletarians who attain to positions of eminence in the party.

2. These considerations do not lack historical corroboration. Their truth is confirmed by a study of the activities of those socialists who were born as members of the aristocracy, or in the upper strata of the bourgeoisie, such as Bakunin and Kropotkin, both Russian nobles and both anarchists, Frederick Engels,[7] Karl Marx.[8] As a rule, in all the great questions with

---

[7] Frederick Engels belonged to an old-established and rich family of manufacturers at Barmen. He performed his military service (1841) in the select corps of the artillery of the guard, as *Einjährig-Freiwilliger* (soldier serving one year at his own expense). We learn from the description given by his old friend Lafargue that the life he led was that of a well-to-do man, fond of study, but also not averse from sport and society life (Paul Lafargue, *Persönliche Erinnerungen an Friedrich Engels,* ''Neue Zeit,'' anno xiii, vol. ii, No. 44).

[8] As is well known, Karl Marx was a Jew, and thus belonged to a race which was not then, nor is even to-day, admitted to the best society in Germany. His father, however, belonged to an aristocratic Jewish family, and was highly respected and well-to-do. It should be noted, also, that Marx's student life was passed during the critical years of Jewish emancipation, at a time when social advance was especially

which the party has to deal the ex-bourgeois socialist is in actual fact one who gives the preference to the most radical and intransigent solutions, to those which accord most strictly with socialist principles. It is of course true, on the other hand, that the history of the working-class movement shows that many "reformist" currents have been strongly permeated by intellectual elements. It is indisputable that even if German reformism was not actually created by the little phalanx grouped round "Der Sozialistiche Student" of Berlin, the reformist tendency was, from the days of its first inception, vigorously and ostentatiously patronized by the members of this group. A closer examination, however, shows very clearly that the strongest impulse to the reformist tendency in Germany was given by the trade-union leaders, by persons therefore of proletarian origin. Moreover, it is the most exclusivist working-class movements which have everywhere and always been most definitely characterized by the reformist spirit. In illustration may be mentioned: the French group of the International Workingmen's Association which assembled round Fribourg and Tolain; the English trade unionists; the "integralists" in France, whose organ was the "Revue Socialiste," edited by the gentle ex-manual worker, Benoît Malon (the note of alarm against this form of socialism was sounded first by the medical student Paul Brousse, next by the intransigent Marxists under the leadership of Paul Lafargue, who had just secured his medical diploma in England, and finally by the man of letters Jules Guesde); the Independent Labour Party with the Labour Representation Committee; the socialists of Genoa, led by the varnisher Pietro Chiesa; the peasants of Reggio Emilia. This tendency has been manifest from the very outset of the modern labour movement. Bernstein says with good reason that, notwithstanding all assertions to the contrary, in the English Chartist movement the intellectuals were distinguished by their marked revolutionary inclinations. "In the disputes among the Chartists, the radical or revolutionary tendency was by no means characteristic of the proletarian elements, or the moderate tendency of the bourgeois elements. The most notable representatives of the revolutionary spirit were members of the bourgeoisie, men of letters, etc., whereas it was leaders of working-

---

easy to a Jew. Moreover, by his love-match with Jenny von Westphalen Marx became connected with the Borussian aristocracy. His wife's brother was celebrated as a Prussian reactionary minister.

class origin who advocated moderate methods." [9] To sum up, and putting aside the question whether the reformist movement has been a good or an evil for the working class, it may be affirmed that generally speaking the working-class leaders of proletarian origin have a special tendency to adopt the reformist attitude. In proof of this assertion it suffices to mention the names of Anseele in Belgium, Legien in Germany, and Rigola in Italy. The term *possibilisme ouvrier* is far from being a malicious invention.

It is not easy to furnish statistical proof of the statement that the socialists of bourgeois origin are more often revolutionaries than reformists. On the other hand, the history of Italian socialism during recent years offers an interesting demonstration of the adverse thesis (the causes of this peculiarity will be subsequently discussed). The official socialist organization of Milan, the Federazione Milanese, suffering from a chronic impecuniosity due to the slackness with which the majority of the members paid their subscriptions, proposed in the year 1903 an expedient which is frequently adopted by the Italian socialists. Henceforward the monthly subscriptions were no longer to be equal for all the comrades, but those who were better off were invited to pay more in proportion to their means. This reform, which was inspired by a thoroughly socialist sentiment, led the Milanese reformists (who in consequence of their differences with the revolutionists had for a long time been on the look-out for an honourable excuse to leave the federation, in which the revolutionary current was predominant) to resign their membership, declaring that they regarded the new system of payment as altogether unjust. On this occasion it appeared that it was the well-to-do members who resigned, so that these, the bourgeois, manifested the reformist tendency.[10] It is also to be noted that during recent years (since 1901) the great majority of Italian socialist intellectuals have definitely declared themselves to be reformists by a more or less unconditional adhesion to the opportunism of Turati. The cases just quoted seem to conflict with the rule previously enunciated that the refugees from the bourgeoisie are adverse to opportunism.

---

[9] Eduard Bernstein, *Zur Theorie u. Geschichte des Sozialismus,* Ferd. Dümmler, Berlin, 1904, 4th ed., part ii, p. 18.

[10] *I Casi di Milane,* a memorial presented by the Milanese federation to the party executive and to the Italian comrades (Stamp. editr. Lombarda di Mondaini, Milan, 1903, p. 18.

But the inconsistency is no more than apparent. It has several times been pointed out that the intransigence of the ex-bourgeois socialist depends upon the circumstance that on his way to join the class-conscious proletariat he has had to make his way through a thorny thicket, struggling violently and suffering many injuries, and his courageous progress proves him to be endowed with an exceptional capacity of sacrifice for the ideal and with the energy of the born fighter. As the years have passed, however, this primal source of revolutionary energy has to a large extent dried up, because the path of the bourgeois adherent to socialism has become so much easier. It is a general law that when we change the soil we change the quality of the fruit. This is what has happened in Italy.[11]

The recent history of socialism shows that the intellectuals are distributed in nearly equal proportions among the various tendencies. Confining ourselves to German examples, we find that it is a doctor of medicine, Raphael Friedeberg, who has inaugurated anarchizing socialism; a similar tendency is exhibited by the Tolstoian-Kantian Otto Buck, doctor of philosophy, and Ernst Thesing, doctor of medicine and at one time a cavalry lieutenant. If among the reformists we find the barrister Wolfgang Heine, the former theological student Richard Calwer, the former student of political science Max Schippel, the pastor Göhre, the sometime gymnasium teacher Eduard David, the doctor of philosophy Heinrich Braun, and many other intellectuals—we find in the opposite camp, that of the revolutionaries, the doctor of philosophy Franz Mehring, the doctor of medicine Paul Lensch, Rosa Luxemburg, Israel Helphant (Parvus), the former student Max Grunwald, the ex-barrister Arthur Stadthagen, the barrister Karl Liebknecht, and Karl Kautsky, who escaped only by chance the disgrace of the doctor's title. We see, then, that in Germany the intellectuals cannot be classed exclusively as revolutionists or as reformists.

* * * * *

The struggle against the intellectuals within the socialist party is due to various causes. It originated as a struggle for leadership among the intellectuals themselves. Then there came a struggle between the representatives of different tendencies: strict logical adhesion to theory versus criticism, opportunism

---

[11] Cf. *supra*, pp. 214, 266-7.

versus impossibilism, trade unionism after the English manner versus doctrinal Marxism as a philosophy of history, reformism versus syndicalism. From time to time these struggles assume the form of attacks made by the bulk of the party upon some small heterogeneous element which has invaded the labour movement.[12] It is not always the genuine manual workers, or those who have been such, that are the first to raise the cry of alarm against the intellectuals. But it is true that the working class has ever been suspicious of those elements in the party who were derived from other social camps.[13] Clara Zetkin writes very justly: "The bourgeois refugee is apt to find himself lonely and misunderstood among his comrades in the struggle. He is at once a stranger and a citizen in the valley of the possessing classes, with which he is associated by education and habits of life; at once, also, a stranger and a citizen upon the heights of the proletariat, to whom he is bound in a firm community by his convictions."[14] The power of tradition presses with peculiar force upon persons of culture.[15]

The coldness of his reception in the new environment seems to him doubly hard. The intellectuals, who have entered the party under the spur of idealism, soon feel humiliated and disillusioned.[16] The masses, moreover, are little capable of appreciating the gravity of the sacrifices which the intellectual often accepts when he adheres to the party. When Paul Göhre related to the Dresden congress how for love of the cause he had renounced his profession and his income, his social position,

---

[12] Cf. *supra*, p. 167.

[13] What the present author has written elsewhere concerning the Italian labour movement (Michels, *Proletariato, etc.*, ed. cit., p. 334) applies perfectly, *mutatis mutandis*, to Germany.

[14] Clara Zetkin, *Geistiges Proletariat, Frauenfrage, u. Sozialismus*, a lecture, Verlag "Vorwärts," Berlin, 1902, p. 32.

[15] "It is precisely those who are inspired by the impulse to swim in the full stream of civilization, and not to stray into the backwater of any sect, that feel with redoubled force the isolation in which they are placed by opposition to the system prevailing in Germany since 1866. They suffer like those who have discarded Christianity and transcendental religion, and who only when they have done so come to recognize to what an extent all our institutions, habits of life, and even the forms of our speech, are permeated with Christian traditions" (Max Maurenbrecher, *Die Gebildeten u. d. Sozialdemokratie*, Leipzig, 1904, p. 26).

[16] Cf. P. J. Troelstra, *Inzake Partijleiding*, ed. cit., p. 103; G. Zepler, *Radikalismus u. Taktik, Nachwort zum Vorwärtskonflikt*, Birk, Munich, 1905, p. 6; Lily Braun, *Memoiren einer Sozialistin*, ed. cit., p. 632.

and even his family, a number of socialist journals answered
that all this was, to put it politely, maudlin sentimentality, and
that the socialist intellectuals, when they made such "sacrifices,"
were not thinking of the cause of the workers but of themselves. In a word, the comrades showed themselves utterly in-
sensible of the greatness of the sacrifice which Göhre had made
for love of them. The truth is that upon this point, as upon
so many others, the intellectuals and the proletarians lack the
capacity of mutual understanding.

In Germany, as in Italy, France, and in some of the Balkan
states, the gravest accusations have been launched against the
intellectuals.[17] There have been times in the history of Ger-

---

[17] We are assured by a Roumanian socialist, B. Librescu, formerly
editor of the socialist journal "L'Unea Noua" of Bukharest, that his
party, which from 1880 to 1885 was strongly represented at the international congresses and had then already two deputies in Parliament,
had been so utterly ruined in consequence of the attacks made upon
the intellectuals that hardly a trace of it remained. He reports: "Because a few intellectuals had left the party in order to secure good
positions, the intellectuals in general were regarded with contempt.
People had no confidence in them, and this sentiment went so far that
the word 'intellectual' became equivalent to a term of opprobrium. But
since our cultured comrades were unwilling to abandon the labouring
masses, they allowed themselves to be maltreated, and did not even
venture to reprove the workers for some of their mistakes. To a working
man everything was permissible. Gradually, however, these tendencies led
. . . into the great and gloomy sea of indifference and death" (B. Librescu,
Il Socialismo in Rumenia, sua Vita e sua Morte, "Il Socialismo," anno
ii, p. 184). At times the self-inflicted humiliations of the bourgeois socialists assume comical forms. There have been periods in the history of the
socialist parties when the ex-bourgeois masqueraded as working men in
order to escape the contempt of their proletarian comrades. It is really
laughable to see how unwilling socialists often are to admit to bourgeois
opponents that there are many ex-bourgeois in their own ranks. A
typical example is recorded in "Het Volk," the organ of the Dutch
socialists (issue of August 21, 1904). In a sketch entitled Overwegingen
van Jan Ralebas over het Internationaal Kongres, we are told of a
peasant to whom certain opponents of socialism have declared that the
leaders of international socialism are all bourgeois. Thereupon the
peasant has the different notabilities in the hall pointed out to him (this
is supposed to be at the international socialist congress of Amsterdam
in August 1904). He then learns that the accusation is quite untrue.
For Molkenbuhr is a cigar-maker, Paul Müller a fore-mast hand, and Clara
Zetkin a gewezen naaister (ex-tailoress)! Thus the writer, instead of
admitting frankly that the dominant personalities in the international
proletariat are derived from the bourgeoisie, leads his imaginary peasant
(and the reader!) by the nose. He does not point out to the peasant

man socialism in which the educated members of the party have been exposed to universal contempt. It suffices to recall the Dresden congress (1903), during which the whole complicated question of tactics seemed to be reduced to "the problem of the intellectuals." Even to-day they are often treated as suspects. There are still intellectuals who think it necessary to demonstrate to the masses that, notwithstanding the aggravating circumstances of their social origin and their superior education, they are nevertheless good socialists. It is surely far from heroic, this persistence with which the intellectuals are apt to deny their true social character and to pretend that their own hands are horny. But we need not be deceived. Merlino hits the bull's-eye when he ironically warns us that this state of affairs lasts only until the moment when the intellectuals succeed in getting control of the working-class movement.[18] They now feel themselves secure, and no longer need wear the mask, at least in their relations with the masses. If they continue, none the less, to assume the posture of the humble demagogue, this is done from a vague fear of being accused as tyrants by the bourgeois parties, but still more in order to ward off the criticism of their working-class competitors.[19]

It is proper to recognize that mistrust of the intellectuals, although in large part an artificial product, has its good side. For this mistrust leads no small number of cranky and eccentric intellectuals, who incline to play a picturesque part in joining the socialists, to turn towards other pastures.[20] Nothing would

the principal orators of the congress, the professors Vandervelde, Ferri, and Jaurès, and the doctors Luxemburg and Adler, whilst with deliberate artifice the names of a few leaders less conspicuous than these are trumpeted as those of "guaranteed proletarians"—and even then the teacher, Clara Zetkin, is presented to us as a tailoress.

[18] F. S. Merlino, *Collettivismo, Lotta di Casse e . . . Ministero!*, rejoinder to F. Turati, Nerbini, Florence, 1904, p. 34.

[19] Cf. *supra*, p. 165 et seq.

[20] "During the second half of the period of anti-socialist legislation. it was not alone men of the stamp of Höchberg who abandoned the possessing classes for socialism, in order to warm themselves in the rays of this rising sun. Misunderstood discoverers and reformers, anti-vaccinators, nature-healers, and other cranky geniuses of all kinds, endeavoured to secure from the working classes, which were displaying so vigorous an activity, the recognition elsewhere denied. Eager to overthrow an outworn world, the class-conscious proletariat was not fastidious, and looked more to the goodwill of those who offered help than to the strength of their loins. Especially vigorous was the current which set towards socialism from academic circles. The traditions of bourgeois radicalism,

be more disastrous for the workers than to tolerate the exclusive rule of the intellectuals. University study is not possible to those choice individuals alone who are endowed with exceptional natural gifts; it is merely a class privilege of persons whose position is economically advantageous. Consequently the student has no right to be proud of his ability and his knowledge. He need not glory in being able to write Dr. before his name or M.A. after it. Every proletarian of average intelligence, given the necessary means, could acquire a university degree with the same facility as does the average bourgeois. Besides, and above all, it cannot be denied, that for the healthy progress of the proletarian movement it would be incomparably better that the mistrust of the workers towards the bourgeois refugees should be a hundred times greater than necessary, rather than that the proletariat should be deceived even once by overconfidence in its leaders. But unfortunately, as we learn from the history of the modern labour movement, even the total exclusion of intellectuals would not save the working class from numerous deceptions.

From the ethical point of view the contempt felt by the non-intellectuals for the intellectuals is utterly without justification. It is a positive fact that even to-day, in many countries,[21] the bourgeois refugee who makes his adhesion to the party of the revolutionary workers, the party of "social subversion," or, as William II expresses it, "the unpatriotic rout of those who are unworthy to bear the name of Germans," suffers serious economic and social damage. On the other hand, the proletarian commonly derives advantage in these respects from joining the party of his own class, and is thus impelled to take this step from motives of class-egoism. Unquestionably the working class, struggling on the political field, needs recruits from its own ranks who can rise to the position of officers in the proletarian army. It is natural, too, that these leaders should be fur-

---

which had persisted among the students since the days of the old *Burschenschaft*, had become extinguished in the political decay of the progressive party. Varying in their inborn tendencies and their social origin, some of the students devoted themselves to a repulsive place-hunting, which at best waved the antisemite flag, whilst others endeavoured to make friends with the socialists" (Mehring, *Geschichte der deutschen Sozialdemokratie*, ed. cit., vol. iv, p. 120). Cf. also *supra*, pp. 94-5.

[21] For example, in northern Germany, Switzerland, the department of the Nord in France, and, for other reasons, in Trieste, Japan, and so on.

nished with adequate means, and that they should be firmly secured in their positions. But it ill becomes the working men who have thus risen in the social scale to look down upon their ex-bourgeois associates, who have descended in the social scale, and have thereby become voluntary *déclassés* for love of the party.

It results from all that has been said that the campaign against the intellectuals in the socialist party, however justified it may be in individual cases, is as a whole utterly unjust, and often inopportune and absurd. Even the German labour movement, despite the high degree of technical organization to which it has attained, could not dispense with intellectuals. Although, as we have seen,[22] its general character is decisively proletarian, and although it has as authoritative leaders such men of proletarian origin as August Bebel, Ignaz Auer, Johannes Timm, Martin Segitz, Adolph von Elm, Otto Hué, etc., it may be affirmed that German socialism would lose much of its prestige if it were to eliminate the intellectuals.

According to Mehring, the use of the intellectuals to the proletariat is not so much to serve as fellow-combatants in the struggle, as to play the part of theorists who illuminate the road. He writes: "If they wish to be practical fighters and not theorists, they become altogether insignificant as adherents to the labour movement; for what could be the import of the adhesion of a few hundred intellectuals to the working-class millions, seeing that the latter are already much better equipped than the former for the rough and tumble of practical life?" On the other hand, he says, the intellectuals are of great value to the proletariat in the elaboration of the theory of the class-struggle; they display the historical nexus between the labour movement and the world-process as a whole; they take care that the workers shall not lose sight of the purposive relationship of individual branches of their movement with the process of world-transformation which it must be their aim to effect with all possible speed. Thus the task of the intellectuals consists in "maintaining the freshness and vigour of the workers in their movement towards their great goal, and in elucidating for them the social relationships which make the approaching victory of the proletariat a certainty."[23]

---

[22] Cf. *supra*, p. 270.

[23] Franz Mehring, *Akademiker u. Proletarier*, II, "Leipziger Volkszeitung," xi, No. 95.

It is not necessary here to undertake a defence of the intelligence of the proletariat against those who, seeing that intellectuals are historically necessary to the socialist party, wish on this account to impugn the political capacity of the manual workers. Any one who has attentively followed the history of the international working-class movement will know how much goodwill and capacity are to be found in that proletarian party which, permeated with class-consciousness, has conceived the design of fighting for its own emancipation; he knows how much intelligence, devotion to duty, calm and indefatigable energy, have been displayed in this cause by the workers of every country. As managers of cooperative societies, employees of trade unions, editors of socialist newspapers, the proletarians have from the technical point of view displayed themselves as models whom the bourgeois who undertake similar activities would do well to imitate.[24] If, notwithstanding all this, we commonly find in the international working-class parties it is to the bourgeois refugees that is usually assigned the task of dealing with theoretical problems and in many cases the supreme guidance in matters of practical politics (although in the latter sphere the proletarians always retain great influence), this phenomenon, far from being a *testimonium paupertatis intellectualis* on the part of the fighting proletariat, finds a perfectly natural explanation in the economic organization of contemporary production. This organization (whilst it permits the wage-earner, when conditions are favourable, to cultivate his intelligence), since it monopolizes the supreme advantages of civilization *ad usum Delphinorum,* makes it impossible for the *intelligent* worker to become an *intellectual.* Unquestionably modern production needs intelligent workers, such as are found among the modern proletariat. But it has need also of intellectuals, that is to say of persons whose natural mental abilities have received suitable training. Now a sufficient supply of these intellectuals is furnished by the master class, from among whose relatives they are recruited. Consequently it is not in the interest of private industry to open for the proletariat all the sluices of instruction. Moreover, as far as agriculture is concerned, many landowners cynically declare that the more ignorant the worker the better does he serve their turn. The consequence of all this is that the socialist of bourgeois origin has enjoyed that

---

[24] Cf. *supra,* pp. 299-301.

which the modern proletarian still necessarily lacks. The former has had time and means to complete his political education; he has had the physical freedom of moving from place to place, and the material independence without which political activity in the true sense of the word is inconceivable. It is therefore not astonishing that the proletariat should still be to some extent dependent upon bourgeois refugees.

In 1894, at the Frankfort congress of the German socialist party, a committee was appointed for the study of the agrarian question, and of the fifteen members of which it was composed no less than nine were intellectuals. This is a manifest disproportion, especially when we remember that among the leaders of the German socialist party there is an exceptional numerical preponderance of working-class elements. But the committee in question had to deal with scientific problems, and these could be solved by those alone who had received a scientific education. The same thing happens whenever legal, economic, or philosophical problems have to be treated with technical competence —in a word, whenever the questions under discussion are not fully comprehensible except by those who have made prolonged and profound preliminary studies. Cases in which the self-taught man is incompetent, present themselves daily. The increasing democratization of state institutions and the progressive socialization of the collective life, together with the securing of better conditions of labour for the workers, may perhaps gradually render the help of the intellectuals less essential. But this is a question for the remote future. Meanwhile, such a movement as that of the modern proletariat cannot afford to await that degree of maturity which would enable it to replace the ex-bourgeois among its leaders by men of proletarian origin.

The bourgeois elements in the socialist working-class party cannot be forcibly eradicated, nor excluded by any resolutions of party congresses; they are integral constituents of the movement for whose existence it is needless to offer any apologies. A political labour movement without deserters from the bourgeoisie is historically as inconceivable as would be such a movement without a class-conscious proletariat. This consideration applies, above all, to the early days of the labour movement; but it is still applicable to the movement in the form in which we know it to-day.[25]

---

[25] Cf. *supra*, p. 238.

PART FIVE

ATTEMPTS TO RESTRICT THE INFLUENCE OF THE LEADERS

CHAPTER I

THE REFERENDUM

In the domain of public law, democracy attains its culminating point in that complex of institutions which exists in Switzerland, where the people possesses the right of the referendum and that of the initiative. The use of the referendum is compulsory in Switzerland upon a number of questions which are statutorily determined. The legislative measures drawn up by the representative body must then be submitted to a popular vote, for acceptance or rejection. In addition, the burghers exercise the power of direct legislation. When a certain number of voters demand the repeal of an existing law or the introduction of a new one, the matter must be submitted to popular vote. These important popular rights are supplemented by the direct popular election of the supreme executive authorities, as in the United States.[1] Although these democratic ordinances have often in actual practice proved but little democratic in their results (the referendum, above all, having frequently shown that the democratic masses possess less democratic understanding than the representative government), and although leading socialists have therefore with good reason sharply criticized these manifestations of democracy,[2] other socialists look to these institutions for the definitive solution of all questions of public law, and for the practical contradiction of the opinion that oligarchy arises by natural necessity, contending that by the referendum and by the initiative the decisive influence in legislative matters is transferred from the representative assembly to the totality of the citizens.[3]

---

[1] Karl Hilty, *Die Bundesverfassung der schweitzerischen Eidgenossenschaft*, Berne, 1891.

[2] Karl Kautsky, *Der Parlamentarismus, die Kolksgesetzgebung u. d. Sozialdemokratie*, Dietz, Stuttgart, 1893; Arturo Labriola, *Contro il Referendum*, ''Critica Sociale,'' Milan, 1897; J. Ramsay Macdonald, *Socialism and Government*, Independent Labour Party, London, 1910.

[3] Giuseppe Renzi, *Gli ''Ancien Régime'' e la Demosrazia diretta*, ed. cit., p. 231.

Now the democratic parties, as far as their internal organization is concerned, have either failed to adopt the principles of direct popular sovereignty, or else have accepted application of these only after prolonged hesitation and in exceptional cases. From the democratic point of view they are therefore inferior to many of the Swiss cantons. For example, the German social democracy does not submit the deliberations of its congresses to ratification by the party as a whole. Moreover, and here the German arrangements differ from those which obtain among the socialists of Italy, France, and England (where the vote is based upon the number of the adherents in the local branches which the delegates respectively represent), in Germany the decisions at the congress are determined by the simple majority of the delegates. Thus we have parliamentarism in place of democracy. It is true that every member of the socialist party has the right of submitting any motion he pleases to the annual congress. But the initiative thus secured is purely nominal. The motions sent in by individuals are hardly ever considered, and they are never passed, and the consequence is that none but a few cranks avail themselves of this right. When the congress is actually sitting, if a new resolution is to be submitted at least ten delegates must demand it. The only institution in the modern socialist parties which corresponds to the right of initiative is that in virtue of which the executive is compelled to summon an extraordinary congress upon the demand of a certain number of the members: in Germany, fifteen sections; in Italy, not less than one-tenth of all the members; [4] in Belgium, two provincial federations or twenty sections.[5]

In the Italian socialist party the referendum was practised for a certain time, especially as regards questions upon which a preceding congress had not come to a decision, or where this decision had been insufficiently clear. From 1904 to 1906 the executive council had recourse to this means on four occasions. In one of these the question submitted was whether in the local branches the minority had the right of secession to form autonomous branches. Of the 1,458 sections consulted, 778 replied (166 for, 612 against). On another occasion it was necessary to consult the party upon the compatibility of freemasonry

---

[4] *Statuto del Partito Socialista Italiano* (1900), Gennaro Messina, *Il Manuale del Socialista*, Nerbini, Florence, 1901, p. 164.

[5] *Programme et Statuts du Parti Ouvrier Belge*, "Le Peuple," Brussels, 1903, p. 14.

with socialism, and to ask whether members of the party could continue to be members of lodges. The participation of the members in this referendum was insignificant, but of the replies received, the majority were adverse to freemasonry.[6] In the two other cases in which the referendum was employed, one related to a local Milanese question and the other to the choice of seat for a congress. Thus the use made in Italy of the referendum has been extremely restricted and the results have been mediocre. In England, many of the trade unions, after having for long made use of the referendum, have now discontinued the practice, on the ground that it led to a loss of tactical stability and was prejudicial to the finances and to the work of administration.[7] In Germany, where, notwithstanding the hesitation of the majority, the referendum was introduced in certain districts for the election of the delegates to the congress, it was soon perceived that those comrades alone had sufficient knowledge to participate in the election of delegates who had taken part in the meetings upon party questions and were familiar with the attitude assumed upon these by the various candidates. Consequently the application of the referendum to the election of delegates came to be regarded as a dangerous measure, tending to withdraw the electoral act from the sovereignty of the assembly.[8] In Holland, where the referendum is obligatory for the election of the executive committee of the socialist party, in 1909 the participation of the rank and file in the election was so small that (notwithstanding the violent internal struggles then agitating the higher centres of the party) not more than one-half of the members exercised their right to vote.[9]

The history of the referendum as a democratic expedient utilized by the socialist parties may be summed up by saying that its application has been rare, and that its results have been unfortunate. The results have been bad owing to the confused manner in which the questions have been formulated and owing to the inadequate participation of the masses. The rare application within the socialist party of this direct appeal to the

---

[6] Ernesto Cesare Longobardi, *Relatione morale e politica della Direzione del Partito*, Stab. Tip. Ital., Frascati, 1906, pp. 5 et seq.

[7] Fausto Pagliari, *Organizzazione operaia in Europa*, Umanitaria, Milan, 1909, 2nd ed., p. 54.

[8] "Volksstimme" of Frankfort, 1908, No. 188, first supplement.

[9] "Het Volk," April 21, 1910.

members is in remarkable contrast with the frequent use made of the referendum by the bourgeois national organism of Switzerland, and it is in flagrant contradiction with the demand which all socialists make of the state for direct legislation by the people through the initiative and right of popular veto. Where party life is concerned, the socialists for the most part reject these practical applications of democracy, using against them conservative arguments such as we are otherwise accustomed to hear only from the opponents of socialism. In articles written by socialist leaders it is ironically asked whether it would be a good thing to hand over the leadership of the party to the ignorant masses simply for love of an abstract democratic principle.[10] The conservative has views which harmonise perfectly with the thought here expressed, but he will speak of the "state" instead of the "party."

The referendum is open to criticism to the same extent and for the same reasons as is every other form of direct popular government.[11] The two principal objections are the incompetence of the masses and the lack of time. Bernstein has said with good reason that even if none but the most important political and administrative questions are to be submitted to the popular vote, the happy citizen of the future will find every Sunday upon his desk such a number of interrogatories that he will soon lose all enthusiasm for the referendum.[12] It is, however, especially in respect of questions demanding a prompt decision that the referendum proves impracticable; it conflicts with the militant character of the party, interfering with easy mobilization. Moreover, in all the more important cases, as when it is necessary to determine the attitude of the socialist

---

[10] Cf. also *supra*, pp. 151–2. The same train of thought is developed by an Italian revolutionist, Arturo Labriola. In the days before his adhesion to syndicalism he wrote a little work against the referendum, in whïch he said: "In politics, as in everything else, it is not truly democratic to hand over power to the many on the plea that right must be on their side; it should be given to those who can best judge the interaction of cause and effect in social life. It is certainly not a revolutionary tactic to entrust the part of Brennus in political life to those who are most attached (as are the peasants) to conservative traditions. But this is what the referendum does" (Arturo Labriola, *Contro il Referendum*, ed. cit., p. 24). In these phrases we have the plainest denial, the most deliberate denunciation, of democracy.

[11] Cf. *supra*, pp. 24 et seq., 43 et seq., 100–1, 151–2.

[12] E. Bernstein, *Zur Geschichte u. Theorie des Sozialismus*, Dümmler, Berlin, 1901, p. 204.

party towards an imminent war, the use of a referendum would be rendered impossible by the forcible opposition of the state. It may be added that it is easy for the chiefs to lead the masses astray by clever phrasing of the questions,[13] and by reserving to themselves the right of interpretation in the case of replies which are ambiguous precisely because the questions have been ambiguously posed. The referendum, through its absolute character and its withdrawal from all criticism, favours the dominion of adroit adventurers. George Sand describes the plebiscite, if not counterpoised by the intelligence of the masses, as an attack upon the liberty of the people.[14] The power of Bonapartism was, in fact, based on the referendum.[15] The institution of the referendum demands for its just working a perfectly conscientious bureaucracy, for the history of this electoral system shows with what ease its results are falsified.[16] Even if the operation should be effected strictly according to rule, the result of a referendum can never have a truly demonstrative value,

---

[13] In 1860, when the unification of Italy was effected by a plebiscite, the Italian petty states being swept away, the alternative proposed in the referendum was between the retention of the ancient and detested petty princedoms and the acceptance of the kingship of Victor Emanuel. In this manner the numerous Italians who desired the unification of Italy in republican form were deprived of the possibility of expressing their true views. (Cf. *supra*, pp. 91 and 229 note 3.)

[14] G. Sand, *Journal d'un Voyageur, etc.*, ed. cit., p. 306.

[15] Result of the plebiscitary elections of Napoleon I (*Idées Napoléoniennes*, ed. cit., p. 19, by Louis Napoleon Bonaparte) :—

	Votes.	Favourable.	Unfavourable.
Constitution of the year 1791, not submitted to popular vote			
Constitution of the year 1793 ...	—	1,801,018	11,600
Constitution of the year III ...	—	1,057,390	49,977
Election as Consul (year VIII)...	3,012,569	3,011,007	1,562
Consul for life (1802)	3,577,259	3,568,888	8,371
Emperor (1804)	3,524,253	3,521,675	2,578

This table is continued on page 338.

[16] Celebrated is the reproach hurled by Victor Hugo at Napoleon III on account of the plebiscite of the year 1851: "Qui a conté? Baroche. Qui a scruté? Rouher. Qui a contrôle? Piétri. Qui a additionné? Maupas. Qui a verifié? Troplong. Qui a proclamé? Vous. C'est à dire que la bassesse a conté, la platitude a scruté, la rouerie a contrôlé, le faux a additionné, la vénalité a vérifié, le mensonge a proclamé" (Victor Hugo, *Napoléon le Petit*, ed. cit., p. 313).

for it always lacks the vivifying influence of discussion. To conclude, it may be said that it can exercise no substantial influence upon the executive.

Plebiscites of Napoleon III

Election to the presidency (1848)	—	5,500,000	1,590,000 (for Cavaignac)
Re-elected president for 10 years (1851)	—	7,500,000	—
Emperor (1852)	—	7,800,000	—

CHAPTER II

THE POSTULATE OF RENUNCIATION

The dissolution of the democratic consciousness of the leaders may doubtless be retarded, if not completely arrested, by the influence of intellectual or purely ideological factors. "So long as the guidance and representation of the party remains in the hands of persons who have grown grey in the great tradition of socialism,"[1] so long, that is to say, as the party is still dominated by vigorous socialistic idealism, it is possible that in certain conditions the leaders will retain their ancient democratic sentiments, and that they will continue to regard themselves as the servitors of the masses from whom their power is derived. We have already discussed the drastic measures that have been proposed to prevent the embourgeoisement of the leaders of proletarian origin.[2] But it is not enough to prevent the proletarian elements among the leaders from adopting a bourgeois mode of life; it is also essential, on this line of thought, to insist upon the proletarianization of the leaders of bourgeois origin. In order to render it impossible for the socialist intellectuals to return to their former environment it has been proposed to insist that they should assimilate the tenour of their lives to that of the proletarian masses, and should thus descend to the level of their followers. It is supposed that their bourgeois instincts would undergo atrophy if their habits were to be in external respects harmonized as closely as possible with those of the proletariat.

This thesis is rooted in the records and experiences of popular history. A life in common awakens sympathy, attenuates the sentiments of class opposition, and may culminate in their entire disappearance. In the equalitarian state of Paraguay, which was founded and administered by the Jesuit order, those who were under tutelage felt themselves to be at one with the Jesuit

---

[1] Heinrich Ströbel, *Gewerkschaften u. Sozialistische Geist,* "Neue Zeit," anno xxiii, vol. ii, No. 44.

[2] Cf. *supra,* p. 126.

fathers who were exploiting them, since there was no distinction between the leaders and the led in respect of clothing or general manner of life.[3] During the French Revolution, the peasantry took the castles of the nobles by storm; it was only in La Vendée that the two classes made common cause in the pitiless struggle with the centralized revolutionary government in Paris, because the patriarchal life in common, the common festivals and common hunting parties, had there effected a close psychological community between the peasants and their lords.[4] Similarly in Italian villages we do not usually find a well-marked hatred of the clergy, for the local curés, good-natured if uncultured individuals, are in no way elevated above the rest of the population, whose habits, and even whose poverty, they usually share.[5]

Numerous measures, both material and ideal, have been proposed to prevent the formation of an oligarchy within the democratic parties. Speaking of the Italian students, Bakunin defines in the following terms the rôle which in his opinion the young refugees from the bourgeoisie ought to play in the ranks of the proletariat. "Ni guides, ni prophètes, ni instructeurs, ni docteurs, ni créateurs. Aux jeunes intellectuels il convient d'être les accoucheurs de la pensée enfantée par la vie même du peuple, et d'élever les aspirations aussi inconscientes que puissantes du prolétariat de l'état de confusion à celui de clarté."[6] Bakunin saw clearly that in certain countries, such as Italy and Russia, the working-class movement could not possibly dispense with the aid of bourgeois intellectuals, but he desired that those who by birth were the natural adversaries of socialism should be subjected to a very strict regime when they adhered to the socialist cause. In this respect he may be considered a precursor of Tolstoi. "La vie domine la pensée et détermine la volonté." It is by this aphorism, essentially based upon the materialist conception of history, that Bakunin defines his attitude to the question under consideration. He continues: "Si un homme, né et élevé dans un milieu bour-

---

[3] J. Guevara *Historia de la Conquista de Paraguay*, Buenos Ayres, 1885.

[4] Adolphe Thiers, *Histoire de la Révolution Française*, Brockhaus u. Avenarius, Leipzig, 1846, vol. ii, pp. 395–6; Karl Kautsky, *Die Klassengegensätze von 1789*, Dietz, Stuttgart, 1889, p. 17.

[5] Cf. the admirable picture given by Bakunin, *Il Sozialismo e Mazzini*, ed. cit., p. 49.

[6] Bakunin, *Lettre inédite à Celso Cerretti*, 1872, "La Société Nouvelle," Brussels, February 1896, No. cxxiv, p. 179.

geois, veut devenir, sincèrement et sans phrases, l'ami et le frère des ouvriers, il doit renoncer à toutes les conditions de son existence passée, à toutes ses habitudes bourgeoises, rompre tous ses rapports de sentiment, de vanité, et d'esprit avec le monde bourgeois, et, tournant le dos à ce monde, devenant son ennemi et lui déclarant une guerre irréconciliable, se jeter entièrement, sans restriction ni reserve, dans le monde ouvrier. S'il ne trouve pas en lui une passion de justice suffisante pour lui inspirer cette résolution et ce courage, qu'il ne se trompe pas lui-même et qu'il ne trompe pas les ouvriers; il ne deviendra jamais leur ami."[7] Thus it was above all for reasons of a psychological order that Bakunin demanded from the "bourgeois socialists," from the "intellectuals," a complete abandonment of their former mode of life. He believed that the outer world exercises a decisive influence upon the world of mental life. Self-renunciation, sacrifice, repudiation of all the forms of bourgeois existence—such were the conditions essential to the labour leader during the long history of the Russian revolution. In 1871 Netchajeff wrote his famous revolutionary catechism, enunciating the principle that the true revolutionary must be a man "consecrated to the cause." In the first paragraph we read: "Il n'a n'y intérêts personnels, ni affaires, ni sentiments, ni attachements, ni propriété, ni même un nom. Tout en lui est absorbé par un seul intérêt exclusif, une seule pensée, une seule passion: la Révolution."[8] Thus the aim was to attain to an absolute forgetfulness of the former bourgeois existence. Even more important than this elusory internal mortification was the external or environmental mortification which, among the Russian socialists, subsequently came to constitute the substratum of their activities, and which Bakunin described as "complete immersion in the life of the people."[9] The suppression of bourgeois instincts, this was the postulate which long dominated the history of Russian socialism. The apostles of the revolution, who were in many cases of the highest birth, must effect this suppression, in accordance

---

[7] Bakunin, *L'Empire knouto-germanique et la Révolution Sociale*, Œuvres de Michel Bakounine, P. V. Stock, Paris, 1897, vol. ii, p. 370.

[8] *Le Catechisme Révolutionnaire*, reprinted by Marx, *L'Alliance de la Démocratie Socialiste et l'Association internationale des Travailleurs*. A. Darson, successeur Foucault, London and Hamburg, 1873, p. 90.

[9] "Il bagno nella vita del populo" (Bakunin, *Il Sozialismo e Mazzini*, ed. cit., p. 24).

with established custom, by living "among the people," by harmonizing their mode of life with that of the proletariat, by confounding themselves with the latter. Such was the theory of the "narodniki" or "populists," and its practical consequences were endured with the greatest heroism. Abandoning their social position, bidding farewell to all the intellectual comforts of the town, renouncing study and bourgeois career, men of science, schoolmasters, nobles, Jewish girl-students, and young women of family, withdrew to remote villages. Working as agricultural labourers, wheelwrights, locksmiths, blacksmiths, etc., they endeavoured to acquire the most intimate knowledge of the common people, to gain their confidence, and whilst still keeping always in view the great revolutionary aim, they became the advisers of the people in the most varied conditions of their lives.[10]

After 1870 an analogous movement, though a somewhat less extensive one, was manifest among the socialist intellectuals of other countries, and more especially among those of Italy, who for this reason were stigmatized by Marx, in a spasm of unjustified anger, as *déclassés*. This term, used in an insulting sense, presents the Italian socialists in a false light. Bakunin spoke of such *déclassement*, not as a historical fact, but as a psychological postulate of the effective socialist action of those who were not proletarians by birth. Thus in Bakunin's view the *déclassé* was not a social outcast, a bankrupt, an ineffectual genius, in a word, an involuntary outcast, but the very opposite, a voluntary outcast, one who has deliberately broken with the society in which he was born, in order to adapt himself to a strange environment and one hostile to that in which he was himself brought up. He is an intentional *déclassé*, and apart from the end which he pursues he must inspire us with respect for his spirit of self-sacrifice and for the invincible firmness of his convictions. It is a historical fact, though one of which the proof cannot be attempted here, that the bourgeois leaders of the early Italian labour movement were *déclassés*, but that they were such almost exclusively in the sense in which the word is used by Bakunin and not in the sense in which the word is used by Marx. Carlo Cafiero, the best-known leader

---

[10] Adolf Braun, *Russland u. d. Revolution*, p. 4.—Among numerous documents relating to this period of the Russian struggle for liberty, cf. also *Geheime Denkschrift über die Nihilistischen Umtriebe im Jahre 1875.* "Deutsche Rundschau."

of the Italian section of the International, derived from an aristocratic and wealthy family, placed the whole of his considerable fortune at the disposal of the party, whilst himself leading the life of a poor Bohemian. He may be considered the prototype of such idealists.[11] Similar political tactics, of which perhaps idealists alone are capable (and these only in periods dominated by strong collective emotion), are based upon the psychological experience that the most ominously dictatorial tendencies of the leaders can be weakened, if not altogether suppressed, by one prophylactic means alone, namely, by the artificial creation of a social homogeneity among the various strata and fragments of which the revolutionary socialist party is composed. It thus becomes a moral postulate that all members of the party should live more or less in the same manner. This homogeneity of life is regarded as a safety-valve against the development of oligarchical forms within the working-class parties.

In our own day the principle that the leaders should practise economic renunciation and should identify themselves with the multitude is advocated only by a few isolated romanticists who belong to the anarchist wing of the socialist movement, and even by them only in timid periphrases.[12] A similar principle, however, continues to prevail in the form of a political postulate, for the demand is made in certain working-class sections of the French and German socialist parties that the leaders should break off all social relationships with the bourgeois world, should devote themselves entirely to the party, and should have no other companions than ''regularly inscribed members.'' In a Guesdist congress held in the north of France a resolution was passed that it was the duty of the socialist deputies to spend their lives among their comrades.[13] In Germany we find traces of the same order of ideas in the absolute prohibition that members of the party shall write for the bourgeois press, or take

---

[11] Cf. Michels, *Borghesia e Proletariato, etc.*, ed. cit., pp. 68 et seq.

[12] Leda Rafanelli Polli, Italian authoress and anarchist agitator, formerly a compositor, maintains in one of her interesting novels that the intellectual cannot become a complete socialist unless he abandon the life of his class. If he is unwilling to effect this renunciation, we can be sure that sooner or later he will leave the proletariat in the lurch (Polli, *Un Sogno d'Amore*, Nerbini, Florence, 1905, pp. 171 et seq.).

[13] *Compte-rendu officiel du IIIᵉ Congrès départmental de la Fédération du Nord du Parti Socialiste, tenu à Loos 1907*, M. Dhoossche, Lille, 1907, p. 41.

any part whatever in bourgeois society. It is obvious that these attempts, which are inefficacious and impractical, can succeed at most in creating party fanaticism. They cannot establish identity of thought and action between the leaders and the proletarian masses.

CHAPTER III

SYNDICALISM AS PROPHYLACTIC

ACCORDING to the syndicalist doctrine, it is essential to transfer the revolutionary centre of gravity of the proletariat from the political party to the trade union. The union is conceived as a politically neutral organism, one which does not adhere to any party, but which is socialist in inspiration and aim.

It is the great merit of the syndicalists that they have understood how disastrous would be isolated syndicalist activity, devoid of any general theory, living simply from day to day; and to have advocated with much energy the indissoluble union of the working class, organized in its trade unions, with the socialist idea as *spiritus rector* and as ultimate aim. The syndicalists desire (and here, for once, they agree with the Marxist politicians) to diffuse among the organized workers the conviction that the trade union cannot attain its aim except by the elimination of capitalism, that is to say, by the abolition of the existing economic order. But the syndicalists also desire (and here they are in open conflict with all the other currents of contemporary socialism) that the trade union should not merely be an asylum for socialist ideas, but that it should also directly promote socialist activity, pursuing not simply a trade-unionist policy in the amplest sense of the term, but in addition and above all a socialist policy. Syndicalism is to put an end to the dualism of the labour movement by substituting for the party, whose sole functions are politico-electoral, and for the trade union, whose sole functions are economic, a completer organism which shall represent a synthesis of the political and of the economic function.[1]

Hence it is not the purpose of syndicalism to do away with organization as the basis of the labour movement. It expressly recognizes that this basis is indispensable. The syndicalists hold, and with good reason, that the dangers of organization

---

[1] Enrico Leone, *Che cosa è il Sindacalismo*, Tip. Industria e Lavoro, Rome, 1906, p. 28.

cannot be eliminated simply by suppressing the organization, any more than we can prevent intoxication of the blood or diseases of the circulation by withdrawing the blood from the vessels. These would be quack cures, alike fatal in their result, for the latter would kill the human organism and the former would kill the political and social organism. The problem rather is to discover an appropriate means for reducing to a minimum the chief defect which seems inherent in organization, namely, the rule exercised by the minority over the majority. Here we find a political school, whose adherents are numerous, able, well-educated, and generous-minded, persuaded that in syndicalism it has discovered the antidote to oligarchy. But we have to ask whether the antidote to the oligarchical tendencies of organization can possibly be found in a method which is itself also rooted in the principle of representation. Does it not rather seem that this very principle is in insoluble contradiction with the anti-democratic protestations of syndicalism? In other words, is not syndicalism itself affected by a manifest antinomy?

The great significance of syndicalism is found, above all, in the clear and penetrating manner in which it has recognized the dangers of bourgeois democracy. With a genuinely scientific scepticism it has stripped away the veils which conceal the power exercised by the democracy in the state, showing that this power is really no more than the hegemony of a minority, and demonstrating that it is in acute opposition with the needs of the working class.[2] "La démocratie prétend continuer l'exploitation des masses productrices par une oligarchie de professionnels de l'intelligence."[3] All the struggles which international syndicalism has undertaken against the German social-democracy, against the Italian and French intellectuals, and against the trade unions constituted upon a bureaucratic basis, may be reduced in ultimate analysis to a struggle against democratic demagogy.[4]

Syndicalism is, however, mistaken in attributing to parliamentary democracy alone the inconveniences that arise from the principle of delegation in general. Mantica is right when he says that the syndicalists themselves have not succeeded in get-

---

[2] Werner Sombart, in his *Sozialismus u. Sozialbewegung* (Fischer, Jena, 6th ed., 1907, p. 129), attributes great importance to this particular aspect of syndicalism.

[3] Georges Sorel, *Les Illusions du Progrès*, ed. cit., p. 263.

[4] Georges Sorel in a letter to Enrico Leone, "Divenire Sociale," v, fasc. 12, 1909.

ting rid of the mental impedimenta with which all those are burdened who belong to any party, whether it participates in parliamentary elections or rejects such participation on principle.[5] *Nolens volens,* the syndicalist party is nothing more than a socialist party inefficiently revised and corrected. The syndicalists wish to stop where logically there is no stopping-place. All that the syndicalists have written upon political parties in general, and upon their big brother the socialist party in particular, applies to themselves as well, because it applies to all organizations as such without exception.

The more syndicalism endeavours to displace the axis of working-class policy towards syndicalist action, the greater is the danger it runs of itself degenerating into an oligarchy. Even in the revolutionary syndicalist groups the leaders have frequent opportunities of deceiving the rank and file. The treasurer of a strike, the secretary of a trade union, even the participator in a conspiracy or the leader upon a barricade, can betray those from whom they have received their instructions far more easily and with much more serious consequences than can a socialist member of parliament or municipal councillor.[6] French syndicalists have frequently insisted with a certain violence upon what they speak of as "direct action" as the only means of bringing the working class into effective operation as an autonomous mass not represented by third persons, and of excluding *à priori* all representation "qui ne peut être que trahison, déviation, embourgeoisement."[7] But they arbitrarily restrict their one-sided theory to the political party alone, as if it were not inevitable that like causes should produce like effects when their action is displayed upon the field of the syndicalist movement. They reason as if they were immunized against the action of sociological laws of universal validity.[8]

---

[5] Paolo Mantica, postscript to an article by Fiorino dal Padulo, *Elezionismo o Anti-Elezionismo?*, "Divenire Sociale," vi, fasc. 19 and 20, p. 272.

[6] We find that this is admitted even by a syndicalist. Cf. Angelo Oliviero Olivetti, *Problemi del Socialismo Contemporaneo*, Cagnoni, Lugano, 1906, vol. i, p. 52.

[7] Cf., *inter al.*, Edouard Berth, *Bourgeoisie et Proletariat dans le Mouvement socialiste italien*, "Mouvement Socialiste," anno ix, series ii, p. 16; and reply by R. Michels, *Controverse socialiste*, in the same review, pp. 282 et seq.

[8] Typical of the ingenuous views of the writer, an ingenuousness which is characteristic of most of the syndicalists, are the words in which

The organic structure of the trade unions is based upon the same foundation as that of the political party of the workers, namely, the representation of the interests of the rank and file by individuals specially elected for that purpose.[9] In the decisive moments of the struggle for higher wages, the masses do not represent themselves but are represented by others. Trade unions without representatives, without some kind of executive, do not exist and are inconceivable.[10]

The management of a trade union is sometimes a post of transition extremely favourable to a political career. In Germany, 35 trade-union leaders sit in parliament, and in England 27. In France the two first permanent secretaries of the Metal-

Gustave Hervé deals with the case of Azeff, the Russian revolutionary who was unmasked as a spy. In an article entitled *L'Affaire Azew* ("La Guerre Sociale," iii année, No. 7), Hervé first of all expresses the view that the Azeff revelations are of a nature "à décourager tout révolutionnaire d'entrer jamais dans une organisation secrète." He then goes on to insist upon the need for the existence of small and secret groups of leaders, saying, among other things: "Il est indispensable qu'une organisation de combat, quel qu'elle soit, ait à sa tête un comité central aussi peu nombreux que possible, et composé de militants aussi inaccessibles à la cupidité et à l'ambition qu'à la peur et à la neurasthénie. . . . Il faut que ses noyaux soient composés de camarades, ayant fait leurs preuves de courage, de discretion, de sobriété, et de désintéressement." Hervé thus consoles himself with regard to the dangers of leadership, which he does not fail to recognize, through the act of faith by which he is assured that syndicalism at any rate will have leaders whose qualities will be proof against all these dangers.

[9] For this reason, too, the criticism which the syndicalists direct against the parliamentary methods of democracy is largely fallacious. For example, Emile Pouget, in a work upon *La Confédération Générale du Travail* (Rivière, Paris, 1908, p. 35), speaks of "l'énorme différence de méthode" between socialism and syndicalism. Whereas, he tells us, the activity of syndicalism must be regarded as the outcome of the work of an enlightened minority, namely that composed of the organized workers, political socialism, which avails itself of the mechanism of universal suffrage, puts power into the hands of the unenlightened majority, or rather of their spokesmen. In reality, however, the activity of the trade union and the activity of the electoral system are governed by the same principle, that is to say, by an electoral right freely exercised. It may be true that the participation of the people in the elections to representative bodies may be somewhat more extensive than is the participation of the organized workers in the election of their leaders, but it would be rash to deduce from this trifling difference the essential inferiority of "political democracy."

[10] Cf. *supra*, pp. 298-9.

lurgical Federation have become deputies.[11] The strike, direct action by the proletariat, which the syndicalists regard as the panacea for all the ills affecting the labour movement, offers to men with a taste for political life, excellent opportunities for the display of their faculty for organization and their aptitude for command. The same may be said of the political strike, the general strike.[12] For the professional leaders of the working-class, the economic strike is often precisely what war is for professional soldiers.[13] Both present a good opportunity for rapid and splendid promotion. Many labour leaders have risen to extremely exalted and lucrative positions because they have directed a great strike, and have thus attracted the attention of the general public and of the government.[14] The political position now [1912] occupied in England by John Burns is largely due to the celebrity he acquired as a strategist when he led the great dockers' strike in London during the year 1889. He then created a solid foundation for his subsequent popularity, and in particular he then gained the confidence of the most important categories of organized workers, and thus paved the way for his elevation from the bench of the working engineer to the rank of cabinet minister.[15] This is one example among many which could be adduced in support of the assertion that very frequently the strike, instead of being a field of activity for the uniform and compact masses, tends rather to facilitate the process of differentiation and to favour the formation of

[11] *Union Fédérale des Ouvriers Métallurgistes de France*, Bourse du Travail, Paris, p. 16.

[12] Even the reformist socialist Victor Adler of Vienna accepts the general strike as a method of public activity suitable for throwing into greater relief, by its reactions, by the fear and respect it arouses in the adversaries of the socialist party, the work of the labour representatives in parliament.

[13] Vilfredo Pareto, *Systèmes socialistes*, ed. cit., vol. i, p. 71.

[14] Cf. *supra*, p. 306.

[15] "In the great dockers' strike of 1889 Burns showed himself to be a notable organizer. Henceforward he was recognized by all parties as one of the most important personalities in English public life" (Carl Stegmann and C. Hugo [Lindemann] *Handbuch des Sozialismus*, 1897, ed. cit., p. 101). "The whole labour movement received during 1889 an immense impetus . . ., above all, from the remarkable series of strikes mostly led and organized by Mr. John Burns."—"The strike [of the London dock labourers] was admirably led and managed by Burns" (Sidney Webb, *Socialism in England*, Swann Sonnenschein, London, 1890, pp. 48 and 53). (Cf. also H. M. Hyndman, *The Record of an Adventurous Life*, ed. cit., p. 407.)

an *élite* of leaders.[16] Syndicalism is even more than socialism a fighting party. It loves the great battlefield. Can we be surprised that the syndicalists need leaders yet more than do the socialists?

The syndicalists reject the system of democratic representation and of bureaucracy. They desire to substitute for it "the more combative tactics of the revolutionary army of liberty, tactics founded upon the tried ability of the leaders." The modern labour leader, they tell us, must not be a bureaucrat. Already to-day, they add, the great strike-leaders arise suddenly from obscurity as did formerly the great leaders of revolution.[17] In so far as it corresponds to historic truth, this conception does not at the best afford more than a general explanation of the institution of leadership. Its adequacy would be far greater were it possible to prove that these strike-leaders, whose necessity is admitted by the syndicalists themselves, when they have emerged from obscurity to fulfil a temporary need, were to prove sufficiently disinterested to undergo a spontaneous eclipse as soon as the strike was over. We know, however, that in general they seize the opportunity to secure a position of permanent influence. No form of strike, however much it may seem to be inspired by the autonomy of the masses, will be able to kill the dragon of demagogy, or even to prevent the formation of a class of independent leaders.[18]

Under certain conditions, the mere theoretical propaganda of the idea of the strike and of direct action has sufficed to secure power and influence for the popular leader, to lift him upon the shoulders of the multitude to a position in which he could pluck at his ease the golden apples of life. Aristide Briand, born at Nantes of a family of small tavern-keepers, hav-

---

[16] During the great strike of the agricultural workers in the Parma district, which took place during the summer of 1908 and which had been organized by the syndicalists, the whole Italian press resounded with the name of a man hitherto unknown, Alceste De Ambris. This brilliant strike-leader succeeded within a few weeks in obtaining for himself among the agricultural population of Emilia a position somewhat similar to that which in the beginning of the seventeenth century Masaniello acquired among the *lazzaroni* of Naples. The popular leadership of De Ambris came, however, to a speedy end, owing to his condemnation for political offences and his flight to America.

[17] Alfonso de Pietri-Tonelli, *Il Sindacalismo come Problema della Libertà operaia*, "Pagine Libere," anno iii, No. 819.

[18] Cf. *supra*, pp. 298–9, 306.

ing joined the socialist party in Paris, speedily acquired fame and power among the workers by his defence of the doctrine of the general strike and the military strike. He soon gained so great a prestige as to require but a few years to climb to the position of premier of France.[19] The starting-point of his triumphal march was the Nantes congress (1894), where he secured the acceptance of the idea of the general strike as part of the official programme of the French trade unions.[20]

Syndicalism is hostile to the "democratic" policy of the socialist party and the "authoritarian" syndicates, for the syndicalists hold that "democracy" affords a mere caricature of the fundamental principle of the labour movement, and they declare that from the democratic soil no fruit can spring but that of oligarchy. No other movement bases itself so energetically as does the syndicalist movement upon the right and ability of the masses for self-government. Where, as in France, the leadership of the labour movement is in their hands, they lay great stress upon the fact that their authority is restricted to carrying into effect the resolutions passed at the sovereign assemblies of the comrades. They assure us that the Confédération Générale du Travail, which sits in Paris, is not a directive organ, but a mere instrument for the coordination and the diffusion of the revolutionary activity of the working class. They describe this body as equally hostile to "centralization" and to "authoritarianism."[21] All impulse to action, we are assured, starts from the masses, and the syndicalist leaders are merely the exponents of this impulse. In strikes, the activity of the Comité Confédéral is not directive in the strict sense of the term; this body is a mere intermediary to ensure the solidarity of the workers, to secure an element of *suractivité* and of *polarization*.[22] Such is the theory. In practice, these same French syndicalists complain that in all decisive questions the masses wait until those above take the initiative, and that in default of such initiative the comrades remain with folded arms.[23]

---

[19] Flax (Victor Méric), *Aristide Briand*, "Les Hommes du Jour," Paris, 1908, No. 26.

[20] Hubert Lagardelle, *Les Origines du Syndicalisme en France*, "Mouvement Socialiste," anno xi, Nos. 215–16, pp. 245–6.

[21] Emile Pouget, *La Confédération Générale du Travail*, ed. cit., pp. 7, 23, 24.

[22] Emile Pouget, *La Confédération Générale du Travail*, ed. cit., p. 30.

[23] After the sanguinary conflict at Draveil between the strikers and

As in all groups characterized by an ostensibly democratic
ideology, among the syndicalists the dominion of the leaders
often assumes veiled forms. In France, the trade union leaders
are forbidden to seek election as deputies, for they must be
preserved from all impure contacts. They must remain in constant communication with the masses, and their activities must
be carried on in the full light of day. It is none the less true
that the necessities of their position often oblige them, in the
interest of the trade unions, to enter into relationships with the
organs of state, in such a way that their antiparliamentary attitude is apt to mean no more than that, instead of treating with
the government in the open, from the summit of the parliamentary tribune, where their actions are, in part at least, visible to
the rank and file, they negotiate mysteriously out of sight in ante-
chambers and passages.[24]

The theory of the masses professed by the syndicalists has
a reverse side to which it is well to pay attention. The trade-
union organizations, taken as a whole, do not include in their
membership more than a minority of the workers susceptible
of organization: in Italy, 11 %; in England, 23 %; in Sweden
(where the proportion is highest of all), 42.21 %. Among the

---

the cuirassiers, the expected general strike did not take place. Regarding
this failure, Emile Pouget wrote as follows in the "Voix du Peuple"
(June, 1908), the chief mouthpiece of the French labour organizations:
"Malheureusement, il faut bien constater que, si, théoriquement, l'idée
de la grève générale a pris corps en France, pratiquement, nous nous
sommes laissés devancer ne serait ce que par la classe ouvrière d'Italie.
Le tort, le tort grave, est de trop regarder au centre et d'attendre de lui
le mot d'ordre. Cette mentalité regrettable décèle chez ceux qui s'y
attardent, une superstition étatique qui, au point de vue révolutionnaire,
est on ne peut plus dangereuse. Au lieu d'agir soi-même on attend un
indication d'en haut. . . . Et l'occasion propice s'échappe!"

[24] The Belgian socialist De Brouckère, writing against the syndicalists,
says very truly: "Le système des Parloirs est assurément très inférieur
à celui des Parlements" (Louis De Brouckère et C. Huysmans, *L'Af-
filiation des Syndicats au Parti Ouvrier. Discours*, Brismée, Brussels,
1907, p. 40). Moreover, in any case, syndicalism is utterly inconsistent
in its attitude towards political democracy. On principle, the syndicalists
regard labour-protection laws as either injurious to the proletariat or
utterly unimportant, and they therefore refuse to raise a finger to secure
the passage of such laws—except in the case of the eight-hours law,
which is warmly advocated by some, though not by all syndicalists. But
whenever labour-protection laws have been actually passed, they do all
they can to maintain them and secure their enforcement. (Cf. A. Keufer,
La Crise Syndicaliste, "Mouvement Socialiste," anno xii, No. 220.)

organized workers, it is once more only a minority which plays an active part in trade-union life.[25] The syndicalists at once lament this fact and rejoice at it, being inspired, in this respect, by sentiments which are by no means logically consistent. They rejoice to be rid of the dead weight of those who are still indifferent or immature.[26] No doubt this attitude is inspired by the old Blanquist idea, that masses too vast and intellectually heterogeneous paralyse all activity by their lack of mobility, and that only alert minorities are enterprising and bellicose. If they were logical, the syndicalists would draw the conclusion that the general movement of the modern proletariat must necessarily be the work of a minority of enlightened proletarians. But the democratic tendencies of our time prevent the formulation of such a conclusion, or at least prevent its frank avowal, for this would bring the syndicalists into open conflict with the very basis of democracy, and would force them to proclaim themselves, without circumlocution, partisans of an oligarchical system. The syndicalist oligarchy, it is true, would not consist (like that of the socialist party) in the dominion of the leaders over the masses, but in the dominion of a small fraction of the masses over the whole. There are a few theorists of syndicalism who already speak unreservedly of socialism as an evolution based upon the action of working-class *élites*.[27]

The oligarchical character of the syndicalist movement is displayed most conspicuously in the demand (made for reasons which have nothing to do with democracy) for absolute obedience to the orders of the organized *élite*. ''Les indifférents, par le seul fait qu'ils ont négligé de formuler leur volonté, n'ont qu'à acquiescer aux décisions prises.''[28] Following the example of the reformist trade unions of Germany and England, those French unions that are inspired by the doctrine of revolutionary syndicalism hold fast to the principle that the organized workers have the right to issue orders to the unorganized.

It may be admitted that the supreme directive organs of the French labour movement do not possess that plenitude of powers which the corresponding hierarchical grades of other countries

---

[25] Cf. *supra*, p. 47.

[26] Pouget, *La Confédération Générale du Travail*, ed. cit., pp. 7 and 34.

[27] Cf. the essays of Angelo Oliviero Olivetti and Alfredo Polledro in ''Pagine Libere,'' 1909–10; especially Polledro's article *Dal Congresso di Bologna alla Palingenesi Sindacalista* (anno iv, 1909, fasc. 14).

[28] Emile Pouget, *La Confédération Générale du Travail*, ed. cit., p. 7.

have at their disposal—above all in Germany. There are various reasons for this difference, such as the national character of the French, the weakness of the organizations, etc. But even in France there is a great difference between theory and practice. In the first place the leaders exercise a powerful influence upon the organized comrades through the newspapers, which, as every one knows, are not edited by the masses. In addition there exists a whole hierarchy of sub-chiefs. The number of trade unionists enrolled in the Confédération Générale du Travail is about 350,000, whilst the number of subscribers to the "Voix du Peuple," the central organ of the Confédération, is no more than 7,000. These subscribers are described as "les plus actifs militants, membres des bureaux et des conseils syndicaux. . . . Par leur intermédiaire se diffuse la pensée confédérale." [29] Here we have a frank confession that there exists a graduated intellectual subordination which conflicts with the syndicalist theory. Even the general strike was primarily conceived in France as a hierarchical procedure. A resolution voted at the Nantes congress (1894) specified that the general strike must be accurately prepared in advance by a central committee of eleven and by a large number of local sub-committees. These were to give the signal and to direct the movement. To-day the syndicalists reject this conception on account of its jacobin character; [30] but in practice they are compelled to conform to the idea, notwithstanding the theoretical contradiction in which they are thus involved. In the works of some of the French syndicalist writers who have a strong tendency towards æstheticism, such as Edouard Berth, we find that the jacobin germs of the theory in question have undergone a full development.[31]

The more syndicalism gathers power, the more conspicuous

---

[29] Ibid., ed. cit., pp. 30 and 33.

[30] Lagardelle, *Les Origines du Syndicalisme, etc.*, p. 247.

[31] Read, for example, the following typical phrases, inspired by a genuine enthusiasm for the policy of the strong hand and by a profound admiration for the grandeur of the creative will: "La bourgeoisie a toujours vu dans l'intérêt de sa classe, l'intérêt national lui-même; elle a toujours identifié sa richesse propre avec la richesse nationale, et avec raison, en définitif: toute volonté forte et créatrice s'érige naturellement en volonté générale, et confond audacieusement, mais légitimement, son intérêt avec l'intérêt général" (Edouard Berth, *Revue critique: un Marx inédit!*, "Mouvement Socialiste," anno vi, series ii, No. 142, p. 100, November 1, 1904).

among the syndicalists become the effects which are everywhere
characteristic of the representative system. From the ranks
of the French syndicalists, leaders have already sprung whose
sensitiveness towards the criticisms of their followers can be
equalled only by that of an English trade-union leader.[32] Youthful syndicalism, although born out of opposition to the authoritarianism of the leaders, is thus quite unable to escape the
oligarchical tendencies which arise in every organization. For
the syndicalist leaders, as for others, the preservation of their
own power becomes the supreme law. So far has the process
already gone in France, that they have abandoned the old tactics
of taking advantage of the prosecutions instituted against them
by the government to make propagandist speeches in court and
to employ the language of heroes and prophets. Instead, on
these occasions, they act with extreme prudence and display
diplomatic reserve.[33] Sorel himself speaks of the ''dégénéres-
cence progressive du syndicalisme.'' And he has declared: ''La

---

[32] One of the best known of the French syndicalist leaders, Victor
Griffuelhes, at that time general secretary of the Confédération Générale
du Travail, in an interview published in ''L'Humanité,'' described
bluntly as ''*braillards*'' his own opponents, and especially those whose
views were voiced in the ''Guerre Sociale,'' although they belonged
to his own section of the trade-union movement. He used still more dis-
dainful terms of his opponents, declaring that their conduct was the
outcome of mere ''demagogy.'' ''Il en est qui se plaisent à parler de
l'opportunisme croissant de la C.G.T. Peu m'importe! J'ai suffisamment
du courage pour braver même cette démagogie-là.'' Here we have the
very language of every holder of power when his adversaries appeal to
Demos, for he regards such an appeal as extremely inconvenient.

[33] During the war in Morocco the antimilitarist propaganda of the
Confédération Générale du Travail was answered by the then premier,
Georges Clémenceau, by the institution of a number of prosecutions
against various noted syndicalist leaders. In the winter of 1907–8, when
Griffuelhes, among others, was prosecuted for antimilitarist views, he
changed his tactics. He gave as a reason for this change the necessity
that he should retain the leadership in his own hands, and that by securing the possibility of an acquittal he should be able to attend the
trade-union congress to be held at Marseilles in the autumn and there
make headway against the reformist tendency. Consequently, in the
proceedings in court the defence was conducted with all that ingenuity
which is calculated to make a good impression on the judge, but which
had hitherto been rigorously eschewed. It was asserted, for example, that
the attacks upon the army had been guided by sentiments similar to those
of the old soldier who declared that in taking part in the war his regi-
ment had been sent not so much to a battle as to a massacre. (Cf.
article in the ''Guerre Sociale,'' 1908, ii, Nos. 11 and 12.)

Confédération Générale du Travail prend de plus en plus l'aspect d'un gouvernement ouvrier." [34]

---

[34] Jean Bourdeau, *Entre deux Servitudes*, Alcan, Paris, 1910, p. 94.— A typical manifestation of the small respect the syndicalist leaders display for the masses, and of the absolute freedom of action they claim whenever their special views do not accord with those of their troops, is afforded by the attitude assumed by Arturo Labriola during the Tripolitan War. In a letter to "L'Internazionale" of Parma (anno v, No. 27), Labriola affirms that the manner in which the syndicalist intellectuals pursue their ideals concerns themselves alone. He says further: "Working-class syndicalists, confined within their unions, must understand once for all the position of syndicalists who are not manual workers, from whom it would be inhuman to demand sacrifices not demanded from others. We cannot fail to have opinions upon questions of civilization, national interests, the moral or religious currents of our time. Naturally these opinions are not and cannot be (and perhaps it is better that they should not be) in conformity with the ideas of an organized manual worker, to whom class questions seem not merely essential, but determinative of his attitude to all others." With these assertions Labriola in effect declares that the leaders are independent of the masses, and discloses a *jemenfichisme* which conflicts with all the duties of political consistency and of obedience to democratic principles. Moreover, this open confession displays the youth (or the senility) of the syndicalist movement. The leader of an ordinary political party might think these things, but he would keep his thoughts to himself.

CHAPTER IV

ANARCHISM AS PROPHYLACTIC

ANARCHISTS were the first to insist upon the hierarchical and oligarchical consequences of party organization. Their view of the defects of organization is much clearer than that of socialists and even than that of syndicalists. They resist authority as the source of servility and slavery, if not the source of all the ills of the world. For them constraint is "synonymous with prison and police." [1] They know how readily the individualism of the leaders checks and paralyses the socialism of the led. In order to elude this danger, anarchists, notwithstanding the practical inconveniences entailed, have refrained from constituting a party, at least in the strict sense of the term. Their adherents are not organized under any stable form. They are not united by any discipline. They know nothing of obligations or duties, such as elections, pecuniary contributions, participation in regular meetings, and so on.

It is a necessary consequence of these peculiarities that the typical anarchist leader differs considerably from the typical socialist leader, the characteristic product of the last twenty-five years. Anarchism has no party organization which can offer lucrative positions, nor does the anarchist pathway lead to parliamentary honours. Consequently there are fewer opportunities for contagion, fewer temptations, and much less field for personal ambition. Thus it may be expected, as a logical consequence of the theory that environment makes character, that in the average anarchist leader idealism should be more conspicuous than in the average socialist leader. The anarchist lives remote from the practice of politics, with all its passions, all its appetites, and all its allurements; consequently he is more objective in his judgment of persons and of things, more contemplative, more self-enclosed—but also more of a dreamer, more remote from reality. Among anarchist leaders we find

---

[1] Ferdinand Domela Nieuwenhuis, *Der staatssozialistische Charakter der Sozialdemokratie*, "Archiv für Sozialw.," xxviii, fasc. i, p. 144.

many learned, cultivated, and modest men who have not lost the sentiment of true friendship, and to whom it is a pleasure to cultivate and nourish that sentiment: sincere and high-minded men, such as Peter Kropotkin, Elisée Reclus, Christian Cornelissen, Enrico Malatesta, and many others less famous.[2] But though the anarchist leaders are as a rule morally superior to the leaders of the organized parties working in the political field, we find in them some of the qualities and pretensions characteristic of all leadership. This is proved by a psychological analysis of the characteristics of the individual anarchist leader. The theoretical struggle against all authority, against all coercion, to which many of the most eminent anarchists have sacrificed a large portion of their lives, has not stifled in them the natural love of power. All that we can say is that the means of dominion employed by the anarchist leader belong to an epoch which political parties have already outlived. These are the means utilized by the apostle and the orator: the flaming power of thought, greatness of self-sacrifice, profundity of conviction.[3] Their dominion is exercised, not over the organization, but over minds; it is the outcome, not of technical indispensability, but of intellectual ascendancy and moral superiority.

Whilst anarchists repudiate the formation of political parties, they adhere none the less to the principle of organization in the economic field.[4] Some of them, even, explicitly recognize the need for the technical guidance of the masses;[5] whilst others

---

[2] We find some admirably drawn character-sketches of anarchist leaders in the work of Peter Kropotkin, *Memoirs of a Revolutionist*, Smith, Elder, London, 1899, vol. ii, p. 196. See also the psychological portrait of an unnamed anarchist in De Amicis, *Lotte civili*, Nerbini, Florence, 1904, pp. 128 et seq.

[3] In some, naturally, we encounter sounding phrases with very little content. "Un besoin de s'épancher, de convaincre, tombe souvent à discutailler où s'écoule en déclamations à l'honneur de sociétés futures. Ailleurs c'est pire: une science rudimentaire s'ébat dans des discours—prêches ou ronronnent les mots d'harmonie, d'amour, et de machinisme" (Zo d'Axa, *A Paterson*, "La Revue Blanche," Paris, 1902, No. 222, p. 10).—Regarding the wealth of empty phrases characteristic of the less serious and less able among the anarchists, consult the critical work of a convinced Italian anarchist, Domenico Zavattero, *Gli Anarchici nel Movimento sociale in Italia*, Iniziativa Edit., Ravenna 1906, pp. 30, 84 et seq.

[4] Cf. Christian Cornelissen, *Op Weg naar een nieuwe Maatschappij, Beginselen en Taktiek van den Klassentrijd*, Becht, Amsterdam, 1902, p. 242.

[5] S. Merlino, *Pro e contro il Socialismo*, Treves, Milan, 1897, p. 268.

declare their conviction that it would suffice to restrict the functions of the leaders to purely administrative work, to eliminate, once for all, the differences, so dangerous to the organization, which arise between the leaders and the led.[6] As if the technical and administrative superiority of the leaders were not alone sufficient to establish their supremacy over the masses in all other respects! Not even Bakunin proposed to exclude the principles of organization and discipline, but he desired that they should be voluntary instead of automatic.[7] He conceived the anarchist regime as a federation of perpetual barricades, and proposed to institute a council of the revolutionary commune, consisting of delegates, one or two in number from each barricade, or from each street or quarter, these delegates having an imperative mandate. The communal council thus composed would nominate from among its own members special executive committees for all the branches of the revolutionary administration of the commune. The capital, having effected a successful insurrection and constituted itself as a commune, would then declare to the other municipalities of the country that it put forward no claim to exercise any supremacy over them. But it would invite them to provide themselves also with a revolutionary organization, and to send delegates to a meeting-place to be determined by agreement, in order to establish a federation of insurgent associations, communes, and provinces, and thus to create a revolutionary power sufficiently strong to oppose any possible reaction. As Marx justly pointed out, these executive committees, if they were to do anything at all, must be furnished with powers, and must be sustained by public force. The federal parliament would have no reason for existence unless it were to organize this public force. Besides, this parliament could, just like the communal council, delegate its executive power to one or more committees, and each of these would in fact be invested with an authoritative character which the needs of the struggle would not fail continually to accentuate. In a word, according to Marx, the whole Bakuninian scheme would be characterized by an ultra-authoritative stamp.[8]

---

[6] Luigi Fabbri, *Sindicalismo y Anarquismo*, Traduccion de José Prat, F. Sempre, Valencia, 1907, p. 169.

[7] Bakunin, *Œuvres*, ed. cit., vol. ii, p. 297.

[8] Karl Marx, *L'Alliance de la Démocratie socialiste et l'Association internationale des Travailleurs*, ed. cit., p. 14.—Regarding the autocratic tendencies of Bakunin see pp. 3, 9, 10–11, 18, 24–5.

Like the syndicalists, the anarchists have extolled "direct action," which, they consider, possesses the value of an ethical principle. Direct action, "in contradistinction to the tactics of negotiation, of mutual compromise, of hierarchical organization, and of the representative system, tends to secure a higher standard of life for the workers, and the emancipation of the proletariat from capitalism and political centralization—to secure these advantages by the immediate self-help of the workers."[9]

Notwithstanding this, anarchism, a movement on behalf of liberty, founded on the inalienable right of the human being over his own person, succumbs, no less than the socialist party, to the law of authoritarianism as soon as it abandons the region of pure thought and as soon as its adherents unite to form associations aiming at any sort of political activity.[10] Nieuwenhuis, the veteran champion of anarchizing socialism with a frankly individualist tendency, showed on one occasion that he had a keen perception of the dangers which anarchism runs from all contact with practical life. At the Amsterdam congress of 1907, after the foundation of the new anarchist international, he raised a warning voice against the arguments of the Italian Enrico Malatesta, an anarchist attached to the school of Bakunin. Malatesta, having dilated upon the strength of bourgeois society, declared that nothing would suit this society better than to be faced by unorganized masses of workers, and that for this reason it was essential to counter the powerful organization of the rich by a still more powerful organization of the poor. "Si tel est ta pensée, cher ami," said Nieuwenhuis to Malatesta, "tu peux t'en aller tranquillement chez les socialistes. Ils ne disent pas autre chose." In the course of this first anarchist congress there were manifest, according to Nieu-

---

[9] Erich Mühsam, *Die direkte Aktion im Befreiungskampfe der Arbeiterschaft,* "Generalstreik," monthly supplement of "Der Freie Arbeiter," anno i, October 1905.

[10] A striking instance of the way in which an anarchist may suffer from the same lust for power and the use of force which he condemns in the working-class leaders of other parties is afforded by the following passage relating to the future socialist state, in which Siegfried Nacht is referring to Bebel, Legien, and others: "If we are to escape the danger that the greatest of all men's struggles for freedom may lead to a new despotism, the first duty of the genuine revolutionist will be to hang to the street-lamps all aspirants to dictatorship" (S. Nacht, *Tod den Schurken!,* "Weckruf," Swiss bi-monthly, June 1905).

wenhuis, the symptoms of that diplomatic mentality which characterizes all the leaders of authoritarian parties.[11]

Ostrogorski has proposed to substitute for party organization, which invariably leads to the institution of anti-democratic forms, a system of temporary associations, which should come into existence only for the attainment of definite ends, and should be dissolved as soon as these ends have been secured (*league system*).[12] He considers that the adoption of this system would tend to restore to political struggles the sincerity, honesty, and clarity which they lack to-day. Now, the analysis of political parties which has been effected authorizes us to doubt the efficiency of the proposed method. Its adoption would not secure any real progress, even were it possible to suppress by a simple decree the organizations which have been brought into existence by the necessary determinants of historical evolution. Whilst anarchism, which presents to us the most abstract and most idealistic vision of the future, has promised to the world an order from which all concentration of power shall be excluded, it has not known how to establish, as a part of anarchist theory, the logical elements of such an order.[13]

---

[11] Ferdinand Domela Nieuwenhuis, *Die Nieuwe Internationale*, ''De Vrije Socialist,'' Hilversum, September 1907, vol. x, No. 71.

[12] M. Ostrogorski, *La Démocratie et l'Organisation des Partis politiques*, ed. cit., vol. ii, pp. 618 et seq.

[13] ''Most once said that only the dictatorial and the servile could be sincere opponents of anarchism. Even if the use of the 'only' be left uncriticized, these words seem to me to display a fatal defect in the psychological foundations of anarchism. For, in view of the natural endowments of human beings, it seems probable that the majority will always continue to belong to one or other of the two types here characterized by Most'' (Walter Borgius, *Die Ideenwelt des Anarchismus*, Dietrich, Leipzig, 1904, p. 58).

PART SIX

SYNTHESIS: THE OLIGARCHICAL TENDENCIES OF ORGANIZATION

CHAPTER I

THE CONSERVATIVE BASIS OF ORGANIZATION

AT this point in our inquiry two decisive questions present themselves. One of these is whether the oligarchical disease of the democratic parties is incurable. This will be considered in the next chapter. The other question may be formulated in the following terms. Is it impossible for a democratic party to practise a democratic policy, for a revolutionary party to pursue a revolutionary policy? Must we say that not *socialism* alone, but even a socialistic *policy*, is utopian? The present chapter will attempt a brief answer to this inquiry.

Within certain narrow limits, the democratic party, even when subjected to oligarchical control, can doubtless act upon the state in the democratic sense.[1] The old political caste of society, and above all the "state" itself, are forced to undertake the revaluation of a considerable number of values—a revaluation both ideal and practical. The importance attributed to the masses increases, even when the leaders are demagogues. The legislature and the executive become accustomed to yield, not only to claims proceeding from above, but also to those proceeding from below. This may give rise, in practice, to great inconveniences, such as we recognize in the recent history of all the states under a parliamentary regime;[2] in theory, however,

---

[1] Especially where there exists universal, equal, and direct suffrage, and where the working-class is strongly organized and is awake to its own interests. (Cf. Franco Savorgnan, *Soziologische Fragmente*, Wagner, Innsbruck, 1909, p. 105). In this case the leaders have every interest in exercising upon the state all the pressure they can to render it more democratic.

[2] Cf., as far as Italy is concerned, the classic work of Marco Minghetti, *I Partiti politici e la Ingerenza loro nella Justicia e nell' Amministrazione*, N. Zanichelli, Bologna, 1881, 2nd ed., pp. 17 et seq. In consequence of the intimate relationships between the popular oligarchy (deputies) and the highest levels of the bureaucratic oligarchy (government), the state officials of the second degree of importance, and especially the prefects, are apt to become entirely dependent upon the popular oligarchy. The deputy threatens, overtly or tacitly, to go over to the

this new order of things signifies an incalculable progress in respect of public rights, which thus come to conform better with the principles of social justice. This evolution will, however, be arrested from the moment when the governing classes succeed in attracting within the governmental orbit their enemies of the extreme left, in order to convert them into collaborators. Political organization leads to power. But power is always conservative. In any case, the influence exercised upon the governmental machine by an energetic opposition party is necessarily slow, is subject to frequent interruptions, and is always restricted by the nature of oligarchy.

The recognition of this consideration does not exhaust our problem, for we have further to examine whether the oligarchical nature of organization be not responsible for the creation of the external manifestations of oligarchical activity, whether it be not responsible for the production of an oligarchical policy. The analysis here made shows clearly that the internal policy of the party organizations is to-day absolutely conservative, or is on the way to become such. Yet it might happen that the external policy of these conservative organisms would be bold and revolutionary; that the anti-democratic centralization of power in the hands of a few leaders is no more than a tactical method adopted to effect the speedier overthrow of the adversary; that the oligarchs fulfil the purely provisional function of educating the masses for the revolution, and that organization is after all no more than a means employed in the service of an amplified Blanquist conception.

This development would conflict with the nature of party, with the endeavour to organize the masses upon the vastest scale imaginable. As the organization increases in size, the struggle for great principles becomes impossible. It may be noticed that in the democratic parties of to-day the great conflicts of view are fought out to an ever-diminishing extent in the field of ideas and with the weapons of pure theory, that they therefore degenerate more and more into personal struggles and invectives, to be settled finally upon considerations of a purely superficial character. The efforts made to cover internal

---

opposition if the minister will not speedily remove from his constituency a prefect to whom he (the deputy) has taken a dislike, and the minister, who has to think of maintaining his majority in the chamber, is apt to give way. (Cf. also Annibale Marazio, *Del Governo parlamentare Italiano*, Unione Tip. Ed. Torinese, Turin, 1904, p. 168.)

dissensions with a pious veil are the inevitable outcome of organization based upon bureaucratic principles, for, since the chief aim of such an organization is to enrol the greatest possible number of members, every struggle on behalf of ideas within the limits of the organization is necessarily regarded as an obstacle to the realization of its ends, an obstacle, therefore, which must be avoided in every possible way. This tendency is reinforced by the parliamentary character of the political party. "Party organization" signifies the aspiration for the greatest number of members. "Parliamentarism" signifies the aspiration for the greatest number of votes. The principal fields of party activity are electoral agitation and direct agitation to secure new members. What, in fact, is the modern political party? It is the methodical organization of the electoral masses. The socialist party, as a political aggregate endeavouring simultaneously to recruit members and to recruit votes, finds here its vital interests, for every decline in membership and every loss in voting strength diminishes its political prestige. Consequently great respect must be paid, not only to new members, but also to possible adherents, to those who in Germany are termed *mitläufer,* in Italy *simpatizzanti,* in Holland *geestverwanten,* and in England *sympathizers.* To avoid alarming these individuals, who are still outside the ideal worlds of socialism or democracy, the pursuit of a policy based on strict principle is shunned, while the consideration is ignored whether the numerical increase of the organization thus effected is not likely to be gained at the expense of its quality.

The last link in the long chain of phenomena which confer a profoundly conservative character upon the intimate essence of the political party (even upon that party which boasts itself revolutionary) is found in the relationships between party and state. Generated to overthrow the centralized power of the state, starting from the idea that the working class need merely secure a sufficiently vast and solid organization in order to triumph over the organization of the state, the party of the workers has ended by acquiring a vigorous centralization of its own, based upon the same cardinal principles of authority and discipline which characterize the organization of the state.[3]

---

[3] Albert Schäffle believes that socialism needs merely to produce a great general at the right moment in order to inherit the power of the centralized military organization (Schäffle, *Quintessenz des Sozialismus,* Perthes, Gotha, 1879, 7th ed., p. 68).

It thus becomes a governmental party, that is to say, a party which, organized itself like a government on the small scale, hopes some day to assume the reins of government upon the large scale. The revolutionary political party is a state within the state,[4] pursuing the avowed aim of destroying the existing state in order to substitute for it a social order of a fundamentally different character.[5] To attain this essentially political end, the party avails itself of the socialist organization, whose sole justification is found precisely in its patient but systematic preparation for the destruction of the organization of the state in its existing form. The subversive party organizes the *framework* of the social revolution. For this reason it continually endeavours to strengthen its positions, to extend its bureaucratic mechanism, to store up its energies and its funds.

---

[4] The same is true of the revolutionary trade unions (French style). "*Un état dans l'état!* C'était bien là, en effet, le bût poursuivi. On voulait que, dans tous les évènements, l'organisation ouvrière pût, à un signal, adopter une attitude identique et, au besoin, prendre l'offensif" (Eugène Guérard, *La Confédération du Travail*, "Mouvement Socialiste," May 15, 1899, p. 555).

[5] Devoting all its energies to the imitation of the outward apparatus of power characteristic of the "class-state," the socialist party allots no more than a secondary importance to psychological enfranchisement from the mentality which dominates this same class-state. This neglect of the psychical factor is disastrous to the democratic principle, especially in so far as it springs from psychological sources. Raphael Friedeberg, who finds fault with historical materialism because it "starts from the monstrous error that the mode of production of material life is the sole cause of all sociological happenings," because it leads to the atrophy of all spiritual faculties, and consequently to the decay of socialist thought, has opposed this doctrine by that which he calls the doctrine of historical psychism, namely, "the psychical enfranchisement of the proletariat from all the intrinsic conditions of class dominion" (see his preface to the German edition of Gustave Hervé's work, *Leur Patrie* [*Das Vaterland der Reichen*], Zurich, 1907, p. vii). But Friedeberg's charge against historical materialism is unsound, for the following reason. This doctrine, based upon the idea of class, teaches the masses of the workers that just as they exist in a state of economic antagonism to the dominant class, so also their spiritual and psychical life (the "superstructure") is (or at least ought to be) in irreconcilable conflict with the spiritual and psychic life of the bourgeoisie. Another argument against historical materialism is adduced elsewhere by Friedeberg. It conflicts, he says, with the class struggle, which depends upon the fact that those who are removed from the mental environment of their material sphere of production become psychical *déclassés*. He goes so far as to maintain that the more independent the human brain becomes, the more manifest

Every new official, every new secretary, engaged by the party is in theory a new agent of the revolution; in the same way every new section is a new battalion; and every additional thousand francs furnished by the members' subscriptions, by the profits of the socialist press, or by the generous donations of sympathetic benefactors, constitute fresh additions to the war-chest for the struggle against the enemy. In the long run, however, the directors of this revolutionary body existing within the authoritarian state, sustained by the same means as that state and inspired by the like spirit of discipline, cannot fail to perceive that the party organization, whatever advances it may make in the future, will never succeed in becoming more than an ineffective and miniature copy of the state organization. For this reason, in all ordinary circumstances, and as far as prevision is humanly possible, every attempt of the party to measure its forces with those of its antâgonists is foredoomed to disastrous failure. The logical consequence of these considerations is in direct conflict with the hopes entertained by the founders of the party. Instead of gaining revolutionary energy as the force and solidity of its structure has increased, the precise opposite has occurred; there has resulted, *pari passu* with its growth, a continued increase in the prudence, the timidity even, which inspires its policy. The party, continually threatened by the state upon which its existence depends, carefully avoids (once it has attained to maturity) everything which

---

is the fallacy of Marxism (R. Friedeberg, *Historische Materialismus und Klassenkampf*, "Polis," a review published at Zurich, 1907, i, No. 5). But this reasoning is erroneous, for in the class situation of the proletariat, a situation clearly recognized by Marxism, there exist all the elements which combine to make the proletariat the natural enemy (in the intellectual sphere) of the bourgeoisie, and thus lead to the "class struggle." Ideologically to remove the members of the working class from the world of their material sphere of production could not mean anything else than to impose upon them an essentially strange mentality, to *embourgeoiser* them. In actual fact this process occurs to-day upon a large scale, not in consequence, however, of historical materialism, but in opposition to it, being due above all to the suggestive influence exercised upon the masses by leaders who have themselves become *embourgeoisés*. It is true that the process of embourgeoisement can itself be explained in conformity with the doctrine of historical materialism, on the ground that it depends upon the changed mode of life and changed position in life of the leaders, upon the organization that is necessary for the conduct of the class struggle, and upon the consequences inherent in this organization which have been studied in the text.

might irritate the state to excess. The party doctrines are, whenever requisite, attenuated and deformed in accordance with the external needs of the organization.⁶ Organization becomes the vital essence of the party. During the first years of its existence, the party did not fail to make a parade of its revolutionary character, not only in respect of its ultimate ends, but also in respect of the means employed for their attainment— although not always in love with these means. But as soon as it attained to political maturity, the party did not hesitate to modify its original profession of faith and to affirm itself revolutionary only "in the best sense of the word," that is to say, no longer on lines which interest the police, but only in theory and on paper.⁷ This same party, which at one time did not

---

⁶ A classical example of the extent to which the fear of injuring the socialist organization will lead even the finest intelligences of the party to play tricks with socialist theory is afforded by the history of that celebrated preface which in 1895 Frederick Engels wrote for a posthumous edition of Marx's book, *Die Klassenkämpfe in Frankreich, 1848-9*. This preface became the subject of great international discussions, and has been justly considered as the first vigorous manifestation of reformism in German socialism. For Engels here declares that socialist tactics will have more success through the use of legal than of illegal and revolutionary means, and thus expressly repudiates the Marxist conception of the socialist revolution. It was not till some years later that Kautsky published a letter from Engels in which the latter disavowed his preface, saying: "My text had to suffer from the timid legalism of our friends in Berlin, who dreaded a second edition of the anti-socialist laws—a dread to which I was forced to pay attention at the existing political juncture" (Karl Kautsky, *Der Weg zur Macht*, Buchhandlung "Vorwärts," 1909, p. 42). From this it would appear that the theory (at that time brand-new) that socialism could attain to its ends by parliamentary methods—and this was the quintessence of Engels' preface—came into existence from a fear lest the socialist party organization (which should be a means, and not an end in itself) might suffer at the hands of the state. Thus Engels was fêted, on the one hand, as a man of sound judgment and one willing to look facts in the face (cf. W. Sombart, *Friedrich Engels, Ein Blatt zur Entwicklungsgeschichte des Sozialismus*, Separat-Abdruck der "Zukunft," Berlin, 1895, p. 32), and was attacked, on the other hand, as a pacifist utopist (cf. Arturo Labriola, *Riforme e Rivoluzione sociale*, ed. cit., pp. 181 and 224); whereas in reality Engels would seem to have been the victim of an opportunist sacrifice of principles to the needs of organization, a sacrifice made for love of the party and in opposition to his own theoretical convictions.

⁷ Maximilian Harden is not far wrong when he compares the revolutionary parties in their attitude towards the state authorities to a cock which is as it were glued to its place because a chalk-line has been drawn in front of its beak, a line which to the bird represents an insuperable obstacle.

hesitate, when the triumphant guns of the bourgeois governors of Paris were still smoking, to proclaim with enthusiasm its solidarity with the communards,[8] now announces to the whole world that it repudiates anti-militarist propaganda in any form which may bring its adherents into conflict with the penal code, and that it will not assume any responsibility for the consequences that may result from such a conflict. A sense of responsibility is suddenly becoming active in the socialist party. Consequently it reacts with all the authority at its disposal against the revolutionary currents which exist within its own organization, and which it has hitherto regarded with an indulgent eye. In the name of the grave responsibilities attaching to its position it now disavows anti-militarism, repudiates the general strike, and denies all the logical audacities of its past.

The history of the international labour movement furnishes innumerable examples of the manner in which the party becomes increasingly inert as the strength of its organization grows; it loses its revolutionary impetus, becomes sluggish, not in respect of action alone, but also in the sphere of thought.[9] More and more tenaciously does the party cling to what it calls the "ancient and glorious tactics," the tactics which have led

---

[8] As is well-known, in 1871 Bebel, in open Reichstag, declared himself opposed to the annexation of Alsace-Lorraine, an annexation which had already been completed, and, with the sole support of Liebknecht, pushed his theoretical opposition to war to the point of voting, in war-time, against the military credits. Bakunin cherished no affection either for the Marxists or for the Germans, but he was unable to refuse his admiration to the youthful Marxist party in Germany, which had had the sublime courage to proclaim "in Germany, in the country where freedom is least known, under the triumphant military regime of Bismarck, its ardent sympathies for the principles and heroes of the Commune" (M. Bakunin, *Il Socialismo e Mazzini*, ed. cit., p. 9).

[9] In this connection it may be observed that the intellectual decadence of the socialist party, and its incapacity for producing men of talent, or at least for attracting such men to its ranks, are often demonstrated by critics who dwell upon the contrast between the present and the past. Ludwig Stein writes (*Die soziale Frage, im Lichte der Philosophie*, Encke, Stuttgart, 1897, p. 438): "The intellectual growth of the socialist party is in inverse ratio to its geographical extension. What an intellectual vacuum has existed since the death of Engels. Millions of votes, but not a single man. A vast number of respectabilities, but not one leading intelligence. The columns of the 'Neue Zeit' are largely filled with matter which is nothing better than an insipid Alexandrianism." A similar opinion by Sombart has been previously quoted (cf. p. 63, note 2).—There is at least this amount of truth in such accusations, that everywhere in the socialist parties the new generation is weakly and intellectually insignificant.

to a continued increase in membership. More and more invincible becomes its aversion to all aggressive action.

The dread of the reaction by which the socialist party is haunted paralyses all its activities, renders impossible all manifestation of force, and deprives it of all energy for the daily struggle. It attempts to justify its misoneism by the false pretence that it must reserve its strength for the final struggle. Thus we find that the conservative tendencies inherent in all forms of possession manifest themselves also in the socialist party. For half a century the socialists have been working in the sweat of their brow to create a model organization. Now, when three million workers have been organized—a greater number than was supposed necessary to secure complete victory over the enemy [10]—the party is endowed with a bureaucracy which, in respect of its consciousness of its duties, its zeal, and its submission to the hierarchy, rivals that of the state itself; the treasuries are full; [11] a complex ramification of financial and

---

[10] In 1893, in a speech at Bielefeld, Liebknecht, referring to the Cologne congress, made a comparison between the political-socialist and trade-union movements, saying: ''I do not believe that the trade-union organizations in Germany will ever attain a degree of development comparable with that of the kindred organizations in England; for I am of opinion that before such a development can be reached the red flag of victorious socialism will be waving over the Bastille of capitalism and the entrenchments of the German bourgeoisie'' (Wilhelm Liebknecht, *Ueber den Kölner Parteitag, etc.*, ed. cit., p. 18). To-day, the German trade unionists are as numerous as the English, while in the intervening years the numerical strength of the socialist movement has more than doubled, but the conquest of power seems more remote than ever.

[11] In the year 1906 the total funds of the German trade unions amounted to about 16,000,000 marks. The richest union, that of the compositors, had accumulated funds amounting to 4,374,013 marks. Next came the bricklayers' union, with 2,091,681 marks; the metalworkers' union, with 1,543,353 marks; and the woodworkers' union, with 1,452,215 marks (Karl Kautsky, *Der neue Tarif der Buchdrucker*, ''Neue Zeit,'' anno xxv, vol. 1, No. 4, p. 129). Since then, notwithstanding the intervening years of crisis involving exceptionally high claims for out-of-work pay, the financial position of the unions has become yet stronger. In 1909 the compositors owned 7,929,257 marks; the bricklayers, 6,364,647 marks; the metalworkers, 6,248,-251 marks; the woodworkers, 3,434,314 marks (*Statistisches Jahrbuch für das deutsche Reich*, 1910, anno xxxi, pp. 376–7). These ample funds are of great importance for defensive purposes, but their value for offensive purposes is extremely restricted. It would be utterly absurd for the union to pursue the policy of heaping up funds in the hope of thus overthrowing capitalism. In Germany there are hundreds of capitalists in whose private treasuries are available means exceeding those of all the unions put to-

moral interests extends all over the country. A bold and enterprising tactic would endanger all this: the work of many decades, the social existence of thousands of leaders and sub-leaders, the entire party, would be compromised. For these reasons the idea of such a tactic becomes more and more distasteful. It conflicts equally with an unjustified sentimentalism and a justified egoism. It is opposed by the artist's love of the work he has created with so much labour, and also by the personal interest of thousands of honest bread-winners whose economic life is so intimately associated with the life of the party and who tremble at the thought of losing their employment and the consequences they would have to endure if the government should proceed to dissolve the party, as might readily happen in case of war.

Thus, from a means, organization becomes an end. To the institutions and qualities which at the outset were destined simply to ensure the good working of the party machine (subordination, the harmonious cooperation of individual members, hierarchical relationships, discretion, propriety of conduct), a greater importance comes ultimately to be attached than to the productivity of the machine. Henceforward the sole preoccupation is to avoid anything which may clog the machinery. Should the party be attacked, it will abandon valuable positions previously conquered, and will renounce ancient rights rather than reply to the enemy's offensive by methods which might "compromise" its position. Naumann writes sarcastically: "The war-cry 'Proletarians of all countries unite!' has had its due effect. The forces of the organized proletariat have gained a strength which no one believed possible when that war-cry was first sounded. There is money in the treasuries. Is the signal for the final assault never to be given? . . . Is the work of preliminary organization to go on for ever?"[12] As the

gether. Moreover, on the present system of depositing savings with private banks, the earnings of this accumulated capital yield profit, not to the trade unionist, but to the enemies of the working class who are shareholders in these banks, so that the trade-union funds are "ultimately employed against the labour movement" (Bruno Buchwald, *Die Gewerkschaftsbank*, "Die neue Gesellschaft," anno iii, fasc. x). Hence the trade-union funds help to strengthen the opponents of the trade unions. For this reason a scheme has long been on foot among trade unionists to institute a bank of their own.

[12] Friedrich Naumann, *Das Schicksal des Marxismus*, "Hilfe," October 11, 1908, p. 657.

party's need for tranquillity increases, its revolutionary talons atrophy. We have now a finely conservative party which (since the effect survives the cause) continues to employ revolutionary terminology, but which in actual practice fulfils no other function than that of a constitutional opposition.

All this has deviated far from the ideas of Karl Marx, who, were he still alive, ought to be the first to revolt against such a degeneration of Marxism. Yet it is quite possible that, carried away by the spectacle of an army of three million men acting in his name, swearing on solemn occasions *in verba magistri,* he also would find nothing to say in reprobation of so grave a betrayal of his own principles. There were incidents in Marx's life which render such a view possible. He certainly knew how to close his eyes, in public at any rate, to the serious faults committed by the German social democracy in 1876.[13]

In our own day, which may be termed the age of the epigones of Marx, the character of the party as an organization ever greedy for new members, ever seeking to obtain an absolute majority, cooperates with the condition of weakness in which it finds itself vis-à-vis the state, to effect a gradual replacement of the old aim, to demolish the existing state by the new aim, to permeate the state with the men and the ideas of the party. The struggle carried on by the socialists against the parties of the dominant classes is no longer one of principle, but simply one of competition. The revolutionary party has become a rival of the bourgeois parties for the conquest of power. It therefore opens its doors to all those persons who may assist in the attainment of this end, or who may simply swell its battalions for the struggle in which it is engaged. With the necessary modifications, we may well apply to the international socialist party the words which de Maupassant puts into the mouth of the *Neveu de l'Oncle Sosthène* in order to describe the essence of French freemasonry: "Au lieu de détruire, vous organisez la concurrence: ca fait baisser les prix, voilà tout. Et puis encore, si vous n'admettiez parmi vous que des libres penseurs, je comprendrais; mais vous recevez tout le monde. Vous avez des catholiques en masse, même des chefs du parti. Pie IX fut des vôtres avant d'être pape. Si vous appelez une

---

[13] Karl Kautsky, Preface to Karl Marx, *Randglossen zum Programm der deutschen Arbeiterpartei* (1875), ''Neue Zeit,'' anno ix, vol. 1, pp. 508 et seq.

société ainsi composée une citadelle contre le cléricalisme, je
la trouve faible, votre citadelle. . . . Ah! oui, vous êtes des
malins! Si vous me dites que la Franc-Maçonnerie est une usine
à élections, je vous l'accorde; qu'elle sert de machine à faire
voter les candidats de toutes nuances, je ne le nierai jamais;
qu'elle n'a d'autre fonction que de berner le bon peuple, de
l'enrégimenter pour le faire aller à l'urne comme on envoie au
feu les soldats, je serai de votre avis; qu'elle est utile, indispensable même à toutes les ambitions politiques parcequ'elle
change chacun de ses membres en agent électoral, je vous crierai:
'C'est clair comme le soleil!' Mais si vous me prétendez qu'elle
sert à saper l'esprit monarchique, je vous ris au nez." [14]

Thus the hatred of the party is directed, not in the first place
against the opponents of its own view of the world order, but
against the dreaded rivals in the political field, against those
who are competing for the same end—power. It is above all
in the electoral agitation carried on by the socialist parties when
they have attained what is termed "political maturity" that this
characteristic is most plainly manifest. The party no longer
seeks to fight its opponents, but simply to outbid them. For
this reason we observe a continual recurrence in socialist
speeches of a claim which harmonizes ill with socialist principles, and which is often untrue in fact. Not the nationalists,
they say, but we, are the best patriots; not the men of the government, but we, are the best friends of the minor civil servants
[in Italy] or of the peasants [in Germany]; and so on. Evidently among the trade unions of diverse political colouring,
whose primary aim it is to gain the greatest possible number of
new members, the note of competition will be emphasized yet
more. This applies especially to the so-called "free unions" of
Germany, neutrally tinted bodies which on principle hold in
horror all definiteness in respect of political views or conceptions
of the world order, and which are therefore distinguishable in
name only (a few trifling terminological differences apart) from
the Christian unions. If we study the speeches and polemic
writings directed by the leaders of the free unions against the
leaders of the Christian unions, we find that these speeches
and writings contain no declarations of principle and no theoretical expositions, but merely personal criticisms and accusa-

---

[14] Guy de Maupassant, *Mademoiselle Fifi*, Libr. Ollendorff, Paris, 1907,
p. 69.

tions, and above all accusations of treachery to the cause of labour. Now it is obvious that these are no more than the means vulgarly employed by competitors who wish to steal one another's customers.[15]

By such methods, not merely does the party sacrifice its political virginity, by entering into promiscuous relationships with the most heterogeneous political elements, relationships which in many cases have disastrous and enduring consequences, but it exposes itself in addition to the risk of losing its essential character as a party. The term "party" presupposes that among the individual components of the party there should exist a harmonious direction of wills towards identical objective and practical aims.[16] Where this is lacking, the party becomes a mere "organization."

---

[15] An article was published not long ago in the "Neue Zeit" (anno xxv, No. 5) entitled *Zur Taktik gegenüber den gewerkschaftlichen Konkurrenz-Organisationen* [Tactics to be employed against the *competing* Trade-Union Organizations].

[16] Antonio Labriola, *Scritti vari di filosofia e Politica* (collected by B. Croce), Laterza, Bari, 1906, p. 321.

CHAPTER II

DEMOCRACY AND THE IRON LAW OF OLIGARCHY

WHILST the majority of the socialist schools believe that in a future more or less remote it will be possible to attain to a genuinely democratic order, and whilst the greater number of those who adhere to aristocratic political views consider that democracy, however dangerous to society, is at least realizable, we find in the scientific world a conservative tendency voiced by those who deny resolutely and once for all that there is any such possibility. As was shown in an earlier chapter,[1] this tendency is particularly strong in Italy, where it is led by a man of weight, Gaetano Mosca, who declares that no highly developed social order is possible without a "political class," that is to say, a politically dominant class, the class of a minority. Those who do not believe in the god of democracy are never weary of affirming that this god is the creation of a childlike mythopœic faculty, and they contend that all phrases representing the idea of the rule of the masses, such terms as state, civic rights, popular representation, nation, are descriptive merely of a legal principle, and do not correspond to any actually existing facts. They contend that the eternal struggles between aristocracy and democracy of which we read in history have never been anything more than struggles between an old minority, defending its actual predominance, and a new and ambitious minority, intent upon the conquest of power, desiring either to fuse with the former or to dethrone and replace it. On this theory, these class struggles consist merely of struggles between successively dominant minorities. The social classes which under our eyes engage in gigantic battles upon the scene of history, battles whose ultimate causes are to be found in economic antagonism, may thus be compared to two groups of dancers executing a *chassé croisé* in a quadrille.

---

[1] Cf. *supra*, p. 41.

The democracy has an inherent preference for the authoritarian solution of important questions.[2] It thirsts simultaneously for splendour and for power. When the English burghers had conquered their liberties, they made it their highest ambition to possess an aristocracy. Gladstone declared that the love of the English people for their liberties was equalled only by their love for the nobility.[3] Similarly it may be said that it is a matter of pride with the socialists to show themselves capable of maintaining a discipline which, although it is to a certain extent voluntary, none the less signifies the submission of the majority to the orders issued by the minority, or at least to the rules issued by the minority in obedience to the majority's instructions. Vilfredo Pareto has even recommended socialism as a means favourable for the creation of a new working-class *élite,* and he regards the courage with which the socialist leaders face attack and persecution as a sign of their vigour, and as the first condition requisite to the formation of a new "political class."[4] Pareto's *théorie de la circulation des élites* must, however, be accepted with considerable reserve, for in most cases there is not a simple replacement of one group of *élites* by another, but a continuous process of intermixture, the old elements incessantly attracting, absorbing, and assimilating the new.

This phenomenon was perhaps recognized at an earlier date, in so far as the *circulation des élites* was effected within the limits of a single great social class and took place on the political plane. In states where a purely representative government prevails, the constitutional opposition aims simply at such a circulation. In England, for instance, the opposition possesses the same simple and resistant structure as the party which holds the reins of government; its programme is clearly formulated, directed to purely practical and proximate ends; it is thoroughly disciplined, and is led by one lacking theoretical profundity but endowed with strategic talent; all its energies are devoted to overthrowing the government, to taking the reins of power into its own hands, while in other respects leaving matters exactly as they were; it aims, in a word, at the substitution of one clique of the dominant classes for another. Sooner or later the competition between the various cliques of the dominant classes

---

[2] W. E. H. Lecky, *Democracy and Liberty,* ed. cit., vol. i, p. 267.
[3] Quoted by J. Novicow, *Conscience et Volonté sociales,* ed. cit., p. 42.
[4] V. Pareto, *Les Systèmes socialistes,* ed. cit., vol. i, pp. 62 et seq.

ends in a reconciliation, which is effected with the instinctive aim of retaining dominion over the masses by sharing it among themselves. The opinion is very generally held that as a result of the French Revolution, or that in any case in the Third Republic, the old order had socially speaking been completely suppressed in France. This view is utterly erroneous. In the present year of grace we find that the French nobility is represented in the cavalry regiments and in the republican diplomatic service to an extent altogether disproportionate to its numerical strength; and although in the French Chamber there does not exist, as in Germany, a declared conservative party of the nobility, we find that of 584 deputies no less than 61 belong to the old aristocracy (*noblesse d'épée* and *noblesse de robe*).

As we have said, the theory that a directive social group is absolutely essential is by no means a new one. Gaetano Mosca, the most distinguished living advocate of this sociological conception, and, with Vilfredo Pareto, its ablest and most authoritative exponent, while disputing priority with Pareto, recognizes as precursors Hippolyte Taine and Ludwig Gumplowicz.[5] It is a less familiar fact, but one no less interesting, that the leading intellectual progenitors of the theory of Mosca and Pareto are to be found among the members of the school against which these writers more especially direct their attacks, namely among socialist thinkers, and especially among the earlier French socialists. In their work we discover the germs of the doctrine which at a later date was elaborated by Mosca and Pareto into a sociological system.

The school of Saint-Simon, while holding that the concept of class would some day cease to be characterized by any economic attribute, did not look for a future without class distinctions. The Saint-Simonians dreamed of the creation of a new hierarchy which was to be founded, not upon the privileges of birth, but upon acquired privileges. This class was to consist of "les plus aimants, les plus intelligents, et les plus forts,

---

[5] Gaetano Mosca, *Piccola Polemica*, "Riforma Sociale," anno xiv, vol. xvii, fasc. 4.—Among the followers of Mosca may be mentioned Carmelo Caristia, who in his book *Analisi odierna del Costituzionalismo* (Bocca, Turin, 1908), whilst he does not deny that an absolutist regime of the old style cannot pass into a modern republican regime by a simple process of gradual differentiation (p. 107), nevertheless concludes that every democratic principle ends by generating an aristocratic principle (p. 229).

personnification vivante du triple progrès de la société," and "capables de la diriger dans une plus vaste carrière."[6] At the head of their socialist state the Saint-Simonians desired to place those whom they termed "hommes généraux," who would be able to prescribe for each individual his quantum of social labour, the individual's special aptitudes being taken into account in this connection; here it is obvious that dependence must be placed upon the discretion of these supermen.[7] One of the most ardent followers of Saint-Simon, an enthusiastic advocate of the "nouvelle dynastie," when forced to defend himself against the accusation that his doctrine paved the way for despotism, did not hesitate to declare that the majority of human beings ought to obey the orders of the most capable; they should do this, he contended, not only for the love of God, but also on grounds of personal egoism, and finally because man, even if he could live in isolation, would always need some external support. The necessity for issuing orders on one side and the necessity for complying with them on the other are furnished with metaphysical justification. Such authority would only be "une transformation politique de l'amour qui unit tous les hommes en Dieu. Et pouvez-vous lui préférer cette triste indépendance qui aujourd'hui isole les sentiments, les opinions, les efforts, et qui, sous un nom pompeux, n'est rien autre chose que l'égoisme accompagnée de tous les maux qu'il enfante?"[8] The Saint-Simonian system is authoritarian and hierarchical through and through. The disciples of Saint-Simon were so little shocked by the Cæsarism of Napoleon III that most of them joyfully accepted it, imagining that they would find in it the principles of economic socialization.

The school of Fourier went further still. With a wealth of detail bordering on pedantry and exhibiting more than one grotesque feature, Fourier thought out a vast and complex system. To-day we can hardly restrain a smile when we study the tables he drew up describing his "spherical hierarchy," consisting of a thousand grades and embracing all possible forms of dominion from "anarchie" to "omniarchie," each of them having its special "hautes dignités," and its appropriate

---

[6] E. Barrault, *La Hierarchie*, in *Religion Saint-Simonienne*, Receuil et Predications, Aux bureaux du "Globe," Paris, 1832, vol. i, p. 196.

[7] *Œuvres de Saint-Simon et Enfantin*, vol. xli, *Doctrines Saint-Simoniennes*. Exposition par Bozard, Leroux, Paris, 1877, p. 275.

[8] E. Barrault, *La Hierarchie*, etc., ed. cit., p. 196.

"hautes fonctions."[9] Sorel has well shown that the socialism of the days prior to Louis Blanc was intimately connected with the Napoleonic era, so that the Saint-Simonian and Fourierist utopias could not live and prosper elsewhere than in the soil of the idea of authority to which the great Corsican had furnished a new splendour.[10] According to Berth, Fourier's whole system presupposes for its working the invisible but real and indispensable ubiquity of Fourier himself, for he alone, the Napoleon, as it were, of socialism, would be capable of activating and harmonizing the diverse passions of humanity.[11]

Socialists of the subsequent epoch, and above all revolutionary socialists, while not denying the possibility, in the remote future, of a democratic government by majority, absolutely denied that such a government could exist in the concrete present. Bakunin opposed any participation of the working class in elections. He was convinced that in a society where the people, the mass of the wage-earners, is under the economic dominion of a minority consisting of possessors, the freest of electoral systems could be nothing more than an illusion. "Qui dit pouvoir, dit domination, et toute domination présume l'existence d'une masse dominée."[12] Democracy is even regarded as the worst of all the bourgeois regimes. The republic, which is presented to us as the most elevated form of bourgeois democracy, was said by Proudhon to possess to an extreme degree that fanatical and petty authoritative spirit (*zèle gouvernemental*) which believes that it can dare everything with impunity, being always ready to justify its despotic acts under the convenient pretext that they are done for the good of the republic and in the general interest.[13] Even the political revolution signifies merely "un déplacement de l'autorité."[14]

The only scientific doctrine which can boast of ability to make an effective reply to all the theories, old or new, affirming

---

[9] Ferdinand Guillon, *Accord des Principes. Travail des Ecoles sociétaires. Charles Fourier*, Libr. Phalanst., Paris, 1850, p. 97.

[10] Preface by Georges Sorel to the work of Fernand Pelloutier, *Histoire des Bourses du Travail*, ed. cit., pp. 7 et seq.

[11] Edouard Berth, *Marchands, intellectuels et politiques*, "Mouvement Socialiste," anno ix, No. 192, p. 385.

[12] Bakunin, *L'Empire Knouto-Germanique et la Révolution sociale*, ed. cit., vol. ii, p. 126.

[13] Proudhon, *Idée générale de la Révolution aux XIX siècle*, vol. x of Œuvres complètes de Proudhon, Paris, 1868, p. 65.

[14] Proudhon, *Les Confessions d'un Révolutionnaire*, ed. cit., p. 24.

the immanent necessity for the perennial existence of the "political class" is the Marxist doctrine. In this doctrine the state is identified with the ruling class—an identification from which Bakunin, Marx's pupil, drew the extreme consequences. The state is merely the executive committee of the ruling class; or, to quote the expression of a recent neo-Marxist, the state is merely a "trade-union formed to defend the interest of the powers-that-be." [15] It is obvious that this theory greatly resembles the conservative theory of Gaetano Mosca. Mosca, in fact, from a study of the same diagnostic signs, deduces a similar prognosis, but abstains from lamentations and recriminations on account of a phenomenon which, in the light of his general political views, he regards not merely as inevitable, but as actually advantageous to society. Aristide Briand, in the days when he was an active member of the socialist party, and before he had become prime minister of the "class-state," pushed the Marxist notion of the state to its utmost limits by recommending the workers to abandon isolated and local economic struggles, to refrain from dissipating their energies in partial strikes, and to deliver a united assault upon the state in the form of the general strike, for, he said, you can reach the bourgeoisie with your weapons in no other way than by attacking the state. [16]

The Marxist theory of the state, when conjoined with a faith in the revolutionary energy of the working class and in the democratic effects of the socialization of the means of production, leads logically to the idea of a new social order which to the school of Mosca appears utopian. According to the Marxists the capitalist mode of production transforms the great majority of the population into proletarians, and thus digs its own grave. As soon as it has attained maturity, the proletariat will seize political power, and will immediately transform private property into state property. "In this way it will eliminate itself, for it will thus put an end to all social differences, and consequently to all class antagonisms. In other words, the proletariat will annul the state, qua state. Capitalist society, divided into classes, has need of the state as an organization of the ruling class, whose purpose it is to maintain the capitalist

---

[15] Angelo Oliviero Olivetti, *Problema del Socialismo Contemporaneo*, ed. cit., p. 41.

[16] Aristide Briand, *La Grève Générale et la Révolution.* Speech published in 1907. Girard, Paris, p. 7.

system of production in its own interest and in order to effect the continued exploitation of the proletariat. Thus to put an end to the state is synonymous with putting an end to the existence of the dominant class."[17] But the new collectivist society, the society without classes, which is to be established upon the ruins of the ancient state, will also need elective elements. It may be said that by the adoption of the preventive rules formulated by Rousseau in the *Contrat Sociale*, and subsequently reproduced by the French revolutionists in the *Déclaration des Droits de l'Homme*, above all by the strict application of the principle that all offices are to be held on a revocable tenure, the activity of these representatives may be confined within rigid limits.[18] It is none the less true that social wealth cannot be satisfactorily administered in any other manner than by the creation of an extensive bureaucracy. In this way we are led by an inevitable logic to the flat denial of the possibility of a state without classes. The administration of an immeasurably large capital, above all when this capital is collective property, confers upon the administrator influence at least equal to that possessed by the private owner of capital. Consequently the critics in advance of the Marxist social order ask whether the instinct which to-day leads the members of the possessing classes to transmit to their children the wealth which they (the parents) have amassed, will not exist also in the administrators of the public wealth of the socialist state, and whether these administrators will not utilize their immense influence in order to secure for their children the succession to the offices which they themselves hold.[19]

---

[17] Friedrich Engels, *Die Entwicklung des Sozialismus von der Utopie zur Wissenschaft*, Buchhandlung "Vorwärts," Berlin, 1891, 4th ed., p. 40.

[18] Many believe with Hobson (*Boodle and Cant*, ed. cit., pp. 587 and 590) that the socialist state will require a larger number of leaders, including political leaders, than any other state that has hitherto existed. Bernstein declares that the administrative body of socialist society will for a long time differ very little from that of the existing state (Eduard Bernstein, *Zur Geschichte, etc.*, ed. cit., p. 212).

[19] Gaetano Mosca, *Risposta ad un' Inchiesta sul Socialismo*, published in the annual "Bios," Marescotti, Milan, 1904.—This is a point to which the critics of collectivism have drawn attention with much emphasis (cf. Paul Leroy-Beaulieu, *Le Collectivisme*, Paris, 1884, vol. i, pp. 350 et seq.; F. S. Merlino, *Pro e contro il Socialismo*, ed. cit., p. 194).—Jean Jaurès proposed a national council of labour which, with many safeguards, was to direct production in the socialist state (Jaurès, *Organisation Socialiste*, "Revue Socialiste," August 1895); such a body, however, would have a fatal ten-

The constitution of a new dominant minority would, in addition, be especially facilitated by the manner in which, according to the Marxist conception of the revolution, the social transformation is to be effected. Marx held that the period between the destruction of capitalist society and the establishment of communist society would be bridged by a period of revolutionary transition in the economic field, to which would correspond a period of political transition, "when the state could not be anything other than the revolutionary dictatorship of the proletariat." [20] To put the matter less euphemistically, there will then exist a dictatorship in the hands of those leaders who have been sufficiently astute and sufficiently powerful to grasp the sceptre of dominion in the name of socialism, and to wrest it from the hands of the expiring bourgeois society.

A revolutionary dictatorship was also foreshadowed in the minimum programme of Mazzini's republican party, and this led to a rupture between Young Italy and the socialist elements of the carbonari. Filippo Buonarroti, the Florentine, friend and biographer of Gracchus Babeuf, a man who at one time played a heroic part in the French Revolution,[21] and who had had opportunities for direct observation of the way in which the victorious revolutionists maintained inequality and endeavoured to found a new aristocracy, resisted with all his might the plan of concentrating the power of the carbonari in the hands of a single individual. Among the theoretical reasons he alleged against this concentration, the principal was that individual dictatorship was merely a stage on the way to monarchy. To Mazzini and his friends, Buonarroti objected that all the political changes they had in view were purely formal in character, aiming simply at the gratification of

---

dency to concentrate power in the hands of a few.—Joseph Sarratne, the reformist socialist, describes the collectivist form of socialist society as "une tâche audacieuse dont on voudrait investir non pas un Dieu, mais un tyran ou un comité de salut publique entre les mains de qui devrait nécessairement abdiquer la nation souveraine" (Sarratne, *Socialisme d'Opposition, Socialisme de Gouvernement et Lutte de Classe*, Jacques, Paris, 1901, p. 46).

[20] Karl Marx, *Randglossen zum Programm der deutschen Arbeiterpartei*, "Waffenkammer des Sozialismus," 10th semi-annual vol., Frankfort-on-the-Main, 1908, p. 18.

[21] Filippo Buonarroti, *Conspiration pour l'Egalité, dites de Babeuf*, Brussels, 1828. Cf. especially p. 48.

personal needs, and above all at the acquirement and exercise of unrestricted authority. For this reason Buonarroti opposed the armed rising organized by Mazzini in 1833, issuing a secret decree in which he forbade his comrades of the carbonari to give any assistance to the insurgents, whose triumph, he said, could not fail to give rise to the creation of a new ambitious aristocracy. "The ideal republic of Mazzini," he wrote, "differs from monarchy in this respect alone, that it possesses a dignity the less and an elective post the more." [22]

There is little difference, as far as practical results are concerned, between individual dictatorship and the dictatorship of a group of oligarchs. Now it is manifest that the concept *dictatorship* is the direct antithesis of the concept *democracy*. The attempt to make dictatorship serve the ends of democracy is tantamount to the endeavour to utilize war as the most efficient means for the defence of peace, or to employ alcohol in the struggle against alcoholism.[23] It is extremely probable that a social group which had secured control of the instruments of collective power would do all that was possible to retain that control.[24] Theophrastus noted long ago that the strongest desire of men who have attained to leadership in a popularly governed state is not so much the acquirement of personal wealth as the gradual establishment of their own sovereignty at the expense of popular sovereignty.[25] The danger is imminent lest the social revolution should replace the visible and tangible dominant classes which now exist and act openly, by a clandestine demagogic oligarchy, pursuing its ends under the cloak of equality.

The Marxist economic doctrine and the Marxist philosophy of history cannot fail to exercise a great attraction upon thinkers. But the defects of Marxism are patent directly we enter the practical domains of administration and public law, without speaking of errors in the psychological field and even in

---

[22] Giuseppe Romano-Catania, *Filippo Buonarroti*, Sandron, Palermo, 1902, 2nd ed., pp. 211–12, 213, 218, and 228.

[23] "There continually recurs the dream of Schiller's Marquis Posa (in *Don Carlos*), who endeavours to make absolutism the instrument of liberation; or the dream of the gentle Abbé Pierre (in Zola's *Rome*), who wishes to use the church as a lever to secure socialism" (Kropotkin, *Die historische Rolle des Staates*, Grunau, Berlin, 1898, p. 52).

[24] Those among the reformists who have been scientifically trained begin to recognize this (cf. Fournière, *La Sociocratie*, ed. cit., p. 10).

[25] Labruyère, *Charactères*, ed. cit., p. 38.

more elementary spheres.[26] Wherever socialist theory has endeavoured to furnish guarantees for personal liberty, it has in the end either lapsed into the cloudland of individualist anarchism, or else has made proposals which (doubtless in opposition to the excellent intentions of their authors) could not fail to enslave the individual to the mass. Here is an example: to ensure that the literature of socialist society shall be elevated and moral, and to exclude *a priori* all licentious books, August Bebel proposed the nomination of a committee of experts to decide what might and what might not be printed. To obviate all danger of injustice and to secure freedom of thought and expression, Bebel added that every author must have the right of appeal to the collectivity.[27] It is hardly necessary to point out the impracticability of this proposal, which is in effect that the books, however large, regarding which an appeal is made, must be printed by the million and distributed to the public in order that the public may decide whether they are or are not fit for publication!

The problem of socialism is not merely a problem in economics. In other words, socialism does not seek merely to determine to what extent it is possible to realize a distribution of wealth which shall be at once just and economically productive. Socialism is also an administrative problem, a problem of democracy, and this not in the technical and administrative sphere alone, but also in the sphere of psychology. In the individualist problem is found the most difficult of all that complex of questions which socialism seeks to answer. Rudolf Goldscheid, who aims at a renascence of the socialist movement by the strengthening of the more energetic elements in that movement, rightly draws attention to a danger which socialism incurs, however brilliantly it may handle the problems of economic organization. If socialism, he says, fails to study the problem of individual rights, individual knowledge, and individual will, it will suffer shipwreck from a defective understanding of the significance of the problem of freedom for the higher evolution of our species—will suffer shipwreck no less disastrous than that of earlier conceptions of world reform which, blinded by the general splendour of their vision,

---

[26] George Sorel, *Dove va il Marxismo?*, ed. cit., p. 17.
[27] A. Bebel, *Die Frau und der Sozialismus*, J. H. W. Dietz Nachf., Stuttgart, 34th ed., 1903, p. 423.

have ignored the individual light-sources which combine to produce that splendour.[28]

The youthful German labour party had hardly succeeded in detaching itself, at the cost of severe struggles, from the bourgeois democracy, when one of its sincerest friends drew attention to certain urgent dangers. In an open letter to the Leipzig committee of the Allgemeine Deutsche Arbeiterverein, Rodbertus wrote: "You are separating yourselves from a political party because, as you rightly believe, this political party does not adequately represent your social interests. But you are doing this in order to found a new political party. Who will furnish you with guarantees against the danger that in this new party the adversaries of your class (*die antisozialen Elemente*) may some day gain the upper hand?"[29] In this observation Rodbertus touches the very essence of the political party. An analysis of the elements which enter into the composition of a party will show the perfect justice of his criticism. A party is neither a social unity nor an economic unity. It is based upon its programme. In theory this programme may be the expression of the interests of a particular class. In practice, however, anyone may join a party, whether his interests coincide or not with the principles enunciated in the party programme. The socialist party, for example, is the ideological representative of the proletariat. This, however, does not make it a class organism. From the social point of view it is a mixture of classes, being composed of elements fulfilling diverse functions in the economic process. But since the programme has a class origin, an ostensible social unity is thereby conferred upon the party. All socialists as such, whatever their economic position in private life, admit in theory the absolute pre-eminence of one great class, the proletariat. Those non-proletarians affiliated to the party, and those who are but partial proletarians, "adopt the outlook of the working class, and recognize this class as predominant."[30] It is tacitly presupposed that those members of a party who do not belong to the class which that party represents will renounce

[28] Rudolf Goldscheid, *Grundlinien zu einer Kritik der Willenskraft*, W. Braumüller, Vienna and Leipzig, 1905, p. 143.

[29] Rodbertus, *Offener Brief, etc.*, in F. Lassalle's *Politische Reden u. Schriften*, ed. cit., vol. ii, p. 15.

[30] Eduard Bernstein, *Wird die Sozialdemokratie Volkspartei?* "Sozial. Monatshefte," August 1905, p. 670.

their personal interests whenever these conflict with the interests of the proletarian class. On principle, the heterogeneous elements will subordinate themselves to the "idea" of a class to which they themselves do not belong. So much for theory. In practice, the acceptance of the programme does not suffice to abolish the conflict of interests between capital and labour. Among the members belonging to higher social strata who have made their adhesion to the political organization of the working class, there will be some who will, when the occasion demands it, know how to sacrifice themselves, who will be able to unclass will continue to pursue economic interests opposed to those of themselves. The majority of such persons, however, notwithstanding their outward community of ideas with the proletariat, the proletariat. There is, in fact, a conflict of interests, and the decision in this conflict will be determined by the relationship which the respective interests bear towards the principal necessities of life. Consequently it is by no means impossible that an economic conflict may arise between the bourgeois members and the proletarian members of the party, and that as this conflict extends it will culminate in political dissensions. Economic antagonism stifles the ideological superstructure. The programme then becomes a dead letter, and beneath the banner of "socialism" and within the bosom of the party, a veritable class struggle goes on. We learn from actual experience that in their conduct towards persons in their employ the bourgeois socialists do not always subordinate personal interests to those of their adoptive class. When the party includes among its members the owners of factories and workshops, it may be noticed that these, notwithstanding personal goodwill and notwithstanding the pressure which is exercised on them by the party, have the same economic conflict with their employees as have those employers whose convictions harmonize with their economic status, and who think not as socialists but as bourgeois.

But there exists yet another danger. The leadership of the socialist party may fall into the hands of persons whose practical tendencies are in opposition with the programme of the working class, so that the labour movement will be utilized for the service of interests diametrically opposed to those of the proletariat.[31] This danger is especially great in countries where

---

[31] Cf. Arturo Labriola, *Riforme e Rivoluzione Sociale*, ed. cit., pp. 225-6.
—Labriola applies his hypothesis to the socialist leaders of bourgeois ori-

the working-class party cannot dispense with the aid and guidance of capitalists who are not economically dependent upon the party; it is least conspicuous where the party has no need of such elements, or can at any rate avoid admitting them to leadership.

When the leaders, whether derived from the bourgeoisie or from the working class, are attached to the party organism as employees, their economic interest coincides as a rule with the interest of the party. This, however, serves to eliminate only one aspect of the danger. Another aspect, graver because more general, depends upon the opposition which inevitably arises between the leaders and the rank and file as the party grows in strength.

The party, regarded as an entity, as a piece of mechanism, is not necessarily identifiable with the totality of its members, and still less so with the class to which these belong. The party is created as a means to secure an end. Having, however, become an end in itself, endowed with aims and interests of its own, it undergoes detachment, from the teleological point of view, from the class which it represents. In a party, it is far from obvious that the interests of the masses which have combined to form the party will coincide with the interests of the bureaucracy in which the party becomes personified. The interests of the body of employees are always conservative, and in a given political situation these interests may dictate a defensive and even a reactionary policy when the interests of the working class demand a bold and aggressive policy; in other cases, although these are very rare, the rôles may be reversed. By a universally applicable social law, every organ of the collectivity, brought into existence through the need for the division of labour, creates for itself, as soon as it becomes consolidated, interests peculiar to itself. The existence of these special interests involves a necessary conflict with the interests of the collectivity. Nay, more, social strata fulfilling peculiar functions tend to become isolated, to produce organs fitted for the defence of their own peculiar interests. In the long run they tend to undergo transformation into distinct classes.

The sociological phenomena whose general characteristics have been discussed in this chapter and in preceding ones

---

gin, whereas, for the reasons previously discussed, it should be made generally applicable, disregarding the social origin of the labour leaders.

offer numerous vulnerable points to the scientific opponents of democracy. These phenomena would seem to prove beyond dispute that society cannot exist without a "dominant" or "political" class, and that the ruling class, whilst its elements are subject to a frequent partial renewal, nevertheless constitutes the only factor of sufficiently durable efficacy in the history of human development. According to this view, the government, or, if the phrase be preferred, the state, cannot be anything other than the organization of a minority. It is the aim of this minority to impose upon the rest of society a "legal order," which is the outcome of the exigencies of dominion and of the exploitation of the mass of helots effected by the ruling minority, and can never be truly representative of the majority.[32] The majority is thus permanently incapable of self-government. Even when the discontent of the masses culminates in a successful attempt to deprive the bourgeoisie of power, this is after all, so Mosca contends, effected only in appearance; always and necessarily there springs from the masses a new organized minority which raises itself to the rank of a governing class.[33] Thus the majority of human beings, in a condition of eternal tutelage, are predestined by tragic necessity to submit to the dominion of a small minority, and must be content to constitute the pedestal of an oligarchy.

The principle that one dominant class inevitably succeeds to another, and the law deduced from that principle that oligarchy is, as it were, a preordained form of the common life of great social aggregates, far from conflicting with or replacing the materialist conception of history, completes that conception and reinforces it. There is no essential contradiction between the doctrine that history is the record of a continued series of class struggles and the doctrine that class struggles invariably culminate in the creation of new oligarchies which undergo fusion with the old. The existence of a political class does not con-

---

[32] This train of reasoning approximates to Mommsen's theory that democracy continually destroys itself.

[33] Gaetano Mosca, *Elemente de Scienza politica*, ed. cit., p. 62.—Among the socialists there are a few rare spirits who do not deny the truth of this axiom. One of these is the professor of philosophy, and socialist deputy of the Swedish Upper House, Gustaf F. Steffen, who declares: "Even after the victory, there will always remain in political life the leaders and the led" (Steffen, *Die Demokratie in England*, Diederichs, Jena, 1911, p. 59).

flict with the essential content of Marxism, considered not as an economic dogma but as a philosophy of history; for in each particular instance the dominance of a political class arises as the resultant of the relationships between the different social forces competing for supremacy, these forces being of course considered dynamically and not quantitatively.

The Russian socialist Alexandre Herzen, whose chief permanent claim to significance is found in the psychological interest of his writings, declared that from the day in which man became accessory to property and his life a continued struggle for money, the political groups of the bourgeois world underwent division into two camps: the owners, tenaciously keeping hold of their millions; and the dispossessed, who would gladly expropriate the owners, but lack the power to do so. Thus historical evolution merely represents an uninterrupted series of oppositions (in the parliamentary sense of this term), "attaining one after another to power, and passing from the sphere of envy to the sphere of avarice."[34]

Thus the social revolution would not effect any real modification of the internal structure of the mass. The socialists might conquer, but not socialism, which would perish in the moment of its adherents' triumph. We are tempted to speak of this process as a tragicomedy in which the masses are content to devote all their energies to effecting a change of masters. All that is left for the workers is the honour "de participer au recrutement gouvernemental."[35] The result seems a poor one, especially if we take into account the psychological fact that even the purest of idealists who attains to power for a few years is unable to escape the corruption which the exercise of power carries in its train. In France, in working-class circles, the phrase is current, *homme élu, homme foutu*. The social revolution, like the political revolution, is equivalent to an operation by which, as the Italian proverb expresses it: "Si cambia il maestro di cappella, ma la musica è sempre quella."[36]

Fourier defined modern society as a mechanism in which the extremest individual licence prevailed, without affording any guarantee to the individual against the usurpations of the mass,

---

[34] Alexandre Herzen, *Erinnerungen*, German translation by Otto Buek, Wiegandt u. Grieben, Berlin, 1907, vol. ii, p. 150.

[35] Félicien Challaye, *Syndicalisme révolutionnaire et Syndicalisme réformiste*, Alcan, Paris, 1909, p. 16.

[36] There is a new conductor, but the music is just the same.

or to the mass against the usurpations of the individual.[37] History seems to teach us that no popular movement, however energetic and vigorous, is capable of producing profound and permanent changes in the social organism of the civilized world. The preponderant elements of the movement, the men who lead and nourish it, end by undergoing a gradual detachment from the masses, and are attracted within the orbit of the "political class." They perhaps contribute to this class a certain number of "new ideas," but they also endow it with more creative energy and enhanced practical intelligence, thus providing for the ruling class an ever-renewed youth. The "political class" (continuing to employ Mosca's convenient phrase) has unquestionably an extreme fine sense of its possibilities and its means of defence. It displays a remarkable force of attraction and a vigorous capacity for absorption which rarely fail to exercise an influence even upon the most embittered and uncompromising of its adversaries. From the historical point of view, the anti-romanticists are perfectly right when they sum up their scepticism in such caustic phraseology as this: "Qu'est ce qu'une révolution? Des gens qui se tirent des coups de fusil dans une rue: cela casse beaucoup de carreaux; il n'y a guère que les vitriers qui y trouvent du profit. Le vent emporte la fumée. Ceux qui reste dessus mettent les autres dessous. . . . C'est bien la peine de remuer tant d'honnêtes pavés qui n'en pouvaient mais!"[38]   Or we may say, as the song runs in *Madame Angot:* "Ce n'est pas la peine de changer de gouvernement!" In France, the classic land of social theories and experiments, such pessimism has struck the deepest roots.[39]

---

[37] Charles Fourier, *De l'Anarchie industrielle et scientifique*, Libr. Phalanst., Paris, 1847, p. 40.

[38] Théophile Gautier, *Les Jeunes-France*, Charpentier, Paris, 1878, p. xv.

[39] The disillusionment of the French regarding democracy goes back to the Revolution. Guizot declared that this terrible experiment sufficed "à dégoûter à jamais le monde de la recherche de la liberté, et sêcher, jusque dans leur source, les plus nobles espérances du genre humain" (F. Guizot, *Du Gouvernement de la France*, ed. cit., p. 165).

CHAPTER III

PARTY-LIFE IN WAR-TIME

NEVER is the power of the state greater, and never are the forces of political parties of opposition less effective, than at the outbreak of war. This deplorable war, come like a storm in the night, when everyone, wearied with the labours of the day, was plunged in well-deserved slumber, rages all over the world with unprecedented violence, and with such a lack of respect for human life and of regard for the eternal creations of art as to endanger the very corner-stones of a civilization dating from more than a thousand years. One of the corner-stones of historical materialism is that the working classes all over the world are united as if by links of iron through the perfect community of economico-social interests which they possess in face of the bourgeoisie, this community of interests effecting a horizontal stratification of classes which runs athwart and supersedes the vertical stratification of nations and of races. The greatest difference, in fact, in the views taken of economico-social classes and of linguistico-ethical nationalities, as between the respective adherents of nationalistic theories and of the theories of historical materialism, consists in this, that the former propound the hypothesis that the concept "nation" is morally and positively predominant over the concept "class," whilst the latter consider the concept and reality "nation" altogether subordinate to the concept "class." The Marxists, in fact, believed that the consciousness of class had become impressed upon the entire mentality of the proletariat imbued with socialist theories.

The war has shattered this theory at one terrible blow. The German socialist party, the strongest, wealthiest, and best organized section of the working-class international, for thirty years past the leading spirit in that international, suddenly and emphatically declared its entire solidarity with the German Emperor. Throughout the proletarian mass there has not been reported a single instance of moral rebellion against the struggle

393

which enlists socialists to fight on behalf of German imperialism and to contend with the comrades of other lands. Unquestionably, the tactics of the German socialists were largely due to the oligarchical tendencies which manifest themselves in modern political parties, because these parties, even if they pursue a revolutionary aim, and indeed precisely because they do so, that is to say because they make war against the existing state-system and desire to replace it by another, have need of a vast organization whose central strength is found in a trusted and stable bureaucracy, the members of which are well paid, and which has at its disposal the powers of a journalistic system and of a well-filled treasury.[1] This organization constitutes a state within the state. Now the forces of party, however well-developed, are altogether inferior and subordinate to the forces of the government, and this is especially true in such a country as Germany. Consequently one of the cardinal rules governing the policy of the socialist party is never to push its attacks upon the government beyond the limits imposed by the inequality between the respective forces of the combatants. In other words, the life of the party, whose preservation has gradually become the supreme objective of the parties of political action, must not be endangered. The result is that the external form of the party, its bureaucratic organization, definitely gains the upper hand over its soul, its doctrinal and theoretic content, and the latter is sacrificed whenever it tends to involve an inopportune conflict with the enemy. The outcome of this regressive evolution is that the party is no longer regarded as a means for the attainment of an end, but gradually becomes an end-in-itself, and is therefore incapable of resisting the arbitrary exercise of power by the state when this power is inspired by a vigorous will.

Inevitably such a party is unable to sustain so terrible a test as that of upholding its faith in principles when the state, determined upon war, and resolved to crush anyone who gets in the way, threatens the party in case of disobedience with the dissolution of its branches, the sequestration of its funds, and the slaughter of its best men. The party gives way, hastily

---

[1] At the end of 1913 the central treasury of the German socialist trade unions owned property amounting to 88,069,295 marks (£4,400,000), whilst the local and independent unions owned 3,152,636 marks (£150,000). Now a rebellion against the government and its foreign policy would have endangered all these funds.

sells its internationalist soul, and, impelled by the instinct of self-preservation, undergoes transformation into a patriotic party. The world-war of 1914 has afforded the most effective confirmation of what the author wrote in the first edition of this book concerning the future of socialist parties.

This natural tendency of the modern political party is reinforced, in the particular case under consideration, by the decision of the German socialists to support their government in all respects, owing to their fear and hatred of Czarism. This invincible aversion, upon which is dependent the general agreement with which the entire Germanic democracy has accepted the war, arises not solely from the foolish prejudice that the Slavs belong to an inferior race, but is also the outcome of a special historical theory held by Marx. Marx, in fact, regarded Russia as responsible for "the reaction" wherever this became manifest. More particularly, he considered that the militarist regime of the Prussian nobles, which he ardently abhorred, was merely the vanguard of the Russian autocracy. He added that the most infallible means for destroying the predominance of the German junkers would be to crush Russia, without whose aid the rule of the Prussian reaction would be impossible. This Marxist conviction had become a party dogma, deep-rooted in the mind of every individual member and diffused in a hundred writings. The German socialists who enthusiastically obeyed the mobilization order issued by the Emperor believed themselves to be fulfilling a sacred duty, not only from the patriotic point of view, but also from the democratic, considering that they were thus hastening the day of their own final deliverance. It was by such a state of mind that were inspired the principal speeches delivered and the most authoritative articles written by the German socialists when William II declared war against the Czar.

Moreover, an attitude which harmonized ill with the theoretical principle of historical materialism was defended by the socialists themselves as absolutely essential for the German proletariat. Substantially what the German socialists said was that, in the event of a defeat of the state to which they belonged, the proletarians would necessarily suffer greatly from unemployment and poverty; consequently it was their supreme interest, and must be the supreme aim of their representatives, to avoid this eventuality; hence it was their first and greatest duty to aid the German army by all the means at their disposal in its arduous task of defeating the enemy. Now, there is no lack of positive clearness about the view which underlies this reasoning. Since the proletariat is an integral part of the state, it cannot but suffer when the state falls upon evil days. Above all, the lot of the workers is dependent upon the degree to which manufacture and commerce flourish. No doubt the most prosperous condition of manufacturing industry does not afford the workers an absolute guarantee that they will receive good wages and be able to enjoy a high standard of life, since there is no proof that the curve of wages will always follow that of industrial profits; indeed, it is notorious that whilst after 1870 the development of German manufacture was rapid and extensive, the condition of the German workers remained stationary for nearly two decades. But if the lot of the workers and that of the manufacturers are not always on the same footing in the matter of good fortune, it cannot be doubted that when bad times come they have to share the same distresses; if manufacturing industry is stagnant, any rise of wages is excluded *a priori*. While, however, this view of a community of interests in the national sphere between the bourgeoisie and the proletariat has a basis of reality, there can be no doubt that not only is it absolutely antagonistic to the *idealism* of class, that is to say, to the fraternal affection which denies national solidarity in order to affirm with enthusiasm the international solidarity of the proletariat, tending and aiming at speedy class-emancipation; but further that it undermines the very *concept* of class. In fact, the theoretical position assumed by the German socialists, and imitated more or less faithfully by their comrades in other lands, is dictated by a criterion altogether different from that which forms the basis of historical materialism. This latter doctrine presupposes the existence of a working class by nature one and indivisible, whereas in the nationalist view there exists only a national proletariat, included within a given state, living within definite geographical boundaries, and subject to all the influences of force or of destiny. Indeed, the social democratic concept of class (as manifested under stress of war by the majority of the German socialists) constitutes the negation of the Marxist concept, in so far as the former degrades the latter, and, instead of becoming the instrument of world liberation as it was conceived by the internationalist theorists, is made the instrument of patriotic, social, and military cooperation. Historical materialism aimed at securing the solidarity of the human race under the guidance of the revolutionary proletariat and through the overthrow of the bourgeoisie and of national governments. The social democratic concept of class aims at the aggrandizement of the fatherland and at the prosperity of the proletariat and of the bourgeoisie therein, through the ruin of the proletariat and of the bourgeoisie of other lands. Between these two conceptions there is, in fact, so great a gulf fixed, that the most learned attempts to bridge it over will inevitably prove futile. If the war has not demonstrated the fallacy of the theory that the working classes of various countries, considered as a whole, possess common interests in opposition to the interests of the various national bourgeoisies also considered as a whole, it has at least demonstrated the non-existence of the reaction which this supposed phenomenon ought to have exercised upon the mentality and consequently upon the activity of the proletariat which prolonged socialist propaganda had endeavoured to indoctrinate with Marxist principles.

But while the German socialists appealed to their right to be guided by strictly economic interests and to make common cause with those who had hitherto been their worst enemies, they had the bad taste to deny this right to their foreign comrades. Paul Lensch, socialist member of the Reichstag, editor of the ultra-Marxist "Leipziger Volkszeitung," has, with a seriousness worthy of a better cause, sustained the following remarkable assertions: that the victory of Germany is necessary for the destruction of militarism, which will become superfluous as soon as the enemies of Germany have been definitely defeated, whilst the defeat of Germany will necessarily provide militarism with new aliment (since Germany will have to take her revenge) ; for the German proletariat, the defeat of Germany would be equivalent to an economic catastrophe, to the loss of the most essential means of subsistence, and to the ruin of the fruits of many years of labour; whereas for the English proletariat, the consequences of the defeat of England would unquestionably be extremely beneficial, by leading to the rapid diffusion of socialist ideas, to the distribution of monopolies, and to "the disappearance of the stupid pride which characterizes the English race." [2] According to this profound thinker, the

---

[2] Paul Lensch, *Die deutsche Sozialdemokratie u. der Weltkrieg*, Buchhandlung "Vorwärts," Berlin, 1915, pp. 26, 42, 58.

same causes would produce different effects in England and France, on the one hand, and in Germany on the other. For Germany a defeat must be avoided at all costs, for its results would be disastrous, whilst in the case of England and France they could not fail to be salutary!

Speaking generally, it may be said that the war has further accentuated the oligarchical character of party leadership. In no country (Italy, of course, excepted, for Italy has had ten months for mature deliberation) were the rank and file of the party active factors in the adoption of a policy for which every single member was accountable; in no country, except Italy, was the great question of the attitude of parties in relation to the problem of peace or war laid before the ordinary members; everywhere the supreme decision was in the hands of the leaders, and the masses had merely to accept an accomplished fact. In most cases the majority of the leaders established their absolute supremacy over the minority by means of the so-called party discipline which obliges the minority to accept the will of the majority. This explains the almost incredible unanimity with which, in the Reichstag, in the memorable August sitting, the German socialist parliamentary group voted the war credits. In the secret session of the group on the eve of the official session the opponents of the war were in the minority, and were therefore compelled on the following day, by the obligations of party discipline, to confound themselves publicly with the majority, and to give a vote which ran counter to their most sincere convictions. This amounts to saying that party life involves strange moral and intellectual sacrifices.

Moreover, by not a few party leaders the war was looked upon as a useful means of propaganda for the attraction of new recruits. This applies above all to the socialist party, eager to overthrow the barriers which separate from the party many sympathizers among the manual, operative, and shopkeeping classes, who are loth to join a party professing internationalist views. In a great public meeting held at Stuttgart on February 22, 1915, Heymann, a deputy to the diet of Würtemberg and one of the best-known leaders of the socialist party in that state, triumphantly declared: ''Many have ardently desired to join our party. But there was an obstacle. Well, that obstacle no longer exists!''[3] Unquestionably principles are often a stum-

---

[3] *Zwei Reden,* by Hildebrand and W. Heine, Dietz, Stuttgart, 1915, p. 44.

bling-block to a party whose main desire is to increase its membership; and to disregard inconvenient principles may bring electoral advantage, if at the cost of honour. The leaders are the first to favour such a tendency, for the more widely extended the foundations of their party, the greater grows their own individual power. In fact, the individual power of the leaders undergoes an immeasurable increase at a time when the majority of the members of all parties are under arms, and for this reason may be considered as politically non-existent because they are unable to exercise any influence upon the executive of the party to which they belong. On the Continent, even those members who have not been summoned to the colours no longer possess any power of controlling their leaders, owing to the suppression of the freedom of the press and of the rights of public meeting and of combination. Wherever martial law prevails, the leader is omnipotent.

CHAPTER IV

FINAL CONSIDERATIONS

"A prendre le terme dans la rigueur de l'acception il n'a jamais existé de véritable démocratie, et il n'en existera jamais. Il est contre l'ordre naturel que le grand nombre gouverne, et que le petit soit gouverné."—
J. J. ROUSSEAU, *Contrat Social.*

LEADERSHIP is a necessary phenomenon in every form of social life. Consequently it is not the task of science to inquire whether this phenomenon is good or evil, or predominantly one or the other. But there is great scientific value in the demonstration that every system of leadership is incompatible with the most essential postulates of democracy. We are now aware that the law of the historic necessity of oligarchy is primarily based upon a series of facts of experience. Like all other scientific laws, sociological laws are derived from empirical observation. In order, however, to deprive our axiom of its purely descriptive character, and to confer upon it that status of analytical explanation which can alone transform a formula into a law, it does not suffice to contemplate from a unitary outlook those phenomena which may be empirically established; we must also study the determining causes of these phenomena. Such has been our task.

Now, if we leave out of consideration the tendency of the leaders to organize themselves and to consolidate their interests, and if we leave also out of consideration the gratitude of the led towards the leaders, and the general immobility and passivity of the masses, we are led to conclude that the principal cause of oligarchy in the democratic parties is to be found in the technical indispensability of leadership.

The process which has begun in consequence of the differentiation of functions in the party is completed by a complex of qualities which the leaders acquire through their detachment from the mass. At the outset, leaders arise SPONTANEOUSLY; their functions are ACCESSORY and GRATUITOUS. Soon, however, they become PROFESSIONAL leaders, and in this second stage of development they are STABLE and IRREMOVABLE.

It follows that the explanation of the oligarchical phenomenon which thus results is partly PSYCHOLOGICAL; oligarchy derives, that is to say, from the psychical transformations which the leading personalities in the parties undergo in the course of their lives. But also, and still more, oligarchy depends upon what we may term the PSYCHOLOGY OF ORGANIZATION ITSELF, that is to say, upon the tactical and technical necessities which result from the consolidation of every disciplined political aggregate. Reduced to its most concise expression, the fundamental sociological law of political parties (the term "political" being here used in its most comprehensive significance) may be formulated in the following terms: "It is organization which gives birth to the dominion of the elected over the electors, of the mandataries over the mandators, of the delegates over the delegators. Who says organization, says oligarchy."

Every party organization represents an oligarchical power grounded upon a democratic basis. We find everywhere electors and elected. Also we find everywhere that the power of the elected leaders over the electing masses is almost unlimited. The oligarchical structure of the building suffocates the basic democratic principle. That which IS oppresses THAT WHICH OUGHT TO BE. For the masses, this essential difference between the reality and the ideal remains a mystery. Socialists often cherish a sincere belief that a new *élite* of politicians will keep faith better than did the old. The notion of the representation of popular interests, a notion to which the great majority of democrats, and in especial the working-class masses of the German-speaking lands, cleave with so much tenacity and confidence, is an illusion engendered by a false illumination, is an effect of mirage. In one of the most delightful pages of his analysis of modern Don Quixotism, Alphonse Daudet shows us how the "brav' commandant" Bravida, who has never quitted Tarascon, gradually comes to persuade himself, influenced by the burning southern sun, that he has been to Shanghai and has had all kinds of heroic adventures.[1] Similarly the modern proletariat, enduringly influenced by glib-tongued persons intellectually superior to the mass, ends

---

[1] Alphonse Daudet, *Tartarin de Tarascon*, Marpon et Flammarion, Paris, 1887, p. 40.

by believing that by flocking to the poll and entrusting its
social and economic cause to a delegate, its direct participation
in power will be assured.[2]

The formation of oligarchies within the various forms of
democracy is the outcome of organic necessity, and consequently
affects every organization, be it socialist or even anarchist.
Haller long ago noted that in every form of social life relationships of dominion and of dependence are created by Nature
herself.[3] The supremacy of the leaders in the democratic and
revolutionary parties has to be taken into account in every
historic situation present and to come, even though only a few
and exceptional minds will be fully conscious of its existence.
The mass will never rule except *in abstracto*. Consequently the
question we have to discuss is not whether ideal democracy is
realizable, but rather to what point and in what degree democracy is desirable, possible, and realizable at a given moment. In
the problem as thus stated we recognize the fundamental problem of politics as a science. Whoever fails to perceive this
must, as Sombart says, either be so blind and fanatical as not
to see that the democratic current daily makes undeniable advance, or else must be so inexperienced and devoid of critical
faculty as to be unable to understand that all order and all
civilization must exhibit aristocratic features.[4] The great error
of socialists, an error committed in consequence of their lack
of adequate psychological knowledge, is to be found in their
combination of pessimism regarding the present, with rosy optimism and immeasurable confidence regarding the future. A
realistic view of the mental condition of the masses shows beyond question that even if we admit the possibility of moral

---

[2] Militant democrats will not admit this publicly. According to them
the power of the masses is unlimited. This unrealistic view, in its application to political elections, will be found in a number of socialist writings,
although its expression is apt to be somewhat veiled. It is only in the
work of Dr. P. Coullery, of La Chaux-de-Fonds, a somewhat eccentric Swiss
internationalist, that we find a categorical expression of the thought: "Par
le suffrage universel le peuple des travailleurs devient tout-puissant"
(Coullery, *Jésus le Christ et sa Vie, sa Doctrine morale, politique, économique et sociale. Les Lois naturelles et le Socialisme*, Schweizer, Bienne,
1891, p. 303). In its application to party organization this same notion
makes no closer approximation to the real facts of the case.

[3] Ludwig von Haller, *Restauration der Staatswissenschaften*, Winterthur,
1816, vol. i, pp. 304 et seq.

[4] Werner Sombart, *Dennoch!*, ed. cit., p. 90. Cf. also F. S. Merlino, *Pro
e contro il Socialismo*, ed. cit., pp. 262 et seq.

improvement in mankind, the human materials with whose use politicians and philosophers cannot dispense in their plans of social reconstruction are not of a character to justify excessive optimism. Within the limits of time for which human provision is possible, optimism will remain the exclusive privilege of utopian thinkers.

The socialist parties, like the trade unions, are living forms of social life. As such they react with the utmost energy against any attempt to analyse their structure or their nature, as if it were a method of vivisection. When science attains to results which conflict with their apriorist ideology, they revolt with all their power. Yet their defence is extremely feeble. Those among the representatives of such organizations whose scientific earnestness and personal good faith make it impossible for them to deny outright the existence of oligarchical tendencies in every form of democracy, endeavour to explain these tendencies as the outcome of a kind of atavism in the mentality of the masses, characteristic of the youth of the movement. The masses, they assure us, are still infected by the oligarchic virus simply because they have been oppressed during long centuries of slavery, and have never yet enjoyed an autonomous existence.[5] The socialist regime, however, will

---

[5] Such an opinion has been expressed by the syndicalist theorists in especial, as, for instance, by Enrico Leone ("Divenire Sociale," vol. v, Nos. 18, 19) in a criticism of my own preliminary studies on this theme, and by Adolpho Momigliano ("Propaganda," Naples, December 2, 1910). Many of the reformists give utterance to a similar opinion. In a lengthy critical examination of my views (whose justice he by no means denies) Fausto Pagliari comes to the conclusion that the oligarchical tendencies of the socialist movement are not indications of what is going to continue in the future, but merely transitional forms of a movement which is still walking in darkness; signs of youth, not of age (*Oligarchia e Democrazia nell' Organizzazione operaia*, "Critica Sociale," February 1, 1909). Others, like the syndicalist Sergio Panunzio, accept my proposition without reserve but fail to apply its consequences to their own theory (*Syndicalisme et Représentation Ouvrière*, "Mouvement Socialiste," anno xii, No. 221). Eduard Bernstein, who also fails to rebut my demonstrations (cf. *Die Demokratie in der Sozialdemokratie*, "Sozial. Monatshefte," 1908, fasc. 18 and 19), reproaches me with overstressing the psychological note, but does not himself fall into the error of the Marxists and syndicalists. He continues to hold to-day the realistic conception of the future which he expressed in 1897, when he compared the process of internal democratic administration with that of industrial production, writing: "At the door of the workshop we may be equal, but are equal no longer when we have gone inside. Here the engineer must issue his orders, and the various subordinate workmen

soon restore them to health, and will furnish them with all the
capacity necessary for self-government. Nothing could be more
anti-scientific than the supposition that as soon as socialists
have gained possession of governmental power it will suffice for
the masses to exercise a little control over their leaders to
secure that the interests of these leaders shall coincide perfectly
with the interests of the led.[6] This idea may be compared
with the view of Jules Guesde, no less anti-scientific than anti-
Marxist (though Guesde proclaims himself a Marxist), that
whereas Christianity has made God into a man, socialism will
make man into a god.[7]

The objective immaturity of the mass is not a mere transitory
phenomenon which will disappear with the progress of democratization *au lendemain du socialisme.* On the contrary, it
derives from the very nature of the mass as mass, for this, even
when organized, suffers from an incurable incompetence for
the solution of the diverse problems which present themselves
for solution—because the mass *per se* is amorphous, and therefore needs division of labour, specialization, and guidance.
"L'espèce humaine veut être gouvernée; elle le sera. J'ai
honte de mon espèce," wrote Proudhon from his prison in
1850.[8] Man as individual is by nature predestined to be guided,
and to be guided all the more in proportion as the functions of
life undergo division and subdivision. To an enormously greater
degree is guidance necessary for the social group.

From this chain of reasoning and from these scientific convictions it would be erroneous to conclude that we should renounce
all endeavours to ascertain the limits which may be imposed
upon the powers exercised over the individual by oligarchies

---

must carry them out. The stoker cannot act according to his own fancy
and draw the fires whenever it pleases him" (*Das demokratische Prinzip
und seine Anwendung,* "Neue Zeit," anno xix, p. 25 [1897]). Bernstein,
however, has not attained to clearness of vision regarding the results of the
division of labour and of the differences in technical competence among the
democratic masses. Consequently he remains faithful to a concept of
democracy which has little more than the name in common with the democracy advocated by the great democratic thinkers of the eighteenth century
and the socialists of the nineteenth.

[6] Cf. Léon Trochet (deputy of Liège), *Socialdémocratie et Anarchisme,*
Discours, Brussels-Ghent-Liège, 1902, p. 42.

[7] Jules Guesde, *La Problème et la Solution,* Libr. du Parti Socialiste,
Paris, p. 17.

[8] Charles Gide et Charles Rist, *Histoire des Doctrines économiques depuis
les Physiocrates jusqu'a nos jours,* Larose et Tenin, Paris, 1909, p. 709.

(state, dominant class, party, etc.). It would be an error to abandon the desperate enterprise of endeavouring to discover a social order which will render possible the complete realization of the idea of popular sovereignty. In the present work, as the writer said at the outset, it has not been his aim to indicate new paths. But it seemed necessary to lay considerable stress upon the pessimist aspect of democracy which is forced on us by historical study. We had to inquire whether, and within what limits, democracy must remain purely ideal, possessing no other value than that of a moral criterion which renders it possible to appreciate the varying degrees of that oligarchy which is immanent in every social regime. In other words, we have had to inquire if, and in what degree, democracy is an ideal which we can never hope to realize in practice. A further aim of this work was the demolition of some of the facile and superficial democratic illusions which trouble science and lead the masses astray. Finally, the author desired to throw light upon certain sociological tendencies which oppose the reign of democracy, and to a still greater extent oppose the reign of socialism.

The writer does not wish to deny that every revolutionary working-class movement, and every movement sincerely inspired by the democratic spirit, may have a certain value as contributing to the enfeeblement of oligarchic tendencies. The peasant in the fable, when on his death-bed, tells his sons that a treasure is buried in the field. After the old man's death the sons dig everywhere in order to discover the treasure. They do not find it. But their indefatigable labour improves the soil and secures for them a comparative well-being. The treasure in the fable may well symbolize democracy. Democracy is a treasure which no one will ever discover by deliberate search. But in continuing our search, in labouring indefatigably to discover the indiscoverable, we shall perform a work which will have fertile results in the democratic sense. We have seen, indeed, that within the bosom of the democratic working-class party are born the very tendencies to counteract which that party came into existence. Thanks to the diversity and to the unequal worth of the elements of the party, these tendencies often give rise to manifestations which border on tyranny. We have seen that the replacement of the traditional legitimism of the powers-that-be by the brutal plebiscitary rule of Bonapartist parvenus does not furnish these tendencies with any

moral or æsthetic superiority. Historical evolution mocks all the prophylactic measures that have been adopted for the prevention of oligarchy. If laws are passed to control the dominion of the leaders, it is the laws which gradually weaken, and not the leaders. Sometimes, however, the democratic principle carries with it, if not a cure, at least a palliative, for the disease of oligarchy. When Victor Considérant formulated his "democratico-pacificist" socialism, he declared that socialism signified, not the rule of society by the lower classes of the population, but the government and organization of society in the interest of all, through the intermediation of a group of citizens; and he added that the numerical importance of this group must increase *pari passu* with social development.[9] This last observation draws attention to a point of capital importance. It is, in fact, a general characteristic of democracy, and hence also of the labour movement, to stimulate and to strengthen in the individual the intellectual aptitudes for criticism and control. We have seen how the progressive bureaucratization of the democratic organism tends to neutralize the beneficial effects of such criticism and such control. None the less it is true that the labour movement, in virtue of the theoretical postulates it proclaims, is apt to bring into existence (in opposition to the will of the leaders) a certain number of free spirits who, moved by principle, by instinct, or by both, desire to revise the base upon which authority is established. Urged on by conviction or by temperament, they are never weary of asking an eternal "Why?" about every human institution. Now this predisposition towards free inquiry, in which we cannot fail to recognize one of the most precious factors of civilization, will gradually increase in proportion as the economic status of the masses undergoes improvement and becomes more stable, and in proportion as they are admitted more effectively to the advantages of civilization. A wider education involves an increasing capacity for exercising control. Can we not observe every day that among the well-to-do the authority of the leaders over the led, extensive though it be, is never so unrestricted as in the case of the leaders of the poor? Taking in the mass, the poor are powerless and disarmed vis-à-vis their leaders. Their intellectual and cultural inferiority makes it impossible for them to see whither

---

[9] Victor Considérant, *Principes du Socialisme. Manifeste de la Démocratie au xix Siècle*, Librairie Phalanstérienne, Paris, 1847, p. 53.

the leader is going, or to estimate in advance the significance of his actions. It is, consequently, the great task of social education to raise the intellectual level of the masses, so that they may be enabled, within the limits of what is possible, to counteract the oligarchical tendencies of the working-class movement.

In view of the perennial incompetence of the masses, we have to recognize the existence of two regulative principles:—

1. The *ideological* tendency of democracy towards criticism and control;

2. The *effective* counter-tendency of democracy towards the creation of parties ever more complex and ever more differentiated—parties, that is to say, which are increasingly based upon the competence of the few.

To the idealist, the analysis of the forms of contemporary democracy cannot fail to be a source of bitter deceptions and profound discouragement. Those alone, perhaps, are in a position to pass a fair judgment upon democracy who, without lapsing into dilettantist sentimentalism, recognize that all scientific and human ideals have relative values. If we wish to estimate the value of democracy, we must do so in comparison with its converse, pure aristocracy. The defects inherent in democracy are obvious. It is none the less true that as a form of social life we must choose democracy as the least of evils. The ideal government would doubtless be that of an aristocracy of persons at once morally good and technically efficient. But where shall we discover such an aristocracy? We may find it sometimes, though very rarely, as the outcome of deliberate selection; but we shall never find it where the hereditary principle remains in operation. Thus monarchy in its pristine purity must be considered as imperfection incarnate, as the most incurable of ills; from the moral point of view it is inferior even to the most revolting of demagogic dictatorships, for the corrupt organism of the latter at least contains a healthy principle upon whose working we may continue to base hopes of social resanation. It may be said, therefore, that the more humanity comes to recognize the advantages which democracy, however imperfect, presents over aristocracy, even at its best, the less likely is it that a recognition of the defects of democracy will provoke a return to aristocracy. Apart from certain formal differences and from the qualities which can be acquired only by good education and inheritance (qualities in which aristocracy will always have the advantage over democracy—qualities which democracy either neglects altogether, or, attempting to imitate them, falsifies them to the point of caricature), the defects of democracy will be found to inhere in its inability to get rid of its aristocratic scoriæ. On the other hand, nothing but a serene and frank examination of the oligarchical dangers of democracy will enable us to minimize these dangers, even though they can never be entirely avoided.

The democratic currents of history resemble successive waves. They break ever on the same shoal. They are ever renewed. This enduring spectacle is simultaneously encouraging and depressing. When democracies have gained a certain stage of development, they undergo a gradual transformation, adopting the artistocratic spirit, and in many cases also the aristocratic forms, against which at the outset they struggled so fiercely. Now new accusers arise to denounce the traitors; after an era of glorious combats and of inglorious power, they end by fusing with the old dominant class; whereupon once more they are in their turn attacked by fresh opponents who appeal to the name of democracy. It is probable that this cruel game will continue without end.

INDEX

A CATALOGUE OF SELECTED DOVER BOOKS
IN ALL FIELDS OF INTEREST

A CATALOGUE OF SELECTED DOVER BOOKS
IN ALL FIELDS OF INTEREST

AMERICA'S OLD MASTERS, James T. Flexner. Four men emerged unexpectedly from provincial 18th century America to leadership in European art: Benjamin West, J. S. Copley, C. R. Peale, Gilbert Stuart. Brilliant coverage of lives and contributions. Revised, 1967 edition. 69 plates. 365pp. of text.

21806-6 Paperbound $2.75

FIRST FLOWERS OF OUR WILDERNESS: AMERICAN PAINTING, THE COLONIAL PERIOD, James T. Flexner. Painters, and regional painting traditions from earliest Colonial times up to the emergence of Copley, West and Peale Sr., Foster, Gustavus Hesselius, Feke, John Smibert and many anonymous painters in the primitive manner. Engaging presentation, with 162 illustrations. xxii + 368pp.

22180-6 Paperbound $3.50

THE LIGHT OF DISTANT SKIES: AMERICAN PAINTING, 1760-1835, James T. Flexner. The great generation of early American painters goes to Europe to learn and to teach: West, Copley, Gilbert Stuart and others. Allston, Trumbull, Morse; also contemporary American painters—primitives, derivatives, academics—who remained in America. 102 illustrations. xiii + 306pp.

22179-2 Paperbound $3.00

A HISTORY OF THE RISE AND PROGRESS OF THE ARTS OF DESIGN IN THE UNITED STATES, William Dunlap. Much the richest mine of information on early American painters, sculptors, architects, engravers, miniaturists, etc. The only source of information for scores of artists, the major primary source for many others. Unabridged reprint of rare original 1834 edition, with new introduction by James T. Flexner, and 394 new illustrations. Edited by Rita Weiss. 6⅝ x 9⅝.

21695-0, 21696-9, 21697-7 Three volumes, Paperbound $13.50

EPOCHS OF CHINESE AND JAPANESE ART, Ernest F. Fenollosa. From primitive Chinese art to the 20th century, thorough history, explanation of every important art period and form, including Japanese woodcuts; main stress on China and Japan, but Tibet, Korea also included. Still unexcelled for its detailed, rich coverage of cultural background, aesthetic elements, diffusion studies, particularly of the historical period. 2nd, 1913 edition. 242 illustrations. lii + 439pp. of text.

20364-6, 20365-4 Two volumes, Paperbound $5.00

THE GENTLE ART OF MAKING ENEMIES, James A. M. Whistler. Greatest wit of his day deflates Oscar Wilde, Ruskin, Swinburne; strikes back at inane critics, exhibitions, art journalism; aesthetics of impressionist revolution in most striking form. Highly readable classic by great painter. Reproduction of edition designed by Whistler. Introduction by Alfred Werner. xxxvi + 334pp.

21875-9 Paperbound $2.25

How to Know the Wild Flowers, Mrs. William Starr Dana. This is the classical book of American wildflowers (of the Eastern and Central United States), used by hundreds of thousands. Covers over 500 species, arranged in extremely easy to use color and season groups. Full descriptions, much plant lore. This Dover edition is the fullest ever compiled, with tables of nomenclature changes. 174 full-page plates by M. Satterlee. xii + 418pp.   20332-8 Paperbound $2.50

Our Plant Friends and Foes, William Atherton DuPuy. History, economic importance, essential botanical information and peculiarities of 25 common forms of plant life are provided in this book in an entertaining and charming style. Covers food plants (potatoes, apples, beans, wheat, almonds, bananas, etc.), flowers (lily, tulip, etc.), trees (pine, oak, elm, etc.), weeds, poisonous mushrooms and vines, gourds, citrus fruits, cotton, the cactus family, and much more. 108 illustrations. xiv + 290pp.   22272-1 Paperbound $2.00

How to Know the Ferns, Frances T. Parsons. Classic survey of Eastern and Central ferns, arranged according to clear, simple identification key. Excellent introduction to greatly neglected nature area. 57 illustrations and 42 plates. xvi + 215pp.   20740-4 Paperbound $1.75

Manual of the Trees of North America, Charles S. Sargent. America's foremost dendrologist provides the definitive coverage of North American trees and tree-like shrubs. 717 species fully described and illustrated: exact distribution, down to township; full botanical description; economic importance; description of subspecies and races; habitat, growth data; similar material. Necessary to every serious student of tree-life. Nomenclature revised to present. Over 100 locating keys. 783 illustrations. lii + 934pp. 20277-1, 20278-X Two volumes, Paperbound $6.00

Our Northern Shrubs, Harriet L. Keeler. Fine non-technical reference work identifying more than 225 important shrubs of Eastern and Central United States and Canada. Full text covering botanical description, habitat, plant lore, is paralleled with 205 full-page photographs of flowering or fruiting plants. Nomenclature revised by Edward G. Voss. One of few works concerned with shrubs. 205 plates, 35 drawings. xxviii + 521pp.   21989-5 Paperbound $3.75

The Mushroom Handbook, Louis C. C. Krieger. Still the best popular handbook: full descriptions of 259 species, cross references to another 200. Extremely thorough text enables you to identify, know all about any mushroom you are likely to meet in eastern and central U. S. A.: habitat, luminescence, poisonous qualities, use, folklore, etc. 32 color plates show over 50 mushrooms, also 126 other illustrations. Finding keys. vii + 560pp.   21861-9 Paperbound $3.95

Handbook of Birds of Eastern North America, Frank M. Chapman. Still much the best single-volume guide to the birds of Eastern and Central United States. Very full coverage of 675 species, with descriptions, life habits, distribution, similar data. All descriptions keyed to two-page color chart. With this single volume the average birdwatcher needs no other books. 1931 revised edition. 195 illustrations. xxxvi + 581pp.   21489-3 Paperbound $3.25

FAIRY TALE COLLECTIONS, *edited by Andrew Lang*
Andrew Lang's fairy tale collections make up the richest shelf-full of traditional children's stories anywhere available. Lang supervised the translation of stories from all over the world—familiar European tales collected by Grimm, animal stories from Negro Africa, myths of primitive Australia, stories from Russia, Hungary, Iceland, Japan, and many other countries. Lang's selection of translations are unusually high; many authorities consider that the most familiar tales find their best versions in these volumes. All collections are richly decorated and illustrated by H. J. Ford and other artists.

THE BLUE FAIRY BOOK. 37 stories. 138 illustrations. ix + 390pp. 5⅜ x 8½.
21437-0 Paperbound $1.95

THE GREEN FAIRY BOOK. 42 stories. 100 illustrations. xiii + 366pp. 5⅜ x 8½.
21439-7 Paperbound $1.75

THE BROWN FAIRY BOOK. 32 stories. 50 illustrations, 8 in color. xii + 350pp. 5⅜ x 8½.
21438-9 Paperbound $1.95

THE BEST TALES OF HOFFMANN, *edited by E. F. Bleiler*
10 stories by E. T. A. Hoffmann, one of the greatest of all writers of fantasy. The tales include "The Golden Flower Pot," "Automata," "A New Year's Eve Adventure," "Nutcracker and the King of Mice," "Sand-Man," and others. Vigorous characterizations of highly eccentric personalities, remarkably imaginative situations, and intensely fast pacing has made these tales popular all over the world for 150 years. Editor's introduction. 7 drawings by Hoffmann.
xxxiii + 419pp. 5⅜ x 8½.
21793-0 Paperbound $2.25

GHOST AND HORROR STORIES OF AMBROSE BIERCE,
edited by E. F. Bleiler
Morbid, eerie, horrifying tales of possessed poets, shabby aristocrats, revived corpses, and haunted malefactors. Widely acknowledged as the best of their kind between Poe and the moderns, reflecting their author's inner torment and bitter view of life. Includes "Damned Thing," "The Middle Toe of the Right Foot," "The Eyes of the Panther," "Visions of the Night," "Moxon's Master," and over a dozen others. Editor's introduction. xxii + 199pp. 5⅜ x 8½.
20767-6 Paperbound $1.50

THREE GOTHIC NOVELS, *edited by E. F. Bleiler*
Originators of the still popular Gothic novel form, influential in ushering in early 19th-century Romanticism. Horace Walpole's *Castle of Otranto*, William Beckford's *Vathek*, John Polidori's *The Vampyre*, and a *Fragment* by Lord Byron are enjoyable as exciting reading or as documents in the history of English literature. Editor's introduction. xi + 291pp. 5⅜ x 8½.
21232-7 Paperbound $2.00

BEST GHOST STORIES OF LEFANU, *edited by E. F. Bleiler*
Though admired by such critics as V. S. Pritchett, Charles Dickens and Henry James, ghost stories by the Irish novelist Joseph Sheridan LeFanu have never become as widely known as his detective fiction. About half of the 16 stories in this collection have never before been available in America. Collection includes "Carmilla" (perhaps the best vampire story ever written), "The Haunted Baronet," "The Fortunes of Sir Robert Ardagh," and the classic "Green Tea." Editor's introduction. 7 contemporary illustrations. Portrait of LeFanu. xii + 467pp. 5⅜ x 8.
20415-4 Paperbound $2.50

AMERICAN FOOD AND GAME FISHES, David S. Jordan and Barton W. Evermann. Definitive source of information, detailed and accurate enough to enable the sportsman and nature lover to identify conclusively some 1,000 species and sub-species of North American fish, sought for food or sport. Coverage of range, physiology, habits, life history, food value. Best methods of capture, interest to the angler, advice on bait, fly-fishing, etc. 338 drawings and photographs. 1 + 574pp. 6⅝ x 9⅜.
22383-1 Paperbound $4.50

THE FROG BOOK, Mary C. Dickerson. Complete with extensive finding keys, over 300 photographs, and an introduction to the general biology of frogs and toads, this is the classic non-technical study of Northeastern and Central species. 58 species; 290 photographs and 16 color plates. xvii + 253pp.
21973-9 Paperbound $4.00

THE MOTH BOOK: A GUIDE TO THE MOTHS OF NORTH AMERICA, William J. Holland. Classical study, eagerly sought after and used for the past 60 years. Clear identification manual to more than 2,000 different moths, largest manual in existence. General information about moths, capturing, mounting, classifying, etc., followed by species by species descriptions. 263 illustrations plus 48 color plates show almost every species, full size. 1968 edition, preface, nomenclature changes by A. E. Brower. xxiv + 479pp. of text. 6½ x 9¼.
21948-8 Paperbound $5.00

THE SEA-BEACH AT EBB-TIDE, Augusta Foote Arnold. Interested amateur can identify hundreds of marine plants and animals on coasts of North America; marine algae; seaweeds; squids; hermit crabs; horse shoe crabs; shrimps; corals; sea anemones; etc. Species descriptions cover: structure; food; reproductive cycle; size; shape; color; habitat; etc. Over 600 drawings. 85 plates. xii + 490pp.
21949-6 Paperbound $3.50

COMMON BIRD SONGS, Donald J. Borror. 33⅓ 12-inch record presents songs of 60 important birds of the eastern United States. A thorough, serious record which provides several examples for each bird, showing different types of song, individual variations, etc. Inestimable identification aid for birdwatcher. 32-page booklet gives text about birds and songs, with illustration for each bird.
21829-5 Record, book, album. Monaural. $2.75

FADS AND FALLACIES IN THE NAME OF SCIENCE, Martin Gardner. Fair, witty appraisal of cranks and quacks of science: Atlantis, Lemuria, hollow earth, flat earth, Velikovsky, orgone energy, Dianetics, flying saucers, Bridey Murphy, food fads, medical fads, perpetual motion, etc. Formerly "In the Name of Science." x + 363pp.
20394-8 Paperbound $2.00

HOAXES, Curtis D. MacDougall. Exhaustive, unbelievably rich account of great hoaxes: Locke's moon hoax, Shakespearean forgeries, sea serpents, Loch Ness monster, Cardiff giant, John Wilkes Booth's mummy, Disumbrationist school of art, dozens more; also journalism, psychology of hoaxing. 54 illustrations. xi + 338pp.
20465-0 Paperbound $2.75

LAST AND FIRST MEN AND STAR MAKER, TWO SCIENCE FICTION NOVELS, Olaf Stapledon. Greatest future histories in science fiction. In the first, human intelligence is the "hero," through strange paths of evolution, interplanetary invasions, incredible technologies, near extinctions and reemergences. Star Maker describes the quest of a band of star rovers for intelligence itself, through time and space: weird inhuman civilizations, crustacean minds, symbiotic worlds, etc. Complete, unabridged. v + 438pp. 21962-3 Paperbound $2.00

THREE PROPHETIC NOVELS, H. G. WELLS. Stages of a consistently planned future for mankind. *When the Sleeper Wakes,* and *A Story of the Days to Come,* anticipate *Brave New World* and *1984,* in the 21st Century; *The Time Machine,* only complete version in print, shows farther future and the end of mankind. All show Wells's greatest gifts as storyteller and novelist. Edited by E. F. Bleiler. x + 335pp. (USO) 20605-X Paperbound $2.00

THE DEVIL'S DICTIONARY, Ambrose Bierce. America's own Oscar Wilde— Ambrose Bierce—offers his barbed iconoclastic wisdom in over 1,000 definitions hailed by H. L. Mencken as "some of the most gorgeous witticisms in the English language." 145pp. 20487-1 Paperbound $1.25

MAX AND MORITZ, Wilhelm Busch. Great children's classic, father of comic strip, of two bad boys, Max and Moritz. Also Ker and Plunk (Plisch und Plumm), Cat and Mouse, Deceitful Henry, Ice-Peter, The Boy and the Pipe, and five other pieces. Original German, with English translation. Edited by H. Arthur Klein; translations by various hands and H. Arthur Klein. vi + 216pp. 20181-3 Paperbound $1.50

PIGS IS PIGS AND OTHER FAVORITES, Ellis Parker Butler. The title story is one of the best humor short stories, as Mike Flannery obfuscates biology and English. Also included, That Pup of Murchison's, The Great American Pie Company, and Perkins of Portland. 14 illustrations. v + 109pp. 21532-6 Paperbound $1.00

THE PETERKIN PAPERS, Lucretia P. Hale. It takes genius to be as stupidly mad as the Peterkins, as they decide to become wise, celebrate the "Fourth," keep a cow, and otherwise strain the resources of the Lady from Philadelphia. Basic book of American humor. 153 illustrations. 219pp. 20794-3 Paperbound $1.25

PERRAULT'S FAIRY TALES, translated by A. E. Johnson and S. R. Littlewood, with 34 full-page illustrations by Gustave Doré. All the original Perrault stories— Cinderella, Sleeping Beauty, Bluebeard, Little Red Riding Hood, Puss in Boots, Tom Thumb, etc.—with their witty verse morals and the magnificent illustrations of Doré. One of the five or six great books of European fairy tales. viii + 117pp. 8⅛ x 11. 22311-6 Paperbound $2.00

OLD HUNGARIAN FAIRY TALES, Baroness Orczy. Favorites translated and adapted by author of the *Scarlet Pimpernel.* Eight fairy tales include "The Suitors of Princess Fire-Fly," "The Twin Hunchbacks," "Mr. Cuttlefish's Love Story," and "The Enchanted Cat." This little volume of magic and adventure will captivate children as it has for generations. 90 drawings by Montagu Barstow. 96pp. (USO) 22293-4 Paperbound $1.95

DESIGN BY ACCIDENT; A BOOK OF "ACCIDENTAL EFFECTS" FOR ARTISTS AND DESIGNERS, James F. O'Brien. Create your own unique, striking, imaginative effects by "controlled accident" interaction of materials: paints and lacquers, oil and water based paints, splatter, crackling materials, shatter, similar items. Everything you do will be different; first book on this limitless art, so useful to both fine artist and commercial artist. Full instructions. 192 plates showing "accidents," 8 in color. viii + 215pp. 8⅜ x 11¼. 21942-9 Paperbound $3.50

THE BOOK OF SIGNS, Rudolf Koch. Famed German type designer draws 493 beautiful symbols: religious, mystical, alchemical, imperial, property marks, ι nes, etc. Remarkable fusion of traditional and modern. Good for suggestions of timelessness, smartness, modernity. Text. vi + 104pp. 6⅛ x 9¼. 20162-7 Paperbound $1.25

HISTORY OF INDIAN AND INDONESIAN ART, Ananda K. Coomaraswamy. An unabridged republication of one of the finest books by a great scholar in Eastern art. Rich in descriptive material, history, social backgrounds; Sunga reliefs, Rajput paintings, Gupta temples, Burmese frescoes, textiles, jewelry, sculpture, etc. 400 photos. viii + 423pp. 6⅜ x 9¾. 21436-2 Paperbound $3.50

PRIMITIVE ART, Franz Boas. America's foremost anthropologist surveys textiles, ceramics, woodcarving, basketry, metalwork, etc.; patterns, technology, creation of symbols, style origins. All areas of world, but very full on Northwest Coast Indians. More than 350 illustrations of baskets, boxes, totem poles, weapons, etc. 378 pp. 20025-6 Paperbound $2.50

THE GENTLEMAN AND CABINET MAKER'S DIRECTOR, Thomas Chippendale. Full reprint (third edition, 1762) of most influential furniture book of all time, by master cabinetmaker. 200 plates, illustrating chairs, sofas, mirrors, tables, cabinets, plus 24 photographs of surviving pieces. Biographical introduction by N. Bienenstock. vi + 249pp. 9⅞ x 12¾. 21601-2 Paperbound $3.50

AMERICAN ANTIQUE FURNITURE, Edgar G. Miller, Jr. The basic coverage of all American furniture before 1840. Individual chapters cover type of furniture—clocks, tables, sideboards, etc.—chronologically, with inexhaustible wealth of data. More than 2100 photographs, all identified, commented on. Essential to all early American collectors. Introduction by H. E. Keyes. vi + 1106pp. 7⅞ x 10¾. 21599-7, 21600-4 Two volumes, Paperbound $7.50

PENNSYLVANIA DUTCH AMERICAN FOLK ART, Henry J. Kauffman. 279 photos, 28 drawings of tulipware, Fraktur script, painted tinware, toys, flowered furniture, quilts, samplers, hex signs, house interiors, etc. Full descriptive text. Excellent for tourist, rewarding for designer, collector. Map. 146pp. 7⅞ x 10¾. 21205-X Paperbound $2.00

EARLY NEW ENGLAND GRAVESTONE RUBBINGS, Edmund V. Gillon, Jr. 43 photographs, 226 carefully reproduced rubbings show heavily symbolic, sometimes macabre early gravestones, up to early 19th century. Remarkable early American primitive art, occasionally strikingly beautiful; always powerful. Text. xxvi + 207pp. 8⅜ x 11¼. 21380-3 Paperbound $3.00

EAST O' THE SUN AND WEST O' THE MOON, George W. Dasent. Considered the best of all translations of these Norwegian folk tales, this collection has been enjoyed by generations of children (and folklorists too). Includes True and Untrue, Why the Sea is Salt, East O' the Sun and West O' the Moon, Why the Bear is Stumpy-Tailed, Boots and the Troll, The Cock and the Hen, Rich Peter the Pedlar, and 52 more. The only edition with all 59 tales. 77 illustrations by Erik Werenskiold and Theodor Kittelsen. xv + 418pp. 22521-6 Paperbound $3.00

GOOPS AND HOW TO BE THEM, Gelett Burgess. Classic of tongue-in-cheek humor, masquerading as etiquette book. 87 verses, twice as many cartoons, show mischievous Goops as they demonstrate to children virtues of table manners, neatness, courtesy, etc. Favorite for generations. viii + 88pp. 6½ x 9¼. 22233-0 Paperbound $1.25

ALICE'S ADVENTURES UNDER GROUND, Lewis Carroll. The first version, quite different from the final *Alice in Wonderland,* printed out by Carroll himself with his own illustrations. Complete facsimile of the "million dollar" manuscript Carroll gave to Alice Liddell in 1864. Introduction by Martin Gardner. viii + 96pp. Title and dedication pages in color. 21482-6 Paperbound $1.00

THE BROWNIES, THEIR BOOK, Palmer Cox. Small as mice, cunning as foxes, exuberant and full of mischief, the Brownies go to the zoo, toy shop, seashore, circus, etc., in 24 verse adventures and 266 illustrations. Long a favorite, since their first appearance in St. Nicholas Magazine. xi + 144pp. 6⅝ x 9¼. 21265-3 Paperbound $1.50

SONGS OF CHILDHOOD, Walter De La Mare. Published (under the pseudonym Walter Ramal) when De La Mare was only 29, this charming collection has long been a favorite children's book. A facsimile of the first edition in paper, the 47 poems capture the simplicity of the nursery rhyme and the ballad, including such lyrics as I Met Eve, Tartary, The Silver Penny. vii + 106pp. 21972-0 Paperbound $1.25

THE COMPLETE NONSENSE OF EDWARD LEAR, Edward Lear. The finest 19th-century humorist-cartoonist in full: all nonsense limericks, zany alphabets, Owl and Pussycat, songs, nonsense botany, and more than 500 illustrations by Lear himself. Edited by Holbrook Jackson. xxix + 287pp. (USO) 20167-8 Paperbound $1.75

BILLY WHISKERS: THE AUTOBIOGRAPHY OF A GOAT, Frances Trego Montgomery. A favorite of children since the early 20th century, here are the escapades of that rambunctious, irresistible and mischievous goat—Billy Whiskers. Much in the spirit of *Peck's Bad Boy,* this is a book that children never tire of reading or hearing. All the original familiar illustrations by W. H. Fry are included: 6 color plates, 18 black and white drawings. 159pp. 22345-0 Paperbound $2.00

MOTHER GOOSE MELODIES. Faithful republication of the fabulously rare Munroe and Francis "copyright 1833" Boston edition—the most important Mother Goose collection, usually referred to as the "original." Familiar rhymes plus many rare ones, with wonderful old woodcut illustrations. Edited by E. F. Bleiler. 128pp. 4½ x 6⅜. 22577-1 Paperbound $1.25

ALPHABETS AND ORNAMENTS, Ernst Lehner. Well-known pictorial source for decorative alphabets, script examples, cartouches, frames, decorative title pages, calligraphic initials, borders, similar material. 14th to 19th century, mostly European. Useful in almost any graphic arts designing, varied styles. 750 illustrations. 256pp. 7 x 10. 21905-4 Paperbound $3.50

PAINTING: A CREATIVE APPROACH, Norman Colquhoun. For the beginner simple guide provides an instructive approach to painting: major stumbling blocks for beginner; overcoming them, technical points; paints and pigments; oil painting; watercolor and other media and color. New section on "plastic" paints. Glossary. Formerly *Paint Your Own Pictures*. 221pp. 22000-1 Paperbound $1.75

THE ENJOYMENT AND USE OF COLOR, Walter Sargent. Explanation of the relations between colors themselves and between colors in nature and art, including hundreds of little-known facts about color values, intensities, effects of high and low illumination, complementary colors. Many practical hints for painters, references to great masters. 7 color plates, 29 illustrations. x + 274pp. 20944-X Paperbound $2.50

THE NOTEBOOKS OF LEONARDO DA VINCI, compiled and edited by Jean Paul Richter. 1566 extracts from original manuscripts reveal the full range of Leonardo's versatile genius: all his writings on painting, sculpture, architecture, anatomy, astronomy, geography, topography, physiology, mining, music, etc., in both Italian and English, with 186 plates of manuscript pages and more than 500 additional drawings. Includes studies for the Last Supper, the lost Sforza monument, and other works. Total of xlvii + 866pp. 7⅞ x 10¾. 22572-0, 22573-9 Two volumes, Paperbound $10.00

MONTGOMERY WARD CATALOGUE OF 1895. Tea gowns, yards of flannel and pillow-case lace, stereoscopes, books of gospel hymns, the New Improved Singer Sewing Machine, side saddles, milk skimmers, straight-edged razors, high-button shoes, spittoons, and on and on . . . listing some 25,000 items, practically all illustrated. Essential to the shoppers of the 1890's, it is our truest record of the spirit of the period. Unaltered reprint of Issue No. 57, Spring and Summer 1895. Introduction by Boris Emmet. Innumerable illustrations. xiii + 624pp. 8½ x 11⅝. 22377-9 Paperbound $6.95

THE CRYSTAL PALACE EXHIBITION ILLUSTRATED CATALOGUE (LONDON, 1851). One of the wonders of the modern world—the Crystal Palace Exhibition in which all the nations of the civilized world exhibited their achievements in the arts and sciences—presented in an equally important illustrated catalogue. More than 1700 items pictured with accompanying text—ceramics, textiles, cast-iron work, carpets, pianos, sleds, razors, wall-papers, billiard tables, beehives, silverware and hundreds of other artifacts—represent the focal point of Victorian culture in the Western World. Probably the largest collection of Victorian decorative art ever assembled— indispensable for antiquarians and designers. Unabridged republication of the Art-Journal Catalogue of the Great Exhibition of 1851, with all terminal essays. New introduction by John Gloag, F.S.A. xxxiv + 426pp. 9 x 12. 22503-8 Paperbound $4.50

THE ARCHITECTURE OF COUNTRY HOUSES, Andrew J. Downing. Together with Vaux's *Villas and Cottages* this is the basic book for Hudson River Gothic architecture of the middle Victorian period. Full, sound discussions of general aspects of housing, architecture, style, decoration, furnishing, together with scores of detailed house plans, illustrations of specific buildings, accompanied by full text. Perhaps the most influential single American architectural book. 1850 edition. Introduction by J. Stewart Johnson. 321 figures, 34 architectural designs. xvi + 560pp.

22003-6 Paperbound $3.50

LOST EXAMPLES OF COLONIAL ARCHITECTURE, John Mead Howells. Full-page photographs of buildings that have disappeared or been so altered as to be denatured, including many designed by major early American architects. 245 plates. xvii + 248pp. 7⅞ x 10¾.

21143-6 Paperbound $3.00

DOMESTIC ARCHITECTURE OF THE AMERICAN COLONIES AND OF THE EARLY REPUBLIC, Fiske Kimball. Foremost architect and restorer of Williamsburg and Monticello covers nearly 200 homes between 1620-1825. Architectural details, construction, style features, special fixtures, floor plans, etc. Generally considered finest work in its area. 219 illustrations of houses, doorways, windows, capital mantels. xx + 314pp. 7⅞ x 10¾.

21743-4 Paperbound $3.50

EARLY AMERICAN ROOMS: 1650-1858, edited by Russell Hawes Kettell. Tour of 12 rooms, each representative of a different era in American history and each furnished, decorated, designed and occupied in the style of the era. 72 plans and elevations, 8-page color section, etc., show fabrics, wall papers, arrangements, etc. Full descriptive text. xvii + 200pp. of text. 8⅜ x 11¼.

21633-0 Paperbound $4.00

THE FITZWILLIAM VIRGINAL BOOK, edited by J. Fuller Maitland and W. B. Squire. Full modern printing of famous early 17th-century ms. volume of 300 works by Morley, Byrd, Bull, Gibbons, etc. For piano or other modern keyboard instrument; easy to read format. xxxvi + 938pp. 8⅜ x 11.

21068-5, 21069-3 Two volumes, Paperbound $8.00

HARPSICHORD MUSIC, Johann Sebastian Bach. Bach Gesellschaft edition. A rich selection of Bach's masterpieces for the harpsichord: the six English Suites, six French Suites, the six Partitas (Clavierübung part I), the Goldberg Variations (Clavierübung part IV), the fifteen Two-Part Inventions and the fifteen Three-Part Sinfonias. Clearly reproduced on large sheets with ample margins; eminently playable. vi + 312pp. 8⅛ x 11.

22360-4 Paperbound $5.00

THE MUSIC OF BACH: AN INTRODUCTION, Charles Sanford Terry. A fine, nontechnical introduction to Bach's music, both instrumental and vocal. Covers organ music, chamber music, passion music, other types. Analyzes themes, developments, innovations. x + 114pp.

21075-8 Paperbound $1.25

BEETHOVEN AND HIS NINE SYMPHONIES, Sir George Grove. Noted British musicologist provides best history, analysis, commentary on symphonies. Very thorough, rigorously accurate; necessary to both advanced student and amateur music lover. 436 musical passages. vii + 407 pp.

20334-4 Paperbound $2.25

AGAINST THE GRAIN (A REBOURS), Joris K. Huysmans. Filled with weird images, evidences of a bizarre imagination, exotic experiments with hallucinatory drugs, rich tastes and smells and the diversions of its sybarite hero Duc Jean des Esseintes, this classic novel pushed 19th-century literary decadence to its limits. Full unabridged edition. Do not confuse this with abridged editions generally sold. Introduction by Havelock Ellis. xlix + 206pp. 22190-3 Paperbound $2.00

VARIORUM SHAKESPEARE: HAMLET. Edited by Horace H. Furness; a landmark of American scholarship. Exhaustive footnotes and appendices treat all doubtful words and phrases, as well as suggested critical emendations throughout the play's history. First volume contains editor's own text, collated with all Quartos and Folios. Second volume contains full first Quarto, translations of Shakespeare's sources (Belleforest, and Saxo Grammaticus), Der Bestrafte Brudermord, and many essays on critical and historical points of interest by major authorities of past and present. Includes details of staging and costuming over the years. By far the best edition available for serious students of Shakespeare. Total of xx + 905pp. 21004-9, 21005-7, 2 volumes, Paperbound $5.25

A LIFE OF WILLIAM SHAKESPEARE, Sir Sidney Lee. This is the standard life of Shakespeare, summarizing everything known about Shakespeare and his plays. Incredibly rich in material, broad in coverage, clear and judicious, it has served thousands as the best introduction to Shakespeare. 1931 edition. 9 plates. xxix + 792pp. (USO) 21967-4 Paperbound $3.75

MASTERS OF THE DRAMA, John Gassner. Most comprehensive history of the drama in print, covering every tradition from Greeks to modern Europe and America, including India, Far East, etc. Covers more than 800 dramatists, 2000 plays, with biographical material, plot summaries, theatre history, criticism, etc. "Best of its kind in English," *New Republic*. 77 illustrations. xxii + 890pp. 20100-7 Clothbound $7.50

THE EVOLUTION OF THE ENGLISH LANGUAGE, George McKnight. The growth of English, from the 14th century to the present. Unusual, non-technical account presents basic information in very interesting form: sound shifts, change in grammar and syntax, vocabulary growth, similar topics. Abundantly illustrated with quotations. Formerly *Modern English in the Making*. xii + 590pp. 21932-1 Paperbound $3.50

AN ETYMOLOGICAL DICTIONARY OF MODERN ENGLISH, Ernest Weekley. Fullest, richest work of its sort, by foremost British lexicographer. Detailed word histories, including many colloquial and archaic words; extensive quotations. Do not confuse this with the Concise Etymological Dictionary, which is much abridged. Total of xxvii + 830pp. 6½ x 9¼. 21873-2, 21874-0 Two volumes, Paperbound $5.50

FLATLAND: A ROMANCE OF MANY DIMENSIONS, E. A. Abbott. Classic of science-fiction explores ramifications of life in a two-dimensional world, and what happens when a three-dimensional being intrudes. Amusing reading, but also useful as introduction to thought about hyperspace. Introduction by Banesh Hoffmann. 16 illustrations. xx + 103pp. 20001-9 Paperbound $1.00

POEMS OF ANNE BRADSTREET, edited with an introduction by Robert Hutchinson. A new selection of poems by America's first poet and perhaps the first significant woman poet in the English language. 48 poems display her development in works of considerable variety—love poems, domestic poems, religious meditations, formal elegies, "quaternions," etc. Notes, bibliography. viii + 222pp.
22160-1 Paperbound $2.00

THREE GOTHIC NOVELS: THE CASTLE OF OTRANTO BY HORACE WALPOLE; VATHEK BY WILLIAM BECKFORD; THE VAMPYRE BY JOHN POLIDORI, WITH FRAGMENT OF A NOVEL BY LORD BYRON, edited by E. F. Bleiler. The first Gothic novel, by Walpole; the finest Oriental tale in English, by Beckford; powerful Romantic supernatural story in versions by Polidori and Byron. All extremely important in history of literature; all still exciting, packed with supernatural thrills, ghosts, haunted castles, magic, etc. xl + 291pp.
21232-7 Paperbound $2.00

THE BEST TALES OF HOFFMANN, E. T. A. Hoffmann. 10 of Hoffmann's most important stories, in modern re-editings of standard translations: Nutcracker and the King of Mice, Signor Formica, Automata, The Sandman, Rath Krespel, The Golden Flowerpot, Master Martin the Cooper, The Mines of Falun, The King's Betrothed, A New Year's Eve Adventure. 7 illustrations by Hoffmann. Edited by E. F. Bleiler. xxxix + 419pp.
21793-0 Paperbound $2.25

GHOST AND HORROR STORIES OF AMBROSE BIERCE, Ambrose Bierce. 23 strikingly modern stories of the horrors latent in the human mind: The Eyes of the Panther, The Damned Thing, An Occurrence at Owl Creek Bridge, An Inhabitant of Carcosa, etc., plus the dream-essay, Visions of the Night. Edited by E. F. Bleiler. xxii + 199pp.
20767-6 Paperbound $1.50

BEST GHOST STORIES OF J. S. LEFANU, J. Sheridan LeFanu. Finest stories by Victorian master often considered greatest supernatural writer of all. Carmilla, Green Tea, The Haunted Baronet, The Familiar, and 12 others. Most never before available in the U. S. A. Edited by E. F. Bleiler. 8 illustrations from Victorian publications. xvii + 467pp.
20415-4 Paperbound $2.50

THE TIME STREAM, THE GREATEST ADVENTURE, AND THE PURPLE SAPPHIRE— THREE SCIENCE FICTION NOVELS, John Taine (Eric Temple Bell). Great American mathematician was also foremost science fiction novelist of the 1920's. *The Time Stream,* one of all-time classics, uses concepts of circular time; *The Greatest Adventure,* incredibly ancient biological experiments from Antarctica threaten to escape; The *Purple Sapphire,* superscience, lost races in Central Tibet, survivors of the Great Race. 4 illustrations by Frank R. Paul. v + 532pp.
21180-0 Paperbound $2.50

SEVEN SCIENCE FICTION NOVELS, H. G. Wells. The standard collection of the great novels. Complete, unabridged. *First Men in the Moon, Island of Dr. Moreau, War of the Worlds, Food of the Gods, Invisible Man, Time Machine, In the Days of the Comet.* Not only science fiction fans, but every educated person owes it to himself to read these novels. 1015pp.
20264-X Clothbound $5.00

A HISTORY OF COSTUME, Carl Köhler. Definitive history, based on surviving pieces of clothing primarily, and paintings, statues, etc. secondarily. Highly readable text, supplemented by 594 illustrations of costumes of the ancient Mediterranean peoples, Greece and Rome, the Teutonic prehistoric period; costumes of the Middle Ages, Renaissance, Baroque, 18th and 19th centuries. Clear, measured patterns are provided for many clothing articles. Approach is practical throughout. Enlarged by Emma von Sichart. 464pp.   21030-8 Paperbound $3.00

ORIENTAL RUGS, ANTIQUE AND MODERN, Walter A. Hawley. A complete and authoritative treatise on the Oriental rug—where they are made, by whom and how, designs and symbols, characteristics in detail of the six major groups, how to distinguish them and how to buy them. Detailed technical data is provided on periods, weaves, warps, wefts, textures, sides, ends and knots, although no technical background is required for an understanding. 11 color plates, 80 halftones, 4 maps. vi + 320pp. 6⅛ x 9⅛.   22366-3 Paperbound $5.00

TEN BOOKS ON ARCHITECTURE, Vitruvius. By any standards the most important book on architecture ever written. Early Roman discussion of aesthetics of building, construction methods, orders, sites, and every other aspect of architecture has inspired, instructed architecture for about 2,000 years. Stands behind Palladio, Michelangelo, Bramante, Wren, countless others. Definitive Morris H. Morgan translation. 68 illustrations. xii + 331pp.   20645-9 Paperbound $2.50

THE FOUR BOOKS OF ARCHITECTURE, Andrea Palladio. Translated into every major Western European language in the two centuries following its publication in 1570, this has been one of the most influential books in the history of architecture. Complete reprint of the 1738 Isaac Ware edition. New introduction by Adolf Placzek, Columbia Univ. 216 plates. xxii + 110pp. of text. 9½ x 12¾.
                    21308-0 Clothbound $10.00

STICKS AND STONES: A STUDY OF AMERICAN ARCHITECTURE AND CIVILIZATION, Lewis Mumford.One of the great classics of American cultural history. American architecture from the medieval-inspired earliest forms to the early 20th century; evolution of structure and style, and reciprocal influences on environment. 21 photographic illustrations. 238pp.   20202-X Paperbound $2.00

THE AMERICAN BUILDER'S COMPANION, Asher Benjamin. The most widely used early 19th century architectural style and source book, for colonial up into Greek Revival periods. Extensive development of geometry of carpentering, construction of sashes, frames, doors, stairs; plans and elevations of domestic and other buildings. Hundreds of thousands of houses were built according to this book, now invaluable to historians, architects, restorers, etc. 1827 edition. 59 plates. 114pp. 7⅞ x 10¾.
                    22236-5 Paperbound $3.00

DUTCH HOUSES IN THE HUDSON VALLEY BEFORE 1776, Helen Wilkinson Reynolds. The standard survey of the Dutch colonial house and outbuildings, with constructional features, decoration, and local history associated with individual homesteads. Introduction by Franklin D. Roosevelt. Map. 150 illustrations. 469pp. 6⅝ x 9¼.   21469-9 Paperbound $3.50

THE PRINCIPLES OF PSYCHOLOGY,
William James

The full long-course, unabridged, of one of the great classics of Western literature and science. Wonderfully lucid descriptions of human mental activity, the stream of thought, consciousness, time perception, memory, imagination, emotions, reason, abnormal phenomena, and similar topics. Original contributions are integrated with the work of such men as Berkeley, Binet, Mills, Darwin, Hume, Kant, Royce, Schopenhauer, Spinoza, Locke, Descartes, Galton, Wundt, Lotze, Herbart, Fechner, and scores of others. All contrasting interpretations of mental phenomena are examined in detail—introspective analysis, philosophical interpretation, and experimental research. "A classic," *Journal of Consulting Psychology*. "The main lines are as valid as ever," *Psychoanalytical Quarterly*. "Standard reading . . . a classic of interpretation," *Psychiatric Quarterly*. 94 illustrations. 1408pp. 5⅜ x 8.

20381-6, 20382-4 Two volume set, paperbound $6.00

VISUAL ILLUSIONS: THEIR CAUSES, CHARACTERISTICS AND APPLICATIONS,
M. Luckiesh

"Seeing is deceiving," asserts the author of this introduction to virtually every type of optical illusion known. The text both describes and explains the principles involved in color illusions, figure-ground, distance illusions, etc. 100 photographs, drawings and diagrams prove how easy it is to fool the sense: circles that aren't round, parallel lines that seem to bend, stationary figures that seem to move as you stare at them — illustration after illustration strains our credulity at what we see. Fascinating book from many points of view, from applications for artists, in camouflage, etc. to the psychology of vision. New introduction by William Ittleson, Dept. of Psychology, Queens College. Index. Bibliography. xxi + 252pp. 5⅜ x 8½. 21530-X Paperbound $1.50

FADS AND FALLACIES IN THE NAME OF SCIENCE,
Martin Gardner

This is the standard account of various cults, quack systems, and delusions which have masqueraded as science: hollow earth fanatics. Reich and orgone sex energy, dianetics, Atlantis, multiple moons, Forteanism, flying saucers, medical fallacies like iridiagnosis, zone therapy, etc. A new chapter has been added on Bridey Murphy, psionics, and other recent manifestations in this field. This is a fair, reasoned appraisal of eccentric theory which provides excellent inoculation against cleverly masked nonsense. "Should be read by everyone, scientist and non-scientist alike," R. T. Birge, Prof. Emeritus of Physics, Univ. of California; Former President, American Physical Society. Index. x + 365pp. 5⅜ x 8. 20394-8 Paperbound $2.00

ILLUSIONS AND DELUSIONS OF THE SUPERNATURAL AND THE OCCULT,
D. H. Rawcliffe

Holds up to rational examination hundreds of persistent delusions including crystal gazing, automatic writing, table turning, mediumistic trances, mental healing, stigmata, lycanthropy, live burial, the Indian Rope Trick, spiritualism, dowsing, telepathy, clairvoyance, ghosts, ESP, etc. The author explains and exposes the mental and physical deceptions involved, making this not only an exposé of supernatural phenomena, but a valuable exposition of characteristic types of abnormal psychology. Originally titled "The Psychology of the Occult." 14 illustrations. Index. 551pp. 5⅜ x 8. 20503-7 Paperbound $3.50

TWO LITTLE SAVAGES; BEING THE ADVENTURES OF TWO BOYS WHO LIVED AS INDIANS AND WHAT THEY LEARNED, Ernest Thompson Seton. Great classic of nature and boyhood provides a vast range of woodlore in most palatable form, a genuinely entertaining story. Two farm boys build a teepee in woods and live in it for a month, working out Indian solutions to living problems, star lore, birds and animals, plants, etc. 293 illustrations. vii + 286pp.

20985-7 Paperbound $1.95

PETER PIPER'S PRACTICAL PRINCIPLES OF PLAIN & PERFECT PRONUNCIATION. Alliterative jingles and tongue-twisters of surprising charm, that made their first appearance in America about 1830. Republished in full with the spirited woodcut illustrations from this earliest American edition. 32pp. 4½ x 6⅜.

22560-7 Paperbound $1.00

SCIENCE EXPERIMENTS AND AMUSEMENTS FOR CHILDREN, Charles Vivian. 73 easy experiments, requiring only materials found at home or easily available, such as candles, coins, steel wool, etc.; illustrate basic phenomena like vacuum, simple chemical reaction, etc. All safe. Modern, well-planned. Formerly *Science Games for Children*. 102 photos, numerous drawings. 96pp. 6⅛ x 9¼.

21856-2 Paperbound $1.25

AN INTRODUCTION TO CHESS MOVES AND TACTICS SIMPLY EXPLAINED, Leonard Barden. Informal intermediate introduction, quite strong in explaining reasons for moves. Covers basic material, tactics, important openings, traps, positional play in middle game, end game. Attempts to isolate patterns and recurrent configurations. Formerly *Chess*. 58 figures. 102pp. (USO) 21210-6 Paperbound $1.25

LASKER'S MANUAL OF CHESS, Dr. Emanuel Lasker. Lasker was not only one of the five great World Champions, he was also one of the ablest expositors, theorists, and analysts. In many ways, his Manual, permeated with his philosophy of battle, filled with keen insights, is one of the greatest works ever written on chess. Filled with analyzed games by the great players. A single-volume library that will profit almost any chess player, beginner or master. 308 diagrams. xli x 349pp.

20640-8 Paperbound $2.50

THE MASTER BOOK OF MATHEMATICAL RECREATIONS, Fred Schuh. In opinion of many the finest work ever prepared on mathematical puzzles, stunts, recreations; exhaustively thorough explanations of mathematics involved, analysis of effects, citation of puzzles and games. Mathematics involved is elementary. Translated by F. Göbel. 194 figures. xxiv + 430pp.

22134-2 Paperbound $3.00

MATHEMATICS, MAGIC AND MYSTERY, Martin Gardner. Puzzle editor for Scientific American explains mathematics behind various mystifying tricks: card tricks, stage "mind reading," coin and match tricks, counting out games, geometric dissections, etc. Probability sets, theory of numbers clearly explained. Also provides more than 400 tricks, guaranteed to work, that you can do. 135 illustrations. xii + 176pp.

20338-2 Paperbound $1.50

JOHANN SEBASTIAN BACH, Philipp Spitta. One of the great classics of musicology, this definitive analysis of Bach's music (and life) has never been surpassed. Lucid, nontechnical analyses of hundreds of pieces (30 pages devoted to St. Matthew Passion, 26 to B Minor Mass). Also includes major analysis of 18th-century music. 450 musical examples. 40-page musical supplement. Total of xx + 1799pp.

(EUK) 22278-0, 22279-9 Two volumes, Clothbound $15.00

MOZART AND HIS PIANO CONCERTOS, Cuthbert Girdlestone. The only full-length study of an important area of Mozart's creativity. Provides detailed analyses of all 23 concertos, traces inspirational sources. 417 musical examples. Second edition. 509pp.

(USO) 21271-8 Paperbound $2.50

THE PERFECT WAGNERITE: A COMMENTARY ON THE NIBLUNG'S RING, George Bernard Shaw. Brilliant and still relevant criticism in remarkable essays on Wagner's Ring cycle, Shaw's ideas on political and social ideology behind the plots, role of Leitmotifs, vocal requisites, etc. Prefaces. xxi + 136pp.

21707-8 Paperbound $1.50

DON GIOVANNI, W. A. Mozart. Complete libretto, modern English translation; biographies of composer and librettist; accounts of early performances and critical reaction. Lavishly illustrated. All the material you need to understand and appreciate this great work. Dover Opera Guide and Libretto Series; translated and introduced by Ellen Bleiler. 92 illustrations. 209pp.

21134-7 Paperbound $1.50

HIGH FIDELITY SYSTEMS: A LAYMAN'S GUIDE, Roy F. Allison. All the basic information you need for setting up your own audio system: high fidelity and stereo record players, tape records, F.M. Connections, adjusting tone arm, cartridge, checking needle alignment, positioning speakers, phasing speakers, adjusting hums, trouble-shooting, maintenance, and similar topics. Enlarged 1965 edition. More than 50 charts, diagrams, photos. iv + 91pp. 21514-8 Paperbound $1.25

REPRODUCTION OF SOUND, Edgar Villchur. Thorough coverage for laymen of high fidelity systems, reproducing systems in general, needles, amplifiers, preamps, loudspeakers, feedback, explaining physical background. "A rare talent for making technicalities vividly comprehensible," R. Darrell, *High Fidelity*. 69 figures. iv + 92pp. 21515-6 Paperbound $1.00

HEAR ME TALKIN' TO YA: THE STORY OF JAZZ AS TOLD BY THE MEN WHO MADE IT, Nat Shapiro and Nat Hentoff. Louis Armstrong, Fats Waller, Jo Jones, Clarence Williams, Billy Holiday, Duke Ellington, Jelly Roll Morton and dozens of other jazz greats tell how it was in Chicago's South Side, New Orleans, depression Harlem and the modern West Coast as jazz was born and grew. xvi + 429pp.

21726-4 Paperbound $2.00

FABLES OF AESOP, translated by Sir Roger L'Estrange. A reproduction of the very rare 1931 Paris edition; a selection of the most interesting fables, together with 50 imaginative drawings by Alexander Calder. v + 128pp. 6½x9¼.

21780-9 Paperbound $1.25

MATHEMATICAL PUZZLES FOR BEGINNERS AND ENTHUSIASTS, Geoffrey Mott-Smith. 189 puzzles from easy to difficult—involving arithmetic, logic, algebra, properties of digits, probability, etc.—for enjoyment and mental stimulus. Explanation of mathematical principles behind the puzzles. 135 illustrations. viii + 248pp.
20198-8 Paperbound $1.25

PAPER FOLDING FOR BEGINNERS, William D. Murray and Francis J. Rigney. Easiest book on the market, clearest instructions on making interesting, beautiful origami. Sail boats, cups, roosters, frogs that move legs, bonbon boxes, standing birds, etc. 40 projects; more than 275 diagrams and photographs. 94pp.
20713-7 Paperbound $1.00

TRICKS AND GAMES ON THE POOL TABLE, Fred Herrmann. 79 tricks and games—some solitaires, some for two or more players, some competitive games—to entertain you between formal games. Mystifying shots and throws, unusual caroms, tricks involving such props as cork, coins, a hat, etc. Formerly *Fun on the Pool Table*. 77 figures. 95pp.
21814-7 Paperbound $1.00

HAND SHADOWS TO BE THROWN UPON THE WALL: A SERIES OF NOVEL AND AMUSING FIGURES FORMED BY THE HAND, Henry Bursill. Delightful picturebook from great-grandfather's day shows how to make 18 different hand shadows: a bird that flies, duck that quacks, dog that wags his tail, camel, goose, deer, boy, turtle, etc. Only book of its sort. vi + 33pp. 6½ x 9¼.
21779-5 Paperbound $1.00

WHITTLING AND WOODCARVING, E. J. Tangerman. 18th printing of best book on market. "If you can cut a potato you can carve" toys and puzzles, chains, chessmen, caricatures, masks, frames, woodcut blocks, surface patterns, much more. Information on tools, woods, techniques. Also goes into serious wood sculpture from Middle Ages to present, East and West. 464 photos, figures. x + 293pp.
20965-2 Paperbound $2.00

HISTORY OF PHILOSOPHY, Julián Marias. Possibly the clearest, most easily followed, best planned, most useful one-volume history of philosophy on the market; neither skimpy nor overfull. Full details on system of every major philosopher and dozens of less important thinkers from pre-Socratics up to Existentialism and later. Strong on many European figures usually omitted. Has gone through dozens of editions in Europe. 1966 edition, translated by Stanley Appelbaum and Clarence Strowbridge. xviii + 505pp.
21739-6 Paperbound $2.75

YOGA: A SCIENTIFIC EVALUATION, Kovoor T. Behanan. Scientific but non-technical study of physiological results of yoga exercises; done under auspices of Yale U. Relations to Indian thought, to psychoanalysis, etc. 16 photos. xxiii + 270pp.
20505-3 Paperbound $2.50

Prices subject to change without notice.
Available at your book dealer or write for free catalogue to Dept. GI, Dover Publications, Inc., 180 Varick St., N. Y., N. Y. 10014. Dover publishes more than 150 books each year on science, elementary and advanced mathematics, biology, music, art, literary history, social sciences and other areas.